UNDERSTANDING AND TREATING ALCOHOLISM

Volume 1

An Empirically Based Clinician's Handbook for the Treatment of Alcoholism

UNDERSTANDING AND TREATING ALCOHOLISM

Volume 1

An Empirically Based Clinician's Handbook for the Treatment of Alcoholism

JILL LITTRELL
Arizona State University

IEA

LAWRENCE ERLBAUM ASSOCIATES, PUBLISHERS

1991   Hillsdale, New Jersey   Hove and London

Lawrence Erlbaum Associates, Inc., Publishers
365 Broadway
Hillsdale, New Jersey 07642

Library of Congress Cataloging in Publication Data

Littrell, Jill
     Understanding and treating alcoholsm / Jill Littrell.
        p.   cm.
     Includes bibliographical references and indexes.
     Contents: v. 1. An empirically based clinician's handbook for the
treatment of alcoholism—v.2 Biological, psychological, and
social aspects of alcohol consumption and abuse.
        ISBN 0-8058-0872-8 (set).—ISBN 0-8058-0870-1 (v. 1).—
ISBN 0-8058-0871-X (v. 2)
        1. Alcoholsm—Treatment. 2. Alcoholsm. I. Title.
     [DNLM: 1 Alcohol, Ethyl—adverse effects.   2. Alcoholism—
genetics.   3. Alcoholism—psychology.   4. alcoholism—therapy.
     5. Risk Factors.   WM 274 L 782u]
     RC565.L57   1991
     616.86'106—dc20
     DNLM/DLC
     for Library of Congress   90-15725
                                                                               CIP

Printed in the United States of America
10 9 8 7 6 5 4 3 2 1

Contents

130987

Preface

In 1981, after having completed my Ph.D. in clinical psychology, I entered the field of alcoholism. I spent a year at the Veteran's Administration Hospital in Phoenix working exclusively in the Alcohol Dependency Department. After this training experience, I went to work in the Alcohol and Drug Dependency Department at CIGNA Health Plan.

While beginning my work, I was impressed by the amount of "factual" information which was voiced by my colleagues and my patients. Having been trained as a scientist, I wondered whether there was research to support the "facts" which seemed to be coin of the realm, and, if there was such research, whether the research justified the conclusions which everyone seemed to believe. I made inquiries of my mentor, Fred Obitz Ph.D., who directed me to empirical sources. The next eight years were spent pursuing these sources.

These volumes are the result of my Odyssey through the empirical literature on alcoholism. In organizing the chapters and selecting the material, I have attempted to provide persons in the field with all the information I wished someone had organized for me before I started. Hopefully, as a result of these volumes, professionals will have a good understanding as to which of the factual statements about alcohol and alcoholism are supported by data and some of the empirically validated ways to proceed with treatment.

I wish to thank my mentor and friend, Robert Cialdini Ph.D. for support and an introduction to empirical work; my clinical supervisor and friend, Fred Obitz Ph.D. for introducing me to this field; my brother, Jordan Tappero M.D. for answering my endless questions about medicine; and my husband, Gus Levine Ph.D. Without the support, patience, enthusiasm, statistical consultation, and conceptual input of Gus Levine this project would not have been attempted.

God grant me the serenity
to accept the things I cannot change,
Courage to change the things I can,
And wisdom to know the difference.

I | THE TREATMENT OF ALCOHOLISM

INTRODUCTION

The section on the treatment of alcoholism is divided into 5 chapters. The first chapter discusses the views of self-help groups and treatment providers with an AA orientation. The first half of the first chapter offers a discussion of the 1946 and 1952 research reports of Jellinek, which verbalized the frame of reference that had been the informal conceptual basis for Alcoholics Anonymous (AA). The stages of alcoholism, and the types of alcoholics, that Jellinek identified, are discussed in detail. The pivotal role of denial in AA thinking is explained, along with other assumptions, including the links between addiction, craving, and loss of control. Recent embellishments on theory provided by professionals with an AA orientation are presented. These ideas include cross addiction to other chemicals, dry drunks, personality traits descriptive of alcoholics, and progression of the disease during periods of sobriety.

The second half of the first chapter examines research pertinent to the ideas advanced in AA. On the basis of numerous studies it is possible to estimate what percentage of untreated alcoholics will recover through abstinence, what percentage will achieve control drinking, and what percentage will die of the disease without having achieved sobriety. In addition to information on what happens to alcoholics over a lifetime, research has addressed whether there are reliable stages in the process of alcoholism. Research has also addressed the issue of the drugs for which the concern regarding cross addiction is justified; the conditions under which alcoholics and others deny, and whether alcoholics are different in that respect; as well as questions pertinent to craving and loss of control. The

1

chapter ends with a discussion of the impact of the disease concept and how it has affected the way in which society at large sanctions and perceives deviant drinking.

The second and third chapters concern treatment. The second chapter outlines characteristic AA oriented treatment. Vernon Johnson has verbalized much of this material, and so is frequently quoted, as are other treatment providers who have been influential in AA based treatment. In addition, the influence of the Hazelden treatment center in Minnesota is represented in the summary of the AA approach. The AA steps, recommended interventions, and how group therapy is conducted, are all covered. In addition, the manner in which relapse prevention in AA based treatment is addressed, is explained.

The second half of chapter 2 compares the AA model with the treatment models advanced by empirically based clinicians such as William Miller and Alan Marlatt. AA's reliance on commitment to maintain sobriety is contrasted with Marlatt's emphasis on the teaching of skills for relapse prevention. The sources of motivation that are tapped by the respective models are discussed and contrasted. The ways in which the models differ in the emphases on, and roles played by, the patient's belief in self efficacy are discussed. There is also brief coverage of differences between the two models in willingness to work with clients who continue to drink, and exploration of differences in the role of the therapist in each model.

Chapter 3 presents a fuller description of empirically based treatment. This chapter draws heavily upon the work of Alan Marlatt presented in his book on relapse prevention. Empirical findings are presented regarding common precipitants to relapse. There is a presentation of the attitude and personality factors (e.g., feelings of self-efficacy, willingness to self-reinforce, expectations concerning the effects from drinking), which differentiate alcoholics who achieve extensive periods of sobriety from those who do not. After presentation of empirical findings concerning common relapse precipitants and relevant personality issues, a discussion of empirically based treatment is offered. Techniques for enhancing feelings of self-efficacy, building coping skills, incorporating self-reinforcement, changing life style, changing positive attitudes toward drinking, and avoiding abstinence violation syndrome, are all included, along with a discussion of which behaviors to self monitor. Consideration is given to differences between the type of alcoholic for whom strengthening feelings of self efficacy is useful, as compared to those for whom reliance on external forces is more efficacious. Treating alcoholics who are continually relapsing presents a problem for group therapy in any model. A discussion of how to handle this type of patient is presented.

The fourth chapter concerns the overarching theme of the many attempts to identify and measure personality traits that are characteristic of, or predictive of, or in some way relevant to, alcoholism. It includes the attempts to define different types of alcoholics, and is specifically concerned with attempts to develop measures for the many personality categories and typologies. The chapter begins with a discussion of personality characteristics that are descriptive of alcoholics. The literature on personality traits is vast and no attempt was made to be exhaustive. A decision was made to limit discussion to (a) those traits that have emerged in the research on children of alcoholics which might constitute part of the temperament precursor to alcoholism and (b) those traits that have generated a body of literature because of their potential importance for treatment. The traits discussed include boredom susceptibility, differences in autonomic nervous system responding, depression, potential for suicide, locus of control, and scale elevations observed on the Minnesota Multiphasic Personality Inventory (MMPI).

There are many ways in which alcoholics might be categorized into types. One particular method for dividing alcoholics is on the basis of demographics: sex, age, and socioeconomic status. Most of the research on alcoholism has been done on gainfully employed males with an average age of 45. This population is therefore heavily represented in the literature reviewed throughout this text. Consequently, consideration of characteristics and other facts that are unique to other alcoholic populations have to be reviewed. That kind of information, specifically on the topics of female alcoholism, geriatric alcoholics, and skid row alcoholics, is covered in this chapter.

In addition to the use of demographics for providing meaningful ways to categorize alcoholics, others have proffered other typologies which might relate to differential treatment outcomes, differential efficacy given various types of treatments, and differential etiological roots. One obvious way in which alcoholics can be distinguished is the pattern of their drinking. Some of the findings investigating differences between bingers and steady state drinkers are discussed. Another way of categorizing alcoholics has been to separate them according to whether their alcoholism was preceded by another major psychiatric disorder. Some of the findings from the literature differentiating alcoholics according to the presence and type of primary psychiatric disorder are discussed. Finally, the responses of alcoholics to the MMPI have also been used to generate types of alcoholics. Some of the major findings from this endeavor are reported.

The discussion of tests and measures in alcoholism is divided according to the purpose of the instrument. Some instruments have been developed to discriminate alcoholics from the general population. Scales specific to this purpose have been constructed. Others have attempted to build scales from the pool of items constituting the MMPI, for the purpose of distinguishing alcoholics from normals or psychiatric patients. In this chapter, some of the more popular methods for identifying alcoholics are discussed. Included in the discussion are the Michigan Alcohol Screening Test, the CAGE, scales from the MMPI including an extensive discussion of the MacAndrew scale, and physiological tests.

Tests that measure specific syndromes associated with alcoholism have also been constructed. Two measures have been developed to help the clinician examine the pattern of an alcoholic's drinking. Both the Comprehensive Drinking

Profile and the Alcohol Use Inventory provide the clinician with information about an individual's unique pattern of drinking and cluster of problems that have developed as a result of the drinking. The Severity of Alcohol Dependence Scale and the Alcohol Dependence Scale assess the extremity of physical dependence on alcohol. The authors of the latter scale recommend its use for identifying patients for whom an abstinence rather than a control drinking goal is most appropriate. Measures similar to the internal/external locus of control have been developed to assess an alcoholic's subjective sense of control over areas in life related to drinking. Two such instruments are discussed. At the end of the chapter several measures that have been developed to identify children of alcoholics are examined.

Chapter 5 considers the outcome literature, beginning with a focus on AA based treatment. The results of three studies in which there was random assignment to AA or a control group are reviewed. Empirical findings from other studies regarding the percentage of treated alcoholics that can be expected to maintain an AA affiliation after treatment are discussed. The literature examining the personality characteristics that distinguish AA affiliates from other alcoholics is also considered.

The same chapter also discusses the differentiating characteristics of alcoholics who seek treatment vs. those who do not. Using material from a number of follow-up studies, the chapter offers expectations for the percentage of clients who can be predicted to be abstinent, control drinking, and relapsed, given a short-term follow-up interval (2 to 4 years). There are a number of studies that empirically examined the issue of whether treatment adds anything (in terms of effectiveness) to simple advice to stop drinking. The results of these studies are also discussed.

In the latter half of the fifth chapter more fine grained questions regarding outcome are examined. Statistics on expectations for drop out rates are provided. The characteristics of patients most likely to drop out of treatment are reviewed. Studies in which procedures for attenuating drop out rates were tested are discussed. The question of whether inpatient vs. outpatient therapy is more effective is explored and the question of group vs. individual therapy is examined. Outcome findings regarding length of treatment are explored. The question of which treatment modalities are preferred by alcoholics is examined. The efficacy of forced treatment is considered. Outcome data on whether matching type of treatment to type of alcoholic improves outcome is presented. Findings relating to aftercare are discussed. Questions regarding aftercare include: the expected percentage who will participate in aftercare, whether aftercare participation is associated with better outcome, procedures that increase aftercare attendance. The topic of patient characteristics (e.g., age, sex, depression, antisocial personality, social stability, cognitive capacity) that are associated with better or worse outcome is considered. Finally, the topic of whether remission of alcoholism correlates with improved functioning in other life arenas is discussed.

1 The AA Perspective

The early mental health reformer and signer of the Constitution, Benjamin Rush, proffered the hypothesis that alcoholism is a disease. Other doctors throughout the 19th century also advanced the disease perspective (Baumohl & Room, 1987). In the 20th century psychiatrists and psychoanalysts generated hypotheses regarding the psychodynamic origins of alcoholism. The contemporary world of alcoholism, however, is dominated by the AA perspective and the teachings and contributions of M. E. Jellinek, a 20th century epidemiologist. Most of those currently working in traditional treatment centers regard the teaching of AA as doctrine. As scientists began investigating alcoholism, many familiarized themselves with AA beliefs. AA assumptions provided the hypotheses for empirical investigation. Jellinek, who developed many of AA's tenets, began his own research in the area by analyzing questionnaires which had been written and responded to by AA members.

AA was founded in 1935 by Bill Wilson, a stock broker, and Robert Smith, an M.D. Both were alcoholics. Bill Wilson had been involved in the Oxford movement, a group of religiously inspired sober alcoholics seeking to reform drinking alcoholics. AA established the tradition of alcoholics staying sober through social support, discussion with each other, and through faith in a Higher Power. The formal AA tenets and program emerged gradually, beginning with Jellinek's verbalizations, but developed further in the course of informal discussions (Baumohl & Room, 1987). Since Jellinek, additional concepts and procedures have been added to what is now considered to be traditional AA based treatment. This is the approach currently offered in most treatment centers.

THE AA POINT OF VIEW

This chapter begins with an overview of the beliefs advanced in traditional alcohol treatment centers. The assumptions adopted by Jellinek inspired a good deal of research on alcoholism, most of which has been conducted by psychiatrists, psychologists, and a few social workers, beginning in the 1970s. As a result there is now data available to critically examine most of the assumptions of AA thinking. Each of the assumptions will be examined in light of the findings of empirical research. By the end of the discussion, the reader should have a sense of which AA beliefs have been more or less supported. Empirical research has not only allowed the field to evaluate AA thinking, but has provided a reservoir of information regarding the contention that there is a common course of development for the disease of alcoholism. Relevant information on this topic is also presented. This chapter ends with a discussion of the impact of one of the basic axioms of Alcoholics Anonymous, viz. that alcoholism is a disease. The social implications of this conceptualization are examined.

The Contributions of Jellinek

Jellinek is known for his typology of alcoholism, for division of the modal temporal course of alcoholism into stages, and for the notion that once particular pathognomonic conditions are established, the alcoholic is committed to an inexorable progression. The empirical support for Jellinek's notions rest on analysis of responses to two questionnaires. The analysis of the first questionnaire was reported in 1946. Results of the second questionnaire were reported in 1952.

The 1946 Stages

Jellinek did not develop the first questionnaire. Rather, he was commissioned to analyze the responses to a questionnaire that had been developed and administered by AA. The questionnaire had been completed by 158 members of AA, a response rate of 10% of the potential sample. The questionnaire requested that respondents report the age at which particular events had occurred in their lives. Many of the items contained jargon phrases such as "loss of control" and "hitting bottom," reflecting a subjective interpretation of events consistent with the assumptions that AA espouses to be true of alcoholics. Jellinek's purpose in analyzing his data was to empirically define a sequence of events that would describe the progression of alcoholism.

The AA belief system suggested that the events in an alcoholic's drinking life would conform to a sequence rather than occurring in random order. To determine temporal ordering, Jellinek analyzed the first questionnaire by computing correlations between responses to items. According to Jellinek's reasoning, a large correlation signified that events occurred in a consistent sequence.

Jellinek's correlations were high (.7 or greater). He thus concluded that there is a dependable sequence of stages in alcoholism. In examining the data, Jellinek selected events that he believed might be construed as signaling the initiation of a stage. Harbinger events were chosen such that most individuals experienced them in the suggested sequence. For those items he assumed to be hallmarks of the beginning of a particular stage, Jellinek reported the percentage of individuals for whom the harbinger event of the particular stage followed the harbinger event of assumed prior stage. Even considering that Jellinek allowed himself to examine the data before selecting events, between one quarter to a half of the sample failed to conform to the predicted sequence. Thus, even in Jellinek's original sample, there was a great lack of correspondence to his predicted sequence. The data was a bit more consistent for hitting bottom. As predicted, hitting one's lowest point occurred prior to going to AA, and followed other events.

In the 1946 analysis, Jellinek also sought to identify a set of events that happen to alcoholics but do not happen to normal drinkers. To aid in identifying events that are unique to alcoholics, Jellinek did include a control group in his 1946 analysis. A group of scientist colleagues were informally interviewed. Since 30% of the control sample had experienced at least one blackout, Jellinek reasoned that blackouts would yield too many false positives to be the diagnostic feature for what he assumed would be an inelutable progression through the stages. Jellinek decided to include a prodromal phase in his staging. Prodromal events are those occurrences that precede later stages but are not predictive of later occurrences. He assigned blackouts to the prodromal stage. Jellinek settled on "loss of control" as the hallmark signifying that a pathological state had begun, as all of the alcoholics in the sample reported this event and none of the control sample reported it. Once the pathological state was entered, progression was described as inevitable.

The 1946 data suggested to Jellinek that there were four stages through which alcoholics would progress. They were: prodromal, basic phase, acute compulsive, and chronic compulsive. The stages and the labels were revised in the 1952 publication. The 1946 terms occasionally seep into parlance, although the 1952 stages have supplanted the 1946 version. In most traditional treatment centers, the Jellinek chart (the names of the stages with attendant symptoms) is posted on the wall.

The 1952 Stages

Included in the 1946 publication was a suggested revision of the original questionnaire which contained additional items and further denoted ambiguous phrases. This revised questionnaire was responded to by 2000 AA members. In a 1952 publication, Jellinek reported a revision of the stages based on an analysis of this amended questionnaire. Unlike the first report, Jellinek did not specify how he analyzed the data from the second questionnaire. No correlation coefficients were reported. No percentages conforming to suggested sequence were provided.

The 1952 version of the stages has received wide acceptance. According to the 1952 Jellinek publication, alcoholism progresses in the following sequence: the prealcoholic symptomatic stage, the prodromal stage, the crucial stage, and the chronic stage. Each stage encompasses its own cluster of symptoms. Since the stages and their correlate symptomotology assume such a meaningful role in the AA perspective, the stages are presented.

The *prealcoholic symptomatic stage* is characterized by growing tolerance to alcohol and drinking motivated by relief of psychological distress rather than social convention. The *prodromal stage* is characterized by recurrent blackouts, planning for the consumption of more drinks than is social appropriate, preoccupation (concern) about the availability of liquor, and gulping the first couple of drinks. Consumption during the prodromal stage is heavy but not conspicuous as it does not result in overt problems. The *crucial stage* (the stage initiating the disease process) is characterized by loss of control over the amount consumed once the first drink is ingested, rationalizations for drinking initially to console the drinker but later to mollify others, social pressures, grandiose behavior to compensate for the loss of self-esteem, blaming the environment, marked aggressive behavior, persistent remorse, periods of total abstinence, changing the pattern of drinking, dropping friends, quitting jobs, concern over whether other activities will interfere with drinking, loss of other interests, reinterpretation of interpersonal relations, marked self-pity, change in family habits, unreasonable resentments, protecting supply, poor nutrition, first hospitalization, jealousy of spouse, decrease in libido, and regular morning drinking. The loss of control is the symptom that must be present to diagnose the stage. The other symptoms are correlates which may or may not be present. The *chronic phase* requires the harbinger of prolonged intoxications or benders for its diagnosis. Correlates of the chronic phase include marked ethical deterioration, impaired thinking, alcoholic psychosis (undefined), drinking with persons far below one's prior social status, drinking unusual sources of alcohol, loss of tolerance, indefinable fears, tremors, psychomotor inhibition, drinking to control the symptoms created by drinking rather than to obtain psychological relief, and seeking solace in religion as rationalizations for one's behavior no longer are satisfactory. Hitting bottom, pathognomoic of the *terminal stage,* is not included in the 1952 publication, although it is included on most charts. According to Marty Mann (1950) the founder of the National Council on Alcoholism and author of *Primer on Alcoholism,* if hitting bottom (which initiates the recovery process and breaks through denial) does not occur, death or insanity will ensue.

In 1946, Jellinek did identify two groups who failed to follow the stage sequence of events: those developing problematic drinking late in life and psychopathic individuals. The former groups followed a more rapid progression.

Jellinek indicated that the older onsetters may have developed their drinking in response to a major life tragedy. The psychopaths differed from the modal pattern in many ways. The psychopaths began problem drinking earlier than the modal alcoholic, began binge drinking before losing control, were often solitary drinkers from the outset, and behaved in an antisocial manner before the onset of significant alcoholic progression.

Jellinek has been the exponent of the inexorable nature of the stages, the assumption that progression is inescapable. The alcoholic cannot return to a prior stage or remain in a particular stage. In the 1946 publication, Jellinek relied upon a high correlation between two events as supporting evidence. The 1952 publication offered no statistical justification.

In both the 1946 and 1952 publications, Jellinek was careful to distinguish those with the disease of alcoholism from those who are nonaddictive alcoholics. He defined those having the disease as those who are addicted. He recognized that there are other heavy drinkers who could be considered to be alcoholics because of the problems caused by their drinking, but who are not addicted, and thus are not considered to have the disease of alcoholism. For Jellinek, the critical distinguishing feature was loss of control. Addictive alcoholics have no choice over getting drunk. Nonaddictive alcoholics are drunk because they want to be. Jellinek was not alone in his thinking. Marty Mann (1950) and later Mark Keller (1972a), an early editor of the *Quarterly Journal of Studies on Alcohol,* made the same distinction. Jellinek (1952) cautioned against the injudicious extension of the disease label to all inebriates because "sooner or later the misapplication will reflect on the legitimate use too and, more importantly, will tend to weaken the ethical basis of social sanctions against drunkenness" (p. 674).

In his 1946 publication, Jellinek affirmed the central AA tenet that rationalizations (denial) are necessary for the disease process. In this earlier writing, Jellinek hedged between the positions of (a) once the alcoholic realizes that he/she has a disease, i.e., that he/she has lost control over consumption, then treatment and recovery will follow (awareness is a necessary and sufficient condition for recovery); and (b) without the realization of disease (i.e., realization of loss of control over alcohol) cessation of drinking is impossible (awareness is a necessary but insufficient condition for recovery). In the 1952 publication, Jellinek endorses the necessary and sufficient condition version. He avers that the alcoholic is enmeshed in a contest to prove to himself/herself that the quantity consumed can be limited. The importance of winning this contest is the motivation fueling the progression of the disease. Once the alcoholic admits that control is not possible, the motivation for the self-delusion is gone, and progressive deterioration is less likely.

With the publication of his book, *The Disease Concept of Alcoholism,* Jellinek (1960) introduced his typology of alcoholics. Jellinek first offered a definition of alcoholism, "any use of alcoholic beverages that causes any damage to the individual or society or both," but cautioned that this definition includes persons who have the disease of alcoholism as well as individuals without the disease. He then discussed the five major types. *Alpha alcoholics* are persons who exhibit a purely psychological reliance upon the effect of alcohol to relieve bodily or emotional pain. The driving force for their behavior is relief of psychological pain. *Beta alcoholics* exhibit physical problems resulting from their drinking (liver disease, gastrointestinal disturbance, etc.) but display no loss of control or physical dependence. *Gamma alcoholics* exhibit acquired tissue tolerance, adaptive cellular metabolism, withdrawal and craving, loss of control with respect to the amount consumed per occasion, and progression. *Delta alcoholics* exhibit acquired tissue tolerance, adaptive cellular metabolism, withdrawal and craving, and loss of control over the decision to consume on any particular occasion, i.e., an inability to abstain. Jellinek specified that disease should be reserved for the gamma and delta alcoholics. Only these alcoholic types display the defining features of a real disease, "the adaptation of cell metabolism and acquired tissue tolerance and the withdrawal symptoms, which bring about craving and loss of control or inability to abstain." The theorizing of the day developing in biochemical circles regarding the process of addiction no doubt inspired Jellinek's distinction regarding the true disease as distinct from a psychological problem.

Later, Jellinek (1960) proffered a fifth type of alcoholic: an episolon alcoholic. An *episolon alcoholic* is a binger. Apparently recalling that binges were the major symptom signifying the beginning of the chronic stage, Jellinek allowed that some gamma alcoholics, who are most likely to display the modal progression, will often become episolon alcoholics. Jellinek cautioned that the binge is "a relapse into a disease, but I must add that the occasion for the relapse is a voluntary one and does not form a part of the disease process" (p. 41).

In 1955, a committee of the World Health Organization chaired by Jellinek was convened to consider the concept of craving and addiction. According to the AA perspective, the excessive consumption of alcoholics is caused by craving for alcohol, a subjective phenomenon not experienced by normal drinkers. Both loss of control given a priming dose of alcohol and resumption of drinking after a period of abstinence were purported to be attributable to craving. Although craving can occur without an identifiable precipitant, one highly probable mechanism for inducing craving is to imbibe even the most minute quantity of alcohol. These AA beliefs were reiterated in the 1955 meeting and were recorded in archival form (Jellinek, 1960).

Criticisms of Jellinek

Jellinek's empirical contributions consisted of the 1946 and 1952 analyses of questionnaire responses. Jellinek's major conclusion from the responses to his questionnaires was that alcoholism is progressive. Stated alternatively, once particular events have occurred, other events will necessarily follow. There are several reasons why the analysis of the original questionnaire does not address the issue of progression. First, Jellinek surveyed AA members. AA members are exposed to schemas which make it likely that they will recall and interpret events in their lives consistent with particular symptomotology. Exposure to doctrine results in the belief that all predicted events have happened. Responses to questions reflect frame of reference, not reality. The second flaw in Jellinek's methodology precluding inferences regarding inexorable staging concerns the lack of a control group. It should be recalled that Jellinek was surveying alcoholics (AA members) who had all hit bottom or at least thought they had hit bottom and then remained in AA. Jellinek had no data on the fate of alcoholics at time two who had exhibited crucial stage symptomotology at time one but who did not become AA members at a later date. He could not know whether some individuals returned to prior stages or arrested at a particular stage.

Jellinek's contributions have largely been theoretical rather than empirical. He did attempt to integrate the contemporary thinking of his day from pharmacology to explain the observed alcoholic phenomenon of tolerance and withdrawal. As the concepts and explanations in pharmacology have changed, the utility of Jellinek's integration has been vitiated. Jellinek can be credited with offering a wealth of testable hypotheses. Perhaps his major contribution has been a heuristic one.

Traditional Ideas Arising after Jellinek

Euphoric Recall

In most treatment centers, patients are told that as the disease progresses, the impact of alcohol on the imbiber's mood changes. For the nonalcoholic drinker, alcohol induces a good mood. After the alcohol is metabolized mood returns to normal. A different processes occurs in the alcoholic. As the alcoholic progression continues, the alcoholic deviates from the normal experience with alcohol. Mood does not return to normal after drinking, but rather slides into the dysphoric range. When the baseline, sober state mood becomes dysphoria, the alcoholic drinks in order to escape the dysphoria. Unlike the early drinking stages, drinking no longer results in a good mood. For the alcoholic, drinking restores to a normal mood state, but no longer induces euphoria. Methaphorically, the drinker is drinking to "get well."

An unusual phenomenon is occurring concomitant with this process. The drinker is not an accurate observer of the change in the nature of the drinking experience. The alcoholic continues to believe that alcohol produces a good mood. This phenomenon is called euphoric recall. Johnson (1980), author of I'll Quit Tomorrow, explains that frequently the alcoholic is in a blackout which precludes accurate recall of his/her mood while drinking. Thus, the drinking mood is remembered as euphoric even though the veridical state was a return to a neutral mood.

Progression of the Disease During Sobriety

Since Jellinek, the notion of progression has received an added embellishment. Father Martin, a priest who has made films on the topic of alcoholism which are shown in traditional treatment programs, states in the film entitled Chalk Talk, that the disease continues to progress even when the alcoholic is not drinking. Should there be a relapse, the alcoholism (undefined) will be worse than it was prior to the abstinent period.

Cross Addiction

Most treatment centers stress the possibility of cross addiction or drug substitution. Citing the cross tolerance of alcohol with barbiturates and benzodiazepines, the case is made that alcoholics are more susceptible than normals to addiction to other chemicals (marijuana, cocaine, heroin, tranquilizers). Conversely, substance abusers are also told that they are more likely than the general population to become alcoholic. Additionally, being under the influence of another chemical is predicted to precipitate relapse to drinking.

Dry Drunks

In AA, the notion of craving has been extended to the related concept of dry drunk (Flaherty, McGuire, & Gatski, 1955). Dry drunks are episodes of unusual behavior without alcohol (sometimes dysphoric mood, sometimes euphoric behavior, sometimes physical sensations of intoxication). Further, in AA based treatment centers, patients displaying resentments or irritations are diagnosed as dry drunks. It is asserted that the diverse mood states encompassed under the term dry drunk, are disguised cravings. All such deviations from the modal state make urges to drink or drinking more likely as well as providing excuses for drinking.

In recent years, AA treatment philosophy has embraced a fillip on the concept of dry drunk, proposed by Gorski and Miller (1982) have suggested that the residual effects of withdrawal will be present throughout the third month postabstinence. Residual withdrawal effects (Post Acute Withdrawal Syndrome, PAW) will be manifested as cognitive deficits, apprehension, irritability, and depression. As in the prior conceptualization of dry drunk, PAW is supposed to increase the probability of a relapse.

Personality Characteristics

AA stresses the salience of resentments in the behavior of alcoholics (Thoreson & Budd, 1987). Vern Johnson (1980) discusses self-pity, grandiosity, selfishness, and perfectionism. Alcoholics are also depicted as highly controlling individuals. In some treatment programs, personality defects are given as much focus as the drinking.

The Definition of Alcoholism

The definition of alcoholism most widely accepted has been the definition proffered by Jellinek and adopted by the World Health Organization. Alcoholism is drinking which creates problems, that is, it is any use of alcoholic beverages that causes damage to the individual or society or both (Jellinek, 1960; WHO, 1952). Jellinek reserved the concept of alcoholism as a disease, for those alcoholics with loss of control and symptoms of addiction. However, currently, in most AA based treatment centers all persons exhibiting any problem created by drinking are considered to have the disease of alcoholism. In today's AA perspective, there are no nondisease forms of alcoholism.

EVIDENCE FOR AND AGAINST THE AA AXIOMS

Craving

An AA assumption is that excessive drinking, loss of control, and indiscreet drinking are mediated by craving. Craving can occur during periods of abstinence but more reliably occurs when a priming dose of alcohol is imbibed. It has not gone unrecognized that this notion is somewhat circular (Pattison, Sobell, & Sobell, 1977). Alcoholics drink excessively because of craving and excessive drinking is prima facia evidence of craving. Nevertheless, the notion of craving has generated testable hypotheses. Three avenues of research can be identified. Researchers have manipulated whether alcoholics received alcohol or placebo and examined the impact on subjective desire for alcohol (craving) and consumption. This vein of research has tested the basic hypothesis that a little bit of alcohol will unleash a compelling motivation to drink. Others have assumed that craving, in some form, does exist and have speculated about the learning phenomenon which can account for (explain) its existence. The demonstration of conditioned learning following alcohol consumption has been advanced as evidence supportive of craving. A third vein of empirical investigation has examined whether recovering alcoholics do experience craving and whether cravings are reliable precipitants to relapse.

Tests of the Basic Hypothesis

One of the first empirical investigations of craving induced by a priming dose of alcohol was conducted by Merry (1966). Merry had access to a sample of hospitalized alcoholics. He sought to determine whether giving alcoholics alcohol disguised and labeled as a liquid form of vitamin supplement would, in fact, unleash an irresistible craving. Merry varied the beverage provided to hospitalized alcoholics over an 18-day period. Drinking days were interspersed between nondrinking days. On each of the 18 days the drink ingested was purported to be a vitamin mixture regardless of veridical content. Each day a measure of subjective craving was taken. The results yielded no support for an association between craving and beverage consumed. Subjects reported no greater craving on days when they had imbibed alcohol than on days when they had not.

Merry's results have been replicated and extended. Engle and Williams (1972) gave alcoholics a liquid mixture on their fifth day of hospitalization. They used a balanced placebo design. Half of the subjects received a mixture containing 1 oz. of 100 proof vodka. The other half received an inert substance. Crossed with the beverage factor was an expectancy factor. Half of the subjects were told they were consuming alcohol while the other half were told they were consuming vitamins. Following consumption, craving measures were taken which were embedded in measures of craving for food and mood measures. Engle and Williams report that the only pairwise comparison that yielded a group difference was between the received alcohol/told vitamin and the received alcohol/told alcohol conditions. Alcoholics reported more craving when they believed they had consumed alcohol. Maisto, Lauerman, and Adesso (1977) report the results of a similar experiment employing hospitalized alcoholics as subjects. A balanced placebo design was utilized and measures of craving were taken. The results indicated that what the subjects believed they were drinking influenced craving although actual content of the mixture consumed did not. Craving, once induced, persisted through the day.

Marlatt, Demming, and Reid (1973) employed a balanced placebo design adding a subjects factor (alcoholic vs. normal subjects) to their study. Each subject was given a priming dose of a beverage purported to be tonic or alcohol before performing a taste rating task. Pretesting indicated that the actual content of the drink was successfully disguised. The purpose of the taste rating task was purported to be an examination of taste sensitivity. The dependent measure was the amount of beverage consumed in the process of making taste discriminations. The beverage available for consumption in the taste testing task varied in accordance with experimental condition, i.e., in those conditions in which the priming dose was alcohol the beverage consumed in tasting was alcohol, whereas when the priming dose was tonic the tasting beverage was tonic. The beverage to be tasted was purported to be alcohol or tonic consistent with what subjects had been told about the priming dose. Results suggested that all subjects, alcoholics and controls, drank more when they believed they were drinking alcohol, regardless of actual beverage content.

A study by Asp (1977) did demonstrate that alcoholics will drink more than normals if they believe that the substance is alcohol. Asp gave alcoholics and normals a priming dose of alcohol and then measured their inert substance consumption which was alleged to be either alcohol or nonalcoholic beverage. Among the normals, beverage label did not influence consumption, but alcoholics drank more when they believed they were drinking alcohol.

There was a study that was somewhat supportive of a pharmacological rather than a beverage label effect for alcoholics. Stockwell et al. (1982) found that severely dependent alcoholics drank more rapidly after receiving real alcohol, regardless of what they believed they had consumed. Expectancy, stemming from the belief that they had drunk alcohol, was associated with stronger statements of a desire to drink after the priming dose.

Further Clarification

The prior studies do call into question the notion that the certain pharmacological impact of alcohol will at all times release an irresistible craving for alcohol. Old beliefs die hard even in the face of irrefutable evidence. Amended versions of the loss of control notion have been proffered. Keller (1972a) suggested that alcoholics will only sometimes experience loss of control. Ludwig and Wikler (1974) suggested that alcohol alone is an insufficient condition for loss of control, although a necessary condition. Certain environmental circumstance must also be present for loss of control to occur. There as been a test of the amended version. Berg, Laberg, Skutle, and Ohman (1981) examined the response to alcohol or an alcohol placebo which was purported to be either alcohol or tonic (balanced placebo design) in a home setting while alcoholics viewed a ball game in groups. (The setting was a response to the issue of the need for a natural setting that had been raised in criticism of earlier studies.) Dependent measures of craving, amount consumed, and rate of consumption were examined. Only what the alcoholics believed to be true about the beverage produced an effect. The actual drunk content made no difference.

The original notion of craving held that the pharmacological impact of alcohol induces unrestrained consumption. The implication was that this unrestrained consumption would not be modified by competing motivations of the alcoholic. Once primed by a dose of alcohol, the need for drink would overshadow other needs. Speaking to this issue has been a large body of research examining the drinking of alcoholics under controlled ward conditions. These studies suggest that alcoholics are more likely to consume in greater quantity when drinking from a cold start rather than imbibing after a priming dose (Cutter, Schwab, & Nathan, 1970). Alcoholics will not consume all the alcohol available but rather will drink to maintain a blood alcohol level around .175 to .25 mg/ml (Mello & Mendelson, 1971; Nathan & O'Brien, 1971; Skolada et al., 1975). The amount consumed will be affected by a variety of environmental circumstances. Alcoholics will defer immediate solitary drinking in order to drink later in an enriched social environment (Bigelow et al., 1974). The amount of work required to earn the alcohol will influence the amount consumed (McNamee, Mello, & Mendelson, 1968). These studies suggest that alcoholics are seeking a particular state when they drink. Further the cost of this particular state will influence how much will be drunk.

Data is also available on drinking habits of alcoholics in the natural environment. According to the self-reports of alcoholics on the amount consumed on any particular occasion, consumption is influenced by a host of contextual variables. Whether drinking occurs with persons who approve of heavy consumption, whether drinking occurs while one is alone, will both influence the reported amount consumed (Choquette, Hesselbrock, & Babor, 1985).

Learning Theory Explanations of Craving

Whereas the prior research investigated the occurrence of craving, others have attempted to understand its causes. Ludwig, Wikler, and Stark (1974) and Pomerleau, Fertig, Baker, and Cooney (1983) have explained craving as a phenomena resulting from respondent conditioning. These authors have primarily focused on delineating unconditioned stimuli and conditioned stimuli and to a lesser extent upon the exact specification of the conditioned response, i.e., the response which is assumed to mediate or be synonymous with craving.

According to the first version of the learning theory explanations of craving propounded by Ludwig et al. (1974) alcoholics undergo a conditioning process each time they withdraw from alcohol. The withdrawal of alcohol is the unconditioned stimulus and the situational context (extended to include internal cues such as bad mood as well as external cues) are the conditioned stimuli. Such situational cues present during the withdrawal process will come to elicit withdrawal symptoms in absence of the physiological process of withdrawal. To explain why the conditioned response of withdrawal symptoms will motivate drinking, Ludwig and Wikler (1974) switch from a respondent paradigm to an operant paradigm. Because the autonomic state associated with withdrawal is aversive, the alcoholic will be motivated to perform some behavior to escape the aversive state. In the past, the alcoholic has learned to escape withdrawal symptoms by further drinking. Having learned to drink to escape the aversive physiological state occurring during withdrawal, the alcoholic will drink to escape this conditioned response state also.

There is data both consistent and inconsistent with Ludwig and Wikler's notion. Consistent with the notion is the fact that there is a correlation between the severity of these withdrawal symptoms and the choice to drink in the laboratory (Kaplan, Meyer, & Stroebel, 1983). Also consistent is a significant correlation between a measure of prior withdrawal symptoms and a measure of prior cravings (Ludwig et al., 1974) and between prior withdrawal symptoms and measures of autonomic reactivity to the presentation of alcohol (Kaplan et al., 1985). Alcoholics who have experienced severe withdrawal evidence greater craving (defined as rapid consumption of a second drink) after a priming dose (Hodgson, Rankin, & Stockwell, 1979). Alcoholics evidence greater salivation (perhaps an index of craving) in response to alcohol placebo than do normals (Monti et al., 1987).

The theory holds that conditioned responses are similar to the autonomic state of withdrawal. Withdrawal is posited to induce a strong compulsion to drink. Here is where Ludwig and Stark's theorizing is not supported by empirical findings. Inconsistent with Ludwig and Wikler's notion is the data suggesting that withdrawal symptoms may not be a strong motivation to drink. Observation of ward drinking by alcoholics under controlled conditions suggests that they will save tokens to purchase a large supply of alcohol later rather than using tokens to escape immediate withdrawal symptoms (Tamerin, Weiner, & Mendelson, 1970). Hershon (1977) found that alcoholics more often reported drinking to relieve dysphoric mood accompanying cessation of drinking than drinking to relieve the physical symptoms (shaking, nausea, etc.). The latter symptoms are probably a better index of withdrawal since the physical symptoms correlated more highly with quantity/frequency of drinking measures than did the mood cluster. Another finding against the conditioned withdrawal hypothesis is the fact that withdrawal severity assessed prior to treatment does not predict relapse during a follow-up interval (Heather, Rollnick, & Winton, 1983).

A second learning theory explanation of craving has been proffered by Pomerleau et al. (1983). This explanation holds that the situational cues present when the alcoholic imbibes come to elicit, via respondent learning (conditioning), the autonomic state associated with actual drinking. (The bar, the martini glass, even the social context, can induce autonomic states associated with drinking.) The autonomic state associated with drinking can be either the state induced by the pharmacological impact of the drug (e.g., tachycardia, increased respiration) or an opponent process opposite in direction to the pharmacological impact, known to occur upon presentation of an alcohol placebo (bradycardia, decreased respiration). Regardless of which autonomic events are elicited by the situational cues associated with drinking (conditioned stimuli), these autonomic events will motivate continued drinking.

There has been demonstration of autonomic activity opposite in direction to the pharmacological impact of alcohol upon presentation of alcohol placebo (Newlin, 1985). Conditioning of this response can occur. It has also been demonstrated that those alcoholics who display a greater degree of conditioned autonomic activity might be construed as more subjectively impelled to drink. Those alcoholics who salivate more when presented with an alcohol placebo are more likely to relapse after treatment (Pomerlau et al., 1983). Those alcoholics who respond with greater magnitude of galvanic skin response (sweating palms) to alcohol presentation, report more subjective response to consumption of alcohol and alcohol placebo (Kaplan, Meyer, & Virgilio, 1984). In addition, alcoholics who display greater autonomic reactivity to alcohol will more often chose it as a reward on operant trials (Kaplan, Meyer, & Stroebel, 1983).

The prior research does establish the occurrence of conditioned events. Further, greater magnitude of conditioned events is found among those with more severe alcohol problems. Although these correlational findings are intriguing, causal links have not yet been demonstrated.

Natural Occurrence of Craving

Another avenue used to investigate the issue of craving has been to monitor the occurrence of the phenomenon in sober alcoholics. Such monitoring can address the issue of whether large percentages of alcoholics experience the phenomenon and whether the phenomenon is temporally associated with relapse.

Mathew, Claghorn, and Largen (1979) examined 46 alcoholics residing in a halfway house who had a mean duration of sobriety of 6 weeks. Eighty-six percent of these individuals reported experiencing cravings of varying severity. Mathew et al. requested subjects to reflect back to their mood state extant while they were experiencing the craving. Similar to the findings of Ludwig and Stark (1974) who found that craving overlapped with symptoms of dysphoria, 85% of subjects reported that at least some of their craving had been precipitated by a negative mood, especially anger/hostility. A measure of trait anxiety positively correlated with intensity of cravings experienced. The severity of cravings dissipated with increased periods of sobriety. Duration of alcoholism was not associated with severity of craving. Another study suggested that craving is usually not a spontaneous phenomenon, but rather is generally a response to external events. A study by Ludwig (1986) found that only 7% failed to identify reliable precipitants to craving.

If craving, defined as compelling thoughts about drinking occurring during periods of sobriety, is an important phenomenon, craving should be a frequent precipitant to relapse. The literature examining the self-report of mood and external factors immediately preceding relapse can be consulted. Cravings should precede and precipitate relapse episodes. In fact, the relapse literature suggests that dysphoric feelings precipitated by external events and encouragement from others to drink are the most frequent precipitants to relapse (Marlatt, 1985b). Subjective desires, cravings, are infrequently mentioned as a condition preceding the relapse (only 1% of Ludwig's 1972 sample).

Summary

Conditioned responses to alcohol and alcohol placebos have been demonstrated. According to the learning theory explanations of the etiology of craving, conditioned events are supposed to underlie craving and motivation to drink. Conditioned events are believed to be evoked by alcohol and alcohol placebos as well as cues (internal and external) which were associated with prior withdrawal episodes. The problem with the learning theories explanation of craving is in bridging from the phenomena of conditioned responses to the notion that these conditioned responses will motivate drinking. Empirical support is lacking. The originators of the theories cite correlational findings of greater choice to drink among those who have sustained severe withdrawal or among those who salivate given alcohol cues. These correlational findings need not imply a causal link between the conditioned response (salivation, conditioned withdrawal symptoms) and strong, overriding motivation to drink. In fact, the relapse literature, suggests that craving, unrelated to external events, is not a frequent precipitant to relapse.

THE EXPECTED COURSE OF DEVELOPMENT OF ALCOHOLISM

Many of the traditional notions (progression until insanity or death, stages, impossibility of control drinking) relate to the issue of the long-term history of alcoholics. According to traditional doctrine, given continued drinking the disease continues to progress until insanity or death occurs. Controlled drinking is impossible. Given continued drinking, a return to less problematic drinking should not occur nor should symptoms plateau.

Several avenues of research have provided a wealth of information as to the long-term fate of alcoholics. Lemere (1953) was original in having selected a group of relatives of 500 alcoholics. He queried these relatives about the eventual fates of their alcoholic relative. Others have begun with general population data bases and have followed those in the sample exhibiting drinking symptomotology over a number of years. The third avenue of research has followed clinic samples, some of whom left before participating in treatment and others who received treatment, over a number of years. Clinic samples have been queried as to the progression of their drinking prior to treatment in order to determine whether events would cluster into stages. They have been followed after treatment to determine the percentages who recovered, continued to drink, died, or became asymptomatic drinkers.

Progression

The notion of progression implies that once an alcoholic process is established it will exacerbate unless arrested through abstinence. Stated alternatively, given events offering clear evidence of alcoholism, then certain other future events are predictable. The proper methodology for addressing the question is to begin with individuals exhibiting particular behavior at time one and assess them at time two to determine if the predicted behaviors have occurred.

Jellinek has suggested that one definition of alcoholism is drinking that is creating problems in some area of life. Assuming that such a definition is valid, one can evaluate the hypothesis of progression by tracking over time a group of individuals selected for exhibiting problems with their drinking. One way to evaluate progression is to begin with groups of undiagnosed alcoholics who are exhibiting problem drinking to determine their future outcomes. A group of individuals who are exhibiting problems at time one, even though they may not have been diagnosed at time one, should continue to display the same or worse level of problem at time two with their drinking, if the progression hypothesis is correct and if problem drinking is a pathognomonic indicator of alcoholism.

Several investigators have longitudinally followed young persons who manifest a large number of alcoholic symptoms. The results of these studies suggest that persons who manifest symptomotology while young adults frequently become nonproblem drinking older adults (Donovan, Jessor, & Jessor, 1983; Fillmore, 1974, 1975; Goodwin, Crane, & Guze, 1971; Vaillant, 1983). In Vaillant's blue collar sample, 25% of those individuals who could be described as exhibiting alcohol abuse without exhibiting the range of problems required for a diagnosis of alcoholism had remitted to asymptomatic drinking before age 35. (That is, their early behavior was symptomatic, while their later drinking behavior lacked symptoms of alcoholism.) In Donovan et al.'s sample, 53% of the men and 70% of the women who exhibited problems became nonproblem drinkers in their early 20s. Fillmore followed up on a college sample 20 years later. The majority of the college problem drinkers had remitted. Goodwin et al. followed up felons identified as problem drinkers in their early 20s. Two thirds of the sample had experienced withdrawal, benders, or cirrhosis. Many (21 out of 93) were drinking nonproblematically at 8-year follow-up. Others have found that those drinking problematically as young adolescents (15 years of age) remit by early adulthood (Andersson & Magnusson, 1988). Vaillant (1983, p. 145) identified a group of alcoholics in his sample of 110 core city alcoholics whom he labeled atypical. These 19 persons did not seem to progress, although they did not remit either. In comparison with the persons Vaillant labeled typical alcoholic, they experienced fewer problems with jobs, money, and families. They more often drank low proof liquor.

The studies just cited suggest that progressive deterioration is not an inevitable outcome for problem drinkers. A second question, is whether it is possible to identify particular subsets of young problematic drinkers who are more likely to become adult problem drinkers. In college samples, severity of drinking problems is a predictor of future alcoholism (Fillmore, 1975). In lower SES (socioeconomic status) samples, where heavy drinking is more frequently expected, severity of problems in the young is not related to future alcoholism (Goodwin et al., 1971). Andersson and Magnusson (1988) found that frequency of drunkenness and attention from authorities at an early age, distinguished the group who remained problematic at ages 18–24.

In addition to longitudinal studies following young adult or adolescent problem drinkers, there are household survey data collected over a 4-year period by Clark (1976) on problem drinkers of various ages. Clark found that the correlation between any particular problem at Time I and that same problem at Time II was low and insignificant. However, there was evidence of some stability over time for persons manifesting particular symptoms at Time I. Seventy-six percent of persons manifesting symptomatic drinking (endorsing such items as sneaking drinking, morning drinking, and drinking more than others) at Time I, reported problematic drinking at Time II. Seventy-eight percent of persons reporting loss of control at Time I, reported problematic drinking at Time II. While these findings suggest stability over the 4 years, they also provide that over 20% of the sample had remitted. In the same sample, half of those with job problems, accidents, and financial problems at Time I, reported no problems with their drinking at Time II although they continued to drink.

The fact that there are human beings drinking problematically at Time I who will continue to drink problematically in the future cannot be disputed. In a sample of young problem drinkers, problem drinking during high school or college did enhance prediction of adult problem drinking (Donovan et al., 1983; Fillmore, 1974). Andersson and Magnusson (1988) found that those exhibiting problematic drinking at 15 were more likely than those in the control group to be problem drinkers in early adulthood. For predictive purposes, problem drinking at Time II is more likely for those who are problem drinking at time I.

The hypothesis of progression can be evaluated in other ways as well. Some might argue that problematic drinking is not a sufficiently stringent definition of alcoholism. Perhaps a sample of unequivocal alcoholics, that is those who present for treatment, constitutes a more appropriate sample for evaluating the hypothesis of progression. The progression hypothesis predicts that alcoholics who continue to drink will deteriorate. They will either display worse symptomotology or die. They should not remain at the same level of problem. Control drinking should not be possible.

Stable Levels of Alcoholism

Alcoholics identified at time one as needing treatment, but who continue to drink during a prolonged follow-up period, constitute a relevant group for evaluating the hypothesis of progression. Some studies suggest that alcoholics can maintain a stable level of problem drinking over many years even after they present for treatment or are recommended for treatment. Kendell and Stanton (1966), following 62 alcoholics who had refused treatment, found that 59% were continuing to drink in a stably problematic manner. The index of social status for the group had not changed in the ensuing mean 6.7 years of the follow-up period. Hyman (1976) conducted a 16-year follow-up of alcoholics who had been in treatment. Ten of Hyman's sample of 54, who at 16-year follow-up were between 46 and 60, continued to drink in a stably problematic fashion. Three of the 10 had changed their consumption pattern to a binge pattern. The lack of deterioration was also consistent with Lemere's finding that only 5% of the alcoholics eventuated in skid row. Twenty-nine percent of Lemere's sample continued to drink problematically throughout their lives, although they did not die of alcohol related conditions. In Vaillant's (1983) community sample of alcoholics tracked for 20 years until age 47, 35 of the 110 living alcoholics were continuing to drink in a chronically problematic fashion.

Retrospective Histories of Alcoholics

If a researcher begins with a sample of alcoholics in treatment and evaluates their histories prior to treatment, a pattern of progression will frequently be found. Many definitions of alcoholism require that an individual exhibit a requisite number of problems across a number of qualitative dimensions (physical symptomotology and social difficulties). Vaillant (1983) defined alcoholism in this way in his examination of patterns in 3 different samples of alcoholics. In Vaillant's contingent of adult alcoholics identified from a community sample, half of the alcoholics had not accumulated enough problems across diverse dimensions to be considered alcoholic until reaching the age of 30 (Vaillant, 1983, p. 132).

Defining alcoholism in terms of accumulated symptomotology across a number of areas (social functioning, family functioning, physical events) may capture the modal pattern for the bulk of alcoholics. The modal age of presentation for treatment or AA is early to mid forties and most alcoholics presenting for treatment have exhibited problems in their drinking for a decade or more (Drew, 1968; Jellinek, 1946, 1952). However, if one selects a particular dimension of alcoholism, viz. severity of dependence, the assumption of a diversity of symptoms over a protracted period of time, breaks down. Orford and Keddie (1986) failed to find a relationship between severity of physical dependence and problem duration. This suggests that for some, physical dependence emerges rather rapidly, without having been preceded by problem drinking which smoldered for years.

Stages

Beyond the issue of whether some persons who at some point have a prior history of problem drinking can unequivocally be labeled alcoholic, is the issue of whether events in their prior history will conform to the sequence that Jellinek has predicted they would. A number of studies have been conducted in which alcoholics in treatment have been asked when and if they experienced the events that define the Jellinek stages.

All of the studies of stages have replicated the grosser findings of Jellinek's sequence of alcohol related problems, but for a large number of events the predicted sequence has not been supported (Jackson, 1957; Park, 1973; Park & Whitehead, 1973; Pokorny, Kanas, & Overall, 1981; Trice & Wahl, 1958). Trice and Wahl report that the symptoms at the beginning (first drink, first intoxication, and first blackout) and the end (hitting bottom, tremors, and convulsions) tend to cluster, although the symptoms in the middle tend to vary across individuals in terms of the order of appearance. Other empirical investigations (Goodwin, Crane, & Guze, 1969a, 1969b) of a specific symptom, the blackout, call into question Trice and Wahl's finding. Examining a sample of 100 alcoholics, Goodwin and colleagues found that a third had never experienced a blackout. Frequency of blackout tended to increase with greater levels of consumption and advancing age. However, frequently first blackout had been preceded by withdrawal symptoms, severe social consequences from drinking, and instantiation of a binge pattern.

Examining a sample of VA alcoholics, Park and Whitehead (1973) reported the number of alcoholics who had not experienced particular symptoms. In their sample, 45% had not experienced frequent hangovers, 66% had not been jealous, 44% had not looked forward to drinking, 40% had not been reproached by their wives, 46% had not changed their friends, 80% had not been aggressive while drinking. These findings suggest that even among alcoholics who had reported a drinking history, predictions about particular events cannot be made with confidence.

Others have examined sequencing in alcoholics from different cultures. Park and Whitehead (1973) compared a sample of Finnish alcoholics with a sample of American alcoholics. The American alcoholics conformed to Jellinek's ordering better than the Finnish alcoholics. Fillmore (1975) examined sequence in college age individuals. She found that among the college age problem drinkers, binge drinking (drinking heavily for protracted periods on weekends) and symptomatic drinking precedes psychological dependence and frequent intoxication. Such discrepancies from Jellinek's findings make salient the caveat to consider the normative drinking styles of the population under consideration. Behaviors that are concomitants of well entrenched problematic drinking in some subcultures, may be initiation rights in other subcultures.

Negative Outcomes: Death, Insanity, or Skid Row?

The fact that some alcoholics do not recover from alcoholism during their lifetime cannot be disputed. Some of these individuals do die of alcohol related causes. Others are institutionalized due to alcohol induced brain damage.

Of Lemere's (1953) 500 alcoholics, 28% had died of alcohol related causes. Part of this 28%, (11% of the total sample) had suicided. In Lemere's sample the mean age of death was 52, which is well below the expected longevity of the general population. Sixteen percent of the sample lived to be older than 75 whereas 12% died before age 40. Hyman (1976) followed 54 alcoholics treated 15 to 16 years earlier in a public treatment facility who at the time of follow up would have been between the ages of 46 to 60. He also found support for the AA notion that alcoholism results in insanity (broadly interpreted as brain damage) or death. Nineteen of 54 were deceased and 5 were brain damaged. Nicholls, Edwards, and Kyle (1974) tracked 114 alcoholics 15 years after treatment. The death rate in the sample was 2.65 times the expected rate for men and 3.07 times the expected rate for women. Ojesjo (1981) followed 96 alcoholics for 15 years. Twenty-seven percent of the sample had died during the follow-up period. However, 84% of those who died were over age 65 at the time of death. McCabe

(1986) followed 55 alcoholics 16 years after treatment, 43% had died with the mean age of death at 60. Vaillant (1983) tracked 120 inner city alcoholics over 20 years when the alcoholics were age 47. By last follow-up, 10 had died.

With a much shorter follow-up interval, Kendell and Stanton (1966) investigated 62 alcoholics a mean of 6.7 years after they had refused treatment at Maudsley hospital. Eighteen percent of the sample were deceased. As in the Lemere sample, the rate of suicide (8%) was striking. The Rand commission tracked alcoholics for 4 years following treatment (Polich, Armor, & Braiker, 1980). Data from 758 alcoholics who had been treated in government funded programs were available. Fourteen and a half percent of the sample had died during the follow-up period. The Rand report indicated that the mortality rate was 2.5 times the expected rate for the general population equated for sex and age.

Higher than average death rates for alcoholics emerges as a finding in all of the longitudinal studies. Whereas poor health and suicide contribute to the increased mortality rate, alcoholics are also 7 times more likely to die in a fatal accident than the general population (Brenner, 1967).

A question that longitudinal studies have frequently failed to address is determination of the deceased's drinking status at time of death. Are those who die more likely to still be drinking at time of death? A study by Ornstein and Cherepon (1985) attempted to assess the drinking status at time of death in those who were found to be deceased at 2 year follow-up. The distribution of abstinent, improved, unimproved drinking was the same among the deceased group as in the total sample. A study by Pell and D'Alonzo (1973) found that abstinence did not alter mortality rate in a sample followed for 5 years. Whether mortality rates decline with extended abstinence is an unanswered question that should be addressed in the future.

Expected Rate of Abstinence

Investigators of alcoholics who have never presented for treatment, and follow-up investigations of alcoholics who have received treatment, offer data on the percentages who remain abstinent. Reports of alcoholics followed over the years suggest that many become abstinent. Of the 62 alcoholics who refused treatment at Maudsley hospital 15% had been sober for over 1 year at 6.7 year follow-up (Kendell & Stanton, 1966). One third of Lemere's sample, most of whom had never been treated, achieved sobriety during their life times. Fourteen and a half percent of McCabe's treated alcoholics who were followed-up at year 16 were abstinent. Of Hyman's 54 blue collar alcoholics who had been treated 15–16 years earlier, 5 were abstinent at follow-up. In Vaillant's sample of alcoholics having grown up in inner city Boston, most of whom had never received treatment, 21 out of 110 had been securely abstinent (not more than one intoxicated bout of less than a week duration per year) for 3 years at time of 20 year follow-up.

Vaillant (1983) reviewed the results of 10 longitudinal studies examining the fate of alcoholics over at least a 10-year time span. The 10 studies included Vaillant's own data following a cohort of inner city, lower class individuals, who had not received treatment, and a cohort of treated inner city clinic males. Unfortunately, the dependent variable category referred to status at follow-up only, making it impossible to infer whether particular individuals had moved into and out of particular categories (e.g., had been sober for an appreciable period and then relapsed) during the years intervening between the initiation of follow-up and the end of the study.

Despite problems precluding some inferences, Vaillant drew several clarifying conclusions. Based on the fact that those studies with longer follow-up periods and hence older subjects at the time of follow-up reported the greater rates of abstinence, Vaillant concluded that if an alcoholic does not die, the chances of recovery (abstinence or control drinking) in late middle age (after 50 to early 70s) are good. Over half the subjects in Vaillant's inner city sample had recovered. Vaillant reported that each year, 2–3% of alcoholics become abstinent and 1% revert to control drinking. Vaillant's findings are consistent with those of Smart (1975–1976) who reviewed findings from several surveys. Smart concluded that across studies recovery rates among nontreated alcoholics vary from 10–42% and each year approximately 33% of alcoholics become abstinent or revert to asymptomatic drinking.

Spontaneous Recovery

Many AA based treatment programs advance the notion that treatment and/or AA participation are necessary conditions for abstinence. Some have amended this position to the prediction that happy, "serene" abstinence can only be achieved in AA. Staying dry without personal equanimity can be achieved without AA, but AA is necessary for contented sobriety, some maintain. There is empirical data available allowing for evaluation of the hypothesis that treatment is necessary for sobriety. Studies in which alcoholics are tracked over time suggest that the majority of alcoholics will become sober outside of treatment or AA. Vaillant's examination of male alcoholics suggests that the majority of those achieving abstinence do so without having sought treatment or help through AA. Those alcoholics achieving sobriety in Lemere's sample (⅓ of those considered) had done so without treatment or AA. Only 2 of the 5 sober alcoholics who had previously received treatment in Hyman's sample were AA members. These findings suggest that some alcoholics do recover without benefit of treatment or an AA program. The issue of personal contentment has not been directly addressed in these studies.

Findings suggesting those factors precipitating a change in drinking habits are available. Marriage, job, and ill health are identified as factors promoting abstinence (Chapman & Huygens, 1988; Lemere, 1953; Ojesjo, 1981; Saunders &

Kershaw, 1979; Vaillant, 1983) and for cutting back to control drinking (Bailey & Stewart, 1967; Saunders & Kershaw, 1979). These same factors tend to be present in persons who seek treatment (Gerard, Saenger, & Wilie, 1962). Those who remit in their 30s more often identify marriage as a factor and less often mention ill health as a factor in motivating change (Donovan et al., 1983; Saunders & Kershaw, 1979); while the converse is true for those remitting later in adulthood (Saunders & Kershaw, 1979).

Results of community surveys suggest that the same reasons heavy drinkers provide for changing their drinking also motivate those who have never received an alcoholic diagnosis. Cahalan, Cisin, and Crossley (1969) in a community sample found that people often mentioned increased problems and responsibility, health, and financial pressures as reasons for a decrease in their consumption. They found that people tend to attribute an increase in their drinking to factors such as a change in friends, having more money, and an increase in free time. In a long-term study of individuals employed in the liquor industry, which has a very high alcoholism rate, Plant (1979) found that persons did decrease their drinking when they left the industry. These findings suggest that changes in life circumstances influence drinking habits at all levels of alcohol consumption.

Data regarding age at which alcoholics present for treatment shed further light regarding the circumstances that promote change. Most of Lemere's sample of recovered alcoholics had quit after they reached the age of 45. Mulford (1977) found that the average alcoholic presenting for treatment had been preoccupied with drinking for 7.3 years, had been aware of criticism from others for over 6 years, and had been debating over whether to do something about the drinking for over 3 years prior to presenting for treatment.

The notion that hitting bottom precipitates abstinence receives partial support from the findings that decisions to recover are made in response to external pressures and the fact that many require a protracted duration of problematic drinking before they consider a change in their behavior. Hitting bottom, defined as experiencing the accumulation of negative consequences, does precipitate attempts to change.

There is a caveat on the concept of hitting bottom. The outcome literature suggests worse outcome among those who have hit bottom as evidenced by their depleted resources (no marriage, no job) (Lemere, O'Hallaren, & Maxwell, 1958). Threat of loss appears to enhance recovery, actual loss seems to be associated with less recovery. Of course, the variables of severity of alcoholism and loss of position and resources due to drinking are confounded, making it difficult to decipher the causal factor in creating a poor outcome. It does appear that serious problems help to focus people's attention on their alcoholism, and can sometimes stimulate recovery. It is not clear that hitting bottom in the sense of losing everything is a health promoting step on the road to recovery.

Mechanisms for Maintaining Abstinence

Vaillant (1983) interviewed the abstinent alcoholics in his sample in an attempt to decipher which factors were associated with their stable abstention. Over half the alcoholics in the sample mentioned will power as a factor in their achievement. There was an association between the severity of alcoholism and attribution of sobriety to will power. Those with the more severe alcoholic histories less often mentioned will power as a factor in sobriety. Vaillant cautioned that although will power was a factor in the subjective perceptions of these alcoholics, other factors emerged for him. Some had become active church members. Some had established stable marital relationships. Some had developed hobbies such as fishing. Although such dramatic changes in life style will probably be apparent in most cases, it is difficult to know what is the cause and what is the effect. When an individual quits drinking, a great deal of time is made available. It is probably a law of human behavior that time will be filled with something.

In Vaillant's study, a particular strategy for maintaining abstention was scrutinized, viz., antabuse. Vaillant (1983) found that very few of those with protracted duration of sobriety relied on antabuse. It appeared to be a strategy employed more often in early recovery.

Attention has been directed to the role of AA in the maintenance of sobriety. Edwards, Hensman, Hawker, and Williamson (1966) found in follow-up of persons who had received traditional (AA) treatment, that only 13% of those strongly exhorted to attend AA will do so on a regular basis (Edwards et al., 1966). In Vaillant's (1983, p. 205) the core city, untreated sample, 17 of 49 abstinent men had attended AA extensively. Vaillant (1983, p. 156) attempted to discern whether AA might be a factor in the sobriety of those persons in his sample who achieved sobriety. Vaillant looked at the association between AA attendance and outcome in his sample of clinic treated alcoholics. In the lower class, unemployed sample (Vaillant did not indicate the percentage which were in half way houses in which AA is mandatory), AA affiliation was greater in the abstinent group. In the employed sample, none of the sober alcoholics were AA members. Hence, AA was not a factor in achievement of sobriety for this latter group.

Control Drinking

Drew (1968) observed that the modal age for alcoholics presenting into treatment centers is in the mid 40s. This caused him to speculate as to explanations regarding this phenomenon. An explanation regarding what happens to alcoholics after 40 seemed required. Possibilities included becoming abstinent, dying or being institutionalized, continuing to drink problematically without seeking treatment a second time, or achieving control drinking. The possibility that for some drinkers alcoholism might be a self-limiting condition had to be examined.

Case reports of control drinking have been published. Davies (1962) and Kendell (1965) published case reports of alcoholics seen at Maudsley hospital who had exhibited severe withdrawal and other related drinking sequale who had remitted to stable nonproblem drinking. Later, however, a follow-up on Davis' 7 control drinkers suggested that only 2 remained in the stably remitted category (Edwards, 1985).

The literature before and after Davies' and Kendell's reports have suggested the presence of some proportion of alcoholics in each sample who remitted to control drinking. The focus has turned to estimating the percentage which will achieve control drinking. Pattison, Sobell, and Sobell (1977) reviewed results from 73 studies that collectively examined data from 11,817 alcoholics. Sixty-four percent of the studies reviewed provided a 1 year follow-up and 33% followed for over 2 years. Studies relied upon self-report corroborated by the report of a significant other. Seventy-seven percent of the examined individuals had received treatment in programs in which the goal was abstinence. Results across studies indicated that 18.25% of individuals were control drinking at follow-up whereas 10.48% of individuals were abstinent. Other reviewers of the literature suggest smaller percentages of control drinkers. Emrick's (1974) review of 271 studies of alcoholics in treatment most of which reported 1- to 2-year follow-up periods suggested that 5% would be control drinking, 33% would be abstinent, with another 24% being abstinent save for occasional lapses. Emrick's report of 5% control drinkers is consistent with Vaillant's (1983) finding of 5% control drinking in a clinic sample of 106 alcoholics followed for 8 years. The Rand report (Polich, Armor, & Braiker, 1981) of 548 patients found that 7% of the sample were drinking without incident over the 4 year follow-up interval. Smart (1978a) found that 6% were social drinkers at 1 year follow-up after treatment in a sample of 1091.

Several studies have followed clinic samples over 15 to 20 years. Hyman (1976) followed 49 blue collar alcoholics. At 16 year follow-up, 19 had died, 4 refused to be interviewed, 6 were mentally deteriorated. Of the 20 who were mentally intact, 5 were drinking daily in an asymptomatic fashion. Five were abstinent. Seven were continuing to drinking to a problematic fashion. Three had switched to a binge pattern.

Nordstrom and Berglund (1987) also followed a sample for a several decade period. They contacted 55 male alcoholics a mean of 21 years after treatment. All of the men had originally met the criteria for alcohol dependence upon admission to treatment. The authors purposefully selected individuals who, as far as they could determine, had not manifested severe problems from their drinking during the intervening period. The 55 followed individuals had been culled from the national health system records. They were selected for not having exceeded normal rates of sick time use and not having been labeled as disabled. Nordstrom and Berglund's purpose was to determine whether the majority of their followed alcoholics had achieved their nonflagrantly problematic statuses through control drinking or abstention. Interviews with the subjects suggested that 11 were abstaining, 21 were social drinking (defined as drinking more than once per month without problem and consuming less than 4 drinks per day), and 23 were abusing alcohol.

Vaillant (1983) has suggested that in studies examining clinic samples, a shorter follow-up period will tend to inflate the rates of control drinking. Since alcoholism by nature is a condition marked by great variability over time, drinking problems will only emerge given sufficient opportunity to do so. Hence, only studies with long follow-up intervals will reveal symptoms arising from drinking. Vaillant also suggests that the rates of control drinking emerging during longitudinal studies will be higher in community sample than in clinic samples. Empirical results have more or less supported Vaillant's view. In Vaillant's community sample, 18 of 110 alcoholics (16%) remitted to asymptomatic drinking during the 20 year follow-up period. In Lemere's sample of 500, most of whom had never been treated, 10% had achieved an asymptomatic drinking status during their life time.

Among alcoholics who do not deteriorate, is control drinking a more likely outcome than abstention? Some 1- to 2-year follow-up studies conclude that control drinking is more likely in those who had received treatment than is abstention (Heather & Robertson, 1981). In longer term follow-up studies, results have varied. Lemere (1953) found asymptomatic drinking in 10% of the sample vs. 33% abstention. Hyman (1976) found that of those outside of institutions who were cognitively intact (n = 20), ¼ were drinking asymptomatically, the same number as were abstinent. Three out of 20 were displaying a binge pattern. In Vaillant's (1983) community sample 21 of the 110 alcoholics (19%) were securely abstinent, defined as having been abstinent for 3 years duration at final follow-up, whereas 16% were control drinking. In the Nordstrom and Berglund (1987) study, the rate of control drinking did exceed the rate of abstention. This was unusual, and their numbers are noticeably different than others. It should be recalled that Nordstrom and Berglund examined a sample of intact alcoholics, rather than all alcoholics who were treated at some point in time.

A major difficulty in generating conclusions regarding whether abstention or control drinking is a more likely outcome for alcoholics is in defining both statuses. Vaillant (1983) remarks upon the high rate of control drinking found in some studies. Finding that many of the control drinkers sustained long hiatuses from drinking, Vaillant suggests that they should have been classified as abstinent. In fact, in most studies, researchers have used frequency and quantity of drinking in order to classify abstinent or controlled drinking. The issue of intention is never assessed. It may be that those who intend to control drink, but only intend to drink very infrequently will be classified as abstainers. It maybe that those who intend to be abstinent but end up drinking with some regularity will be classified as control drinkers. It is not clear which category will be inflated by current practices of assigning to categories.

In most traditional treatment programs, influencing intention constitutes the major focus of treatment. Convincing alcoholics that they must aspire to abstain is the critical message. Even though intention is a highly unreliable phenomenon, that is, difficult to measure reliably, it might be related in meaningful ways to outcome data. Future research might profitably address this factor and explore methods for measuring intention.

Predictors of Control Drinking

The fact that control drinking is possible is not of much use to a clinician without knowledge enabling prediction of which alcoholics are most likely to be able to control drink in the future. Although there is no basis for making dependable individual predictions, there are some clear group trends that are informative.

An interesting question is whether family history of alcoholism alters the probability of achieving control drinking. Here the findings are inconsistent. In his 20 year follow-up, Vaillant (1983, p. 225) found no difference on family history between those who were drinking asymptomatically and those who displayed a progressive pattern (remitted to abstention or continued to abuse alcohol). In the 20 year follow-up study of Nordstrom and Berglund (1987) no differences of family history were observed in those remitting through asymptomatic drinking vs. those remitting through abstention. Sanchez-Craig, Wilkinson, and Walker, (1987) report that FHP (family history positive) alcoholics drank less after control drinking training than did FHN alcoholics, although in another study number of alcoholic relatives was a factor mitigating against control drinking (Miller & Joyce, 1979). With their 8 year follow-up, Goodwin, Crane, and Guze (1971) found that young alcoholic convicts were more likely to become asymptomatic drinkers if they have fewer alcoholic relatives. Some of the inconsistencies in the studies might be a function of the duration of the follow-up period. Whereas Sanchez-Craig and Miller and Joyce followed alcoholics for several years, Vaillant and Nordstrom and Berglund observed people into middle age.

Women are more likely to become control drinkers than are men (Heather & Robertson, 1981; Helzer et al., 1985; Miller & Joyce, 1979). In skid row populations, the rate of control drinking is lower than the rate in stably employed populations (Vaillant, 1983, p. 124–125). A number of investigators have found that those who are more socially stable at intake (stable employment and marriages) as opposed to the socially unstable are more likely to be in the control drinking category at follow-up (Hyman, 1976; Nordstrom & Berglund, 1987; Smart, 1978a).

There are some intake findings that seem to distinguish those who are more likely to become control drinkers. Those who are more motivated when they enter treatment, are more satisfied with themselves, and who display favorable attitudes toward abstinence are more likely to achieve control drinking (Smart, 1978a). At intake, those who are confident about their ability to abstain are more likely to achieve control drinking (Orford et al., 1976). Eventual control drinkers are less likely to have evinced early life ASP features (truancy, school problems, etc.) (Nordstrom & Berglund, 1987; Vaillant, 1983). They have families who are more recreationally oriented (Finney & Moos, 1981). Whereas the preceding characteristics are more prevalent among the control drinkers, persons with chronic health problems (EEG abnormalities, hypertension, psoriasis) are more likely to remit through abstention (Chapman & Huygens, 1988).

Age has not been consistently related to probability of eventual control drinking. A study by Sanchez-Craig (1980) found that their relatively young subjects displayed more favorable outcomes when taught to control drink than when treated with the conventional abstinence goal. Vogler, Weissbach, and Compton (1977) followed-up at 2 years, a group treated with control drinking training. At follow-up they found that the mean age in those who were control drinking was 37 vs. 45 in the abstinent group and 37 in the relapsed group. Others have found that younger persons are more likely to remit to control drinking over time (Clark, 1976; Moberg, Krause, & Klein, 1982; Smart, 1978a) or have found no relationship (Helzer et al., 1985; Orford, Oppenheimer, & Edwards, 1976).

There are intuitively plausible reasons why there should be inconsistent findings with age. Youthful problematic drinking is not necessarily predictive of adult alcoholism. Many young problem drinkers do mature out of their problems. If they were followed-up after they had surpassed the age when the norms for heavy drinking had changed, many would have reverted to control drinking. If they were followed-up while still young when the norms apposite to the young were still in force, they would be likely to still be problem drinking and to be hard to convince that there was a problem, since their drinking might well conform to the expected drinking patterns for their age and subcultural norms.

The relationship between age at which drinking became a problem and whether a control drinking status would be achieved has been examined. Helzer et al. (1985) followed alcoholics 5 years after treatment. He found that those alcoholics who had developed problems with drinking early in life were less likely to become control drinkers. His procedure assessed drinking at 5 year follow-up in a diverse age range sample. Vaillant (1983) assessed a community sample all in middle age at the time and a clinic sample who were heterogeneous in age. Vaillant also found that those with younger age of onset were less likely to become control drinkers in both the clinic sample followed for 8 years and the community sample followed for 20 years. Chapman and Huygens (1988) compared control drinkers at 18 months with those who were problem drinking or abstaining. The control drinkers more often had received their first admission for alcoholism after the age of 45.

The duration of problem drinking is a slightly different variable than the age at which drinking became a problem. It can reflect earlier age of onset, although it may not. If a relationship exists between the variable of duration of problem drinking and whether remission occurs through control drinking or abstention, it may just reflect the fact that remission through one pathway takes longer to achieve than the other. Vaillant (1983) found that those who remitted through control drinking had displayed fewer years of loss of control than those who either never recovered or remitted through abstention. In a study by Orford et al. (1976) at 2 year followup, duration of problem drinking assessed at intake did not relate to control drinking at follow-up.

Many studies with short-term follow-ups (2–5 years) have found that those whose drinking is less severe at intake are more likely to become control drinkers (Finney & Moos, 1981; Heather & Robertson, 1981; Helzer et al., 1985; Maisto, Sobell, & Sobell, 1980; Miller & Joyce, 1979; Mulford, 1977; Orford, Oppenheim, & Edwards, 1976; Popham & Schmidt, 1976; Smart, 1978a; Sanchez-Craig et al., 1984; Vogler et al., 1977). In the Helzer et al. (1985) study, future control drinkers, at intake, had displayed less severe and less diverse symptomotology, had more often been identified in an alcohol rehabilitation unit as opposed to a medical/surgical hospital, and had developed alcoholism at a later age than those who in the future became abstinent.

There are two long-term studies that address the issue of the relationship between accumulated number of alcohol symptoms and attaining a control drinking status. Nordstrom and Berglund (1987) tallied number of alcoholic symptoms throughout life for 55 patients who were successfully functioning 20 years after having been diagnosed as alcoholic. They found a curvilinear relationship to control drinking. Those high and low in number of alcoholic symptoms were likely to become control drinkers. Those remitting through abstention were more likely to be in the middle range. A related finding was that those who were in the control drinking category tended to remit later, that is, they lived with alcoholic problems for a longer period before ceasing to have problems with alcoholism. In Vaillant's (1983) 20-year longitudinal sample of individuals selected from the community, those who became control drinkers could be differentiated from those alcoholics who exhibited a progressive pattern (i.e., who either continued to drink alcoholically or who achieved sobriety). The control drinkers were less likely to have been hospitalized for alcoholism, were less likely to have been diagnosed by a physician, and were less likely to have displayed a binge pattern. They did not differ on medical complications resulting from drinking, i.e., perceived loss of control, complaints by relatives, barroom fights or violence, or blackouts, although they were less often sociopathic (Vaillant, 1983, p. 170).

There are studies in which household surveys were conducted at 2- to 4-year intervals. The finding that those with more severe drinking problems are less likely to remit through control drinking are echoed in population surveys. Hermos et al. (1988) in a community sample assessed in 1973 and again in 1982, found that the following items were predictive of control drinking, as opposed to abstention: Not self-labeling drinking as problematic in 1973, having been married in 1973, and higher socioeconomic status. Clark's (1976) community survey found that those who remitted in problems while continuing to drink vs. those who continued to exhibit problems were distinguished by consuming lower quantities at time one, less often drinking in the morning, less often endorsing loss of control, and less often drinking to relieve hangovers.

In addition to severity, those with clear psychological precipitants to drinking may be more likely to remit through control drinking. In a household survey, Bailey and Stewart (1967) found that those who developed alcoholism in response to situational precipitants, were more likely to become control drinkers.

In summary, with the exception of the Nordstrom and Berglund (1987) study, the research supports a factor that consistently relates to eventual success with control drinking. Those whose drinking problems are less severe, and who experience less alcohol related symptomotology, appear to be stronger candidates for eventual control drinking. Stated another way, those with more severe alcohol related problems should be more strongly discouraged from attempting control drinking.

Differences in Mental Health and Access to Economic and Social Resources at Initial Assessment.   Beyond the variable of severity of alcoholism, there are many factors that might be expected to influence whether an individual will recover through abstention or control drinking. For example, those with stable jobs and marriage are more likely to recover (Costello, 1975a). There are studies in which those who eventually become abstinent vs. those who eventually become control drinkers vs. those who remain problem drinkers, have been differentiated on resources (marital status, employment, SES) at initial assessment. Assuming that resources at intake reflect a person's general status independent from severity of alcoholism, findings from these studies could suggest how resources impact on outcome.

Moberg, Krauss, and Klein (1982) examining a population of alcoholics targeted for rehabilitation in a work setting, found that the background characteristics of control drinkers and the abstinent were similar in terms of socioeconomic status, marital status, and mental health, but different from those who continued to drink problematically. Helzer et al. (1985), examining a population in which one third were unemployed, found that control drinkers could be differentiated from the abstinent or relapsed. The control drinkers were more often employed and married than those who became abstinent or remained problem drinkers. Others have also found greater social stability (job and marriage) and higher income to be predictive of control drinking (Hermos et al., 1988; Heather & Robertson, 1981; Vaillant, 1983).

Nordstrom and Berglund's (1987) data suggest that divergent paths to remission (abstinence and control drinking) may be taken by specific subtypes of alcoholics. Those alcoholics displaying less social stability and more features of sociopathy were most likely to find remission via abstinence. They required a mean of 10 years post hospital admission prior to establishing stable remission. Two groups of those remitting through control drinking could be differentiated. The two groups differed in terms of duration of time required to establish stable remission. Some of those who were control drinking at follow-up had begun their remission by abstaining completely. (The mean was 3 years of initial abstention.) This group required a mean of 2 years to establish stable remission. Others who were found to be control drinking at follow-up had not sustained an initial period of abstention. They required a mean of 16 years before establishing stable remission.

Are the Occurrences of Relapse More Frequent Among Those Who Choose Control Drinking Versus Those Who Choose Abstinence?

In the Rand report (N = 220) (Polich et al., 1981) and a report of VA alcoholics (Gottheil, Thornton, Skoloda, & Alterman, 1982) (N = 156) no differences were found between the abstainers and control drinkers at 6 months in the rate of their relapse during the extended follow-up period (4 years in the Rand report, and 2 years in the Gottheil et al. study). These reports differed from a large outcome study executed by Paredes et al. (1979) (N = 279), an outcome study by Finney and Moos (1981) (N = 131), and a smaller study by Moberg et al. (1982). Control drinking at 3 or 6 months vs. the abstinent at 3 or 6 months were more often relapsed at final follow-up. A study by Barr, Antes, Ottenberg, and Rosen (1984) failed to detect differences in mortality rates at 8 years post-treatment between those abstinent and control drinking at 2 years.

The Rand report (Polich et al., 1980) found that many variables interacted to determine whether people were better off at 4 year follow-up if they were control drinking or abstinent at 18 months. Degree of alcohol dependence, age, and marital status at intake moderated whether control drinkers remained stably remitted at follow-up. The over 40, severely dependent, and married displayed fewer problems related to drinking during follow-up when they abstained. The under 40, less severely dependent, and single were less likely to display problems due to drinking given a control drinking agenda. In their 21-year follow-up study, Nordstrom and Berglund (1987) report findings consistent with better outcome among those who control drink. Those who had established a year of stable remission (no problems created by drinking during the year) via abstention were compared with those who had established a year of stable remission via control drinking. Subsequent relapse was more common for the abstainers. These findings probably reflect that fact that the more severe alcoholics are more likely to select abstinence than to attempt to control drink.

Two studies looked at the relationship between *expressed* goal (abstention or control drinking) and relapse. In Elal-Lawrence et al.'s (1987) sample 36% of those who at time of discharge endorsed a control drinking goal vs. 26% of those endorsing an abstinence goal were in the relapse category at 1 year follow-up. In contrast to the Elal-Lawrence et al. data, Orford (1973) found that those endorsing an abstinence goal at intake were more heavily represented in the worst outcome categories at followup.

Do Those Recovering Through Control Drinking vs. Abstention Display Greater Improvement in Other Areas of Life?

Some studies have examined whether control drinkers display better functioning than abstainers on mental health variables. Of course, any obtained differences will be correlational, precluding a causal interpretation. Since many studies suggest that those with more severe alcoholism recover through abstention rather than control drinking, and severe alcoholism might be expected to produce troubles in diverse areas of life, initial severity of alcoholism could account for difference found at follow-up between the two routes to recovery. Nevertheless, findings are intriguing.

Patients graduating from an AA based abstinence oriented treatment program (Brissett et al., 1980) were compared at 3 years follow-up. Some of these patients were drinking nonproblematically, some were abstinent, and others were drinking problematically. On self-assessment measures, the problem drinkers were doing worse than the other two groups. Comparisons between the abstinent and the control drinkers are thought provoking. The abstinent perceived themselves as having a duller life, were less optimistic about the future, saw themselves as less favorably regarded by friends, reached out and accepted more help, and relied more on their Higher Power. The nonproblem drinkers compared to the abstinent saw themselves as more able to assume responsibility, as enjoying life more, as having a better self-image, but as less able to cope with problems. Results from another study are also available. Elal-Lawrence et al. (1987) found no difference in the social and life functioning between those remitting through control drinking rather than abstention.

A study by Mayer and Myerson (1970) suggests that family members are more comfortable with abstention than control drinking in the weeks immediately following treatment. Improved spousal relationships at 3- to 4-week follow-up were more often found among those who were abstaining than in the control drinking group.

Patterns of Control Drinking in Former Alcoholics

Vaillant (1983) remarked upon the ritualized nature of drinking that was exhibited by those alcoholics in his sample whom he classified as control drinking. Many drank in gregarious contexts only in which the norms regulating consumption were clear and definite. Vaillant's findings are mirrored in the findings of others. Those who remit to nonproblematic drinking are not frequent drinkers. In moving from a problem to nonproblem status, they have attenuated the amount consumed per occasion. Often they have switched to low alcohol content beverages.

Of the 10% of Lemere's (1953) sample who became control drinkers, 14 out of 49 were regular consumers whereas the other 35 drank only on special occasions. Among the control drinkers identified by Bailey and Stewart (1967), many maintained several months of abstinence. Eighty-six percent of Elal-Lawrence's (1987) control drinkers were setting conscious limits on the amount they drank. The treated alcoholics who remitted to control drinking identified by Nordstrom and Berglund (1987) consumed a mean of 25 drinks per month and were abstinent a mean of 19 days per month. They most often consumed low alcohol content beverages and drank only in the company of others. Popham and Schmidt (1976) found that those who successfully reduced the amount they consumed per occasion also reduced their frequency of consumption. Vaillant (1983, p. 230) reported that 7 of his 22 asymptomatic drinkers limited the frequency of consumption to once per week and drank only beer.

In their community survey, Bailey and Stewart (1967) found that some control drinkers, who had been definite gamma alcoholics displaying loss of control and no clear situational precipitant to drinking, mentioned the acquisition of non-drinking friends, no longer frequenting bars, and no longer experiencing the same subjective response to alcohol, as factors in attenuating their consumption. Elal-Lawrence (1987) and Vogler et al. (1975) found that control drinkers had switched to lower alcohol content beverages. Whereas prior to treatment, the control drinkers had drunk in bars, after treatment they more often drank at home.

The prescription for control drinking that emerges from the evidence dictates the use of low content alcoholic beverages, and very limited amounts of drinking at each occasion. In addition, infrequent drinking, occurring in new contexts (for example in a social situation with people who do not drink to excess) is also related to success.

A theoretical point raised by Pattison, Sobell, and Sobell (1977) may be relevant here. Pattison et al. have suggested the possibility that for alcoholics who can be considered cured, the expectations or psychological significance of alcohol has changed. Some clinical observations of the author suggest the way in which the psychological significance of alcohol needs to change for control drinking to be a viable option. Many of the alcoholics treated by the author, on initial visits, have voiced the opinion that they would not wish to drink if they were limited to one or two drinks per occasion, because they would not realize a mood change until they had consumed considerably more than 2 drinks. (In fact, these anecdoctal findings are consistent with Gottheil et al.'s, 1972a, ward drinking study in which alcoholics who were limited to one drink, preferred abstention.) Perhaps those who are going to control drink, which usually means limiting consumption to small quantities, can no longer pursue the experience they once had with alcohol in the past. This anecdotally supports the Pattison, Sobell, and Sobell contention that for those alcoholics who have achieved control drinking, the motivations for drinking may have changed. Perhaps they have been able to change the alcoholic proof of their beverages, the number of drinks they consume, and the speed with which they consume them, because they have come to seek different things from their drinking experiences.

The Desirability of an Initial Period of Abstinence

Nordstrom and Berglund's (1987) study suggested that the most likely, safe path to control drinking is through an initial period of abstention. Over half of those eventually achieving control drinking status reported at least 1 year of abstention. The mean period of abstention was 3 years prior to resumption of drinking. Further, it took a mean of 2 years posttreatment to establish a stable remission for those who found their way to control drinking via initial abstention vs. 16 years for those who chose not to initially abstain. The mean age of remission was 38 in the initial-abstaining-eventual-control-drinking group vs. 51 years in those who had no abstinence period but eventually achieved control drinking (defined as a year of problem free drinking of less than 4 drinks per day if regular drinking occurred and less than 6 drinks per day if sporadic drinking occurred).

The Nordstrom and Berglund (1987) study finding that control drinking would be achieved more quickly if preceded by a substantial period of abstention has been replicated. Elal-Lawrence et al. (1987) found that those who became successful control drinkers more often complied with an initial period of sobriety that was recommended in their control drinking group, than those who had attempted to control drink but were found to have relapsed at follow-up. Finney and Moos (1981) found that those who sustained a period of abstinence prior to control drinking were less likely to relapse in a 2 year follow-up period than were those who initiated control drinking directly subsequent to treatment. Kendell and Stanton (1966) found that 3 of their 5 subjects who had been control drinking for at least 3 years, had been abstinent for at least 1 year prior to returning to imbibing.

Control Drinking Programs

Presently, few attempts to teach alcoholics to control drink have been presented in the literature. Sobell and Sobell's (1978b) classic Patton state hospital study is a notable exception. The Sobells followed their subjects for 2 years and found that there were fewer relapses among their control drinkers than among those who have been treated with the traditional abstinence goal. Caddy, Addington, and Perkins (1978) followed the Patton state hospital subjects through the third year. Those who received the control drinking treatment displayed greater improvement at follow-up than controls. Pendery et al. (1982) did a later 10 year follow-up of these same subjects and found that they were doing quite poorly, although the control group was not followed so it is difficult to assess the effect of treatment. The Sobells' study was a first attempt, and a controversial one. Its implications are no longer clear, and so the rest of the literature has to be consulted for conclusions that are less likely to be disputed.

Ewing and Rouse (1976) represent another early attempt at a control drinking program. They found that over half the subjects approached were unwilling to try the control drinking program, often remarking that it is easier to quit drinking than to attempt to regulate. Following up on the patients who did participate in the program for between 27 to 55 months, most of the patients displayed crapulous drinking at some point during the follow-up period. The authors indicated that the control drinking program was a route to abstention for some. Nine out of 14 patients embraced an abstinence goal by the end of the follow-up period.

Others, selecting populations with less severe alcoholism have been more successful in their control drinking approaches. Alden (1988) reported results of a 12-week program of social support or control drinking training based on the procedures outlined in Miller and Munoz self-help book *Control Your Drinking*. Alden selected drinkers who were problem drinkers but who had never displayed dependence. Results from the program were encouraging. Fifty percent of the individuals were in the control drinking category at follow-up (defined as a weekly consumption of less than 21 drinks per week without ever exceeding a peak BAL of .10). Sanchez-Craig and her colleagues (1987) have also been pioneers in this area.

Some interesting findings have emerged from the studies in which drinkers have been instructed in control drinking techniques. In the Patton state hospital subjects, there was a trend for the number of days abstinent during the follow-up period to be greater in those having been instructed in control drinking than in the abstinence oriented treatment group (Caddy et al., 1978; Maisto, Sobell, & Sobell, 1980; Sobell & Sobell, 1976). Sanchez-Craig et al. (1987) report that during follow-up those in control drinking programs actually drink less than those in abstinence treated programs. Further, as Ewing and Rouse found, frequently, control drinking treatment is a route to the embracing of an abstinence goal.

Which Groups are Most Likely to Select Control Drinking?

Data is available suggesting which type of patients are likely to be interested in control drinking as a treatment goal at intake. Many have found that those with less severe drinking histories were more likely to be interested in control drinking (Booth et al., 1984; Heather & Robertson, 1981; Ojehagen, Skjaerris, Berglund, 1988; Orford, 1973; Orford & Keddie, 1986; Pachman, Foy, & Erd, 1978). Hingson, Scotch, and Goldman (1977) found that the tendency of severe alcoholics to gravitate towards the abstinence goal is there even with some encouragement to move toward a control drinking goal. Hingson et al. informed alcoholics in treatment of the Rand commission findings suggesting that alcoholics can achieve control drinking. Most of the alcoholics responded that they did not believe the Rand commission findings were applicable to them.

There is a contrary finding regarding the severe alcoholics being resistant to a control drinking goal. Cannon, Baker, and Ward (1977) authored a study in which severe alcoholics were more likely than less severe alcoholics to choose control drinking. In this study, the majority of their subjects were in detoxification and did not accept referral to any treatment, hence the meaning of their finding is equivocal.

Other characteristics associated with choice of control drinking have been identified. Pachman et al. (1978) found that those choosing control drinking were more confident as to the success of their treatment, were better educated, and had short problem drinking histories. Men have been found to be more interested in control drinking programs than are women (Orford & Keddie, 1985). Younger patients have been found to be more interested in control drinking (Booth et al., 1984; Pachman et al., 1978).

A study by Ojehagen and Berglund (1989) allowed flexibility, permitting choice of control drinking or abstinence as the treatment goal, the choice being offered at specific times throughout treatment. They treated alcoholics as outpatients for 2 years. Each quarter the alcoholics were given an opportunity to decide whether they wished to maintain abstinence or choose a control drinking goal. (Control drinking was defined as not more than 4 drinks per day if drinking occurred more than twice per week. If drinking occurred only twice per week, then 6 drinks per occasion was admissible.) Most of the alcoholics were of high socioeconomic status and there was little attrition (14% over the 2-year period). In their study, 84% initially chose abstention as their goal. This figure dropped to 64% by the last quarter in the study. Consistent with other studies, those consistently choosing abstention were distinguished by greater alcoholic dependence at intake. In terms of outcome, the number of abuse days during the 2 years did not differ between the control drinkers and the abstinent. However, those who had chosen abstention as their goal did drink more on abuse days than those who chose to control drink. This latter finding probably reflects the greater severity of problem drinking among those choosing abstention.

Is There a Relationship Between the Path to Recovery and Exposure to AA Philosophy; Between Path to Recovery and Belief in AA Philosophy?

Findings suggest that those who become control drinkers less often express belief in AA articles of faith. Those achieving recovery through control drinking vs. those achieving recovery through abstention, less often endorse the belief that one drink will result in uncontrolled drinking (Heather & Robertson, 1981; Chapman & Huygens, 1988). Those who recover through a control drinking path, have had less exposure to AA concepts (Heather & Robertson, 1981; Nathan & Skinstad, 1978). They less often affiliate with AA (Heather & Robertson, 1981; Chapman & Huygens, 1988). In community samples, those who sought treatment (where they are exposed to AA concepts) are more likely to be abstinent whereas those who have not sought treatment are more likely to be control drinkers (Saunders & Kershaw, 1979). It would seem from these findings that belief systems are consistent with the paths people choose for themselves.

Making the Decision for Abstinence or Control Drinking

Treatment providers working with alcoholics are forced to confront the issue of treatment goal. One way to avoid the dilemma is to allow the patient to select his/her own goal. The fact that those with more severe problems tend to recognize that control drinking is not an option for them, suggest that the alcoholic should be a full partner in the decision about which road is best. The treatment professional can supply the information about the relationship between severity and control drinking success, as well as a professional estimate of the individual's relative status. In addition, the information should be shared about the behavioral and setting changes that are needed to support control drinking. The apparent importance of an initial prolonged period of abstinence, even with a long-term goal of control drinking, should probably be stressed both in regard to the decision and in related planning.

Ultimately, patients determine their own goals anyway, since treatment providers cannot force abstinence on alcoholics. Therapists can assist the patient in exploring the possibilities. Further, the patient can be helped in ascertaining why he/she might select control drinking as the goal. Does the patient wish to control drink because he/she does not believe in his/her ability to become abstinent or is drinking still attractive? Is the decision to control drink consistent with the patient's other values? If the patient decides to control drink, the therapist can guide the patient in selecting criteria for when the goal should be abandoned.

Denial

Traditional doctrine ascribes pivotal significance to the role of denial. According to AA and Jellinek, the factor that allows alcoholics to continue drinking in a problematic fashion, is their stubborn refusal to recognize a problem. Once alcoholics have admitted that they cannot control their drinking, the probability of recovery is greatly enhanced.

Results of studies speaking to the issue of denial have accumulated. There are data on whether alcoholics do deny their alcoholism. There are data addressing whether there is an association between denial and recovery. There are data on whether admission of alcoholism is necessary for abstention. Further, information exists on the impact of treatment on denial.

Do Alcoholics Deny?

A large literature has developed examining whether alcoholics provide accurate self-report about their drinking. The answer to the question of whether alcoholics deny or not will vary as a function of which population is assessed, the type of question asked, and the circumstances of the interview.

The Population.   Bailey, Haberman, and Sheinberg (1966) assessed denial in a sample of problem drinkers identified in the context of a household survey. Each household was queried twice, with a time lapse of 8 years. Questions concerning alcohol were embedded among items addressing other issues. Bailey et al. found that 25% of those who admitted to an alcohol problem at Time II had denied the problem 8 years previously, although other responses at Time II suggested that the problem was extant at time I. More generally, the authors reported that half of those who reported problems at either time, had not been consistent, suggesting denial among about half of the alcoholics. Tempering this conclusion, however, is the finding from the same study that problem drinkers were more likely than their wives to report their drinking problem.

In treatment populations, Guze and Goodwin (1972) have found that those with more extensive problems created by alcohol, are more likely to be consistent over time in their endorsement of problem areas created by drinking. Cooper, Sobell, Maisto, and Sobell (1980) have found that inpatients inflate their endorsement of alcohol related events (hospitalizations, arrests, DWIs) relative to official records, whereas the converse is true for outpatients. They also found that heavier drinking frequently occurs in the period immediately preceding treatment admission, such that estimating prior consumption of drinking from the period just preceding treatment, will yield an inflated estimate.

In samples of pregnant women, those with heavier consumption patterns are more likely to provide inconsistent reports of their drinking behavior (Czarnecki, Russell, Cooper & Salter, 1990; Streissguth, Martin, & Buffington, 1976). In a study examining which patients would reveal their alcoholism to a doctor, Helzer and Pryzbeck (1988) found that those men with severe problems, and women, were more likely to admit. Both Vaillant (1983) and Helzer and Pryzbeck (1988) have observed that sociopaths are less likely to reveal problems.

In interviews with medical patients, clinicians arrive at more false negative decisions than false positive decisions regarding alcoholism (Thompson, Orvaschel, Prusoff, & Kidd, 1982). The disagreement between probands and their relatives as to a diagnosis is no greater for alcoholics than for other psychiatric classifications, however (Thompson et al., 1982).

The Relationship Between the Question and Denial.   When alcoholics in treatment are asked about the consequences of their drinking or whether particular events have or have not occurred, they provide valid reports. Alcoholics are more likely to affirm alcohol problem questions than are their relatives (Babor, Stephens, & Marlatt, 1987; Guze, Tuason, Stewart, Picken, 1963; Skolada et al. 1975). Alcoholics are just as likely to over report than to under report drunken arrests and DWIs (Sobell, Sobell, & Samuels, 1974). In a community sample, in which both the alcoholic husband and the wife were queried, although the husband was less likely to view himself as having neglected obligations or to label himself as a problem drinker, alcoholics reported more legal, social and work problems than their wives reported (Leonard, Dunn, & Jacob, 1983).

In a skid row population asked the same question 2 weeks apart, Summers (1970) found that about half the answers changed regarding assessment of age of first drink, subjective response to first drink, and history of blackouts. Annis (1979), querying a skid row population after withdrawal who had been admitted to 2 detox centers, within a 6-month interval found good test–retest reliability on responses to frequency of drinking questions. There was little reliability on typical amount consumed per occasion, treatment history, employment history, and involvement with the law. Examining a population of alcoholics who had not experienced withdrawal symptoms, interviewing them twice, with a 6-week interval, Sobell, Maisto, Sobell, and Cooper (1979) found good test–retest reliability in response to questions, although estimates of the duration of problem drinking increased on the second assessment. For heavy drinkers, reliability is better for frequency of alcohol consumption than for assessments of amount consumed per occasion (Czarnecki et al., 1990).

When asked questions requiring a subjective judgment about objective facts, there is more evidence of denial in alcoholics in treatment. Wives of alcoholics in treatment report a significantly longer duration of problem drinking than do their alcoholic husbands (Orford, 1973). On measures of perceived incapacity to regulate drinking, drinkers endorse a less extreme view of their loss of control than do their relatives (Orford & Keddie, 1986). In community samples, alcoholics are more likely to say they are normal drinkers when their wives label them alcoholics. Alcoholics are also more likely than their wives to believe friends and relatives view them as normal drinkers (Leonard, Dunn, & Jacob, 1983). Alcoholics do make external attributions for their drinking, citing external factors as the reason for their drinking, although they do not differ from normals in this regard (Vuchinich, Tucker, Bordini, & Sullwold, 1981).

When asked about the specific amount of alcohol they have consumed, alcoholics are inaccurate. Intoxicated alcoholics report having consumed less than their blood alcohol levels suggest (Sobell, Maisto, Sobell, & Cooper, 1979). In a population of individuals with liver disease, alcoholics have been found to deny alcohol consumption when urine analysis and blood alcohol readings suggest drinking, although denial of drinking was more likely when blood alcohol levels were low (Orrego, Blendis, Blake, Kapur, & Israel, 1979). In Summers (1970) study of alcoholics in detoxification, most of the alcoholics could not estimate how much they had consumed.

The importance of the nature of the question is brought home in a study by Morrow-Tlucak, Ernhart, Sokol, Martier, and Ager (1989). Prior to pregnancy women responded to a self-report measure that allowed for identification of their problem drinking. During pregnancy, it was found that problem drinkers did underreport their drinking. Although admitting their problem drinking, they were dishonest about the specific amount of their drinking during pregnancy.

Although alcoholics are notoriously unreliable in their estimates of the amount they have consumed, underreporting is not unique to them. Survey data suggest that test–retest reliability on exact amount consumed is poor for normal drinkers as well (Edwards, Hensman, & Peto, 1973). Lack of reliability over time is not unique to alcoholics either. In a general population survey by Edwards et al. (1973) normals decreased their endorsement of drinking problems and the magnitude of their consumption when tested on the second occasion, 2 weeks after the first interview.

There have been studies investigating the veracity of alcoholic's self-report of drinking following treatment. Pokorny, Miller, and Cleveland (1968) found that friends and relatives (collaterals) were less likely to assign a global improvement rating at 1 year follow-up than were alcoholics. This study, however, was contradicted in a study by Freedberg and Johnston (1980), who compared the year follow-up global rating assessment of the alcoholic, the spouse, and the counselor. In each case the alcoholic provided the less favorable assessment. There was most agreement between the spouse and the alcoholic. Maisto, Sobell, and Sobell (1979) found that collaterals and alcoholics agree when the alcoholic is abstinent and when he is obviously relapsed. There is less agreement ($r = .49$) on the number of drunk days (defined as consumption greater than 3 oz. of alcohol per day) during the follow-up period. Greater disagreement is found when the alcoholic and collateral have had little contact. Those days which the collateral labels drunk days, the alcoholic reports having control drunk or having been institutionalized. At 18 month follow-up, greater than 10% discrepancy has been found between patients and collaterals, with alcoholics more often reporting drinking and collaterals more often reporting abstention (Chapman & Huygens, 1988). In assessing veracity of alcoholics report at follow-up, Sobell, Sobell, and VanderSpek (1979) did find that 44–55% of non-DWI clients who had positive blood alcohol levels denied consumption (46–65% truthful). Only 14.3% of drinking DWI offenders were truthful about their positive blood alcohol levels. Watson, Tilleskjor, Hoodecheck-Schow, Pucel, and Jacobs (1984) followed up on VA alcoholics after treatment. They compared global ratings of drinking (totally abstinent, controlled half of the time, totally uncontrolled) between alcoholics and collaterals. They found only 74% agreement. In 75% of the cases where disagreement occurred, the alcoholic had provided the more favorable rating.

There have been studies determining whether alcoholics and their relatives will agree on a diagnosis of alcoholism. Levenson, Oyama, and Meek (1987) recruited children of alcoholics by having students respond to the Michigan Alcoholism Screening Test (MAST) assessing the behavior of their parent. After identifying children of alcoholics in this way, Levenson et al. had the parent complete the (MAST). There was more agreement for alcoholic fathers than for alcoholic mothers. Correlations were .85 for the child and the father and .52 for the child and the mother.

The concept of denial connotes dissembling specifically in regard to the consequences of drinking, the impact of drinking, and the label of alcoholic. In the psychological literature the global personality trait of defensiveness and social desirability has received considerable attention. Defensiveness and social desirability refer to a general tendency to deny all problems and to present oneself in a favorable light. Data fail to suggest that alcoholics are distinguished by more defensiveness than other populations (Donovan & O'Leary, 1983).

The Style of the Interviewer. Another factor increasing the veracity of self-report is the conditions under which questioning occurs. Sobell and Sobell (1981) find that individual interviews produce more valid responding than group interviews. Computers vs. interviewers have been found to elicit higher report of consumption with community samples (Duffy & Waterton, 1984), and alcoholics presenting for inpatient treatment (Lucas et a., 1977), but not in male outpatient alcoholics (Skinner & Allen, 1983b).

Use of a bogus pipeline (a machine or procedure that the subject believes can detect alcohol use) will increase accuracy of reports of amount consumed (Babor et al., 1987). Self-report of alcohol consumption by pregnant women, not all of whom are alcoholic, doubles when they are told that blood tests will be employed to validate self-report (Lowe, Windsor, Adams, Morris, & Reese, 1986). In a community sample, alcoholic husbands were more likely to report alcohol problems when they believed that their wives would be queried after them (Leonard et al., 1983).

Community survey studies comparing diary methods with weekly report find that the former method yields an estimate on average 22% higher than the weekly method. The discrepancy between methods is greater for heavier consumers (Lemmens, Knibbe, & Tan, 1988).

Comment. There have been many reviews of the literature assessing whether the self-report of alcoholics should be trusted (see Midanik, 1988). Midanik (1982) indicates that in each area of investigation (validating self-report against collateral report, official records, laboratory tests, and records of official sales of alcohol), there are studies in which self-report yields the higher estimate of consumption as well as studies in which the opposite is the case. Fuller, Lee, and Gordis (1988) suggest that using self-report of amount of drinking after treatment will result in too positive an evaluation of outcome. The studies these authors reviewed investigated VA alcoholics. Whether their conclusions can be generalized to other populations is unknown.

The literature suggests a mixed picture regarding whether alcoholics are untruthful about their drinking. In their reviews of the literature, Polich (1982) and Babor et al. (1987) conclude that alcoholics tend to be truthful about the consequences of drinking. Alcoholics tend to be more favorable than their relatives about subjective judgments regarding drinking (whether they have lost control). Alcoholics, like normals, tend to be unreliable about the amount they have consumed. This is particularly likely to be the case, if they are cognitively impaired or drunk at the time of assessment (Babor et al., 1987).

Perhaps the more critical issue pertinent to denial is the question of whether alcoholics are aware of the need for a change. The data on which populations are likely to select a control drinking goal rather than an abstinence goal is relevant here. The findings, cited earlier in the sections on control drinking, suggest that unambiguous alcoholics do value the goal of sobriety, are not easy to dissuade, and often do recognize that they have a problem.

Whereas the empirical findings suggest that those whose alcoholism is unambiguous do not exhibit denial, those with the more equivocal symptoms do exhibit denial defined as endorsement of a control drinking goal, with the implicit assumption that they can handle their drinking. For those adopting the AA philosophy of treatment, any individual who has experienced alcohol related problems has a progressive disease which can only be arrested by abstinence. Suggesting that she or he can control drink is thus an example of denial, and is merely a way of delaying the single road to remission. The data, however, suggest that many alcoholics with less severe alcoholism can remit to nonproblem drinking. The previously cited studies on the mechanisms employed by persons who eventually achieve control drinking suggest that attempts to cut down through drinking low alcohol beverages, and confining their drinking to particular settings, etc., can be successful for some people. In that sense, some alcoholics whose problems of alcohol abuse are more moderate, may be correct in their self-assessments, even though these assessments might be labeled as denial by treatment professionals with an AA orientation.

The previously cited literature on spontaneous recovery does suggest that many alcoholics arrive at a decision to alter their drinking behavior through ill health or an accumulation of pressures in life (employment and financial problems, increased responsibilities). Problems created by alcoholism, for example ill health, can take a good deal of time to develop. This suggests that attitudes about the acceptability of "having a few drinks" may change over time for many alcoholics who do not experience the more serious negative effects in the early stages. Longitudinal studies tend to bear out this change in thinking. Hingson et al. (1982) conducted a community survey 2 years apart. Those who were problem free on the first but not the second occasion vs. those who reported problematic drinking on both occasions, were more likely on the first occasion to endorse the view that 4 drinks per day was admissable behavior. Denial, in the sense of saying "I can control my drinking," may thus reflect a personal point of view that follows from the alcoholic's current belief that there is no serious problem. This is consistent with the AA expectation that denial will be present. On the other hand there does appear to be a tendency for the underlying attitudes towards the problem to change, and a tendency for the problem to gradually be recognized, at least for some alcoholics, given the opportunity for the problems to impact the alcoholic. The AA emphasis on the avoidance of enabling, of care being taken to avoid shielding the alcoholic from his or her problems, would appear to be good advice in this context. However, perhaps contrary to AA assumptions, the empirical literature suggests that, for at least some alcoholics, denial may dissipate naturally in the face of gradually increasing problems.

Is Breaking Down of Denial Necessary for Abstention?

Assume the simplest definition of denial, that is, does a person with clear problems resulting from alcohol abuse deny the label of "alcoholic." Is it necessary for such an admission to take place, for abstention to be maintained? Only a few outcome and long-term follow-up studies in which patients are categorized as abstaining, control drinking, or drinking uncontrollably have queried subjects regarding whether they label themselves as alcoholic. In an informal survey of alcoholics who became abstinent without treatment, Tuchfeld (1981) found that many quit drinking without resolving the issue of whether they were alcoholic. The rate of abstention in control drinking programs, in which no one is told that they cannot drink in a controlled manner, is just as high as it is in abstention oriented programs (Miller & Caddy, 1977). In a sense, the control drinking program reinforced denial but in the abstention oriented program, denial was systematically attacked.

According to traditional belief, those with less denial should display better outcome. Some data gainsay this prediction. Equal percentages of the relapsed and abstinent do not label themselves as alcoholic and do not subscribe to the notion that alcoholics can never drink again (Watson, Jacobs, Pucel et al., 1984). Others find that those who define themselves as alcoholic at intake vs. those who do not are more likely to be in the relapsed category at follow-up (Orford, 1973; Rossi, Stach, & Bardley, 1963; Moberg et al., 1982). Those who are in the control drinking category at follow-up were found to be less likely to have accepted the disease model or their own alcoholism, than either the abstinent group, or the relapsed group (Pfrang & Schenk, 1985–1986; Polich et al., 1980). Denial of the label correlates with a less severe drinking problem and less general self-deprecation (Skinner, Glaser, & Annis, 1982). Further, lack of denial may indicate demoralization. Moore and Murphy (1961) found that a substantial proportion of those who did not deny their alcoholism but who relapsed, more often suicided. Lemere et al. (1958) found that wanting to be sober related to treatment outcome, but labeling oneself as alcoholic did not relate to outcome.

In contrast to the earlier studies, are those studies that relate to outcome not whether an individual self-labels as alcoholic, but whether an individual views alcohol as having created problems. Willems, Letemendia, and Arroyave (1973a, 1973b) found that those who did not view their drinking as problematic, did not improve at follow-up. Gillis and Keet (1969) found that refusal to recognize a problem related to worse treatment outcome. Smart (1978b) found that alcoholics who greatly underreported their intake levels were less likely to be improved at follow-up. Sannibale (1989) found in a sample of young alcoholics that those who did not wish to decrease the frequency of their drinking or did not wish to become abstinent, did not realize any treatment gains.

Another seminal notion in traditional treatment is that denial is a precursor to relapse. Alternatively stated, uncertainty regarding the alcoholic identity or that deleterious consequences will always occur, is the major precipitant to relapse. Although there have been few direct investigations of this hypothesis, scattered findings exist. Ludwig (1972) finds that 7% of relapse precipitants fell into a curiosity category which included such reasons as "trying to drink socially" and "wanting to test myself." Across addictions (that is, including both drug and alcohol abusers), Marlatt (1985b) reports that 11% of relapses were associated with a test of personal control, i.e., wanting to see if deleterious consequences could be avoided this one time.

In summary, the assumption that self-labeling as an alcoholic is necessary for abstention appears to be incorrect. On the other hand, denial of the existence of problems stemming from alcohol does seem to be associated with poor prognosis. This dovetails with the material cited earlier suggesting that remission is facilitated by the alcoholic experiencing problems from drinking.

The Impact of AA Oriented Treatment on Denial

Bauman, Obitz, and Reich (1982) found that upon entry into an AA oriented treatment program, patients indicated they were similar to a person described as an alcoholic, whereas by the end of treatment this rating of similarity had decreased. The results of this study suggest that in the course of treatment patients distance themselves from the alcoholic label. If this is not an anomalous finding, it would suggest that treatment may increase rather than decrease denial. Of course, if treatment helps, people may simply no longer wish to label themselves as alcoholic, once the symptoms are no longer present.

Perspective on Denial

All clinicians will encounter alcoholics who are not motivated to change their drinking behavior even when the consequences have been severe. AA treatment providers would explain the lack of motivation by invoking denial, that is the alcoholic does not recognize the gravity of the problem, and does not value the goal of a sober life. Those alcoholics who are not actively seeking to change their behavior, somehow do not believe that past occurrences are predictive of future occurrences. They do believe they are capable of drinking in a controlled fashion. That is, they do not value the goal of sobriety. This is the traditional view.

An alternative explanation for the lack of motivation exhibited by some alcoholics would incorporate consideration of an alcoholic's expectations regarding the probability of being able to achieve sobriety or the probability that sobriety might improve the situation. Perhaps severely alcoholic, unmotivated individuals fail to attempt to alter their behavior because they believe that they cannot be successful in doing so. Lack of efficacy, rather than denial, could explain why people appear complaisant in the face of obvious need for change. Another variant of efficacy is that alcoholics do not believe that sobriety will improve their lives. Clinicians may find it difficult to believe that sobriety would not be perceived as an improvement. However, some alcoholics may think of themselves as dull when they are sober, or have come to expect depression when sober because of the pharmacological effects of long-term alcohol abuse, or otherwise find life difficult and alcohol comforting.

It is hard to know why people continue to drink in the face of real problems from it. One could simply ask alcoholics why they continue to drink, although it is not clear that they really know themselves. Gerard et al. (1962) did however ask the question directly. They summarized the answers they received in the following way: (a) the negative consequences from the drinking were infrequent; and (b) life was so bad that abstinence would not improve things. One could categorize the first (a) response as a form of denial, but the second (b) response sounds more like hopelessness. This could be a reflection of the depression that long-term alcoholics often experience.

Most theories of motivation suggest that goal directed behavior will be a function of the attractiveness of the goal and the expectations regarding the probability of attaining the goal (Weiner, 1972). The literature on this subject suggests that people will often fail to address a difficult or frightening problem unless they believe there is a viable solution to the problem. It is possible that this analysis is applicable to alcoholism. If it is a correct analysis, it would suggest additional therapeutic approaches. It would imply that the patient must be made to believe that it is possible to maintain sobriety before lack of sobriety can be recognized as a problem. Techniques would need to be developed for making the goal of sobriety itself attractive to people who clearly have not perceived sobriety as offering the promise of an improved existence.

EVIDENCE ON POST-JELLINEK AA PERSPECTIVES

Cross Addiction

AA based treatment centers advocate abstention from all mind altering chemicals, except coffee and nicotine. They advance the positions that (1) alcoholics are at greater risk to abuse other drugs than are nonalcoholics, such that recovered alcoholics are likely to switch addictions becoming addicted to alternative substances; and (2) if recovering alcoholics ingest mind altering chemicals they will be more vulnerable to relapse. The relevant findings are reviewed in this section.

Theoretical Reasons for Cross Addiction.   Data regarding the nature of the predisposition to alcoholism, which is inherited by those at genetic risk for alcoholism, suggest that the inherited factor predisposes to drug use in general. Adopted out children of antisocial personality parents and adopted out children of alcoholic/nonantisocial personality parents both display high rates of drug abuse (Cadoret, Troughton, O'Gorman, Heywood, 1986). In the rat literature, rats bred for alcohol preference display preference for other drugs as well. Alcohol preferring rats display little sedation when drinking alcohol. They are also inured to the sedating effects of other sedative drugs (Hellevo, Kiianmaa, Juhakoski, & Kim, 1987; McIntyre & Alpern, 1985).

Data on Alcoholics Using Other Drugs.   A review of the literature by Ciraulo, Sands, and Shader (1988) concluded that across studies, 3 to 41% of alcoholics have been noted to use benzodiazepines. This rate is larger than the percentage in the general population (9.7–16%) but about the same as in a psychiatric population (17–36.9%). Two of the reviewed studies by Ciraulo et al. examined escalation beyond prescribed amount, impaired functioning, or illicit use rather than mere use. In one study, abuse was found in only 5% of cases and in the other only 10.3%. In the first study, it was found that 90% of those alcoholics who used tranquilizers, who were followed for a year, averaged consumption under 100 mg per day.

Vaillant (1983) examined drug use in his sample of males who had grown up in the inner city. He found that the abstinent and the alcoholic were equally likely to use tranquilizers and in both groups the rate exceeded use among the moderate drinkers. Lewis, Rice, and Helzer (1983) found that the rate of drug abuse in their alcoholic sample did not exceed the rate in their control group, after they removed the alcoholics who were also sociopathic.

Goodwin, Davis, and Robins (1975) found that 13% of the opiate users in Viet Nam had been alcoholic prior to service induction. Of those who were opiate abusing in Viet Nam, 16% returned to alcoholism after service discharge.

Is Risk for Drug Abuse Particular to Subsamples of Alcoholics?   There is a suggestion that the increased use of drugs sometimes reported in studies may be peculiar to particular subgroups of alcoholics. Ashley, le Riche, Olin, Hatcher, Kornaczewski, Schmidt, and Rankin (1978), in their sample of 1001 alcoholics, compared the 228 who abused additional drugs vs. the 773 who did not. The drug abusers were younger, had experienced an earlier age of onset of their alcoholism, and were of lower socioeconomic status. Ogborne and Kapur (1987) also found that among alcoholics admitted to a detox center, drug abuse was higher among the younger alcoholics. Von Knorring, Palm, and Andersson (1985) found that drug abuse was greater in the early onset alcoholics. In a sample of young, problem drinking, Navy enlistees, those abusing other drugs differed from those only abusing alcohol in being more immature, more noncon-forming, and having more friends who abused drugs (Kolb & Gunderson, 1980).

If middle class samples of alcoholics are examined, females and unmarried alcoholics are more likely to use sleeping pill and tranquilizers than are married, male alcoholics (Bromet & Moos, 1976; Curlee, 1970). Because among the middle class, female alcoholics are more likely to be primary depressed, second-ary alcoholics (Schuckit, 1979), the increased use of tranquilizers in this group may reflect self-medication for primary depression. Tranquilizers were also seen as the middle class drug of choice in a study by Mendelson, Miller, Mello, Pratt, and Schmitz (1982). In a sample of 3411 alcoholic patients admitted to Raliegh Hills facilities across the country (Raliegh Hills draws a middle class clientele), tranquilizer use was frequently encountered. However, Mendelson et al. did make the distinction between use and abuse, and found that only 2% abused.

In general population surveys, drug use and type of drug use seems to be dictated by the norms governing behavior of particular age groups in particular subcultures. Mellinger et al. (1978) found that age was the strongest predictor of type of drug used. Younger men relied on alcohol to cope with psychological stress, but not prescription tranquilizers. Older men relied on benzodiazepines but tended not to drink. In a college age sample, Ritson and Plant (1977) found that those who took illicit drugs were more likely to be heavy smokers and drinkers. In a population of gynecological patients, within the age group 40–59, women who have consumed a psychoactive drug at least once during the prior month vs. those who had not were less likely to be classified as heavy drinkers (defined as consuming on average 2 or more drinks per day). The reverse was the case among women younger than 40 and older than 60 (Russell & Coviello, 1988). Although Ross (1989) found no difference in drug abuse between male and female alcoholics, the sexes differed in the type of drug used. Males more often smoked cigarettes or marijuana, whereas females more often abused barbiturates, sedatives, and tranquilizers.

Cross Addiction with Nicotine. There is support for a strong link between cigarettes and alcohol. Alcoholics are more likely to be smokers than nonalcoholics (Ayers, Ruff, & Templer, 1976; Maletzky & Klotter, 1974; Walton, 1972). Alcoholic smokers consume more cigarettes per day than do nonalcoholic smokers (Maletzky & Klotter, 1974). There is a stronger correlation between alcohol consumption per day and cigarette consumption per day among alcoholics than among nonalcoholics (Maletzky & Klotter, 1974). Cigarette consumption, however, does not increase following recovery in alcoholics (Maletzky & Klotter, 1974).

There is some tentative suggestion that the genetic predisposition to alcoholism may place at risk for nicotine consumption as well. High MacAndrew scale alcoholics (the case was advanced in the genetics section that these individuals are the alcoholics who inherit risk for alcoholism) smoke more than low MacAndrew alcoholics (Willis, Wehler, & Rush, 1979). If alcoholics who become control drinkers are truly a different breed than those who cannot control drink, cigarette consumption is a distinguishing feature here too. Vaillant (1983, p. 137) found that alcoholics who become control drinkers smoked fewer cigarettes per day than alcoholics who displayed a progressive pattern (either never recovering or become abstinent).

Another stimulant, caffeine, is also consumed in greater quantities by alcoholics (Ayers, Ruff, & Templer, 1976; Istvan & Matarazzo, 1984).

Are Drug Abusers Likely to Become Alcoholics? There has been scant investigation of whether rates of alcoholism increase following recovery from drug abuse. Freed (1973) reviewed 48 studies yielding 15,447 cases of persons addicted to some drug including alcohol. In 20% of the cases, evidence of concomitant abuse of chemicals or sequential abuse of chemicals was noted. Unfortunately, Freed did not differentiate cases in terms of primary drug of abuse. He did note that addicts were more likely to be alcoholic than was the reverse.

There is substantial evidence of cross addiction between opiate use and alcohol use. High rates of alcoholism among addicts who are no longer using opiates have been noted (Belenko, 1979; Lewis, Croughan, Whitman, & Miller, 1983; Rounsaville, Weissman, & Kleber, 1982). In women, the increased risk for alcoholism after opiate cessation has been found to be limited to those displaying antisocial personalities (Lewis et al., 1983a). Interestingly, the two substances were generally not used simultaneously in male samples (Goodwin, Davis, & Robbins, 1975; Lewis, et al. 1983a).

Answer to the Question of Whether Alcoholics are at Greater Risk to Abuse Other Drugs.   The foregoing summary suggests that alcoholics do tend to use other drugs, but, with the exception of nicotine, and possibly caffeine, there is not a clear picture of what could be called cross addiction. Rather, the picture of modest increased use of other drugs, above that of nonalcoholic populations emerges. This can be contrasted with those who are addicted to opiates. Here we see true cases of cross addiction in that alcoholism follows withdrawal from the opiates. The reverse is not the common pattern, alcohol deprivation in an alcoholic does not commonly lead to opiate addiction. The cases of nicotine and caffeine, on the other hand, do appear to be cases of cross addiction with alcohol.

Although the general picture is not that of cross addiction for other drugs of abuse, there is evidence of some cross addictions among subpopulations of alcoholics. For example, young, sociopathic, family history positive alcoholics are more likely to abuse other chemicals. Those women alcoholics who are primary depressives might be inclined to self-mediate, given availability of a variety of substances. Future research should clearly delineate the subpopulations of alcoholics, in order to identify consistent patterns, and also clarify whether the behavior can be classified as true addiction, noncompulsive frequent use, or experimentation.

Does Drug Exposure Enhance the Risk of Relapse?   On a theoretical basis, Wise (1988) argues that use of any drug will stimulate craving and will render relapse to all drug use more likely. Wise maintains that all drugs that are self-administered by animals derive their reinforcing property through agonist action at the same brain locus (ventral tegmental area). In an extinguished animal, administration of any drug with agonists properties at the ventral tegmental area will reinstate drug responding. Extrapolating to humans, Wise suggests that recovering alcoholics should eschew all reinforcing drugs (cocaine, heroin, tobacco) that might stimulate the ventral tegmental area.

Wise's speculation is certainly theoretically consistent with experimental data. However, the majority of recovering alcoholics seem to smoke without succumbing to relapse. Hence, stimulation of the ventral tegmental area, which may indeed instigate craving, does not seem to present an insurmountable problem for staying sober. On the other hand, however, it is known that those alcoholics who have quit smoking, display higher rates of recovery from alcoholism (Battjes, 1988).

The image of drug exposure increasing the risk of relapse, is implicitly one of a recovering alcoholic secretly taking some other drug, thus causing a drinking relapse. An ideal test of this would appear to require a comparison of recovering alcoholics who on their own take some other drugs, who can then be compared to other recovering alcoholics who are known to be drug free. There are two studies that approximate this. Elal-Lawrence et al. (1987) measured tranquilizer use in alcoholics in 3 outcome categories. Eighteen percent of control drinkers, 33% of the abstinent, and 70.5% of problem drinkers were consuming tranquilizers. In Vaillant's (1983) study a small fraction (5/38) of those maintaining sobriety for over a 3-year period were taking tranquilizers.

There is more definitive information on how drug consumption impacts relapse risk in a different type of study. Not all treatment providers have assumed that drug exposure will create relapse. In fact some consider drug therapy to be an important adjunct for some patients. There are studies of such attempts to deliberately introduce other drugs into the treatment. Bromet, Moos, Bliss, and Wuthmann (1977) investigated the efficacy in various types of treatment programs of using ataraxic (anxiety reducing) drugs adjunctively. They did not find any demonstrated efficacy, but they did not find any increase in relapse either. A study by Chapman and Huygens (1988) found decreased relapse among those receiving sedatives. Others have found that when tranquilizers are used adjunctively, they will decrease dropouts from therapy (Powell & Viamontes, 1974; Rosenberg, 1974).

Prior studies suggest that the adjunctive use of tranquilizers to the treatment of alcoholism, does not impact drinking outcome. Some studies have examined whether tranquilizers used to treat alcoholism become a problem in their own right. Here, there is support for the view that when tranquilizers are provided as part of the treatment, alcoholics use them in the manner prescribed. Rothstein, Cobbie, & Sampson (1976) treated 150 alcoholics with therapeutic doses of librium for 1.5 years. Only 5% of their sample misused (escalated dosage or experienced problems in social functioning) during the time period. Over 50% voluntarily abstained for over 30 days at some point during the 1.5 years. Seventy-five percent discontinued use of their own accord.

It does seem clear from the evidence that the assumption that drug exposure enhances the risk of relapse, is incorrect.

Euphoric Recall of Intoxication

According to Vern Johnson's hypothesis, alcoholics remember their intoxicated state as happy and halcyon. There is evidence allowing for an evaluation of Johnson's hypothesis. Researchers have examined the expectations that alcoholics hold regarding alcohol.

In some regards, Johnson's hypothesis of a positive view of drinking is substantiated. Evidence suggests that alcoholics have an expectation of greater enhancement of positive mood states and greater tension relief from alcohol than do normals (Brown, Goldman & Christiansen, 1985; MacAndrew, 1979b). There are some further specifications, however. MacAndrew (1979b) sought to assess empirically the expectations alcoholics hold about the impact of alcohol on their persona. He had sober alcoholic subjects respond to Q sorts of their ideal, intoxicated, and sober selves. The results suggested that alcoholics expect to be more resentful, more selfish, and more irresponsible when drunk than when sober. These findings imply that alcoholics do not expect to behave like nicer people when they are drinking. Some positive effects of alcohol were also noted, however. It was found that alcoholics expect that their drinking self will be more persuasive, forceful, and self-confident (MacAndrew 1979b; MacAndrew & Garfinkel, 1962).

Whereas the prior research evaluated the beliefs that alcoholics harbor regarding the impact that alcohol will have on them, others have evaluated alcoholics under the influence to directly observe the effect. Specifically, the issue of how being under the influence of alcohol impacts the self-concept of alcoholics has been addressed. Results have been inconsistent. Berg (1971) found a more charitable self-evaluation when alcoholics were drinking. Vanderpool (1969) reported more negative self-evaluation.

Results from empirical investigation suggest that Johnson is partially correct in his hypothesis that alcoholics anticipate a positive impact from alcohol. The research also suggests, however, that alcoholics appreciate some of the deleterious impact of alcohol on their behavior as well.

Does the Disease Continue to Progress During Periods of Abstinence?

The AA perspective incorporates the notion that alcoholism will progress periods of abstinence. If a relapse occurs the consequences of drinking will be much graver for the drinker following a relapse than the consequence which redounded from drinking before the initiation of sobriety. The prediction fails to specify which particular dimensions of the sequale of drinking will be worse. One can speculate though that two dimensions can be involved: Both more abuse (larger amount of drinking), and more negative physical consequences. There is little direct evidence to support this notion, or to refute it. However, it may reflect long experience of those who are associated with alcoholics who relapse after long dry periods. Assuming that this observation is in fact correct, there are explanations for what is observed, other than a progression of alcoholism.

Burish et al. (1981) induced nonproblem drinking college students to voluntarily abstain from drinking for a month long period. Following abstinence, Burish et al. found that these college students drank more than they had been drinking before abstention. They also drank more than a control group who had not voluntarily abstained. One explanation for the phenomenon is reactance. That is, whenever freedom of choice is restricted, the proscribed behavior will appear more attractive (Brehm & Brehm, 1981). Reactance theory would predict that postabstinence, imbibing should seem like a more attractive behavior and be engaged in with greater frequency. This constraint on behavior will affect both alcoholics and nonalcoholics alike.

A second explanation for increased frequency and magnitude of drinking following enforced abstinence is provided by the phenomenon of self-fulfilling prophecy. AA treatment programs make it clear to patients that one drink will lead to a drunk. Consequently, when an individual makes the decision to relapse, he/she may view himself/herself as deciding to get drunk rather than to have a drink. That such a phenomenon obtains for persons imbued with the traditional notion is supported by the finding that members of AA experience more severe relapses than non-AA members after controlling for initial problem severity (Ogborne & Bornet, 1982), and the fact that persons receiving treatment in AA oriented programs are less likely to be control drinkers at follow-up (Nathan & Skinstad, 1987).

The third explanation for the phenomenon of more severe alcoholism after relapse concerns the physical consequences of drinking. If an individual relapses after a protracted period of abstinence, e.g., after 15 years of abstinence, that individual will, of course, be older. Older people are more heavily impacted by drugs of all sorts. Given the same level of consumption the older drinker will feel worse than the younger drinker. Rather than the disease continuing to progress during periods of abstinence, the reason for more severe physical sequale from drinking after abstinence could be that the aging process has continued to progress.

Of course, these explanations, like the AA explanation, are speculative, and they could all be incorrect. They do, however, provide plausible alternative views for what may be observed clinically.

THE DEFINITION OF ALCOHOLISM

What is alcoholism? Many definitions for alcoholism exist. The World Health Organization defines alcoholism as any drinking which results in problems (WHO, 1952). Gitlow (1973) places emphasis on continuing to drink despite the fact that alcohol has created problems. According to this definition those who quit drinking after problems have redounded are not alcoholic. The DSM-III does not define alcoholism but does offer criteria for alcohol abuse and alcohol dependence. The criteria for alcohol abuse is problematic drinking for over a 2-month period. Alcohol dependence requires demonstration of tolerance and withdrawal.

According to Vaillant (1983), there is consensus on the diagnosis of alcoholism for persons exhibiting a broad spectrum of alcohol related problems across diverse domains. There is also consensus that persons who drink without exhibiting any problems are not alcoholic. There is less consensus with regard to individuals who display any one particular problem but not a broad range of problems. Vaillant, examining a population of middle age, working class individuals, finds that with one exception no particular problem related to drinking is more highly correlated with the entire scale than any other problem. Vaillant suggests that it is the number of problems, regardless of the nature of the problem, which should be considered in rendering a diagnosis. The one exception to this rule is the presence of withdrawal symptoms. Diagnosing alcoholism among persons who have experienced withdrawal yields few false positives, although requiring withdrawal symptoms for the diagnosis will yield some false negatives.

Empirical findings suggest that there are a number of alcohol related behaviors which are poor diagnostic indicators of alcoholism. At least 40% of social drinkers have experienced blackouts, and 33% of medical students have experienced at least one blackout (Goodwin, Powell, & Stern, 1971; Schuckit & Russell, 1983). Hence using blackouts as a diagnostic criterion will yield many false positives. Approximately one-third of social drinkers have experienced problems created by drinking (Schuckit, 1986). In a recent survey, 21% of the general population reported tangible consequences from drinking and 20% had experience tangible consequences in the year prior to the survey (Hilton, 1987). Seven and a half percent of nonproblem drinkers report early morning drinking and 8.8% report needing more drink to experience the same effect (Glatt, 1961 cited by Chick, 1980a). In Schuckit, Gunderson, Hectman, and Kolb's (1976) sample of young general population Navy enlistees, 18% reported occasional morning drinking, 8% drank on the job, and 4% had binged. Vaillant (1983) and Fillmore (1974, 1975) find that many nonproblem drinkers exhibit psychological dependence, i.e., they report drinking to feel better. Using the complaints of friends or relatives will also yield many false positives as well as false negatives (Bailey, Haberman, & Alksne, 1965; Vaillant, 1983).

Jellinek's criteria for the disease was the documentation of the phenomenon of loss control. Loss of control does require a subjective judgment either on the part of the alcoholic or the observer. Chick (1980a, 1980b) reports that interviewers of alcoholics in treatment failed to demonstrate agreement on whether loss of control had or had not been experienced.

Another problem was highlighted in the Chick study. Loss of control presumes that an individual has tried to exert control but has failed in doing so. In a sample of recently hospitalized alcoholics, Chick (1980a, 1980b) found that the concept of exerting control was alien. Many indicated they had never set limits or consciously made a decision not to drink. Chick's 1980 study was a factor analysis of drinking items from which an alcohol dependence scale was derived. Loss of control did not correlate sufficiently with any other set of items to be contained on any factor scale. Self-identification as an alcoholic did not necessarily mean that the individual would report loss of control.

Whereas Chick's study questions whether alcoholics view the concept of loss of control as germane, studies of light drinkers have found that some of them report loss of control. Harburg, Gunn, Gleiberman, Roeper, DiFranceisco, and Caplan (1988) reported results of a general population survey. They found that 87% of males, and 92% of females, responding "no" to the item "Are you able to stop drinking when you want to?" were light drinkers. Their results suggest that factors other than heavy consumption influence the perception of loss of control.

There is some suggestion that quantity and frequency indices of drinking may yield accurate classification into alcoholic and nonalcoholic categories. Vaillant (1983, p. 114–118) beginning with a blue collar sample containing non-alcoholics as well as alcoholics, found that no one in the sample drank more than 5 drinks per day without experiencing problems in some life domain. Orford (1973) found that wive's objections to drinking corresponded to husband's consumption of over 5 pints of beer per day. Sanchez-Craig (1986) categorized a group of alcoholics who had received treatment according to whether they were drinking problematically or nonproblematically at time of follow up. Consumption levels did vary between the groups and a quantity/frequency index was useful in correctly identifying the problem from the nonproblem drinkers. The criteria of 4 drinks per occasion with a frequency of 2–3 occasions per week achieved maximal discrimination between the groups. Either frequency or quantity criteria was equally effective alone, and employing both criteria was best in discriminating between the groups. Sanchez-Craig cited data suggesting that these criteria have been established as the cutoff points at which the risk for cirrhosis is increased.

Whereas the foregoing suggests that amount consumed might be a good criteria for alcoholism, Cahalan and Room (1972) report that amount consumed does not necessarily correlate with problem drinking. Half of the heavy drinkers identified in community surveys did not experience problems. Only half of those who experienced social problems from their drinking were regular heavy consumers.

There are some individuals who would be classified as alcoholic by virtually anyone's criteria. There are many others who would be classified as alcoholic by some, but not by others. Whether and what to label those persons in the middle of the alcohol problem continuum remains a question. It is these individuals for whom, given continued drinking, prognosis is less certain. Invoking the label alcoholic for these individuals may help to convince them that abstinence is imperative, although the validity of the imperative is unsubstantiated. Invoking the label may encourage some individuals in this problem range to seek treatment, but it may discourage others. Perhaps this is the group that is in need of new forms of treatment. For example, whereas the traditional abstinence road appears advisable for those with severe alcohol problems, if control drinking is ever advisable, it would appear to be so primarily with those evidencing more moderate symptoms. Perhaps, for this group, the issue of label is not a relevant concern.

Is Alcoholism a Disease?

In 1956 the American Medical Association officially declared that alcoholism is a disease. Vaillant (1983) discussed the question of whether this was an appropriate label. His discussion raised the issue of what is meant by a disease. He pointed out that physicians have a great deal of difficulty determining whether a condition such as hypertension is a disease. Researchers and academicians tend to think it is not whereas general practicioners are happy to include it under the general definition. Vaillant (1983), and Pattison, Sobell, and Sobell (1977, p. 13), both view the medical profession as invoking the category of disease for "any deviation from a state of health, particularly when there is a characteristic train of symptoms associated with that process." If a disease is properly encompassed by this definition, alcoholism then satisfies the definition. Alcohol consumed in large quantities has a reliable impact on health, mood, and behavior both when it is in the system and following heavy consumption. It should be recognized, however, that given this conceptualization of disease many conditions that may not be currently thought of as diseases (e.g., aging, learning disabilities, and mental retardation) will qualify.

Vaillant (1983) attributes significance to the findings of high correlations among diverse assessment measures of alcoholism, some scales emphasizing the social consequences of drinking and others emphasizing the physical consequences. Vaillant believes this constitutes proof of a unitary syndrome and establishes alcoholism as a bonafide disease. Unfortunately, Vaillant's high correlation among scales was probably a consequence of the population from which the data were generated: a blue collar, heavy drinking subculture. The norm in this subculture is to drink heavily and behave in a rowdy fashion. The heavy drinking would create the physical problems. The cultural norms would pressure the social problems. Had Vaillant tested his hypothesis of internal consistency in a middle or upper class group of alcoholics, he may not have obtained high correlations among the scales.

Indeed, other researchers examining problem drinking in more diverse cultural groups find less consistency across the range of alcohol problems. Although a correlation between alcohol dependence and social problems was not reported, Hasin, Grant, and Endicott (1988) found that older alcoholics and depressed alcoholics were most likely to report alcohol dependence. Younger alcoholics and those manifesting social problems unrelated to drinking were more likely to display social/occupational problems due to drinking. Protean variety among alcoholics has been noted. Bailey, Haberman, and Alksne (1965) found that 63/99 alcoholics reported health problems, 45/99 reported family arguments caused by drinking, 17/99 reported job problems, 23/99 reported money problems, and 4/99 reported trouble with police. Particularly among the upper social classes, women, older persons, and better educated, using social problems as a criteria for alcoholism will fail to identify many alcoholics who are identified by relatives and clinicians (Bailey et al., 1965; Mulford & Fitzgerald, 1981b). Each type of criteria for alcoholism will identify a different cluster of alcoholics (Clark, 1966; Rousaville et al., 1986; Tarter, Arria, Moos, Edwards, & Van Thiel, 1987).

Impact of the Disease Concept

Aside from the niceties of reliable definition, is the issue of the impact on the public and the alcoholic when alcoholism is assumed to be a disease. The major rationale for classifying alcoholism as a disease is that it removes the moral stigma. However, the empirical issues need to be established. Is there a moral stigma, and is it diminished through the disease concept? Linsky et al.'s public opinion survey suggested that few people view alcoholism as a moral problem. The most frequent views expressed were the disease notion or the notion that alcoholism is a response to internal or externally generated stress (Caetano, 1987; Linsky, Colby, & Straus, 1986). Knox (1971) surveyed VA psychologists and psychiatrists. The majority viewed alcoholism as a behavior problem and not a disease. These professionals believed that treatment in a group setting or AA was preferable to sanctions through the courts or the correctional system.

In fact, data suggest there is a great deal of confusion in the views on alcoholism. Some researchers have found that both the moral and disease view are held simultaneously by some people (Blum, Roman, & Bennet, 1989; Mulford & Miller, 1964). Those who endorse the statement that alcoholism is a disease, do not necessarily view it as progressive or incurable (Rodin, 1981).

Perhaps it can be assumed that some hold a moralistic, punitive view of alcoholism. A more constructive view would be desirable. It is by no means clear whether having a disease is a more benign interpretation than being morally weak. There are numerous diseases whose victims are held in low esteem (schizophrenia, Pick's disease). Perhaps the old stigma was better than the new one. There are a few empirical findings on the issue of the impact of the alcoholic label. Sobell and Sobell (1975a), in a public survey, found that portraying the perpetrator of a nonspecified violent crime as alcoholic results in more severe sentencing despite the fact that half the sample endorsed the disease concept. However, when the crime is specified as rape or wife beating, information that an individual was drunk during commission of the crime did attentuate the sentence rendered (Richardson & Campbell, 1978). In still another study intoxication attentuated perception of responsibility and blameworthiness for heinous behaviors, but not the punishment meted out (Critchlow, 1985). Rule and Phillips (1973) studied the perceptions of high school students. They found that the critical variable in determining whether a problem drinker is viewed favorably is whether his drinking condition is presented as mutable. The disease vs. behavior problem depiction did not make a difference as to how the drinker was regarded.

Presumably, one's view of alcoholism (an internal problem, a moral weakness, a disease, a psychological problem, etc.) will correspond with notions of what should be done about the problem (Brickman et al., 1982). Here, Linsky et al. (1986) found confusion in the public. As will be seen, this confusion extends to the professional community.

Those who view a deviant act as beyond the control of the deviant due to a disease process should prefer rehabilitation to punishment. Operation of a similar principle would predict that those who view alcoholism as a disease would opt to rehabilitate rather than sanction. Treatment professionals do recommend treatment rather than job loss. However, coupled with the notion of treatment is the concept of enabling. Most AA oriented treatment professionals believe that only through hitting bottom will the alcoholic realize that he or she is an alcoholic, and that this is the critical step in motivating abstinence. Along with this notion is the belief that alcoholics would hit bottom faster were it not for enablers who rescue the alcoholic from the consequences of his/her behavior. In such treatment programs counselors compete for who can avoid enabling the most and provide the "toughest love." Given this ethic, alcoholism counselors probably would make more severe recommendations for punishment than even the lay public. Indeed, Weisner and Room (1984) have noted that treatment professionals providing service to the court for drunk drivers have encouraged the court to commit persons to treatment for protracted periods in order to counter the perception that drunk drivers were not being held accountable. Perhaps the impact of the disease concept is more punishing than what it replaced.

The notion that alcoholism is a disease does connote that the doctor should provide the treatment. For most diseases, the patient assumes a passive stance, taking a pill or sleeping through the operation. A study by Fisher and Farina (1979) reveals differential impact on behavior depending on whether people are taught to view mental health problems as stemming from faulty social learning or physiological imbalance. Persons with the social learning orientation (in comparison to the physiological orientation) report they would be more likely to seek help for their own future problems; they would rely less on drugs and alcohol to modify mood; and they believe their efforts to solve their problems would be more effective. There were no differences between those holding the psychosocial orientation and those with the physiological orientation in terms of derogation toward those with problems. These data suggest that a psychological conceptualization of problem drinking might promote greater help seeking.

Fingarette (1988) voices concern regarding another ramification of the disease concept. He feels that viewing alcoholism as a disease creates a dichotomy of those who are alcoholics vs. those who are not. Those who fail to display the more flagrant aspects of alcoholism may be lulled into complaisance regarding their heavy drinking, falsely believing that if they are not alcoholic there is no reason for concern. Indeed, Fingarette suggests that the liquor industry will advance the disease concept because it legitimizes social drinking. The concept of alcoholism as a disease antedates its official recognition by the American

Medical Association, the concept extending back to 1870 (Blumberg, 1977). It is probably going to continue as a label for alcoholism. The important question is how that label will be used. Its removal of a moral stigma, when it functions that way, is useful. However, since the alcoholic plays a large role in achieving remission, the question of whether the disease concept encourages or discourages personal effort is an unanswered question. The AA concept of putting one's self in the hands of a "Higher Power" similarly can cut both ways.

Many diseases start out with only a limited percentage of people recovering. As treatments improve, larger numbers are cured or go into remission, until eventually the disease is conquered. This analogy for the disease concept of alcoholism has perhaps not been fully recognized. There is insufficient concern about the large percentage of alcoholics who are not helped by current procedures. If this were any other disease, treatment professionals would be far from proud of their current efforts. When the treatments fail for other diseases, the treatment provider feels in some way responsible. In alcoholism treatment, it is the patient that is held responsible for failure. This seems strangely at variance with a disease concept. Perhaps the concept should be taken more seriously in the cases of failure. Perhaps we should be looking more diligently for new approaches to utilize for those who are not helped by the traditional AA approach.

2 AA Oriented Treatment and its Differences from Empirically Oriented Treatment

Movements similar in philosophy and structure to AA were prevalent throughout the 1800s. Although none of these groups established a national organization, these forerunner organizations (e.g., Oxford group, the Washingtonians) ran halfway houses in urban areas (Baumohl & Room, 1987). Not until the 1950s did it become common for alcoholics to be treated in state hospitals, where they were housed with patients suffering from other disorders. Therapies (psychoanalysis and group therapy) employed in the treatment of other disorders were applied to alcoholism. Some states also financed half way houses for alcoholics (Weisner & Room, 1984). City missions, financed through charities and church, provided sustenance and religious reform for those alcoholics lacking employment and families. AA, founded in 1935, was available but did not achieve the large reception it enjoys presently.

The 1970s witnessed the deinstitutionalization of both treatment for alcoholism and treatment for mental illness. The time was one of reform. The focus was on the development of community mental health centers to allow for treatment on an outpatient basis. Prevention, identification, and treatment of early stage problems was to be achieved through a public awareness campaign. Paraprofessional providers were encouraged as a mechanism for reaching the large numbers in need.

In 1970, the Comprehensive Alcohol Abuse and Alcoholism Prevention, Treatment, and Rehabilitation Act (Public Law 91-616), was passed. This act established the National Institute of Alcoholism and Alcohol Abuse (NIAAA) as a separate entity, no longer under the National Institute of Mental Health. NIAAA was charged with the task of dispersing federal matching funds to states, and establishing standards for state programs. NIAAA encouraged insurance companies to extend benefits for alcohol and drug treatment. The laws governing federally subsidized Health Maintenance Organizations required coverage for alcohol and drug abuse. With the availability of funds, the industry of alcohol and drug treatment was sired. Again, the concern was with prevention and early identification. Persons drinking at levels that might not have been identified as problematic in the past, were labeled alcoholic (Mulford, 1979; Weisner & Room, 1984).

The AA doctrine was the only well articulated model of treatment prepared to meet the new demand for treatment. The precedent for the use of paraprofessionals had been established in mental health. Recovering alcoholics, active in AA, were ready to provide care. This sharply contrasted with the professional community which had not addressed alcoholism as a treatment issue. Relatively little knowledge gleaned through empirical research was available. Courses addressing alcoholism were not part of professional curriculums. Lacking guidance from the usual disciplines charged with the task of treating personal disturbance, the Jellinek perspective coupled with religious tradition inspired specific treatment for alcoholism. This perspective represents the modal form of treatment in this country today. Halzelden and the Johnson Institute, two early Minnesota treatment centers, which published their perspectives, became the treatment models for the rest of the country.

Concomitant with the development of traditional treatment models, was the development of Employee Assistance Programs for business and industry. Trice and Roman, both sociologists embracing AA concepts, have been the major publicists of the Employee Assistance movement. The model is one of prevention. An individual called an employee assistance professional, often a recovering alcoholic, is employed by a company. The employee assistance provider trains supervisors in the identification of alcoholism. Supervisors are instructed in techniques for confronting troubled employees and referring them to treatment programs rather than terminating their jobs. Participation in treatment, usually treatment in an AA oriented program and AA attendance, is required for job retention (Roman, 1988).

With the emerging public focus on alcoholism, the courts began using alcoholism treatment as a means of dealing with a wide variety of social problems. Individuals were mandated by courts into alcoholism treatment and/or AA after commission of a wide variety of offenses, including DWIs, family violence, child abuse, robbery, forgery, and assault. Although AA had originally developed to work with voluntary clients, AA treatment perspectives accommodated to the new demand and availability of public funding. AA oriented treatment professionals developed strategies for "breaking through denial," that is, convincing individuals that they were alcoholic and that the treatment was relevant to them (Weisner & Room, 1984). With the advent of the private, for profit, alcoholism treatment industry, treatment centers began marketing services to family members as well as to the alcoholic; offering family members an external aid and ally in control of the alcoholic's drinking and related troubling behaviors (Weisner & Room, 1984).

The scientific disciplines of psychology and psychiatry with their epistemological traditions of knowledge through controlled research have played no role in the development of AA oriented treatment for alcoholism. In the 1970s, the academic psychologists were experiencing, and acting in accord with, the behavior modification zeitgeist. Psychologists trained in behaviorism did develop treatments for alcoholism. During that period reports of aversion therapy, blood alcohol level discrimination training, and token economies for alcoholics appeared in the literature. Throughout the 1970s psychologists also contributed to the alcoholism field through basic research. This empirical research, much of which was reviewed in the previous chapter, cast doubt on the assumptions inspiring AA oriented treatment, though not necessarily invalidating the treatment procedures, which could be helpful, but incorrectly rationalized. The basic research has also yielded a reservoir of information about the natural paths of excessive drinking and drinking related phenomenon. These findings have been available for reference in developing alternative treatment perspectives, or even suggesting ways in which AA oriented therapy programs might be improved.

Presently, within the psychological community, there is growing consensus on how to treat alcoholism and the addictions. The emerging psychological perspective in the treatment of alcoholism receives its inspiration from behavior modification (skills training, assertion training, etc.) and the principles of social psychology. Relapse prevention, and positive ways of dealing with relapse, have emerged as an organizing focus for treatment.

In his book, the term empirically based treatment is used to refer to treatment based on psychological principles that have some empirical support. The term traditional treatment is used to refer to AA oriented treatment. The empirically based approach is exemplified by William Miller and Alan Marlatt, two well published university based clinicians. Their work is heavily referenced in this chapter and the next.

This chapter begins with an overview of what usually occurs in traditional treatment. Following with, a comparison and contrast of traditional empirically based treatment is presented. The differences in philosophical perspective on the change process, as well as the role of the therapist in this change process, are highlighted. Whereas this chapter, which contrasts the two approaches, only details the traditional approach, the following chapter is devoted to a detailed presentation of empirically based treatment.

DETAILS OF TRADITIONAL TREATMENT

Discussion now turns to a description of what might typically happen in a traditionally oriented treatment center. The major sources for this discussion are the Big Book of AA and Reverend Vern Johnson's (1980) *I'll quit tomorrow*. Reverend Johnson helped to develop the Minnesota model of treatment, and founded his own treatment center, the Johnson Institute. Both the Johnson Institute and Hazelden have been models for traditional treatment. Johnson's views have been adopted whole cloth by many traditional treatment providers. At one point, *I'll quit tomorrow* was the major text used by those studying to be accredited as certified alcoholism counselors in Arizona. This accreditation had developed on a state level, although never written into state laws, as a way of certifying the legitimacy of recovered alcoholics and paraprofessionals in providing services to alcoholics.

Interventions

Traditional treatment often begins with an intervention (Johnson, 1986). An intervention consists of an assembly of relevant persons in the life of an alcoholic (wife, children, friends, employer, physician) who have been brought together for the purpose of confronting the alcoholic with information confirming his alcoholism in a manner that "breaks through the denial." The significant others have met with the therapist prior to the confrontation to receive coaching in presenting factual vingettes, offering detail without value judgments. Each individual presents his/her episode in a brief period (about 5 min apiece). Along with the factual account significant others are instructed to include information pertinent to how they felt during the particular incident and a statement of concern or love for the alcoholic. Sometimes contingencies are included to the effect that if the alcoholic does not enter treatment the job will be lost or the wife will sue for divorce, although empty threats are discouraged.

The alcoholic is often brought to the intervention under some ruse. Upon discovering what is about to happen, the therapist requests that the alcoholic be reasonable, and offer no response while each significant other proceeds through his/her prepared speech. At the end the alcoholic is offered a choice of which treatment center he/she would like to enter. Possible objections have been anticipated ("I have to work") and necessary arrangements have already been made. The bags have been packed prior to the intervention.

Patient Education

In most traditional treatment centers a good deal of didactic information is presented. "The alcoholic must educate himself about his disease." Generally, there is a lecture on the physical sequale of alcoholism. The following ideas are imparted: the disease concept including notions of progression ineluctably resulting in insanity or death if abstinence does not eventuate; the notion that the disease continues to progress even when the alcoholic is not drinking such that after relapse the situation (unspecified) will be worse than before the onset of abstinence; the notion that one drink will result in a loss of control and a return to debauchery; and the notion that alcohol removes the intellect and leaves the emotions unbridled.

There are a number of nationally distributed films that are standard in most treatment centers. Father Martin's Chalk Talk is probably the most widely distributed of films. Rather than imparting information or logical argument, Father Martin presents an emotional appeal for sobriety. He is humorous and avuncular in his presentation, and warmly welcomes the alcoholic into the AA community.

AA and the Steps.   In addition to films and lectures, most traditional treatment centers encourage AA attendance. They include the caution that failure to attend AA will result in relapse, or if this prediction is not made, patients are told that without AA they might achieve abstinence but not sobriety. (Sobriety, in this frame of reference, connotes good mental health as well as abstinence.) Most treatment centers in some way incorporate the steps of AA. (See Alcoholics Anonymous World Services, Inc. 1985.) The twelve steps to AA are listed below:

1. We admitted we were powerless over alcohol—that our lives had become unmanageable.
2. Came to believe that a Power greater than ourselves could restore us to sanity.
3. Made a decision to turn our will and our lives over to the care of God as we understood Him.
4. Made a searching and fearless moral inventory of ourselves.
5. Admitted to God, to ourselves, and to another human being the exact nature of our wrongs.
6. Were entirely ready to have God remove all these defects of character.
7. Humbly asked Him to remove our shortcomings.
8. Made a list of all persons we had harmed, and became willing to make amends to them all.
9. Made direct amends to such people wherever possible, except when to do so would injure them or others.
10. Continued to take personal inventory and when we were wrong promptly admitted it.
11. Sought through prayer and meditation to improve our conscious contact with God as we understood Him, praying only for knowledge of His will for us and the power to carry that out.
12. Having had a spiritual awakening as the results of these steps, we tried to carry this message to alcoholics, and to practice these principles in all our affairs.

The first step requires a personality expressed litany of incidents which exemplify how the individual has become powerless over alcohol. This confession is usually presented in front of a group. Treatment centers that address additional steps arrange for the alcoholic to admit to a counselor the exact nature of past wrongs (4th and 5th steps). If the 9th step is included, the patient makes apologies to wronged individuals while in the program. Patients may be encouraged to make daily inventories of their transgressions, continuing to take a searching moral inventory (the 10th step).

The Role of Guilt

Traditional treatment centers do utilize guilt as a tool of influence. Vern Johnson states directly that guilt is a desirable goal of treatment. In providing instructions to the confessor hearing the searching moral inventory, Johnson advises:

> Here perhaps it should be pointed out to the listener that he must allow the speaker to experience the pain he is attempting to describe. This is not the time to reassure or minimize, but rather to draw out what has so long been hidden. What the speaker experiences rather than what the listener says is the therapeutic agent involved. (p. 178)

Johnson also regards dispositional attributions for past wrong doing (viewing one's behavior as caused by being a particular type of individual) as the goal. Rather than attributing the past wrong, to the drinking, Johnson wants the alcoholic to view the past wrong as arising from some stable personality trait, which he/she is incapable of changing. Johnson cautions the counselor listening to the fourth step,

> when sentences begin with 'When I was drinking, I' . . . . , the listener will stop the speaker promptly and call attention to what is happening. The goal is to have the alcoholic speak of himself directly and unequivocally. Thus he might summarize with some such thought as, 'I did those things because I am this kind of person, God help me. (p. 178)

According to Johnson, recuperation of self-esteem will occur when the third step is completed and God is entreated to remove character defects.

Whereas, traditional AA doctrine ascribes a central role to guilt in the recovery process, there is some recognition that depression and learned helplessness can result. According to the AA discussion of the moral inventory, (Twelve Steps and Twelve Traditions):

> If temperamentally we are on the depressive side, we are apt to be swamped with guilt and self-loathing. We wallow in this messy bog, often getting a misshapen and painful pleasure out of it. As we morbidly pursue this melancholy activity, we may

sink to such a point of despair that nothing but oblivion looks possible as a solution. Here, of course, we have lost all perspective, and therefore all genuine humility. For this is pride in reverse. (p. 45)

The process that will attenuate guilt feelings once induced is not clearly delineated in the traditional literature. However, the expectation that the patient will not remain depressed is conveyed. Traditional philosophy suggests that God is forgiving and that faith is exemplified in happy gratitude.

Vehicle for Treatment

Most traditional treatments rely on groups as a vehicle for treatment. Johnson advocates a verbal confrontational approach in group treatment. The therapist and group are advised to make descriptive statements about the behavior of the individual focused upon. Along with the descriptive statement, members in the group are encouraged to include comments regarding their own affective response to the individual's behavior. The group is trained to observe for defense mechanisms (defined here as an individual's frequent expression of a particular emotion such that it becomes a characteristic posture) as well as stylistic behaviors (e.g., self pity, resentment, arrogance). Advice-giving or speculation as to the etiology of the particular behavior are avoided.

AA groups and Traditional treatment centers proffer a taxonomy of traits which are believed characteristics of alcoholics. These include self-pity, resentment, grandiosity, trying to control or fix other people, trying to control external events, bursts of unsustained enthusiasm, perfectionism, hypersensitivity, and selfishness (Johnson, 1980, p. 82). Contradictory positions are expressed regarding whether these traits caused the alcoholism (AA, 1976, p. 554) or whether the drinking caused the traits (Johnson, 1980, Chapters 7 & 8; p. 5). Terry Gorski, a traditionalist of some renown, takes the position that resentments are no more characteristics of alcoholics than other people. However, alcoholics, unlike other people, cannot afford to harbor resentments because resentments lead to relapse. (These views were expressed at a workshop in Phoenix in 1982 which the author attended.) Regardless of theory as to etiology, these traits constitute the schemas that direct observations for the members of the group in traditional group therapy sessions.

Most traditionally trained alcohol counselors have been imbued with the perspective that alcoholics early in new-found sobriety lack the cognitive capacity necessary for making good judgments in their life. Alcoholics are advised against making major life decisions. If an alcoholic is also an "adult child of an alcoholic," he/she is told not to explore the emotional turmoil of his/her childhood until achieving a year of sobriety. Part of the fragile emotional state and poor judgment is attributed to Post Acute Withdrawal Syndrome (see prior chapter). The idea that the alcoholic progression arrested emotional and cognitive development is also advanced (Kinney & Leaton, 1982, p. 151–152). If the onset of the alcoholism was in adolescence, then the alcoholic is assumed not to have matured beyond this state.

What Happens at AA Meetings

There are several types of AA meetings. At a speaker's meeting, a designated individual tells his/her story. The norm is to fully articulate details rather than glossing over them. The focus is on the drinking days rather than on what has occurred since the advent of sobriety. At step meetings, one of the 12 steps is selected and each participant speaks to the relevance or personal meaning of the step. Sometimes an AA slogan or concept (First things, first; Let go and Let God; Just for Today; But for the Grace of God; Little by Little; Live and Let Live; Easy does it; One day at a time; hitting bottom; getting off the pity pot; stinking thinking), one of the traditions, or a chapter in the Big Book is used as a point of departure for group discussion. Generally each person is given an opportunity to speak in turn. Advice giving is discouraged and no feedback is provided in response to a self-disclosing monolog. The meetings conclude with the Lord's prayer. Most AA groups celebrate sobriety anniversaries. Chips are given for sobriety landmarks (1 month; 5 months, etc.).

Newcomers are encouraged to find sponsors. Sponsors are recommended to have at least a year's sobriety and to be of the same sex. Initiates are encouraged to do whatever their sponsor tells them in "working" their program. Generally 90 meetings in 90 days are advised. Sponsors generally have at least weekly contacts with their pigeons (the slang term for new initiates; see Room, 1989). New initiates are encouraged to provide service to other alcoholics. In Phoenix, AZ new initiates provide rides from the city detox center to AA meetings implementing the 12th step, which exhorts AA members to provide service to others.

Comments

The initiation rights of AA (90 meetings in 90 days; the term pigeon for initiates; the recommended obedience to a sponsor) manifest many of the components of initiation into a college fraternity. During the college hazing process initiates similarly bear implicitly low status with the promise of eventual high status in the group for those who remain. As in a college fraternity, AA members are proud of their affiliation as evidenced by AA bumper stickers, AA key chains, and AA book markers. The "anonymous" component lives on primarily in the name.

The psychological principles of cognitive dissonance and self-perception theory provide explanation for behavior change mediated by self-perception. Both theories posit that if a person chooses to act in a particular manner then that person's view of himself/herself will change to incorporate traits exemplified in the action (Fazio, Zanna, & Cooper, 1977). The change in self-concept will produce subsequent behavior consistent with the new view of self. There are several limiting conditions. No change will occur when individuals believe their behavior was caused or forced by external factors, i.e., when external explanations for behavior are available. (Differences between cognitive dissonance and self-perception are discussed, later when distinctions between the theories are germane.) Research has substantiated the principles of cognitive dissonance theory and self-perception theory. Research has shown that people behaving in ways that conflict with their attitudes, will shift their attitudes to favorably accommodate the new behavior if they believe that their behavior was voluntary. Inducing action consistent with a desired attitudinal shift, is a standard attitude change procedure known to social psychologists (Baron & Byrne, 1981).

AA procedures, without recognizing the principles, exploit cognitive dissonance and self-perception. New initiates who are uncomfortable with recommendations or AA philosophy are encouraged to "fake it, until you make it." The dubious are encouraged to maintain an open mind, and try to believe, acting as if they do believe, until they are able to believe (See Big Book Chapter on advice to agnostics). This encourages behavior in accord with the desired new attitudes. Defiance is seen as a necessary first step to recovery (Johnson, 1980, p. 77) and is interpreted as such. By interpreting defiance as part of the process, the traditionalist changes the patient's dispositional attributions about his/her own behavior leaving the individual confused about his/her real feelings. That is, defiant behavior is defined as pro AA rather than antagonistic to AA. Every possible response that a patient might make is defined as pro AA. Thus, regardless of the patient's reactions, the traditional therapist will convince the patient that he/she is acting in ways that are favorable to AA. The dubious are made comfortable by the reassurance that many now avid AAs began as skeptics, thus the initiate's skeptical behavior is redefined as fitting the mold. In addition to cognitive dissonance mechanisms for attitude change, AA relies on more direct methods as well. Newcomers are encouraged to suspend judgment and thought. An AA slogan is provided for those raising points of logic, "you can be too smart to take advantage of this simple program, but you can't be too stupid."

In recent years, given the great number of treatment centers for alcoholics that have arisen around the country, a massive infusion of people has been sent to AA. Because of the emphasis on prevention, many individuals who in the past would not have been labeled alcoholic, receive the diagnosis today. Another trend has been the reliance of the courts and industry on AA as a mechanism for social control (Weisner & Room, 1984). Whereas AA began as a community of largely gamma alcoholic voluntary affiliates, at any meeting today a large number of alcohol abusers and involuntary persons will be found.

There is good reason to wonder whether the infusion of new populations will change the fundamental organization of AA. Whereas an alcohol dependent alcoholic in the past would have found that the bulk of AA members were similar to himself/herself, today the majority may be alcohol abusers. Perhaps the organization may not be as helpful today as in the past in providing an opportunity for positive identification to the gamma alcoholic. Another question concerns the impact of a large number of coerced individuals at any AA meeting. Perhaps the large contingent of obviously disgruntled individuals sent by the courts will block the operation of cognitive dissonance principles and vitiate the organization's efficacy. A final question concerns the ratio of old timers to initiates needed for preserving the fundamental operation of the organization. Whether the organization will retain a large enough critical mass of members who are familiar with the AA philosophy to preserve its fundamental orientation, is a question that can only be answered with time.

DIFFERENCES BETWEEN TRADITIONAL AND EMPIRICALLY BASED TREATMENT

The following discussion endeavors to make salient some of the major distinctions between traditional and empirically based treatment. Four areas where the differences are clear and important are addressed. The first is in regard to information that is given about traits of alcoholics; the second is in the assumed tasks and strategies of therapy; the third is in the sources of motivation that are tapped by the two approaches; and the fourth is in differences on the issue of working with alcoholics while they continue to drink.

Information about Traits of Alcoholics

The prior section presented the list of personality traits that are purported to be characteristic of alcoholics. Most of these traits are presented with a pejorative tone by the traditional treatment provider, suggesting that the alcoholic should endeavor to change them. As will be seen in the chapter on personality, there are few, if any personality traits, which are uniquely descriptive of alcoholics. Empirically based treatment does not present patients with stereotypic beliefs about their behavior. Most professional schools also train clinicians in assuming a nonjudgemental posture. It is for the patient to decide, which, if any, trait constitutes a character defect. The therapist does not set up a standard to which the patient should aspire. Further, some schools of therapy (e.g., Gestalt) believe that problems are created when people create standards for themselves and judge themselves contingently. Although professionally trained persons will vary on the issue of whether or not it is useful for patients to have standards and to judge themselves by these standards, most professionals are trained to remain neutral on the issue when talking with the client.

Traditional treatment is also full of interpretation about the alcoholic's behavior. Depression or irritability are interpreted as a dry drunk. Lack of enthusiasm for AA attendance is interpreted as a reinstatement of the denial process. Empirically based treatment does not engage in this interpretation. As yet, the impact of the interpretations of traditional treatment on the alcoholic and his/her family has not been assessed. The question of impact is an interesting one. What is the ramification of the alcoholic's spouse viewing the alcoholic's occasional irritability as a "dry drunk" or "typical alcoholic behavior" rather than perhaps communicating something about the immediate situation? Perhaps future research will address these questions.

In empirically based treatment, alcoholics are not imbued with the idea that a drink will necessarily lead to a drunk. Patients are not told that drinking will unleash an irresistible craving, or that relapses are inevitably severe. Patients are told that should a first drink occur, they can and should immediately take steps to reinstate the goal of sobriety. Here the data are supportive of not setting up a self-fulfilling prophecy. Patients who do and do not become AA affiliates, equated on the severity of their drinking at intake, have been followed up. AA affiliates experience fewer relapses; however, those that occur are more severe and last longer (Ogborne & Bornet, 1982).

The Task: Attitude Change vs. Exploration

In traditional treatment, the patient is cast in the role of learner. He/she is imbued with a new perspective. The individual who is not fully convinced that there is a problem and/or that he/she has lost control over alcohol, is repeatedly presented with the viewpoint that he/she is in the early stages which will surely progress to eventual destruction. Traditional treatment assumes that denial clouds the patient's judgment in such a way that the patient's thoughts and perspective on the matter become irrelevant (Johnson, 1980, p. 27). The patient need only surrender and listen as the therapist explains the true nature of the situation.

In traditional treatment, there is a great deal of pressure to, in essence, join the group by admitting that one is an alcoholic. Generally, the self-labeled alcoholics in the group are concerned, helpful people, so that group affiliation should seem attractive. Denial is disparaged or even ridiculed, thereby redounding in further pressure to self-define as an alcoholic. Attitude change procedures are brought to bear by encouraging the patient to make public statements consistent with the treatment philosophy.

In empirically based treatment, the individual's motivation is explored more fully. Rather than assuming the patient needs to be converted to a particular point of view, the patient is assisted in identifying his/her objections to drinking, as well as the factors that maintain it, or preclude commitment to sobriety. The pros and cons for drinking are assessed by the patient in terms of how they correspond with the patient's more fundamental values. Denial is not assumed. The patient is viewed as capable of making decisions about himself/herself and is trusted to evaluate. Exploration leading to a treatment decision, rather than conversion, is the goal.

A related difference between the two approaches is the issue of who controls the therapy. In traditional treatment, the control of the therapy is the purview of the therapist. (However, the therapist is not overtly assumed to be responsible for motivation or outcome.) Control of therapy is a salient issue. For example, it would not be unusual for a therapist to make a diagnostic comment such as the following to colleagues: "he [a particular patient] is trying to control his treatment." Such a statement might be made when the patient says he cannot come to inpatient treatment, or would like marital therapy instead. It is possible that this closing off of patient control at times makes the task of effecting change harder. There are seminal studies demonstrating that treatment compliance is enhanced when the client has a choice in selecting the treatment (Champlin & Karoly, 1975; Gordon, 1976; Kanfer & Grimm, 1978). By contrast, for empirically based therapists, it is important for the patient to feel responsible for decisions that are made. The patient actively participates in, for example, goal selection (abstinence versus eventual control drinking).

Strategy: Reliance on Commitment to Maintain Change vs. Teaching Skills for Relapse Prevention

Most of the energy in traditional treatment is expended on attitude change and securing commitment to the AA group. Commitment to AA is equated with commitment to sobriety. At AA meetings, individuals participate in repetitive affirmations of their original commitments. It is assumed that those who believe in the group, who sincerely desire to be sober, and who follow their sponsor's advice will stay sober. Commitment and conversion will suffice to achieve the goal of sobriety. There is little need to identify the precipitants of drinking or factors maintaining it. There is no focused development of skills for coping with situations that precipitate drinking.

Ways in which Traditional Treatment Addresses Relapse

Traditional treatment has not incorporated, as part of treatment, a systematic behavioral analysis of the factors eliciting relapse, or the teaching of new coping behaviors. Such processes necessitate listening to the individual case with the attendant danger of reinforcing excuses. In recent years, however, AA has begun to pay attention to potential precipitating factors of relapse. AA members are exhorted not to be hungry, angry, lonely, or tired (HALT acronym). Though sometimes hard to follow, this is good advice.

Although traditional treatment does not systematically address relapse prevention, there are some adventitious features mitigating against relapse which might be expected to follow from AA affiliation. Three clear ways in which AA decreases the probability of relapse are the following:

1. For those who have the social skills requisite to elicit social support, AA offers this resource. The social support will be there for those who know how to access it. Stress, a precipitant to drinking, can be buffered by social support.
2. For those whose social life becomes AA, AA affiliation constitutes a life style change. The new life style will be incompatible with the drinking.
3. For those lucky enough to become group leaders a new source of self-esteem will eventuate.

All foregoing mechanisms constitute powerful mechanisms for decreasing the chances of relapse. For some they may be enough.

Terry Gorski (Gorski & Miller, 1982) has labeled his treatment approach, relapse prevention. According to Gorski relapse begins long before the first postsobriety drink is imbibed. Two major categories of relapse indicators are recognized: waning enthusiasm for AA or treatment, and bad moods. Waning enthusiasm for the AA program is equated with waning enthusiasm for sobriety. Bad moods are interpreted as part of the disease, viz., dry drunks or postabstinence withdrawal symptoms. The antidote for bad moods or other dry drunk symptoms is renewed commitment, not coping skills. For Gorski, commitment to AA and treatment are the same. The patient cannot value one and not the other.

In making predictions about relapse, empirically based clinicians also would take into consideration an individual's commitment to sobriety. A person not valuing her/his sobriety will probably relapse. A distinction is made, however, between valuing sobriety and commitment to therapy or AA. (For example, a patient may want to achieve sobriety, but not find her/his therapist compatible.) Further, in making predictions, it is recognized that motivation is only half the story. Equal emphasis is given to an individual's quality of, range of, and confidence in her/his skills for coping with relapse precipitants.

As previously suggested in passing, part of the reason why traditional treatment may not have incorporated an individual assessment of the forces precipitating relapse, is that such a procedure lends credence to excuses for drinking. In traditional treatment, excuses are viewed as rationalizations, which dissipate the alcoholic's guilt over drinking, decrease the pain of hitting bottom, and hence undermine the motivation to cease drinking. Excuses and rationalizations are to be avoided.

In psychological treatment, identification of external forces or internal mood precipitants to drinking is encouraged. First, this process allows the alcoholic to know when he/she will be vulnerable to relapse and offers signals suggesting when coping skills should be remembered. Second, following failure (relapse) attributions to external factors or to internal, controllable, unstable factors can prevent any change in self-percept, which would undermine motivation to try again. Evidence suggests that excuse making after failure diminishes the psychological pain and averts subsequent behavioral deterioration (Snyder & Higgins, 1988). From a self-concept perspective, believing a relapse was caused by a fight with one's spouse or that it was caused by a bout of the flu is better for long-term sobriety than attributing it to an inability to stay sober.

The differing perspectives on excuses between the traditional and psychological approaches reflects a more fundamental divergence on what motivates people to change. From the empirically based perspective, motivation for sobriety is seen as broader based than the shame and guilt arising from internal attributions for drinking. It is assumed that patients are likely to eventually realize that the major negative consequences of drinking cannot be escaped even if means of decreasing guilt for any particular drinking episode are found. It is considered unlikely that anyone will devalue sobriety simply because shame for a particular drinking incident is escaped.

Sources of Motivation

Traditional treatment programs view hitting bottom as fundamental to the process of change. Patients are seen as changing to avoid further punishment and/or the negative states of shame, fear, loss. Consistent with the traditional model of change, traditional treatment induces fear via details of the progression of the disease or by detailing medical sequale. Shame is increased through the litany of the first step. Films depict the destruction occurring in families and imply that even if these events have not yet occurred they are imminent given continued drinking.

There are several psychological literatures that suggest when fear and shame will be useful strategies. Fear appeals have been the focus of a great deal of attitude change research (Leventhal, 1971). The moderator variable of having an available efficacious coping strategy determines whether fear appeals will produce the intended impact on behavior. For individuals who have a clear alternative path available, appeals to fear will be efficacious. For those who do not view themselves as having an option, fear appeals are ignored or produce no impact on behavior (Leventhal, 1971; Rogers & Mewborne, 1976; Rogers & Thistlethwaite, 1970).

In the area of employee assistance, there has been some attempt to identify those aspects of an employee/supervisor meeting that are most effective for inducing the alcoholic employee to enter treatment and recover. Studies evaluating the efficacy of confrontation in work settings allow the drawing of conclusions regarding which strategies work best for bringing people into treatment and improving work performance. In their study, Trice and Beyer (1984) surveyed supervisors who had arranged meetings with heavily drinking employees to encourage their involvement in the company's employee assistance program. Supervisors indicated the number of topics that had been discussed at the meetings. Topics were divided into three qualitative categories: (1) confrontational (demanding changes in employee's behavior and performance, suggesting possible disciplinary action, and discussing negative effects on other employees); (2) constructive topics (opportunities for expression of the employee's explanation of his/her own behavior, explanation by the supervisor of the relevant features of the Employee Assistance Program, and discussion of the employee's personal problems); (3) informing the employee of formal disciplinary actions. Trice and Beyer then performed a discriminant analysis to identify those variables that best discriminated the following outcome groups: those accepting treatment, those refusing treatment, and those leaving the company. (The authors indicated that job performance at the time of the meeting had been entered into the analysis first, such that this variable was controlled when evaluating the impact of subsequent variables.) Results suggested that receiving treatment was associated with less confrontation and more constructive discussion. Leaving the company was associated with more confrontation and discipline. The mean for confrontational topics was lower in the receiving treatment group, next highest in the refusing treatment group, and highest in the group leaving the company.

A separate regression analysis predicting employee performance improvement suggested that participating in treatment was related to improvement. In this analysis, after controlling for employee's performance at the time of the meeting as well as all other variables, introduction of confrontation topics did relate to improved performance; however, formal disciplinary action was associated with lack of improvement in job performance. Clearly, if the employer wishes to keep the employee, disciplinary action is not desirable. A constructive approach works best, and confrontation, though it may improve job performance, may not be a good long-term strategy because it appears to have a negative effect on treatment motivation.

There are additional reasons mitigating against confrontation. Confrontation can create or enhance a patient's self-percept of being in an adversarial role with the therapist (or supervisor). Further, any intervention that forces patients to acknowledge aspects of themselves that they would rather forget, can induce a cognitive dissonance change. That is, patients might change their attitude to a more positive view of the behavior, if they are convinced that the behavior is truly characteristic. Unlike traditional treatment, psychologists are cautious in utilizing confrontation (i.e., reminding the patient of some unfavorable behavior he/she has performed) as a motivating tactic. Self-labeling in keeping with undesirable attitudes or behaviors, is recognized as a potentially negative influence.

In traditional treatment, all patients must feel bad (surrender, be humble, feel guilty, be contrite) before they can feel good. In psychological treatment, although it is recognized that many will come to treatment feeling badly for past transgressions, which may be inevitable for socialized human beings, there is no need to further enhance these feelings to promote recovery. If anything, these emotional postures are viewed as sometimes being a threat to feelings of self-efficacy and the commitment to change, especially for those with fragile self-esteem.

The efficacy of techniques that induce shame have been investigated in alcoholic populations. Alcoholics have been exposed to videotapes of their own drunken behavior. When these videos have depicted moderately intoxicated behavior, there has been support for efficacy on measures of subsequent drinking (Baker, Udin, & Vogler, 1975; Paredes, Ludwig, Hassenfeld, & Cornelison, 1969). However, when the videotapes have depicted very drunken behavior, efficacy has not been demonstrated. Schaefer, Sobell, and Mills (1971) found that those alcoholics who watched videotapes of themselves during extreme intoxication, professed the goal of abstinence. However, they were more likely to drop out of treatment and under experimental drinking conditions shortly after the videotapes, there was no suppression of drinking. At 12 month follow-up, there were no differences between the video group and the control group on drinking measures, although there was a tendency for the former to attend more AA meetings (Schaefer, Sobell, & Sobell, 1972).

The studies examining the impact of the videotapes were conducted on low status alcoholics, possibly those most lacking in self-efficacy. One possible interpretation of the videotape studies is that eliciting extreme shame is not useful for those with low self-efficacy, i.e., those who believe they have no option other than continuing to drink uncontrollably. They believe they lack capacity for sobriety. Perhaps alcoholics who possess a high degree of self-efficacy and/or high self-esteem might be benefited by the goad of the reminder of their negative behavior. There is a study in the literature suggesting that for individuals who do not presently hold a particular negative self-perception, accusing them of such, i.e., confronting them with the possibility of negative behavior, will goad them to perform in an exaggerately positive manner. Steele (1975) accused persons who were subsequently asked to donate time to charity of being socially apathetic. Those individuals who had been accused, were more likely to comply with the subsequent request than those who were not accused. Unfortunately, Steele's study did not assess the impact of an insulting accusation when the accusation might be consistent with self-perception. For those alcoholics who perceive themselves as incapable of love or who believe they are unworthy degenerates, reminding them of what they believe they are may have a negative impact.

Psychological treatment views the motivation for change as broader based than traditional treatment does. Hitting bottom is not seen as necessary and is seen as counterproductive for some individuals, viz. those who cannot envision themselves as having achievable positive alternatives. Rather than offering such negative motivations as shame or guilt, empirically based treatment offers positive motivations, aspiration rather than avoidance, the carrot rather than the stick. Helping a patient identify other people in her or his environment who successfully function in ways that the patient admires, can sometimes inspire the patient, offering hope that there is an alternative. Cynicism about the possibility of change is an important stumbling block for many people. Helping them to recognize the coping skills that they can call upon, and seeing how others do it, can lessen that cynicism. Then detailed discussions of how to achieve the change can become a fundamental part of the therapy. In general then, the approach in empirically based therapy is on how to bring about changes rather than emphasizing the disgust with the drinking life, getting patients to think positively about their psychological resources for change so that they will then be more willing to recognize the necessity for change.

The Role of Self-Efficacy

As emphasized in the preceding section, in psychological treatment a great deal of emphasis is placed on self-efficacy. Treatment is geared to enhancing the patient's belief in his/her ability to maintain sobriety. This contrasts sharply with traditional treatment. In AA and traditional treatment, self-efficacy is irrelevant since God is charged with the task of maintaining sobriety rather than the patient. In fact, patients professing confidence in their ability to recover without external assistance are corrected in their "misperceptions." Attributions concerning will power are discouraged.

In traditional treatment, whether God will bestow grace becomes the issue. In some religious systems, grace can be entreated through faith and prayer. For most alcoholics, AA subscribes to this version, viewing faith as instrumental in securing God's support. Relapses are attributed to lack of spiritual effort (AA, 1976). In at least one other religious system, Calvinism, those worthy of grace from God are preordained and individual entreaty has no impact. For a minority of unspecified alcoholics AA implicitly endorses this latter position. AA indicates that there are those who are born incapable of honesty and faith (AA, 1976, p. 58). For such unfortunates, sobriety will not ensue. It seems plausible that the chronic, skid row alcoholic who is wet despite protracted experience with AA might well conclude he is one of the constitutional unfortunates.

Religious counselors are probably well equipped to help people change through religion. Most other mental health workers and treatment professionals are not charged with the task of helping people change through religion. However, treatment professionals with an AA orientation might reasonably see this as part of their mandate. For others in the mental health field, a related appropriate task might be to identify those individuals who might be particularly amenable to change through religion. There are suggestions in the research literature that some persons will function better when the responsibility for effecting outcome is placed in an external force. Persons can be differentiated on the dimension of resourcefulness. Resourcefulness taps a tendency toward the making of dispositional attributions (the identification of personal traits) for success, and general self-efficacy. Empirical findings suggest that those scoring high on a resourcefulness index respond well to treatment for depression when the treatment trains the patients in the use of coping strategies. Those scoring low on resourcefulness do better when given a pill (Rosenbaum & Smira, 1986). By extrapolation, individuals who are low in resourcefulness might be best off relying upon the external strategy of entreating God. If such individuals can be convinced that God will view them as worthy of grace, turning it over to God and the social support and precepts of AA may provide the strength and confidence that might not otherwise be experienced.

It is possible that both change attributed to self and change attributed to God will have the same impact. Empirical investigation has not yet assessed whether persons who have strong convictions that they will be helped by God to stay sober, will develop enhanced sense of capacity to effect outcome in other areas of their lives. AA does imply that those who develop faith will display serenity, happiness, and gratitude for their perceived high quality of life. Belief in God may enhance belief in one's ability to affect outcomes in general. Such a circuitous route would produce the same outcome viz., self-efficacy, which psychological treatment attempts to produce directly.

Working with Clients who Continue to Drink

Another area where traditionalists and empirically based clinicians strongly diverge is on the issue of working with a drinking client. A traditionalist would view working with a drinking client as enabling. Enabling is especially likely when this client expresses ambivalence over whether he/she wants to quit drinking. According to traditional thinking, the therapeutic encounter is believed to engender good feelings in the drinker. If good feelings are engendered while the drinker continues to drink, the traditionalist would argue that the drinker is being robbed of the bad feeling state needed for hitting bottom. Thus, the therapist is enabling. Patients who drink in the course of treatment, especially when there is an absence of contrition over the drinking, are discharged from treatment. The one criteria for membership in AA is a sincere desire to be sober (AA, 1976, p. 564). By implication, alcoholics who are uncertain of their goals are denied membership.

By contrast, in the empirical literature there are reports of therapists working with clients who are attempting to control drink. The therapist's goal can be assisting in learning how to control drink or helping the client to acquire the motivation to embrace an abstinence goal. People in control drinking programs often emerge embracing the goal of abstinence.

Ojehagen and Berglund (1986, 1989) report the results of an innovative treatment in Scandanavia in which psychosocial goals as well as drinking goals were the foci of treatment. Therapists were willing to work with patients who were attempting to control drink as well as those embracing an abstinence goal. The treatment was structured to continue for 2 years. Over the course of the 2 years, 10% of the patients were in the category of moving from a control drinking goal to an abstinence goal. Some alcoholics, most often those who were not physically dependent, displayed improvement in the first year. Others displayed improvement in the second year. The drinking improvement was most often preceded by positive changes in social functioning. The group displaying improvement in the second year was more often the Type 2 alcoholic (a label of Cloninger's discussed in the genetics chapter which refers to early onset alcoholism). Without a tenacious commitment on the part of the therapists to continue working with patients who were drinking, improvement in this group may not have been realized. This study suggests that working with drinking clients can result in positive change.

Again, differences in perspective on whether to work with drinking clients derives from the therapist's view of motivation. Is motivation a factor which, if present, the client always brings to therapy or is it sometimes a product of the process that occurs between the therapist and the client? Sterne and Pittman (1965) have recognized the salience of motivation in the philosophy of traditional treatment. The concept of hitting bottom implies that motivation emerges from the pain of the consequences of drinking. Sterne and Pittman sought to further specify how traditional treatment providers thought about motivation. They found that about half of those interviewed viewed motivation as a stable trait of the alcoholic rather than a static trait subject to influence during treatment. Further, about half inferred a patient's motivation through the occurrence of those behaviors which motivation was believed to influence. That is, motivation was not assessed independently from the patient's drinking. Finally, there was a correlation between viewing motivation as a stable trait and moralistic attitudes toward alcoholism (defined as endorsing such statements as, "alcoholism is a spiritual problem," "a person who turns to alcoholism must not have a very strong religious faith," "an alcoholic is always worried about the days he spends in treatment but he didn't worry about the days he spent drinking").

In the psychological literature motivation is viewed as deriving from two phenomena: how much value is placed on the goal and perceived self-efficacy in attaining the goal (Weiner, 1972). Miller (1985) has pointed out that the traditionalist will often be mislead in predicting which patients are most motivated and which patients will be successful. Research suggests that therapists view patients who are compliant and accepting, who are dependent, and who are more psychologically distressed as more motivated for treatment (Miller, 1985). Whereas these factors may be correlates of how much the abstinence goal is valued, they are probably negatively related to self-efficacy. Thus, alcoholics who evince great distress at the consequences of their alcoholism, as is often the case in those on skid row, may be the ones with the worst motivation and outcomes because they lack belief in self-efficacy.

A view of motivation by those with an empirically based treatment orientation, is that it can be a product of the process of therapy. The process of therapy can impact both upon the value of the goal to the patient and on the patient's feelings of self-efficacy. Research suggests that severe alcoholics present to treatment choosing an abstinence goal. For this group, the patient comes in valuing the goal. Motivating this type of patient will consist of enhancing belief in self-efficacy. Techniques for enhancing belief in self efficacy are presented in chapter 3.

The patient who presents for therapy with a control drinking objective obviously does not value the goal of sobriety. The experience in control drinking programs has been that those who are unsuccessful in their learning to control drink, later choose abstention (see prior chapter). Perhaps experience is a good teacher.

Differences in the Roles and Responsibilities of the Therapist in the two Treatment Approaches

In traditional treatment the therapist's role is to carry the message of disease to the patient. The patient has the responsibility for changing. Traditional therapists also view themselves as applying the sanctions of the larger society. They are careful to reward good behavior (sobriety) and to avoid being construed as approving bad behavior (drinking). They are agents of social control.

In psychological treatment the therapist collaborates with the patient in exploring whether sobriety is a desirable goal. Pattison (Pattison, Sobell, & Sobell, 1977) has brought to the attention of the treatment community the fact that not everyone is better off with sobriety. The data on which patients select abstention vs. a control drinking goal does support the view that the severely dependent do select abstention (Ojehagen & Berglund, 1989, 1986). Listening to the patient is critical. The patient makes her/his own choice.

The therapist offering empirically based treatment intervenes to create behavioral change which will make the goal attainment more likely. Although one way to influence behavior is for the therapist to show strong disapproval for drinking, most such therapists would not use this method. It is highly redundant with the natural consequences of drinking; it enhances the patient's sense of guilt and shame at a time when efforts toward problem solving would better serve the end goal; it will cast the therapist in the role of adversary; and if a return to drinking reflects a change in the patient's desired goal, it undermines the therapist's task of helping the patient explore why he/she had a mind change about trying to achieve abstention, or lost the resolution that had been present for a time. The patient would have reason to assume that a disapproving therapist would not be able to understand the reasons for the slip.

Allowing the patient to choose his/her own goal sharply contrasts with the approach of some traditionalists. Trice and Sonnenstuhl (1988), who have published in the area of employee assistance programs, argue that coercion is an effective and inevitable component in inducing a behavioral change. They suggest that there is no such thing as a truly voluntary referral to a drinking program because all persons quit drinking out of fear of reprisals (family disapproval, health concerns, etc.). Further, more overt coercion can be effective. Pertinent data is available on the issue of how coercion impacts treatment efficacy. Data from a study by Rosenberg and Liftik (1976) suggest that the drop-out rate for court-ordered patients is lower than for self-referred patients. However, in this study when the court order ended, only 16% of the court-ordered patients continued with treatment. The existence of skid row alcoholics, who at one time were threatened with loss of job and family, but did not respond to the threat, attests to the fact that even coercion will fail for some. Coercion can bring people into treatment, but since society only sustains coercion forever with life sentences to jail, we generally have to face the question of what happens after the coercion.

Trice and Sonnenstuhl (1988) have a point in that no rational person would decline a pleasure (alcohol) were there not some negative factors associated with the pleasure. What they have done however, is taken a good point, and taken it too far by refusing to recognize some important distinctions. For example, we can begin by recognizing that we are all products of our environment. Thus, in some way, we can say that everything we do is a function of our past experience, of our upbringing, past reinforcement, even our genetic make-up. Thus none of us is ever really free. On the other hand, we can recognize that there are vast differences between the freedoms experienced in successful democracies, and the lack of such freedoms in oppressive dictatorships. There are large differences in the freedom of the employer to take the day off, and the employee in a time of high unemployment to take the day off. Clearly, there are differences in degrees of free choice. There are, most importantly for this discussion, differences in the subjective impression of free choice. Further, distinctions concerning the subjective impression of free choice have been shown to have behavioral implications. Some of the behavioral differences that emerge when a person does or does not have a subjective experience of free choice, are highly relevant to people's responses to attempts to influence their behavior, as in therapy.

Several literatures speak to the folly of making it obvious that there has been external influence in a person's decision, when the goal is to create a change in the individual that will still be there after the external sanctions are faded out. The over justification literature (Lepper, Greene, & Nisbett, 1973) has demonstrated that children who are rewarded for behavior they are already performing will subsequently decrease their behavior. The forbidden doll experiment (Freedman, 1965) demonstrated that children who were warned of severe consequences should they play with the doll, were more likely to play with the doll than those merely requested not to play with the doll, after the experimenter had left the scene.

The overjustification literature and the forbidden doll experiment yield an important principle. When people can attribute their behavior (reinforced behavior in the overjustification literature or failing to transgress after heavy threat in the forbidden doll experiment) to some obvious external sanction, they will fail to make dispositional personal attributions. That is, they will not feel that their behavior is something that is voluntary, they will not identify with the behavior that they manifested under the subjective experience of coercion. Further, given the external sanction, the patient may be convinced that he/she is antagonistic to the sanctioned behavior. Self-perception principles would operate to make the patient feel all the more strongly about her or his wanting to behave in opposition to the coercion. It has previously been suggested that cognitive dissonance can operate positively in changing attitudes towards drinking in the context of AA attendance, where patients are encouraged to say things even when they do not mean them. The research literature on cognitive dissonance effects is very clear in showing that the subjective experience of the behavior being voluntary is critical to achieving attitude change. To the extent that alcoholics feel coerced into their verbal behaviors in AA meetings, or in pleasing judgmental therapists, they would not be likely to adopt the points of view they are verbalizing. Thus, regardless of the ultimate philosophic truth of whether we are ever really free, the subjective experience of freedom is important to the success of most therapeutic interactions.

A therapist taking into consideration the principles pertinent to influencing the self-concept will avoid obvious disapproval for drinking or external sanctioning. When approval for abstinence is given it should be couched in terms of helping the client to be proud of meeting his/her own goal, celebrating and emphasizing the patient's pride in achieving his/her own goal (the goal having been selected by the patient). With this approach (which emphasizes a subjective sense of freedom and personal decision making), it is clear that anything that causes the patient to believe that the goal belongs to the therapist rather than to the patient will defeat the objectives.

A further distinction between the therapist in traditional and psychological treatment, is in who accepts responsibility for failure. For traditionalists once the message is heard, the patient has the responsibility for sobriety. An AA quote reflects the attitude toward those persons who fail to respond to AA: "Rarely have we seen a person fail who has thoroughly followed our path. Those who do not recover are people who cannot or will not completely give themselves to this simple program, usually men and women who are constitutionally incapable of being honest with themselves" (AA, 1976, p. 58).

An alternative view of responsibility is that treatment failures are attributable to the inadequacy of the treatment method, given it is clear that the patient wanted to be sober. Of course, establishing whether a patient desires sobriety is usually a subjective judgment. However, when a patient takes time and money, and voluntarily goes for help, there is reason to assume that there is some real motivation. How strong is the motivation? All emotions vary in strength from time to time, so there is little reason to force a label on people that suggests they were not sufficiently motivated. If they are forced to go for others, and agree only after coercion, there is no reason to assume motivation at that point in time. But given any sign of personal motivation, it can be seen as the therapist's job to try to increase it.

Some patients agree that sobriety offers a better existence that would allow for more positive feelings about the self. They fail, however, to meet their goal due to skill deficits when encountering relapse precipitants, or due to a lack of confidence in their ability to utilize the skills they possess. Therapists can take at least some of the responsibility for this type of failure. It can be seen as their job to help to develop the needed skills, or to increase self-confidence and feelings of self-efficacy. It is reasonable that there should be regret that available treatment has not been more impactful.

Two incidents that occurred in a traditionally oriented treatment center illustrate the differences in assumptions about the treatment provider's responsibilities, from the points of view of those offering traditional and those offering empirically based treatment. The incidents illustrate how differing perspectives dictate separate courses of action, and also suggest some of the differences in the types of relationships that are likely to exist between patients and therapists, given the different orientations.

In a treatment center in which this author worked, therapy was provided on an outpatient basis, although patients occasionally requested inpatient treatment, believing that the latter would be more impactful. Given consumer pressure, a decision was made to offer inpatient treatment for some individuals. The staff was requested to generate criteria for inpatient treatment. Having recently read Miller and Hester's (1986) article on this subject, and agreeing with their perspective, I suggested that one criterion might be to admit as inpatients those persons who had failed to respond to outpatient therapy. The rationale for this criterion is that when one approach fails, other approaches should be applied in an attempt to find something that will work. My colleagues, all traditionalists, responded in a way typified by the following quote: ". . . aren't we then saying that the patient isn't responsible for quitting drinking?" The belief was advanced that those persons who drank during the outpatient program should not receive our symbol of approval, viz., inpatient hospitalization. Willingness to help the patient curtail the drinking through provision of inpatient treatment might imply that treatment providers have some responsibility to stop patients from drinking. In contrast, the usual manner of dealing with a drinking patient in that facility was to dismiss the patient from treatment, which clearly placed the responsibility for not drinking on the patient and not the staff.

The traditional staff then advanced the reasonable position that the very distressed and those without social support should be hospitalized. Patient distress, a factor cuing the therapist's perception of motivation in the patient (Miller, 1985), was deemed worthy of approval. Given limited inpatient facilities, the final decision in this example was not a bad one (and I did not oppose it). However, the response to the suggestion of inpatient treatment for those who continue to drink despite participation in outpatient therapy, was instructive in offering a clear glimpse of one of the basic assumptions of the traditional approach, and how it differs from assumptions that are considered in empirically based perspective. Although traditional treatment assumes a disease model, the patient rather than the therapist is seen as the responsible person given treatment failure.

The next vignette illustrates yet another difference in assumed responsibilities. A nurse had referred herself for treatment of prescription drug abuse. My colleague, a traditionalist, was treating the nurse. Upon learning the magnitude of the patient's drug consumption, the therapist decided that she should breach confidentiality and report the patient to the nursing board. In explanation, the author's colleague expressed concern both about her obligation to the larger society (a concern shared by both traditionalists and other treatment professionals), and her belief that she would be guilty of enabling were she not to report the nurse (a concern of traditionalists only).

In traditional treatment, the accusation of enabling is a looming threat for spouses and therapists. Enabling is behavior that protects the substance abusers from suffering the consequences of the addiction. By protecting the substance abuser from punishments that might follow from an addiction, the enabler is inhibiting the forces that will motivate recovery.

The concept of enabling induces confusion. Many in the traditional treatment community fail to make the distinction between interfering with the natural consequences of substance abuse and actively causing these consequences to occur. A traditional therapist in the service of eschewing enabling may actively arrange punishment for the patient. Thereby, the therapist relinquishes the freedom conferred by being a neutral party. By in effect assuming a surveillance role, the therapist assumes responsibility for the agonizing decisions of a judge. As the patient self-discloses, the therapist must assess whether enough rules have been violated to warrant sanction. Being in such a position may tempt the therapist to discourage disclosure.

There are benefits to not being in a surveillance or sanctioning role. Not being in a position to sanction, the issue of enabling is a non-sequiter. Of course, the Tarasoff decision has called into question whether therapist working with any disorder can avoid a surveillance role. Although the larger society has the capacity to mandate this function to clinicians, the benefits of not functioning in this capacity have been recognized. Without the assurance of confidentiality patients will be grossly limited in what they are willing to discuss. The process of therapy will be cripped by assigning the therapist a surveillance task already adequately fulfilled by other persons in the society.

Comment

The preceding discussion has highlighted the differences between traditional therapists and empirically based clinicians. It suggests that there are major differences in the assumptions that are made about alcoholism, and that these differences affect treatment. These differences include whether the practitioner is willing to work with drinking clients; whether the emphasis is placed on skill development and the sense of self-efficacy vs. the concern for the commitment of the alcoholic; whether commitment is to the goal of sobriety or to the AA group; and whether guilt and fear are used as motivating tools.

In a seminal article, Kalb and Popper (1976) presented their perspective on the differences between traditionalists and psychologists. They reached a very pessimistic conclusion as to whether the two camps could ever work together in harmony. Having attempted to reconcile the two perspectives in clinical practice, I share at least some of their pessimism. However, there are also some shared characteristics that could help to promote accommodation.

SHARED CHARACTERISTICS

Patients who are in traditional and empirically based treatment are placed in the role of the adult learner, being advised to seek out the facts and make informed decisions. Both orientations provide optimism and a sense of hope that the problem can be ameliorated, an aspect that Jerome Frank (1974) views as common to all therapies. Both approaches offer social support. Both dispel worry and some guilt by offering a sense of the universality of particular sequale of heavy drinking (feeling paranoid and depressed, becoming violent, not remembering well). Both create enthusiasm and energy for the process of maintaining abstinence. Both encourage patients to assess their own contribution to problems and what they can do rather than complaining about others. Both share a commitment to assisting patients to better their way of life.

Those practicing empirically based therapy can recognize the value of some of the operating principles of the traditional approach. Tiebout (1953) summed up traditional treatment as a conversion process. Indeed, AA was modeled after the fundamentalist movement (Blumberg, 1977) and traditional treatment, inspired by religion, embraces the features common to spiritual movements. Social psychologists have long recognized the power of the principles harnassed by these movements (Festinger, Rieckew, & Schachter, 1956). While recognizing the power of the conversion experience, and while occasionally exploiting a particular principle when it is most likely to be especially efficacious, those utilizing research based therapies bring a different perspective and strategy to the treatment of alcoholism. It is this approach to treatment that is discussed in the next chapter.

3 Research-Based Treatment

The prior chapter has contrasted the philosophy of traditional alcoholism treatment with the philosophy behind the treatment offered by research based professionals. In this chapter, the specifics of research based treatment are more fully discussed, with an emphasis on treatment interventions geared to an abstinence goal. Although a control drinking goal might be appropriate for some patients, in most cases an initial extended period of abstinence of 1 to 3 years generally increases the chances for later successful control drinking (see the discussion of control drinking in chapter 1, where the factors associated with successful and unsuccessful control drinking are reviewed). Miller and Munoz's (1976) book *How to control your drinking* or Sanchez-Craig et al.'s (1987) excellent work on this topic, offer helpful information on how to proceed when the decision is to attempt control drinking.

It is assumed that patients enter a program with at least an initial commitment to either sobriety or controlling their drinking. Whichever goal is selected, the problem is relapse. Therefore, this chapter on research-based treatment is centered on the issue of relapse. First, the data on relapse frequencies are given: How soon after a commitment to sobriety do relapses most frequently occur? What can be expected in terms of repetitions of relapse? What are some of the specific factors that are associated with relapse? These facts offer an orientation that can be helpful in understanding the relapse process. The chapter closes with a final section specifying the interventions that can make the occurrence of relapse less likely.

Because the issue of relapse follows after an assumed commitment, a few words should be stated on the issue of commitment, and about the initial sessions in general. It is given that an initial assessment process, and some goal setting, characterizes most initial interactions with patients. These stages are briefly discussed, before moving on to relapse occurrence and prevention.

ASSESSMENT

Some patients present for an intake already having decided to pursue sobriety. Others present wishing to seek information, and to reflect upon and evaluate their drinking. For patients at the undecided, "let's evaluate" stage, there has been empirical comparison of traditional interviewing techniques with an approach called motivational interviewing developed by William Miller and colleagues (Miller, 1989). Motivational interviewing has been incorporated into a two interview protocol called the drinker's checkup (Miller, Sovereign, & Krege, 1988). To evaluate the approach, Miller (1989) recruited a sample of persons responding to an ad in the paper for a therapeutic session to reflect and evaluate potential changes in drinking habits. Motivational interviewing consisted of a nonjudgemental discussion of drinking along with feedback regarding liver functioning. No one was told to quit drinking or labeled alcoholic. Compared to traditional approach, those exposed to the drinker's check-up approach decreased their drinking to a greater extent at follow-up (Miller, 1989). Further, 93% of those who came to the first interview presented for the second interview. There was evidence that the approach had influenced drinkers to regard the magnitude of their drinking problems in more severe terms. Miller's data suggested that the two interview sessions alone were efficacious in decreasing drinking. The approach might also be used as a method for referring people to control drinking or abstinence oriented treatment programs.

Whereas some patients present for treatment in an exploration stage, other patients present for treatment acknowledging a drinking problem. Assume for the moment that the patient has an obvious, acknowledged drinking problem. An assessment process is still necessary in order to determine the factors (attitudes, social forces, stressors, environmental cues) which might be supporting the drinking. Miller and Marlatt's (1984) Comprehensive Drinking Profile assessment measure provides a useful tool, allowing the therapist and the patient to evaluate the drinking and gather the information needed for creating change.

Most therapists would be willing to collaborate in attenuating or eliminating the drinking, even if the modal features of alcoholism are not present, and even if the drinking problem is not severe. With the advent of a great deal of publicity regarding early diagnosis of alcoholism, more patients than in the past are diagnosing themselves as alcoholic when few experts would concur with their perception of a problem. Whereas there is no harm in helping a patient achieve abstinence regardless of his/her prior drinking habits, there may be harm in embracing a label (alcoholism) that is not applicable. Given such a situation, the therapist's task is to assess whether the label is appropriate, and if it is not appropriate, whether it may be harmful. For some, it may be more expedient to focus on changing the drinking behavior, rather than pondering over which diagnosis is most apposite.

GOAL IDENTIFICATION AND COMMITMENT

Assuming that some assessment of the situation has been made, it is normally useful to quickly identify the goal of therapy in regard to drinking. As discussed later, this goal is not written in concrete; it is possible to change and adjust goals at a later point in life. However, this issue is often on the minds of patients who come to therapy with concerns about their drinking. Prochaska and DiClemente (1983) have recognized that most clients, in or out of therapy, engage in a contemplation stage (considering options in regard to what they wish to do about their drinking) prior to a decision about entering therapy. For those patients still struggling with that issue when they enter therapy, goal identification is likely to be an engaging issue. It is often helpful to discuss the client's larger values in this context, with the purpose of selecting the most individually appropriate goal. It is sometimes possible to identify hidden reservations or barriers to goal implementation in these discussions. In fact, there are research findings suggesting that anticipating barriers to commitment and anticipating potential satisfactions resulting from a fulfilled commitment, literally listing the pros and cons, does enhance the probability that the commitment will be maintained (Hoyt & Janis, 1975).

The goal-setting stage may be revisited later in the therapeutic process. Signs of ambivalence signal the patient's return to the decision process, self-questioning about whether she/he can, or wants to, stop drinking completely, and whether she/he just might be able to control drink. Whereas traditional treatment would view such reconsiderations as evidence of denial, an alternative view is that people do change their minds. Returning to the exploration process will clarify motivations and goals. Often a renewed commitment to sobriety will result.

One critical objective of the initial process is securing commitment. Commitment is a statement of behavioral intention made by a person who believes he/she has a good chance of following through. The possibility of change must be envisioned before commitment becomes possible. Since the change takes place through personal commitment, the client must believe in his/her ability to sustain the commitment and implement some required actions. This implies some sense of self-efficacy. Techniques for enhancing belief in self-efficacy are discussed in the section on interventions for preventing relapse. These techniques can be utilized at these early stages as well to develop the sense of self-efficacy needed for the initial commitment.

RELAPSE PREVENTION

The major thrust of research-based treatment for alcoholism has been in the area of goal implementation, i.e., relapse prevention. Once the patient makes the decision to quit drinking, the focus is on how to implement the decision, i.e., to keep from taking the next drink. Research illuminating the nature of the relapse phenomenon (when does it occur, what are the precipitants, in whom is it most likely to occur) is reviewed next. Interventions to prevent relapse can be extracted from the empirical findings.

Relapse as Function of Time

National statistics indicate that 80% of persons who participate in an abstinence oriented treatment program relapse within a 2-year period (Marlatt, 1985a, p. 26). In Vaillant's (1983, p. 185) sample of 110 alcoholics, 20 maintained abstention between 6 months to 24 months but later returned to drinking. Eighty percent of those who qualify as relapsed by 2 year follow-up, begin their drinking during the first 6 months post discharge (Vallance, 1965). The bulk of individuals (47 to 90% across studies) will relapse within the first 4 months following treatment (Ludwig, 1972; Orford et al., 1976; Sussman et al., 1986; Vallance, 1965).

In terms of prolonged periods of abstinence before relapse, Lemere reported that 8% of his sample of 500 alcoholics had relapsed after 3 years or longer of sobriety. It may be that different variables control relapse among persons who maintain long versus short periods of abstinence. For example, a person who has maintained abstinence for 20 years may possess requisite coping skills for staying sober. Other mechanisms (e.g., making a statement to a significant other with the relapse, for example, you are not being supportive enough) may account for the relapse.

Although statistics on cumulative relapse offer information about the difficulty of maintaining abstinence, they obscure information about treatment success. Some patients reinstate an abstinence goal after a relapse. Others return to drinking after a relapse and then reenter treatment at a future time. Statistics support this view. Although all 149 in the sample of patients treated at Hazelden had relapsed at least once by 3 year follow-up, 80 of these patients were abstinent by the end of the 3-year study (Brisset et al., 1980). Ludwig's (1972) 18 month follow-up, found that on cumulative graphs 70% had experienced a relapse by 3 months and 90% had experienced a relapse by 12 months. Thus, early relapses are common. However, between months 7 to 18, 45% of the 176 patients were sober suggesting that many had reinstated abstinence after an early relapse. Orford et al. (1976) found that their entire sample had relapsed in the course of a little over 2 years, however, 20% of the sample had drunk unacceptably under 10 days during the 2-year period. Litman, Eiser, and Taylor (1979b) examining individual patterns in Orford et al's data, found that of 65 individuals who oscillated between recovery and relapse, 53 achieved at least 1 month of recovery subsequent to relapse. If short-term follow-up periods are employed, then relapse does predict less success at the end of the follow-up interval (Polich et al., 1980). However, longitudinal studies allowing for examination over several decades suggest that recovery rates are surprisingly high, and those recovering include many of those individuals who had been unsuccessful in their earlier attempts within the context of treatment programs (Vaillant, 1983). Further, there is some evidence that the probability of achieving longer term abstinence improves with repeated attempts, or at least there is some association between multiple attempts and final success. Mulford (1977) found that more attempts to quit drinking prior to treatment predicted treatment success. Gillis and Keet (1969) found that those alcoholics who were not first admissions to their treatment program were doing better at follow-up than were the first admissions. These findings are consistent with the findings pertaining to other addictive behaviors. Schachter (1982) in his investigation of persons who quit smoking or lost weight outside of treatment, found that many had made several attempts at their goals before eventually achieving success. Although these data do not imply that eventual success is achieved because of prior attempts (alcoholism may just burn out with time as Drew, 1968, had suggested), these data do suggest an optimistic long-term prognosis. Given a long-term perspective, relapse does not preclude eventual success.

Considering relapse over a short-term follow-up period, Marlatt (1985a, p. 27) presented two alternative explanatory models for relapse. One model assumes a passive patient and a powerful treatment. This model predicts that the effects of the powerful treatment will dissipate with time. A greater number of relapses will occur as a function of time since discharge. Marlatt (1985a) cites data illustrating that this model predicts response to aversion therapy. The second model assumes an active patient in a learning role. As time elapses posttreatment, patients encounter potential threats to their sobriety. They learn how to successfully cope with these threats, thereby decreasing the risk of relapse as a function of time. Marlatt (1985a) cites data illustrating that this model predicts response to therapy targeted toward social skill development. Social skills are developed as coping strategies which defuse the eliciting capability of relapse precipitants (Chaney, Leary, & Marlatt, 1978).

There are many unanswered questions about relapse. Little information is available regarding whether persons who relapse to former drinking habits do so in a sanguine fashion. According to the disease model of alcoholism, denial is a necessary condition for drinking. No data is available examining whether persons who have relapsed posttreatment have decided that they are not alcoholic, and therefore do not anticipate deleterious effects from their drinking or, alternatively, whether they realize they are alcoholic but feel that there is no alternative to drinking.

Precipitants to Relapse

A great deal of empirical investigation has been directed toward identifying the conditions that precede relapse. Investigators have examined relapse across a variety of addictive behaviors (smoking, weight reduction, drinking, heroin use). For the most part, the situations precipitating relapse appear to be similar regardless of the addictive behavior investigated.

Marlatt and associates (Marlatt, 1985) identified precipitants of relapse in 3 samples: dieters, smokers, and alcoholics. Negative emotions and social influence were the categories accounting for the largest number of relapses. Positive emotions, and tests of personal control also were identified as precipitants.

Negative Emotions.   According to Marlatt's (1985b) data, negative emotions precipitate 59% of the relapses among alcoholics. Marlatt distinguished between negative emotions which were intrapersonal and those negative emotions that were interpersonally generated. Negative emotions of an intrapersonal nature accounted for 38% of relapse situations. Included in this category were frustration, anger unrelated to a particular individual, fear, loneliness, sadness, boredom, worry, anxiety, depression, loss, personal misfortune, and evaluation apprehension when not associated with any particular individual or individuals. Negative emotions precipitated by interpersonal conflict accounted for 18% of relapses. Included in this category were conflicts that stimulate thoughts and feelings associated with lack of appreciation, guilt, reactance (e.g., wife tells patient that he better not be drinking), and perceived unjust accusation. Negative physical states accounted for 3% of the relapses.

There was one suggestion in research with opiate addicts that different types of negative emotion trigger relapse at different times during the recovery process. Chaney et al. (1982) found that negative emotions attributable to interpersonal conflicts were more likely to stimulate relapse in later abstinence.

Negative emotions precipitating relapse can often be conceptualized as responses to external stress. Several researchers have examined the association between stress and relapse. In Rosenberg's (1983) sample of recovering alcoholics, persons who experienced more negative life changes and fewer positive life changes were more likely to relapse. Hore (1971) found no association between life events and relapse in the total sample, however, in examining individual cases there was a subset of alcoholics for whom negative life events seemed to evoke relapse. Hore speculated that particular individuals may be more sensitive than others to the impact of negative events. Event sensitivity may constitute an important subject variable in predicting relapse.

Tucker, Vuchinich, and Harris (1985) proffer a more complex hypothesis regarding stress and relapse. Their data suggested that persons whose drinking had disrupted their resources in a particular life area would be particularly vulnerable to stressful events. For example, those alcoholics who had disrupted their family support system were more likely to relapse given a negative event in the family. These alcoholics seemed to lack a buffer for stress. Furthermore, relapses associated with stressful events were more severe than those unassociated with a specific stressful event.

Hull, Young, and Jouriles (1986) also advanced an interaction hypothesis predicting a relationship between a particular type of stressor and relapse for specific individuals. Hull posited that for alcoholics high in self-consciousness, the experience of ego threatening events would result in relapse. Hull's results, which yielded a significant correlation between ego threatening events and relapse for those alcoholics high in self-consciousness but not for other alcoholics, was consistent with the hypothesis.

The results of a laboratory study by Miller, Hersen, Eisler, and Hilsman (1974) support the view that negative emotions can precipitate heavy alcohol consumption for alcoholics. In this laboratory demonstration, alcoholics and normals were allowed to work for alcohol under pleasant conditions and under stressful conditions. The alcoholics and normals did not differ on the degree of effort expended for alcohol under convivial conditions, however, under the stressful conditions the alcoholics expended greater effort than the normals.

In summary, as is commonly believed, stress can be a factor in precipitating or increasing drinking, but there are individual personality differences, and the source of stress may also make a difference.

Social Pressure.   Marlatt's (1985b) second largest relapse precipitant category, accounting for 18% of the relapses, was social pressure. Social pressure can be direct, such as when a friend encourages drinking or ridicules for not drinking. Social pressure can be indirect as well. Indirect social pressure includes the influence of social modeling. It also includes the state of deindividuation, a blending in with the crowd such that self-awareness is reduced, releasing the individual from the pressure to act in accordance with his/her value system (Baron & Byrne, 1981, p. 420). Chaney et al.'s (1982) findings suggest that among opiate addicts social pressure is a more likely relapse precipitant in early abstinence.

Tests of Personal Control.   Eleven percent of relapses investigated by Marlatt (1985b) were associated with a test of personal control, i.e., relapsers reported that they wanted to see if they could control their drinking or whether they could avoid the negative consequences just this once.

Positive Emotions.   Only 3% of relapses reviewed by Marlatt (1985b) were associated with positive emotions in interpersonal situations. There were no reports of intrapersonal positive emotion precipitants. Positive emotions include a sense of celebration, freedom, and excitement.

Although positive moods accounted for only a small percentage of relapses among Marlatt's subjects, the principles regarding positive mood would predict that good moods should induce a state of subjective invulnerability for many individuals. A state of subjective invulnerability connotes a feeling of being in control and a sense of optimism. When persons are in a good mood they are more likely to self-indulge. Negative consequences are less readily accessed from memory, sometimes resulting in the temporary perception of invulnerability. Perceived coping capacity is enhanced (Bower, 1981).

Good mood may create proneness to relapse in particular individuals only. For those whose sobriety is motivated by fear of long-term consequences, good mood should undermine this fear-based motivation. If no other source of motivation (e.g., pride in being sober) is operative, the motivation for sobriety given a good mood should be very low. Given these particular circumstances, persons who do not have alternative avenues for self-indulgence, might exercise their habitual form of indulgence, viz., drinking. In fact, in a recent study (Strack, Carver, & Blaney, 1987), a relationship between a greater frequency of positive events and an increase in dropping out of aftercare, which the authors suggest is usually attributable to a return to drinking, emerged. Empirical research does then offer tentative support for concern over good mood as a relapse precipitant.

Cravings and Urges.   Urges and cravings were identified in 11% of alcoholic relapses (Marlatt, 1985b). It is possible that the rather small percentage of relapses that are preceded by cravings and urges may be attributable to the way in which Marlatt and others have collected their data. Niaura et al. (1988) provide trenchant criticism of the procedure of asking alcoholics to retrospectively identify relapse precipitants and the fact that only one precipitant per relapse occasion is counted. It is possible that retrospectively, alcoholics will discount internal events. Further, these authors question whether retrospective recall accurately reflects reality.

Research has addressed how urges and cravings that are acted upon (lead to relapse) differ from those urges and cravings that are not acted upon. Shiffman (1982) has presented relevant analysis for smoking relapse. In gregarious contexts, persons more often acted upon their urge when in the presence of a smoking model and when drinking. When alone, persons more often acted upon their urges when in familiar anxiety eliciting circumstances.

Apparently Irrelevant Decisions.   Marlatt discusses apparently irrelevant decisions. AA captures the broad notion of apparently irrelevant decisions and ambivalence with its use of the unfortunate term "stinking thinking." According to Marlatt (1985b), apparently irrelevant decisions are those decisions that set the person up to drink (e.g., purchasing liquor for the ostensible purpose of being prepared for guests who might arrive; cessation of antabuse because it is inconvenient). These decisions are usually made with partial awareness of the motivation to drink. Unfortunately, Marlatt did not report the frequency with which apparently irrelevant decisions precede relapse. Pomerleau, Adkins, and Pertschuk (1978) found that those exsmokers who seek situations in which they are exposed to risk are more likely to relapse.

Unanswered Questions. There are a number of unanswered questions regarding precipitants of relapse. No one has empirically investigated whether relapse precipitants will vary as a function of the drinking patterns prior to drinking. For example, persons who are more likely to drink in a bad mood, might be more likely to drink when alone or when under stress. Contexts in which drinking generally occurred (drinking while watching TV vs. drinking in bars or at parties) may be predictive of cues that elicit relapse. Persons who were more likely to drink in a good mood rather than a bad mood might be particularly vulnerable to relapse when in convivial contexts or when a good mood is induced by dint of achievement. Preliminary supportive data is available. Chaney et al. (1982) found that relapse to opiate use for its positive effect more often occurred in convivial contexts.

Research suggests that alcoholics and heavy drinkers differ from moderate drinkers in their expectations regarding the effect of drinking (Leigh, 1989). It may be that expectations regarding particular salubrious effects of alcohol might predict when an individual would be most vulnerable to relapse. In the smoking literature it has been noted that persons who associate smoking with relief from dysphoric mood are more likely to relapse, although precipitants to relapse (e.g., being in a bad mood) were not investigated (Pomerlau et al., 1978). Eastman and Norris (1982) report a positive association between relapse and the expectation that alcohol will enhance self-esteem. The authors did not investigate whether situations threatening esteem were more likely to precipitate relapse in those holding the view that alcohol would enhance esteem. The picture in terms of causal relationships is somewhat muddled by the finding in the Eastman and Norris study that those holding positive expectancies for alcohol were lower on self-esteem than the other alcoholics.

Another unexplored area is whether planned relapses differ from impulsive relapses in terms of duration or severity. Furthermore, the thought processes associated with planned relapses have not received much examination. Some persons may question whether they are alcoholic and whether abstinence is an appropriate goal. Others may know they are alcoholic, but feel they can no longer maintain what they are experiencing as white knuckle sobriety. They may relapse, fully expecting their drinking to result in disastrous consequences, but believing they have no choice, as the situation could not get worse than it already is. Some persons may plan their relapses, believing they are alcoholic, but believing they will drink for a short hiatus during which they hope to escape the more dire consequences they know could be associated with protracted drinking. These diverse cognitions may be associated with differential relapse outcomes.

A further question with regard to planned relapses concerns the expectation or intention of the individual upon initiating the relapse. It could be that persons who plan their relapses begin their drinking with an intention or an expectation about how much they will drink. Some may plan a binge while others may plan to control drink. Whether such intentions influence the result of the relapse also should be explored.

No one has investigated whether motivations for abstinence will predict when persons are likely to relapse. For example, it is possible that persons who quit drinking fearing health consequences, might be less likely to access this type of motivation when in a good mood. Persons who quit drinking to please their family, might be likely to relapse when they feel they have been unfairly treated or rejected by a family member. Those who quit drinking because they wish to reinstate their pride and live a better life, might be vulnerable to relapse when depressed and experiencing low levels of general self-efficacy.

Characteristics of Relapsing and Nonrelapsing Alcoholics

A number of investigations have examined those qualities that distinguish relapsers from nonrelapsers. The findings from these investigations are reviewed under the following topics: feelings of self-efficacy, predisposition toward positive reinforcement, attitudes, and coping skills. The issue of will power is discussed within the larger topic of coping skills.

Feelings of Self-efficacy

In Bandura, Adams, and Beyer's (1977) classic paper on self-efficacy, beliefs about oneself are ascribed causal status in determining whether an individual will behave in a particular manner. Self-efficacy implies two affirmations: (1) I am capable of, and likely to act in a particular way; (2) When I act in a particular manner, a particular outcome is likely to result. Bandura's self-efficacy notions are consistent with Bem's theory of self-perception. The major thesis of self-perception theory is that people act consistently with their beliefs about themselves (Bem, 1972). Self-efficacy is a specific corollary of the more general central tenet of self-perception theory. The theory predicts that given valuing of some goal (say sobriety), people who *believe* they can achieve the goal (that is, stay sober), will more often do so.

Investigations of individuals in treatment suggest that they themselves are good predictors of whether they will relapse and the situations in which they will relapse (Chapman & Huygens, 1988; Condiotte & Lichtenstein, 1981; DiClemente, 1981; McIntyre, Lichtenstein, & Mermelstein, 1983). There have been, however, inconsistent reports. For example, Burling et al. (1989) found in a mixed group of alcohol and drug abusers, that the amount of increased self-efficacy (change between intake efficacy and discharge efficacy) predicted relapse. Low efficacy ratings for particular relapse situations corresponded to actual relapse precipitating event. Mean differences on discharge efficacy scores between the relapsers and abstainers were not found, however. With regard to the confusion in empirical findings, Baer and Lichtenstein (1988) advise that inconsistencies in the literature may be attributable to varying times at which assessment occurs. Beyond being able to predict whether they relapse, people make accurate predictions as to whether they will successfully employ particular coping skills in place of drinking (Condiotte & Lichtenstein, 1981; Rist & Watzl, 1983). An interpretation of these findings consistent with self-perception theory is the following. People's optimistic predictions about their abstention or ability to withstand pressures to drink, are causal factors in the maintenance of sobriety. Supportive of this interpretation are the self-observations of persons who experience urges to drink which they successfully resist. Such individuals report that in resisting urges to drink they invoke images of themselves behaving in self-efficacious manner, e.g., imagining themselves refusing a drink (Litman et al., 1979a).

Some related findings as to the association of self-efficacy with drinking relapse comes from a particular measure employed to assess alcoholics. This measure, identified by the acronym DRIE, assesses components of self-efficacy. The measure taps self-perceived ability to withstand the internal and external pressures to drink, to withstand the pressure arising from interpersonal turmoil, as well as the belief that one's sobriety is determined by chance or fate factors external to the self. This measure does correlate with particular factors of the Alcohol Use Inventory (see Chapter 4). People taking the DRIE can be distinguished in terms of their own subjective guess as to the probability of their succumbing to pressure to drink. Donovan and O'Leary (1983), using the DRIE, divided alcoholics into those who judged themselves as having a high probability of succumbing to pressure to drink, and those who did not, and compared them on drinking related behaviors. Alcoholics judging themselves as having a high probability of succumbing, reported drinking in a more sustained, obsessive fashion; had used more external resources to stop; reported a higher incidence of loss of control when drinking; had experienced more physical and perceptual symptoms during withdrawal; and had evidenced significantly greater physical, psychosocial, and psychological deterioration as a consequence of drinking. The DRIE has not been found to relate to outcome, however, alcoholics become more internal on the DRIE as a function of treatment (Donovan & O'Leary, 1983). Those viewing their sobriety as determined by fate or chance factors (low on internality of control over drinking) are more likely to drop out of treatment (Donovan & O'Leary, 1983).

Further data is available in other areas of addictive behavior on the issue of self-efficacy. Blittner, Goldberg, and Merbaum (1978), in a smoking study, conducted a test of whether an intervention to influence self-efficacy directly could alter probability of a smoking relapse. Some patients had been given bogus personality feedback suggesting that they were strong willed. Those patients who were informed that they were strong willed experienced fewer smoking relapses post treatment. In another smoking study, Chambliss and Murray (1979) found that providing people with positive feedback about their ability to quit smoking increased positive results among people high in internal locus of control, but not for those high in external locus of control (those who feel that their fate is in the hands of others or chance). The general literature suggests that a high sense of self-efficacy is a factor in good outcome when trying to overcome addictions. However, as seen in the Chamblis and Murray study, when attempts are made to enhance self-efficacy, only those persons whose self-concepts allow for the possibility of individual influence on their fates (those high in internal locus of control) may be benefited.

What about Complacency?

Traditional doctrine offers the notion of the "pink cloud." A pink cloud is the belief that after attending treatment the drinking problem is totally resolved. There is no need for further worry. Drinking will never occur again. Further skill development is unnecessary. A pink cloud is viewed as an ominous sign in traditional treatment programs and would probably also be ascribed ominous import by treatment personnel with other orientations as well.

In fact, there is data supporting the view that those persons who enter treatment with confidence in their ability to resist relapse precipitants remain in treatment for a shorter duration of time and are more likely to be discharged prematurely for rule violation. Perhaps a certain degree of lack of confidence is necessary to induce a person to take advantage of the treatment program (Burling et al., 1989).

The caution regarding the pink cloud may seem contradictory to the validated salubrious impact of feelings of self-efficacy. The apparent contradiction between the view of self-efficacy as desirable and a pink cloud as undesirable may be resolved by identifying where the placement of confidence should occur. In Bandura's paper, he did not specify those particular behaviors in which feelings of self-efficacy should be invested. It was unclear as to whether it was important to believe one could affect the outcome (e.g., I can pass the test) or whether it was more important to believe one would and could perform the behaviors requisite to affecting the outcome (I can study each night for 2 hours). For most situations in which coping skills rather than will power is required, self-efficacy in regard to performing the behaviors requisite for success may be the more important in determining outcome. With regard to recovering alcoholics, patients who believe that they can perform those behaviors that constitute coping skills (refuse a drink when offered, stay away from heavily drinking friends, not enter the bar, etc.) are likely to display better outcomes than those who believe they will stay sober "somehow."

In the domain of learning and skill utilization, the impact of confidence (self-efficacy) has been empirically assessed. Positive feedback (a direct influence on self-efficacy) on easy tasks seems to impair performance and to decrease effort and vigilance (Halisch & Heckhausen, 1977). Imagining failure seems to increase effort and improve performance (Campbell & Fairey, 1985; Sherman et al., 1981). This is the case, however, only for particular individuals, viz., those who make dispositional attributions for their success (attributing success to personal traits) (Halisch & Heckhausen, 1977) and/or who are high in self-esteem (Campbell & Fairey, 1985). It would seem that an expectation that hard work will be needed coupled with general self-efficacy/high self-esteem is the best recipe for success.

There are certain conditions under which negative feedback or imagining failure will result in worse performance. When the task is difficult, for persons who display low self-efficacy even when anticipating an easy task, and for persons making dispositional attributions for failure (I failed because I'm an ineffectual person), negative feedback does not enhance performance (Campbell & Fairey, 1985; Halisch & Heckhausen, 1977). Under such conditions, any negative feedback will destroy self-efficacy and instigate capitulation.

There are many considerations pertaining to the situation and personality variables that will influence whether contemplating failure will result in greater vigilance and effort or capitulation. In the section on treatment intervention specific suggestions are made for optimally instructing persons so that they will avoid the negatives of contemplating failure while realizing the benefits.

Is Self-Efficacy More Appropriate for Some than Others?

External locus of control refers to a personality factor of believing that events in general are beyond one's personal control. External individuals may see outcomes in the world as caused by powerful others or determined by random events. There are some findings that suggest that instilling the possibility of personal self-efficacy in externals creates anxiety (Harackiewicz, Sansone, Blair, Epstein, & Manderlink, 1987; Strentz & Auerbach, 1988). For this group, it has been demonstrated that attributing smoking cessation to a pill rather than self-efficacy produced better long-term results (Chambliss & Murray, 1979). It is possible that approaches that attribute sobriety to an external force (perhaps the Higher Power, the doctor, or antabuse) may produce better results for externals. It is possible that for those external in locus of control, identifying efficacy in the therapist, or therapeutic community (such as AA), may be more effective than attempts at increasing feelings of self-efficacy.

Comment.   The general issue of self-efficacy is a complex one. Generally people with self-efficacy avoid relapse. However, efficacy is probably best placed in optimistic views on developing skills rather than a simple abiding faith that everything will work out well regardless of whether one invests energy or not. The advisability of developing efficacy in treatment is a complex issue. Some people become anxious when it is implied that they have control over their own outcomes. For these people, more indirect ways of developing self-efficacy, for example developing belief in the program, AA, antabuse, or the Higher Power, may be a more personality-compatible strategy.

Orientation Toward Positive Self-reinforcement: The Carrot rather than the Stick

Another personality dimension that differentiates the successful from the unsuccessful in treatment programs for addictive behaviors is orientation toward positive self-reinforcement, as opposed to self-punishment. A measure of general proclivity to rely on positive self-reinforcement rather than self-punishment has been developed. Individuals working at a verbal recognition memory task can be differentiated as to whether they consequate themselves with punishment or positive feedback. This self-regulation measure predicted successful vs. nonsuccessful dieting. Those who lose weight rely more on positive self-reinforcement and less on self-punishment in the laboratory task (Rozensky & Bellack, 1976). This general personality trait seems to be reflected in the findings specific to the behavioral patterns of nonrelapsers. Individuals who incorporate rewards for abstinence into their daily routines experience fewer relapses (Glasgow et al., 1985). There are some caveats, however. Carroll, Yates, and Gray (1980), in another weight control study, found that although positive self-reinforcers do better in behavioral programs, such is not the case in other types of programs. Without specific behavioral instruction, the self-reinforcers may positively consequate the wrong behavior, leading to less weight loss.

There are additional data suggesting that positive reinforcement strategies work better than punishment strategies. Confronted with an urge to relapse, people recall the original source of motivation for their abstention (Litman et al., 1983). The motivation for sobriety can be dimensionalized into wanting to avoid negative consequences (poor health, divorce, job loss), and wanting to achieve positive consequences (pride, a life consistent with one's values, heightened awareness in the external environment). Litman, Stapleton, Oppenheim, and Peleg (1983) have factor analyzed a menu of strategies for avoiding relapse. They identified the following factors: (a) positive mechanisms exemplified by recalling positive benefits of sobriety and recalling past methods of self-deception; (b) negative mechanisms exemplified by the recall of past wrong doings; (c) distraction/avoidance; (d) utilizing social support. Litman et al. (1983) found that the positive mechanisms factor best differentiated those who avoided relapse from those who did relapse. Those avoiding relapse relied upon recall of the benefits of sobriety. Consistent with this finding, research on smoking relapse suggests that those who think about their new sense of pride are more successful than those who recall health hazards or who disdain themselves for imagined relapse (Glasgow et al. 1985; Shiffman, 1984). Those able to sustain abstention from smoking made self-statements emphasizing positive images (I'm setting a good example) whereas the less successful made negative statements (I'm weak if I give in) (Glasgow et al., 1985: Shiffman, 1984).

Whereas the above data are correlational, others have manipulated use of positive vs. negative strategies to determine their impact on relapse. In the area of weight reduction the effect of instructing subjects to employ negative images of themselves (e.g., fat self) vs. positive image (e.g., thin self) as a means of sustaining commitment to diet were tested (Horan et al., 1975). The positive image group lost the most weight. The negative image group quickly learned to quit thinking about the negative thought.

Another related variable has been identified. Having a generally optimistic attitude toward life is relevant. This variable positively related to greater success in treatment (Strack, Carver, & Blaney, 1987). Possibly related to the variable of proclivity toward self reinforcement, Yung, Gordis, and Holt (1983) have found that alcoholics who consume more sugar and carbohydrates post treatment manifest better drinking outcomes.

Coping Skills

Marlatt (1985b) assigns a major role to coping skill deficits in determining relapse. Coping skills constitute a broadly encompassing category. The category includes all those behaviors that decrease the probability of relapse given the occasion of a relapse precipitant. Coping skills are those skills that attenuate those moods that can precipitate relapses, or that alter situations that tend to prompt relapses, or those behaviors that decrease the probability of encountering cues and situations that tend to precipitate relapses.

Coping Skills of Non-Relapsers.   Nonrelapsers report employing a greater number and diversity of coping mechanisms than the relapsers (Litman, Eiser, Rawson, & Oppenheim, 1979a; Perri, Richards, & Schultheis, 1977; Shiffman, 1982). Persons using both cognitive and behavioral strategies display the lowest relapse rates, although use of one or the other is more predictive of success than no coping skill (Shiffman, 1984).

Whereas the research discussed in the preceding paragraph assessed coping after the fact, a study by Chaney et al. (1978) assessed coping strategies manifested during treatment. Chaney et al. measured the number of coping strategies generated by alcoholics in treatment after being presented with a hypothetical relapse precipitating situation. Both the number of strategies and the reaction time for the strategies were related to relapse during the subsequent follow-up interval; more and quicker strategies were associated with less likelihood of relapse. Unfortunately, Chaney et al. did not statistically covary intelligence and cognitive impairment, nor did they control these factors, which could have been the causal factors in this finding. That is, those who were less intelligent, or more cognitively impaired from their drinking, may have been the ones tending to relapse, and also the ones who could not verbally produce as many coping strategies, nor respond as quickly with verbal responses.

There is another study in which feelings about ability to cope as assessed during treatment predicted subsequent relapse. This study allowed for a more exact statement regarding a specific coping skill. Rist and Watzl (1983) found that although feelings about the capacity for (probability of and comfort with) general assertion, was *not* related to risk for relapse, feelings of self-efficacy in specifically refusing alcohol in a social situation, did predict future relapse. Feelings of self-efficacy were measured through questionnaires that asked about expectations of the patients' own behavior as well as about comfort with the assertive behaviors. (The patients were female alcoholics.)

Some other research has offered more fine grained analyses of which coping skills are most likely to be implemented and/or effective at particular times. Shiffman (1982) found that when depressed, people are less likely to employ coping skills. However, when depressed individuals do implement a coping strategy, the cognitive, although not the behavioral strategies, were effective in decreasing the incidence of relapse. Litman, Eiser, Rawson, and Oppenheim (1979a) found that in response to the relapse precipitant of negative mood, the coping strategies of self-punitive thoughts and distraction are implemented but are not effective in avoiding relapse. In response to the relapse precipitant of social anxiety, persons most often implement avoidance as a coping strategy. Avoidance as a response to social anxiety tends to be effective.

Litman, Stapleton, Oppenheim, and Peleg (1983) have differentiated between relapse precipitating situations in which individuals have the capacity to influence external events and those in which they do not have control. In situations of control, greater strength in coping strategies is associated with (does predict) an absence of relapse. In those situations beyond the control of the individual, a more positive general self-concept, but not a stronger coping repertoire, predicts successful abstention.

There has been some attempt to determine whether the coping strategies change as a function of duration of abstinence. Prochaska and DiClemente (1983) found that early smoking quitters rely on frequent reminders of self-efficacy, social support, and self-reinforcement. Nonrelapsing alcoholics in the early stage of sobriety rely on avoidance (not going to places where they might be tempted to drink) as a coping skill (Litman et al., 1979a). Smokers who have been abstinent for some duration have found other ways to structure time and have removed smoking cues from their environment (Prochaska & DiClemente, 1983).

Is Will Power a Coping Skill?   Will power is a concept that receives a great deal of attention in AA and traditional treatment. In AA circles, will power is assumed to be an index of character, but not an index of ability to resist drinking. The case is advanced that will power cannot overcome craving. No conclusions can be drawn about the will power or character of alcoholics based on their intemperate drinking. (If will power were assumed to have some relationship to ability to resist drinking urges, it could then imply that alcoholics with a great deal of will power could control drink, and that would contradict a basic assumption of the AA position.) Marlatt (1985c), a major exponent of a research based approach to treatment of alcoholism, also discounts the importance of will power in preventing drinking.

There is another view of will power that might be invoked. There are differences in individuals. Some can delay gratification longer than others. Some people can do things that they do not want to do more readily than others. Some explanation is needed for these observations of differences between people. In these instances lay people generally accept will power as an explanation. The problem with its use by responsible professionals, is that the concept is vague, and there is no analysis of how it works. When a vague concept, working in unknown ways, is used as an explanation, the result is an apparent explanation that in fact does not illuminate anything.

The concept of coping skills can be used in place of will power in the area of drinking relapse. Coping skills are specific, and it can be seen just how they can sometimes prevent relapse. For example, the literature investigating resistance to temptation suggests how coping skills can function in a way that conjures will power. Specifically, observations of children who stay task directed rather than being distracted by an attractive toy, demonstrate that they spend less time thinking about the toy, which is the reward for task completion, and make more self-statements directing themselves to focus back on the task (Mischel & Mischel, 1976). In this situation, what looks like will power, is an elegant strategy for not allowing the reward to distract the child from the task that has to be completed to obtain the toy. A lay person without all the facts, merely seeing some children succeed in not being distracted by the toy, might say that such children have exercised will power. In fact, they have utilized a specific coping strategy that works.

Resistance to temptation in adults is open to similar analyses. Rosenbaum and Smira (1986) have examined the cognitive styles of individuals on kidney dialysis who successfully comply with restrictions on liquid intake. Those adults who are successful resistors of temptation display a general self-efficacy, more coping skills, they engage more problem-solving strategies when confronted with a problem, and they make dispositional attributions for success (take personal credit for success).

The specification of particular behaviors as present when people behave in ways that would otherwise be labeled as exercising will power, offers a method of analysis that should be used in all such circumstances. The needed behaviors for coping in particular situations have to be defined, and those attitudes that are helpful also have to be identified. Such specification then yields the prescription for self-efficacy, that is, good coping skills, which may appear to uninformed observers as "will power."

Expectations Toward Alcohol and Attitudes Toward Drinking

Eastman and Norris (1982) have found that alcoholics holding more positive expectations regarding alcohol (concerning enjoyment and mood) are more likely to relapse. Those who manifest more conditioned autonomic responses (salivation, increased heart rate, etc.) upon presentation of alcohol are more relapse prone (Niaura et al., 1988). Autonomic response to alcohol presentation is correlated with greater expectation of a positive mood given drinking, increased urges to continue to drink once imbibing has occurred, and increased alpha wave production post consumption (Niaura et al., 1988).

Attitudes toward drinking and abstention are believed to have causal significance in allowing the development of alcoholism (Vaillant, 1983). Specifically, toleration and perhaps secret admiration of intoxication (those who party-hardy to use common parlance) can assist in the development of crapulous drinking. All of these attitudinal factors need to be addressed in treatment. In the course of treatment, changing attitudes and expectations toward alcohol and toward alcohol related behaviors can be a productive strategy for decreasing relapse.

Treatment Goal as a Predictor of Relapse

A recent study has found that embracing an extreme goal during treatment may be associated with less relapse. The authors of the particular study in fact interpreted their findings as evidence that commitment to sobriety may be the most important factor in predicting future relapse. Hall, Havassy, and Wasserman (1990) examined subjects who had attended an AA based treatment program for heroin addiction, alcoholism, or smoking cessation. They found that the strongest predictor of whether a patient slipped or not, or whether once slipped the patient's slip would meet criteria for relapse was whether the patient had endorsed the most stringent treatment goal, "I will never use again ever." Although mood and symptoms were related to relapse when these were tallied over the follow-up interval; mood, life events, and hassles tallied for the previous week failed to predict relapse occurring within the subsequent week time-frame. The authors drew the strongest conclusion suggesting that their data implied that never envisioning relapse at all is the best strategy.

The results of the Hall et al. study are intriguing. However, caution in interpretation is necessary. All subjects in the study had attended an AA model treatment program in which the total abstention directive is strongly advanced. Indeed, 58% of the sample had endorsed the total abstention goal. It probably takes a very deviant, nonconforming individual to attend an AA treatment program and reject the goal that is so strongly advanced. Consequently, rather than reflecting a causal link between commitment to abstinence and relapse, the data may reflect a relationship between personality style and relapse.

Another way of looking at the findings from the Hall et al. study is also available. It is probably the case that patients who do not wish to be abstinent will not be. There are probably some patients in traditional treatment who wish to pursue a control use goal and who will do so whether such behavior is approved of by the staff or not. Hall et al.'s definition of relapse was 4 days of use within a week period. This definition does not necessarily imply crapulous drinking. It is possible that patients embracing a nonabstinence goal were successfully control drinking. These patients would have been classified as relapsed in the Hall et al. study. It should not be surprising that these patients did not embrace an absti-nence goal during treatment. Hence, it is difficult to surmise from the Hall et al. study, how to interpret the findings.

Descriptors of the Lives of Non-Relapsing Alcoholics

The preceding discussion reviewed the literature identifying personality charac-teristics of persons who emerge as the more successful in treatment programs for addictions. Feelings of self-efficacy, a propensity to use positive self-reinforce-ment and positive images (offering themselves thoughts of the benefits of so-briety, and experiencing pride in accomplishment when maintaining sobriety), and the possession of strong coping skills were recognized as important. Atten-tion is now directed toward those features of living style, and social support, which have been found to be predictive of positive outcome.

Life Style Changes

Life style can be differentiated from other coping skills in the following way. Whereas coping skills are implemented given specific relapse events, life style changes are regularly occurring behavioral routines which do not depend on the presentation of a relapse precipitant for their occasion.

In the alcoholism literature, changes in life style preceding extended periods of sobriety have been identified. Vaillant (1983) found that those alcoholics who had been sober many years, had developed an abiding interest that filled the time previously devoted to drinking. For some it was church; for others it was a hobby. Marlatt and colleagues (Marlatt, 1985e, pp. 327–329), who have specifically instigated life style changes in their clients, have found that meditation and running are effective in decreasing relapse rates for persons with control drinking goals.

The mechanisms by which life style changes decrease relapse have not yet been identified. It may be that life style changes achieve their efficacy through a self-perception mechanism. For example, being a runner, a new identity, might be incompatible with viewing oneself as a drinker. Alternatively, it may be that life style changes influence relapse by precluding exposure to cues that previously precipitated relapse and by arranging new contingencies. A third possibility is that life style change decreases stress while increasing coping skills. Identification of the mechanism by which any particular life style change decreases relapse could suggest which life style change would be most useful for those who are vulnerable to relapse in particular ways.

Along with life style change is the consideration of whether an alcoholic's social support system (friends and spouse) hold favorable attitudes toward alcohol. Often, alcoholics come from families in which heavy drinking is normative. As such, when they recover, they either have to develop very good coping skills for dealing with the scorn they are likely to encounter for their sobriety, or they have to avoid familiar social contacts and develop new sources of support. The choices are sometimes very difficult.

Social Support

A warm family environment and an intact social support system is associated with reduced relapse (Orford, Oppenheimer, Egert, Heinsman, & Guthrie, 1976; Wright & Scott, 1978). Nonrelapsers perceive themselves as having a more comfortable living environment and a more extensive social support network (Rosenberg, 1983). A decrease in smoking relapse is found among those whose spouses made positive comments, talked the smoker out of a cigarette, did not complain about withdrawal irritability, and did not closely monitor the smoking (Mermelstein, Lichtenstein, & McIntyre, 1983).

There are several hypothetical models for explaining the association between social support and better outcomes. Perhaps a supportive environment presents less stress and therefore fewer relapse precipitants. Perhaps social support operates by buffering the impact of the stress which is experienced without reducing the level of stress encountered. Perhaps social support offers an ongoing reinforcement for behavioral gains. Alternatively, social support may not be a causal mechanism in reducing relapse. It may be that persons who have the capacity for developing salubrious interpersonal relationships are those who also have the capacity for coping with relapse precipitants.

In smoking cessation research and weight reduction programs, enlisting the systematic encouragement of the spouse or a buddy has resulted in superior treatment gains (Brownell et al., 1986; Janis, 1983; Lichtenstein, 1982). Those smokers whose significant others attended treatment were less likely to relapse, as were those who viewed their partners as supportive (Lichtenstein, 1982). Weight reduction programs in which reinforcement is delivered by a significant other rather than a therapist result in more weight loss for an extended period of time (Israel & Saccone, 1979).

There are some difficulties in extrapolating from smoking cessation and weight reduction to alcoholism. Alcoholic drinking is more likely to have elicited strong spouse disapproval than some other addictive problems. Enlisting a spouse to focus or attend to sobriety may carry different implications. Most treatment data suggests that involving the family in treatment is positively associated with outcome. However, data regarding how spouses can be most helpful is lacking. Given insufficient general information on this topic, it would seem advisable to allow the alcoholic to convey his/her beliefs about what will be helpful to the spouse.

The Psychology of a Relapse Episode

There are some psychological principles that can be invoked in explanation of the relapse process, which can help to explain why it is sometimes more severe than other times. In this section some thoughts on this topic are shared. It is helpful to begin with a distinction that is sometimes made between a "lapse" and a "relapse." Brownell et al. (1986) make this distinction. They aver that a lapse implies a continuous process (a backsliding, worsening, or subsiding). It is less serious than a relapse. A relapse suggests a dichotomous event, and due to the lack of gradation in severity, implies a more ominous status.

Another distinction between a lapse and a relapse is that the individual's goal or commitment changes after a relapse. A lapse, even when the consequences of a particular drinking episode are regretable, will not be a relapse if the individual reinstates prior coping mechanisms and renews his/her commitment to sobriety. A lapse becomes a relapse when the individual abandons the goal, either because he/she feels a lack of self-efficacy or because he/she no longer regards the goal as appropriate.

Marlatt (1985c) also uses the term lapse to refer to something that is less severe than a relapse. He identifies and describes a process he believes may be responsible for turning a lapse into a relapse. He calls this process an "abstinence violation syndrome," because he believes that the situation can worsen as a function of the alcoholic's interpretation of, and conclusions from, observing herself/himself once again drinking after an attempt at sobriety. Abstinence violation syndrome is a type of all or nothing thinking which undermines the commitment to sobriety by equating a small lapse in deviation from goal with a total abandonment. A decrease in feelings of self-efficacy and an increase in dysphoric feelings of guilt and helplessness accompanies the perception that one has failed at abstinence. Lacking feelings of self-efficacy, and feeling defeated, can create exactly the kind of mood that many alcoholics would characteristically try to dissipate with alcohol. Marlatt (1985c, p. 160) hypothesizes that the magnitude of the abstinence violation mood (the bad mood created by observation of oneself having failed), will be a function of the duration of the preceding sobriety, the commitment to the sobriety, and the importance of the sobriety. Marlatt invokes two areas of social psychological theory to explain the absti-

nence violation effect: attribution/self-perception theory and cognitive dissonance. The principles of these social psychological theories can be used to
understand what is happening, and then to fashion treatment procedures that can
lessen the negative effects of relapse on eventual outcome.

Self-perception theory and cognitive dissonance both make the same prediction about one particular domain of behavior. When an individual chooses to
behave in a manner that is inconsistent with prior beliefs about the self, the
beliefs about the self will change to be congruent with the new behavior. Internal
attributions for the behavior are necessary in both theories. That is, in both
theories the individual must view himself/herself as having had free choice in
performing the behavior. There are differences between the two theories, which
suggest that each might account for differing responses to a slip.

Cognitive dissonance accounts best for change after the performance of some
behavior that is radically disparate from the prior self-concept rather than being
only slightly different from one's prior self-concept (Fazio, Zanna, & Cooper,
1977). Cognitive dissonance induced change is arousal driven. It has been demonstrated that change will not eventuate in a person who is imbibing alcohol
(Steele et al., 1981). If the individual misattributes the arousal (e.g., believing
his/her arousal was caused by a pill he/she had ingested) then no change is
induced (Fazio, Zanna, & Cooper, 1977). Cognitive dissonance change extends
to attitude as well as behavior. Not only will the individual regard himself/herself
in a new way, but his attitude will be altered such that he will be pleased with the
change. Cognitive dissonance is a theory regarding attitude change whereas self-
perception theory describes changes in self-concept only.

Self-perception theory accounts best for change after the performance of
behavior that is inconsistent with, but not radically inconsistent with, the prior
view of the self (Fazio, Zanna, & Cooper, 1977). Self-perception change is
mediated by new information about the self provided by self-observation; arousal
is not required. The induced change in self-perception need not be associated
with a change in attitude. The individual might well be dismayed or ashamed of
his new image.

An individual is most likely to experience cognitive dissonance arousal the
day after drinking. Dissonance arousal will not develop while the drinking occurs
because the alcohol precludes the dissonance induced change. But when next
sober, upon realizing that he/she has violated a commitment to abstinence,
dissonance arousal (a bad feeling) will eventuate. This dissonance arousal is
likely to induce an attitude change. The relapsed alcoholic's attitude toward
sobriety may be altered. (Remember, cognitive dissonance is a theory of attitude
change.) One might conclude that sobriety is no longer a desirable aspiration.
Couched in traditional language, the denial process would be enhanced.

Self-perception change can occur while the alcoholic is drinking since it does
not require the presence of appropriately attributed arousal. While drinking, the
alcoholic's self-perceptions regarding capacity to maintain abstinence or his/her

identity as a recovering alcoholic will be threatened. When internal attributions for the lapse are made (this happened because of something about me), a change in self-concept will occur. Commitment to sobriety, requiring feelings of self-efficacy, will be vitiated. The individual will feel badly about the drinking. Both the bad feelings (bad mood) and the reinstated self-perception as a wet alcoholic will increase the chances of continued drinking.

There are data concerning opiate addiction consistent with self-perception theory regarding when a lapse will evolve into a relapse. Persons who have available obvious situational precipitants for their lapses to opiate use display shorter durations of relapse (Chaney, Roszell, & Cummings, 1982). That is, as suggested by cognitive dissonance theory and self-perception theory, if they can blame their relapse on an external event, they do not have to see themselves as unable to maintain their long-term goal of sobriety. If this reasoning is correct, it means that there are times when "excuses" are actually a positive factor in eventual outcome.

TREATMENT

Research examining the characteristics of relapsing individuals and the research identifying precipitants to relapse suggest avenues for preventing relapse. These literatures as well as other findings discussed throughout the book are consulted in developing treatment strategies in the following sections. Presentation of interventions are organized according to their objectives. The following categories are considered: interventions to enhance feelings of self-efficacy, interventions to increase coping skills, interventions to alter life styles, interventions to develop self-reinforcement for success, interventions to strengthen commitment, and interventions to alter attitudes toward drinking. The topic of objective self-awareness as it relates to relapse prevention is also considered.

Interventions Enhancing Feelings of Self-efficacy

Feelings of self-efficacy stem from experience and beliefs about the self. The principles of self-perception theory offer suggestions of how to induce an individual to believe that he/she possesses a particular trait or ability. A desired trait can be incorporated into an individual's self-perceptions by reminding him/her of occasions when he/she has acted consistently with that trait; by emphasizing particular aspects of behavior consistent with the desired trait; by responding to the individual in a way that suggests he/she possesses the desired trait (Fazio, Effrein, & Falender, 1981; Swann & Hill, 1982).

Feelings of self-efficacy can be restored, or conceived of, as a high estimate of the probability of one's behaving in a desired manner. The work of Tversky and Kahneman (1974) offers suggestions on how to influence such probability judgments. Their principle, the availability heuristic, provides that when individuals have imagined a particular event, that is, had a clear mental image of the occurrence of the event, then they are more prone to believe that the event is likely to occur. With regard to the self, it has been empirically demonstrated that if persons are induced to imagine themselves acting in a particular manner, they increase their estimate of the probability of their acting in that manner in the future. Further, under some conditions, they are more likely to then act consistently with that image (Gregory, Cialdini, & Carpenter, 1982). (The step from seeing oneself as someone who is likely to act a particular way, and actually acting that way, is logically traversed with self-perception theory.) The availability heuristic can be recruited in changing alcoholics' feelings of self-efficacy. Alcoholics can be induced to imagine themselves turning down drinks, resisting urges to drink, and experiencing the first anniversary of their sobriety. All of these procedures should increase their belief that they will act in a manner conductive to sobriety, bolstering their feelings of self-efficacy. Similar techniques have been suggested by Klinger (1987), who labels these techniques covert self-modeling, and by Curry and Marlatt (1987).

Interventions to Increase Coping Skills

Most psychological treatment incorporates the teaching of coping skills for confronting relapse precipitants. A reasonable question is which coping skills should be developed. There are data on common precipitants to relapse, and these could be targeted. For example, normative data from relapse literature suggest that coping skills for refusing drinks, coping skills for dissipating anger, guilt, disappointment are needed. In addition, individual patients can be interviewed to determine which events they believe will be precipitants specific for them.

The data comparing individually tailored coping skill packages vs. broad brush approaches are scant. No data has been adduced as to whether the patients own prediction regarding relapse are superior to prediction based on normative findings. Baer and Lichtenstein (1988) examined whether contexts or smoking situations prior to adopting a smoking cessation goal would predict relapse situations. They found no relationship between an individual's pretreatment smoking behavior and the type of situation in which they relapsed. Therefore, they advise the broad brush strategy.

Regardless how the decision is made to select potential relapse precipitants, after a set of relapse precipitants is identified, persons are trained in coping mechanisms. Instruction, modeling, and role playing are frequently utilized. For example, one particular coping skill needed by all alcoholics is a comfortable strategy for refusing a drink. Practice, role playing, and observation of how to turn down a drink at a party should be incorporated into treatment. Persons reaction times for generating lists of coping skills and details of their articulation of coping skills can offer clues for additional training.

Within the area of coping skills, skills for coping with dysphoric states are a necessity. A combination of problem focused coping (strategies for changing the situation causing the bad mood) and emotion focused coping (strategies for altering or containing the mood, i.e., controlling the symptoms) should be included. Empirical research has suggested that coping strategies aimed at making changes in objective circumstances are associated with positive mood changes (Folkman & Lazarus, 1988; Scheier, Weintraub, & Carver, 1986). For people in general, problem focused coping constitutes a successful strategy. One group is made anxious by thoughts about affecting change in objective reality. For externals, the suggestion that a new objective world can be created through personal action induces anxiety (Strentz & Auerbach, 1988). For externals, the notion of changing circumstances rather than reacting to them would constitute a significant alteration in self-perception. For this group, passive rather than active coping skills may constitute a better strategy for preventing relapse.

Interventions to Alter Life Style

It has been recognized that a choice to drink will depend in part on the availability of alternate paths either to reducing aversive states or finding pleasure (Cox & Klinger, 1988; Vuchinich & Tucker, 1988). The issue of building alternative sources of reinforcement is a very broad one, indeed encompassing the existential question of what to do with life. To aid in this task, Cox and Klinger (1988) recommend a motivational assessment instrument, which can assist the alcoholic and the therapist in setting salient goals and identifying personally congruent values that preclude drinking and provide alternative sources of satisfaction.

In most treatment centers for alcoholism, therapy usually occurs in a group. A group offers a particularly useful vehicle for developing life-style changes. If the group is comprised of individuals with diverse backgrounds, a wide variety of ways in which to structure time will be represented. If the group lacks models for creative use of free time, the therapist can supplement by suggesting activities. A discussion of life before alcohol, if there are alcoholics in the group who developed their alcoholism later in life, might also be profitable.

Interventions to Develop Self-reinforcement for Success

Findings regarding nonrelapsing individuals vs. the relapsing suggest the former more often provide positive consequences for abstinence. They offer themselves positive reinforcement, self-congratulations, and opportunities for other pleasures when they have succeeded in their goal of abstention. Further, nonrelapsers rely on positive images (sober self) rather than negative ones to resist temptation and sustain motivation. These findings imply that alcoholics should be instructed in positively consequating their behavior. Alcoholics in early recovery often feel so guilty for prior transgressions that they feel unworthy of allowing themselves any pleasure. Stressing the importance of self-rewarding for recovery may be necessary for some alcoholics. The drinking process may have narrowed the range of reinforcing activities in which the alcoholics engage, such that few reinforcements come to mind. Encouraging the sampling of a menu of potential reinforcers to identify pleasurable activities may aid in the process of learning to self-reinforce.

Developing a sense of pride in sobriety might also reduce the probability of relapse. There are often many barriers to pride in sobriety. Many alcoholics feel ashamed of their drinking and do not feel entitled to pride based on changing behavior, which they believe should not have been happening in the first place. Perhaps the development of positive regard for other alcoholics in the group can alter the negative attitude toward one's own alcoholism. To date, interventions for developing pride in sobriety have been neglected.

Interventions to Strengthen Commitment

Commitment is a statement of behavioral intention made by a person who expects to successfully execute the intention. The act of commitment includes envisioning success at the goal in the sense of believing, at least for the moment, that you are the kind of person who would work to achieve that goal. Self-perception theory would predict that the act of commiting may be a causal factor in reducing relapse (we act in accordance with how we see ourselves). The envisioning of oneself acting to achieve sobriety is the causal component. If the act of commiting is of causal importance in maintaining sobriety, enhancing the salience of the commitment might enhance its potency. In order to obtain the maximum impact on self-perception, a patient might want to incorporate some highly conspicuous, frequently performed behavior into the commitment process—to be reminded of how much valuing sobriety is a defining characteristic of the self.

AA provides many useful suggestions for building in daily reminders of commitment to sobriety. New AAs are sometimes given marbles to carry in their pockets. When a decision to take a drink is made, the new AA member is to give the marble away, symbolizing the loss of his/her proverbial marbles. Chips carried in the back pocket are another mechanism for providing reminders of one's commitment. Additional behavioral reminders of a commitment might include adherence to an exercise plan, keeping a diary of observations on a sober life, etc.

Reminders of commitment can be symbols such as the marble, or can be behaviors. If it is a behavior, the behavior should be defined with sufficient latitude such that minor lapses in commitment will not be experienced as failures. Research in the area of studying plans suggests that plans work best to increase studying, when criteria for fulfillment is left vague. Given some minor lapse in studying, if the criteria for fulfillment is vague, the individual is less likely to conclude that he is not conforming to the plan and to then abandon the plan entirely (i.e., to experience an abstinence violation syndrome) (Greiner & Karoly, 1976; Kirschenbaum, Humphrey, & Malett, 1981; Kirschenbaum, Tomarken, & Ordman, 1982). Extrapolating from the study research suggests that the behavioral commitment might achieve its best effect if the criteria for defining failure is somewhat loose.

In the area of alcoholism, the broader the range of behavior, which is perceived as consistent with commitment to sobriety, the less likely a perception of goal abandonment will be. Behavior that might jeopardize sobriety (e.g., failing to shun former drinking friends, failing to attend an AA meeting in any particular week) should not be characterized as goal abandonment. If the decision is made to include a highly conspicuous well-defined behavior in the commitment, the temporal specifications for its performance should be broad.

The issue of whether commitment should include never envisioning the possibility of relapse is an intriguing one. The study by Hall et al. (1990), which was previously discussed, found that endorsing the view "I will never use again ever" was associated with less relapse during the follow-up interval. Does this mean that AA's advice of "one day at a time," and teaching relapse prevention is counterproductive? That is, should the possibility of relapse never be contemplated? In fact, it may be the case that people can be illogical. They can simultaneously view themselves as completely successful while making plans for dealing with failure. Indeed, Shelly Taylor (colloquium at ASU in the spring of 1990, has found evidence of simultaneously held contradictory beliefs in cancer patients. They state, "I will never get cancer again, and if I do. . . ." Perhaps positive illusions and realistic plans constitute the best strategy.

Attitude and Expectancy Change

Alcoholics holding more positive expectations regarding impact of alcohol are more likely to relapse (Eastman & Norris, 1982). Heavy drinkers, as a group, expect more positive effects from drinking than do light drinkers (Leigh, 1989). Given the fact that alcoholics hold specific beliefs about the salubrious nature of drinking, it would be well to identify particular expectations regarding the impact of alcohol held by particular alcoholic individuals. Expectancies can be assessed with the standard instruments developed for this purpose (Brown et al., 1980; Christiansen et al., 1982; Farber et al., 1980). Completion of an adjective checklist for the drinking and nondrinking self might also provide clues as to expectation.

Once positive expectations for drinking have been identified, intervention can occur. Sometimes positive expectations are not substantiated by the empirically identified effects of alcohol. In such a case, individuals can be disabused of their expectancies. Sometimes positive expectations may be accurate (i.e., the positive expectancy may correspond with the impact of alcohol suggested by the empirical literature). Under such conditions it may be futile to try to convince individuals that they are wrong. Rather, an orientation toward developing the ability to experience the desirable effects of alcohol (e.g., arousal, affective awareness, loquaciousness, decreased self-consciousness) in the sober state might be useful.

Many of the early behavioral treatments for alcoholism focused on altering the alcoholic's conditioned visceral response to alcohol. Both shock and emetics have been paired with the ingestion of alcohol. Emetics have met with greater success than shock (Cannon et al., 1981). Behavior modifiers have also experimented with nonaversive techniques, which extinguish desire to drink given exposure to environmental cues normally associated with drinking. The procedure consists of exposing the alcoholic to alcohol cues while restraining drinking behavior. Blakey and Baker (1980) present successful case studies of persons in whom drinking had decreased at 9 month follow-up. Treatment facilities that have the resources to provide such conditioning procedures might find their incorporation beneficial for altering the alcoholics' subjective orientation to alcohol.

The prior discussion has concerned expectations regarding the impact of alcohol. Alcohol is also associated with a broad network of attitudes concerning the symbolic nature of drinking. Drinkers and abstainers are both represented in cultural stereotypes. Research suggests that cultural attitudes toward drinking are factors in the etiology of alcoholism (Vaillant, 1983). Persons who are scornful or distrustful of abstainers and who are admiring or tolerant of intoxication, who view heavy drinking as a sign of virility, are more likely to drink problematically. Not only are such attitudes factors in the development of alcoholism, but such attitudes might also make it more difficult to resist encouragement to drink from a friend (fearing that one will be viewed as a boring abstainer). Any relapse prevention program might wish to incorporate procedures for altering those attitudes that encourage heavy drinking.

As part of relapse prevention, treatment programs might profitably incorporate attitude change procedures. Public statements of the desired attitude can alter attitude (Cialdini, 1984). Best's (1975) investigation on attitude change procedures utilized for persons attending a smoking cessation clinic suggest that timing and initial patient variables are important in optimizing efficacy of public statements of commitment. Having patients engage in attitude change procedures prior to the quit data (viz., having the patient deliver a speech on why smoking is bad), was found to be effective for those patients who hold negative views toward smoking and who are high in self-efficacy regarding their ability to quit. For patients low in self-efficacy and holding positive views of smoking, the same attitude change procedure worked best when instituted after the patient had quit smoking. These latter patients may have needed to first gain some feelings of self-efficacy concerning their ability to quit, before they could allow themselves to consider the desirability of quitting. The authors speculated that the speech delivery prior to quitting, for those low in self-efficacy and high in positive attitudes, may have increased resistance.

A second attitude change procedure can also be used for those patients who have favorable attitudes toward drinking. A discussion of the lack of choice individuals usually have in developing their own attitudes (attitudes are usually inculcated from the peer group) might move the client to a more positive view of sobriety. The psychological reactance literature has demonstrated that when people perceive their choices as constrained or limited, they more highly value the eliminated choice. This phenomenon is called reactance (Brehm & Brehm, 1981). Reactance can be recruited to alter attitudes. Depicting the way in which the culture precluded a positive view of abstention might create psychological reactance motivating the client to develop new attitudes. The eliminated choice, positively viewing abstention, might be more heartily embraced, or at least less resisted. Clinically, creating reactance through sensitizing 7th graders to the pressure provided by their peers to smoke has been demonstrated as effective in decreasing smoking (Evans et al., 1978).

In addition to attitude change, the therapist might want to strengthen the new attitude. McGuire has found that exposing individuals to counter arguments and helping them to debate against the counter arguments has an inoculating effect (see Baron & Byrne, 1981, p. 119). When patients move out into the world in which they must encounter old friends with enticing favorable attitudes toward heavy drinking, they are more likely to remain consistent with their favorable attitudes toward sobriety if they have received training in mustering counter arguments.

Strengthening the Link Between Attitude and Behavior

Even if negative attitudes toward heavy drinking and positive attitudes toward abstention are developed, they will not be of use if situational forces (e.g., importuning friends) are the predominating force at a critical moment. Mechanisms for helping the person keep future behavior consistent with attitudes do exist. One way is to make the person's behavioral understanding of the attitudes highly specific. There should be clarity as to which behaviors to avoid and which to engage in (although, as previously suggested, there should be some freedom in terms of when behaviors should occur so as not to set up an easy experience of failure). Second, dangerous situations that will challenge the new attitudes should be identified. That is, the situational factors that could make it tough to maintain the resolution to be sober should be specified. This type of clarity can aid in the resistance of situational forces (Higginbotham, West, & Forsyth, 1988). The individual will have the mental schema "this situation offers a test of my values." They will be alerted to the need for specific vigilance in maintaining the commitment to sobriety.

Maintaining a State of Objective Self-awareness

In their review of treatment of self-control behaviors, Kirschenbaum and Tomarken (1982) ascribe importance to self-monitoring. They cite data that relapse (to unrestrained eating or decreased studying) is often preceded by a lapse in monitoring and recording the behaviors identified by the therapist (Condiotte & Lichtenstein, 1981). Kirschenbaum and Tomarken (1982) suggest that self-monitoring establishes a state of objective self-awareness. When in a state of objective self-awareness, the individual assumes an observer perspective with regard to himself/herself. In such a state, individuals are more likely to conform to a standard of values. The probability of attitude consistent behavior is increased. For this reason, an objectively self-aware individual might be less likely to relapse. With specific regard to alcoholism, Kennedy, Gilbert, and Thoreson (1978) found that alcoholics taught to self-monitor precipitants to drinking decreased their drinking to a marginally significant degree more than those in a discussion group.

If patients are to self-monitor it becomes important to ask which behaviors it is most useful to monitor. For patients maintaining abstinence, drinking is not a behavior available for self-monitoring. Self-monitoring of urges to drink may not be beneficial. Objective self-awareness literature suggests that when individuals are focused on themselves, their emotional states are more likely to be enhanced (Scheier & Carver, 1977). Focusing on urges, might very well intensify urges. Focusing on those behaviors that are not desired (apparently irrelevant decisions, lacking enthusiasm for program participation) might very well cause the patient to conclude that he/she lacks motivation. Such will be the case when dispositional attributions (I guess I don't value sobriety) are made for the undesired behavior. Such attributions impact on the self-concept. However, when external attributions for the thought are made (that apparently irrelevant decision must have been suggested to me by my friend), no impact on self-concept occurs. Unless the patient has been trained to make external attributions for undesired thought, focusing on their occurrence may produce undesired effects.

With regard to the issue of which behaviors should be the focus of the monitoring process, monitoring the behavior that is desired might offer the best course of action. If a patient notices the urge to drink, the focus might be profitably switched to the coping skills the patient can bring to bear on the situation. For example, the patient might keep a list of the ways in which he/she refused a drink or the patient might keep a list of strategies that have worked to decrease craving. Monitoring situations and thoughts that could precipitate relapse can be useful if the monitoring incorporates how the situations are successfully handled.

Additional Treatment Components

Many programs incorporate assertion training, relaxation training, aversion therapy, etc. All of these interventions have been empirically validated in their own right. Bellack, Rozensky, and Schwartz (1974) report that the addition of endless therapy components can vitiate motivation. It is probably wise to select from the menu of these various therapies based on the individual needs of the client rather than incorporating everything.

Decreasing Abstinence Violation Syndrome

Apprising patients of the fact that relapse has not been found to be predictive of long-term success may innoculate the patient against psychological defeat. Marlatt (1985d) conceptualizes recovery as a journey. Each turn in the road offers a new learning situation which enables one to better prepare for the rest of the journey. Sharing Marlatt's view of the road to sobriety as consistent with a learning model may be useful. The concept of learning from relapses rather than seeing one's self as having relinquished the goal, is more constructive; and given the frequency of relapse, more practical.

Once an individual consumes the first gulp of alcohol the task becomes one of limiting the relapse and developing safety devices so that the individual, when next sober again, reinstates his/her goal of sobriety. Self-perception theory and cognitive dissonance theory explain the phenomenon that occurs in relapse. The theoretical literature in both these areas explains how the change in self-concept to that of a wet alcoholic can occur, as well as suggesting mechanisms to prevent such change from occurring.

Steele and Liu (1983) found a way to block the attitude change induced by cognitive dissonance. Steele and Liu blocked attitude change through adding a simple little procedure after the cognitive dissonance induction. They demonstrated that persons participating in a cognitive dissonance induction procedure (that is performing some abhorrent action) will fail to change their attitudes if they are asked to recall instances of positive behavior in areas of their life not relevant to the attitudinal area addressed by the dissonance induction. Steele and Liu induced their subjects to freely choose to write essays that espoused notions abhorrent to them. (According to dissonance theory the composition of the essay should create aversive arousal.) Then, some subjects were asked to recall instances of positive behavior. On outcome measures of attitude change, those subjects who recalled the positive behavior failed to manifest the usual cognitive dissonance induced attitude change. They did not manifest the attitude change evidenced by the subjects who did not experience the interpolated positive memory procedure.

The Steele and Liu procedure might be adapted for relapsing alcoholics who are vulnerable to a cognitive dissonance induced change upon recalling their drinking the morning after the relapse. The fact of a relapse will create cognitive dissonance, a pressure to change the sobriety goal and to view drinking in a positive light. If alcoholics who lapse can be induced to recall positive behavior in their life, or read a list of their positive traits that they have written during treatment, attitude change might be avoided. Having a list to read of positive traits (which the patient believes to be true), might short circuit the dissonance procedure. This could prevent the loss of the sobriety goal (which is under pressure to change from the tensions caused by dissonance).

The self-perception/attribution theory literature also suggests mechanisms for preventing a change in self-perception after a person observes himself/herself behaving in a negative manner. Self-perception theory posits that a change in self-perception will occur only if the individual attributes her/his behavior to internal, stable attributions. If the individual views her/his behavior as externally caused or makes attributions to internal traits that are not assumed to be enduring (temporary factors such as effort or mood) then no self-perception change will occur. Consistent with this view, the data suggest that those who attribute a relapse to external factors experience shorter, less severe relapses (Goldstein, Gordon, & Miller, cited by Brownell et al., 1986).

In keeping with the findings of this literature, Marlatt (1985c) recognizes that there is some utility in external attributions for lapses, as well as attributions to controllable, internal, unstable factors (e.g., a deficit coping skill or effort). Marlatt is concerned not only with a change in self-percept (cognition) but also with the affect associated with particular attributions. He is concerned to pre-clude the guilt or helplessness that might results, since an alcoholic might con-tinue drinking to dissipate the mood.

Attributions to external factors for a relapse (e.g., I drank because my friend wanted me to) can block guilt. Such attributions further avoid a change in self-perception which might be demoralizing (see, I just can't do it). There is also a case to be advanced for attributions for failure due to a lack of effort.

The attribution literature has investigated the type of affect associated with various attributions after failure (Russel & McAuley, 1986). Attributions to internal, controllable, unstable factors (such as effort) do create guilt. Although guilt can be counterproductive if there is no prospect of a future opportunity to redeem oneself, when the individual orients to the next opportunity, attributions to effort (which creates guilt) can redound in enhanced persistence (Steenbarger & Aderman, 1979). A study in which children had been taught to attribute lack of success to effort, demonstrated that they display enhanced persistence in the face of negative feedback (Dweck, 1975). Those children believing their failure meant they were not working hard enough, worked harder.

There is another critical factor in determining how an individual will be effected by failure. There is evidence that there is a crucial stage between failure and the behavioral performance decrement which often follows. This necessary stage is self-focus. That is, the individual's mind wanders to thoughts about the self rather than generating better solutions for the next challenge (Mikulincer & Nizan, 1988). If an individual can be oriented to problem solution, behavioral deterioration can be averted.

Kuhl (1981) has suggested that after failure many of the deleterious effects can be avoided if the individual immediately focuses on problem solving for suc-cessful response to the next occasion on which he/she will be tested. Such focus can dissipate the guilt, depression, and resultant tendency to give up after failure (Carver, Blaney, & Scheier, 1979). A study by Elliot and Dweck (1988) illustrated the impact of differences in focus of attention following failure. This study sought to determine whether instructional set would alter the impact of negative feedback. Some children were taught to view the task performance as an opportunity for demonstrating or measuring current skill level. Given failure, the children with cognitive set of honing skills were not impaired, whereas those with the cognitive set of measuring themselves, worked less effectively and progressively displayed worse outcome over trials. Apparently, the successful children were oriented to using the information as feedback for strategizing for the next trial.

The attribution literature has primarily investigated cognitive skill situations. Experiments examining the principles with alcoholics have not occurred. The principles can be extrapolated to alcoholics, however. If alcoholics can be trained to utilize relapse as a learning situation for developing better responses, abstinence violation syndrome may not ensue.

Additional Suggestions for Attenuating Relapse

Agreements can be reached with friends and relative as to contingency plans should a relapse occur. An example of a plan might be that a friend would call or visit the alcoholic should he not appear at a scheduled therapy group session. Such a plan might limit the duration of the relapse. It is important to arrange the contingency plan prior to the relapse. A friend's intervention requested by the alcoholic before the relapse is less likely to create reactance and resentment. An intervention deriving from prior agreement is also likely to remind the individual of his/her prior commitment.

Another procedure for decreasing the probability of a lapse turning into a relapse would be to have the alcoholic compose a letter to himself/herself to be read in the event of relapse. Properly composed this letter would remind the alcoholic of his/her good feelings about this commitment to sobriety. Others have experimented with supervised relapse, i.e., having the alcoholic drinking during the therapy session. The purpose of the supervised relapse is to demonstrate that a relapse need not eventuate in a disaster. Such supervised relapse has been found to precipitate unsupervised relapse for smokers (Brownell et al., 1986). Until the benefits of such an approach have been empirically demonstrated, such procedures should not be routinely incorporated into therapy.

Where Should the Relapsing and the Lapsing Receive Treatment

In traditional treatment centers, group rather than individual therapy is most often the vehicle by which treatment is delivered. The impact on other members in the group of individuals who are experiencing frequent relapse while continuing to endorse the goal of sobriety, and the impact of individuals who are no longer working toward the goal of sobriety, but wish to continue in treatment to address other goals, has not been empirically assessed. The clinician, however, has to consider the issue.

Individuals who experience frequent relapse and individuals who no longer endorse abstinence as a goal constitute a big threat to the therapeutic process of others in therapy delivered according to the traditional model. Those who relapse despite going to AA, disprove the AA slogan "keep coming back, it works." Those who continue to drink, when they do not become immediate disasters, call into question the notion that alcoholics can never become control drinkers. Deviance can weaken the group norm. To the extent that the group norm of sobriety rather than personal motivation is the force behind the patient's staying sober, the norm's vitiation can be damaging. AA does not require sobriety for attendance at meetings. However, many traditional treatment centers require abstinence as a condition of continued treatment. The lapsing and the relapsing are expelled.

The continually lapsing and the relapsed constitute a threat to group therapy conducted from a research-based model of treatment as well. The type of negative impact of such individuals on other group members will probably vary according to whether the drinking member has (a) changed her/his goal or (b) has failed to meet her/his goal without abandoning it. By having a control drinker in a group with abstainers, there is danger of the group's goal becoming less clearly defined, rendering the goal less attractive to its members (Higginbotham, West, & Forsyth, 1988). The presence in a group of a person who wants to be sober but repeatedly fails demoralizes others. One member's failure might jeapordize feelings of self-efficacy of other members. ("If he/she can't make it, maybe I can't either.")

It is probably best to treat those with a control drinking goal in one group and those with an abstinence goal in another. The question of what to do with the individual who wants to be sober but is unsuccessful is less clear. Of course, the presence of a drinking member can provide opportunities as well. Analysis of the forces contributing to the perpetual relapses of a particular group member may provide valuable insights for other group members. Despite mechanisms for handling the problems created by relapsing members, it is probably best to limit group composition in terms of the ratio of lapsing to successful. The lapsing can be seen individually rather than in the group context.

SUMMARY

The psychological literature offers a wide range of treatment techniques and considerations for a practitioner who does not operate from a traditional perspective. Specific relapse precipitants should be identified and coping skills should be taught. Feelings of self-efficacy generally need to be enhanced, as do attitudes conducive to a sober life. Life style changes and social support commonly need to be discussed and developed. Further, the patient should be prepared for handling relapse should it occur.

In addition to all these interventions aimed at decreasing the risk or severity of relapse, it should be remembered that alcoholics will probably need assistance in negotiating the challenges of daily living as well. For many alcoholics life will present more than the normal number of challenges as a result of the aftermath of the drinking. Bosses and spouses may be angry. Spouses may create reactance by forbidding the alcoholic to drink. In treatment, these issues should be discussed and coping strategies developed. In the appendix section of this book (Appendix C) a list of group topics for drinkers groups is presented. This list can serve as a check list from which the items specific to any particular patient can be selected.

4 Personality Characteristics, Personality Types, Tests

In this chapter, personality characteristics which have been identified for the modal alcoholic are examined. There is consideration of descriptive characteristics of distinctive types of alcoholics (female alcoholics, geriatric alcoholics, skid row alcoholics, etc.). Instruments specifically developed for either differentiating alcoholics from the general population or for assessing syndromes associated with the alcoholic process are discussed.

We begin with a discussion of some of the personality characteristics that are descriptive of alcoholics. Mark Keller (1972b, p. 1147) has averred that "The investigation of any trait in alcoholics will show that they have either more or less of it." Obviously, the information distinguishing alcoholics from others is vast, and I have not attempted to exhaustively review the literature. Discussion is limited to (a) those traits that have emerged in the research on children of alcoholics that might constitute part of the temperament precursor to alcoholism, and (b) those traits that have generated a body of literature (e.g., depression and internal/external locus of control) because of their potential importance for treatment.

There are many ways in which alcoholics can be categorized into types. One way is to distinguish alcoholics on the basis of demographic characteristics (sex, age, socioeconomic status). Most of the research findings in this book have been generated from the modal category of alcoholic: male, middle aged, and blessed with an income. Not all alcoholics fit the demographic modal pattern. A brief discussion of the highlights from research findings investigating female alcoholics, older alcoholics, and skid row alcoholics is presented.

Some have sought to ascertain dimensions along which alcoholics might be categorized to yield types that relate to differential treatment outcomes, differential efficacy given various types of treatments, and differential etiological roots. One obvious way in which alcoholics can be distinguished is the pattern of their drinking. Some findings investigating differences between bingers and steady state drinkers are discussed. Another way of categorizing alcoholics has been to separate them according to whether their alcoholism was preceded by another major psychiatric disorder. That literature differentiating alcoholics according to the presence and type of primary psychiatric disorder is reviewed. Finally, the responses of alcoholics to the MMPI (Minnesota Multiphasic Personality Inventory) have also been used to generate types of alcoholics. Some major findings from this endeavor are reported.

Discussion of tests and measures in alcoholism is divided according to the purpose of the instrument. Some instruments have been developed to discriminate alcoholics from the general population. Scales specific for this purpose have been proffered. Clinicians have attempted to construct scales from the pool of items constituting the MMPI for the purpose of identifying alcoholics from normals or psychiatric patients. In this chapter, the more popular methods for identifying alcoholics are discussed. Included in the discussion are the Michigan Alcohol Screening test, the CAGE, scales from the MMPI, and laboratory tests that are used to identify alcoholics.

Tests that measure specific syndromes associated with alcoholism have also been developed. Two measures have been designed to help the clinician examine the pattern of an alcoholic's drinking. Both the Comprehensive Drinking Profile and the Alcohol Use Inventory provide the clinician with information about an individual alcoholics' unique pattern of drinking and problems developing from the drinking. The Severity of Alcohol Dependence Scale and the Alcohol Dependence Scale assess the extremity of physical dependence on alcohol. They may aid in selecting patients for whom an abstinence rather than a control drinking goal is most appropriate. Measures, similar to the internal/external locus of control have been developed to assess an alcoholic's subjective sense of control related to drinking. Two such instruments are discussed.

At the end of the chapter several measures that have been developed to identify children of alcoholics are examined.

DISTINGUISHING TRAITS OF ALCOHOLICS

Boredom Susceptibility

In a sample of 18-year-old Swedish army inductees, von Knorring, Oreland, von Knorring (1987) found that the alcohol abusers and abusers of multiple substances could be differentiated from other recruits on boredom susceptibility, an extraversion/impulsivity scale developed by Eysenck, and on an impulsivity and monotony avoidance measure. (They were higher on all measures.) The multiple substance abusers could be further distinguished on lower MAO values. Although some have failed to distinguish alcoholics from normals on the basis of the sensation seeking scale, Malatesta, Sutker, and Treiber (1981), in a population of public intoxicants, found that high sensation seeking was related to the number of public intoxication charges. Further, the sensation seekers more often reported initially using alcohol for pleasure rather than to fit in with peers. Others have noted low MAO levels in alcoholics who have sustained protracted abstention (Faraj et al., 1989).

Differences in Autonomic Nervous System Responding

When alcoholics in general are examined, many investigators have found that their sympathetic nervous system responses are retarded and attenuated in magnitude (Kissen, Schenker, & Schenker, 1959; Knott & Blumer, 1985; Rubin, Gottheil, Roberts, Alterman, & Holstine, 1977; Rubin, Gottheil, Roberts, Alterman, & Holstine, 1978). There have been inconsistent findings in samples of alcoholics who have been screened such that those who have suffered head injury are eliminated. Although Knott and Blumer (1985) found attenuated responding, Chandler, Parsons and Vega (1975) observed a different pattern of activity. Chandler et al. found that alcoholics in response to a stress inducing stimulus, display an augmented GSR response and greater heart rate variability. Lovallo, Parsons, and Holloway (1973) found that whereas normals given an interpolated mind engaging task while being exposed to a painful stimulus, will display an attenuated stress response, alcoholics will display an augmented response. The autonomic responding of alcoholics takes longer to return to baseline poststress than it does in normal subjects (Tarter, Alterman, & Edwards, 1985).

There has been speculation that the unreliable, sometimes exaggerated autonomic responding observed in alcoholics, has implication for how they will perform behaviorally. When feedback from autonomic activity is erratic or excessive, perhaps it will be ignored. There are data consistent with this thinking. Whereas normals seem to rely on kinesthetic nervous system cues to determine behavior, a lack of correspondence between kinesthetic events and differential overt behavior is found in alcoholics. Several types of paradigms have been recruited to demonstrate the lack of correspondence between kinesthetic events and overt behavior.

In general, after consuming a large amount of liquid, people will subsequently drink less. They seem to rely upon internal sensations of fullness, to determine how much they will drink. Brown and Williams (1975) have demonstrated that alcoholics are influenced to a lesser degree by a water preload when subsequently presented with a pleasant tasting nonalcoholic beverage. Consistent with this finding, is the demonstration that alcoholics are less accurate in estimating the amount of water they have consumed than are normals (Heilburn, Tarbox, & Madison, 1979). Parsons, Tarter, and Edelberg (1972) speculate that the deficit ability of alcoholics to turn a knob slowly may be reflect impairment in the capacity to integrate kinesthetic and proprioceptive feedback.

A punishment paradigm constitutes a second situation in which kinesthetic feedback seems to mediate the response of learners. In a punishment paradigm, it is believed that persons learn to avoid because they experience a conditioned anxiety, which has been associated with external cues signaling the occurrence of shock if behavior is not altered. The conditioned anxiety, elicited by the external cue, is necessary for learning. Given a punishment or avoidance paradigm, alcoholics are much slower to learn to avoid an aversive event than are normals (Vogel-Sprott & Banks, 1965; Weingartner & Faillace, 1971). It may be that this slower learning is attributable to a lack of reliance on signals from the autonomic nervous system which inform the learner that an aversive event is about to occur. Tarter, Alterman, and Edwards (1985) have suggested that failure to integrate kinesthetic feedback reflects another facet of a general temperament, which underlies the genetic predisposition to alcoholism.

In addition to greater variability and sometimes heightened responsivity of the autonomic nervous system, alcoholics have been observed to be stimulus augmenters (von Knorring, 1976). In normals, if stimuli of increasing intensity are presented (e.g., lights that become progressively brighter in intensity), the EEG magnitude will habituate or adapt such that the magnitude of the response plateaus rather than tracking the increase in the stimulus intensity. In alcoholics' the EEG magnitude augments to track the magnitude of the stimulus rather than plateauing.

There is good evidence, then, that the autonomic nervous systems and the reliance of alcoholics on internally generated information follow a distinctive pattern. The significance of the particular autonomic nervous system activity, utilization of internal information, and the stimulus augmentation in the etiology of alcoholism are discussed in the section on genetics.

Possible Reactance

Another explanation for the failure of alcoholics to learn to avoid punishment has been offered. Okulitch and Marlatt (1972) placed alcoholics in a situation in which they were first taught to make a response for reinforcement but were then punished with shock for making the response. Alcoholics were slower to quit responding than were normals. Whereas the behavior of the alcoholics was consistent with the idea that they were failing to rely upon kinesthetic feedback (anxiety response), it is also possible that their behavior could reflect cognitive events. Okulitch and Marlatt found that the alcoholics verbalized the perception that their nerves were being tested. They seemed to display a stubborn determination to persist in their responding despite the fact that they were being punished for doing so. This sample of alcoholics seemed to be more determined to resist suppression of their behavior than were those in the normal control group.

This particular study suggests that alcoholics might be more resistant to having their behavior constrained by others. If true, this particular characteristic might be taken into consideration in designing treatment options.

Depression

During detoxification and in the first few weeks of treatment, depression is frequently observed in alcoholics (Behar, Winokur, & Berg, 1984; Overall, Reilly, Kelley, & Hollister, 1985; Weingold, Lachin, Bell, & Coxe, 1968). Brown and Schuckit (1988) report that across studies 28–98% of alcoholics are depressed during the initial period of treatment. Depression remits within 3–4 weeks of sobriety. By the fourth week, only 10% of Overall's sample continued to display depression. Brown and Schuckit (1988) assert that the sharpest decline in depression occurs around the second week.

In contrast to the reported decline in sobriety, Penick et al. (1988) failed to observe remission in depression in over half their sample of VA alcoholics over a 1-year period. In this sample, although many reported improvement in their drinking, precise consumption levels were not ascertained such that it was possible that continued depression reflected the continuation of heavy consumption. In a sample of alcoholics in AA, all sober for at least a year, Behar et al. (1984) found that 15% were depressed. Provision of tricyclic antidepressant medications has not been observed to increase the percentage of those alcoholics' whose depression remits (Shaw, Donley, Morgan, & Robinson, 1975).

The conclusion that heavy sustained drinking can induce chemical changes in the brain which manifest as depression emerges from the ward drinking studies. In these studies, alcoholics became depressed, irritable, and anxious, as they were observed drinking heavily over a protracted period (McNamee et al., 1968; see discussion in Tamkin et al., 1987). The idea that something about protracted heavy consumption induces depression is consistent with the observation of a correlation between depression and other indices of heavy consumption (sleep disturbance, hangover incapacitation, neurological signs) (Nakamura et al., 1983).

Helzer and Pryzbeck (1988) did find that the presence of an additional psychiatric diagnosis increased the rate of help seeking in alcoholics. Hamm, Major, and Brown (1979) have cautioned that depression may be confined among those alcoholics who seek treatment. In populations selected from the community and populations of male, young, physically intact alcoholics, higher rates of depression, have not been observed (Hamm et al., 1979; Woodruff, Guze, Clayton, & Carr, 1973). Others have queried community samples regarding symptomotology occurring at any point during their life time. In Weissman, Myers, and Harding's (1980) sample of community alcoholics, 44% qualified as having been depressed at some point during their life. Helzer and Pryzbeck (1988) investigated current depression in a community sample of alcoholics. They reported that the rates of depression in male alcoholics exceeded general population values by a small margin (5% vs. 3%), although in women alcoholics rates are considerably higher than in the general population (19% vs. 7%). These community studies support the view that alcoholics regardless of their treatment status are more likely to be depressed than others. However, the incidence of depression in community samples is not as high as in those presenting for treatment.

There have been attempts to use intake variables to discriminate between those whose depression remits over the first 3 weeks of treatment and those whose depression fails to remit. Nakamuara et al. (1983) found that alcoholics' whose social life had revolved around drinking were less likely to recover from depression following protracted sobriety. Overall et al. (1985) and Brown and Schuckit (1988) found that the nonremitting were distinguished by the lack of an intact social support system.

There have also been attempts to estimate the parameter of manic-depressive illness among alcoholics. In a review of the literature, Freed (1970) reported that 1.2 to 32.8% have been diagnosed as MDI (manic-depressive illness). Although large sample data is not available on the issue, Reich, Davies, and Himmelhoch (1974) have observed that bipolar depressives tend to drink during the manic phase rather than the depressive phase of their illnesses.

Other studies have examined correlates of depression in alcoholics. Consistent with increased depression, a sample of alcoholics usually are lower in self-esteem than normals (Berg, 1971; Charalampous, Ford, & Skinner, 1976). Although alcoholics can be characterized as deficient in self-esteem, in a sample of middle class alcoholics, Heilburn and Swartz (1980) observed that alcoholics employ the cognitive coping mechanisms of inflating the value of their positive traits while selectively forgetting their negative traits. Twentyman et al. (1982) found no differences in social skills between alcoholics and normals, save for deficit skill in refusing a drink.

Suicide

Between 5–27% of all deaths in alcoholics are attributable to suicide. Between 15–47% of all suicides are committed by alcoholics; and between 13–50% of suicide attempters are alcoholic (Berglund, 1984; Goodwin, 1973). Attempts have been made to determine whether alcoholics who commit suicide can be identified from those who do not. Some have found that additional diagnoses (depression and ASP) are more frequent in those who eventually commit suicide (Berglund, 1984). Those who commit suicide more often have peptic ulcers (Berglund, 1984). Hesselbrock et al. (1988) found that depression, drug abuse, ASP, a positive family history for alcoholism, and earlier onset of alcoholism distinguished the male suicide attempters. Beck, Steer, and Trexler (1989) began with a group of alcohol abusers who had all attempted suicide. There was a factor that differentiated those suicide attempters who eventually committed suicide from those who did not. This factor was the extent to which the attempter had taken precautions to avoid detection at the time of the initial attempt.

Data suggest that suicide is committed by alcoholics in middle age rather than later in life, although Sundby's data (discussed by Goodwin, 1973) suggested that suicide is still relatively high among alcoholics who have surpassed middle age and in whom social status has not declined (Goodwin, 1973). Often a major loss or threat of major loss precedes the suicide (Murphy & Robins, 1967). In one study, 32% of alcoholic suicides had experienced a disruption of affectional ties within 6 weeks preceding their suicide attempt (Murphy & Robins, 1967). Goodwin (1973) has advanced the hypothesis that having something to lose is usually associated with alcoholic suicide. Among those who are on skid row or have lost everything, suicide is no longer a risk.

Beyond increased risk of suicide in alcoholics, 25% of persons committing suicide have been drinking at the time of commission (Goodwin, 1973). Mayfield and Montgomery (1972) indentify two patterns. One pattern is a suicide in a person who has been binge drinking for a protracted period. Binge type of drinking is usually done alone and brings on anxiety and depression later in the drinking episode. The anxiety and depression then precipitate the suicide attempt. The second pattern is a suicide precipitated by an interpersonal altercation in which the attempter is intoxicated. Interestingly, Mayfield and Montgomery (1972) indicate that many suicide attempters who were intoxicated at the time of the attempt, when sober denied suicidal intention. Often, when sober they failed to recall the suicide attempt. Several days after the event, many are not depressed.

Differences in Locus of Control

The construct of locus of control has received wide attention since its introduction by Rotter in 1966. A number of instruments have been developed to measure the concept. The I–E scale published by Rotter has been factor analyzed by Mirels. Two factors were yielded: controllability over political events and controllability of events in one's personal life. Whereas the Rotter instrument assesses expectations, Tiffany has developed an instrument assessing perceived control over past events. In addition to measures assessing control over events in general, several instruments have been developed to measure control over precipitants to drinking.

Although there has been inconsistency across studies, major reviews of this literature conclude that as a group alcoholics either do not differ from normal populations or are more external than nonalcoholics (Donovan & O'Leary, 1983; Rohsenow, 1983; Rohsenow & O'Leary, 1978b). Increased externality seems to be the case for the overall Rotter scale as well as for the Tiffany experienced events scale. Donovan and O'Leary (1983) caution that the meaning of these findings must be evaluated taking into account the fact that assessment is most often made at treatment outset. Immediately prior to treatment, events veridically have probably been externally controlled. Hence the findings may reflect the state of alcoholics in the beginning of treatment rather than a personality trait characteristic of alcoholic populations.

Attention has been given to the association between measures of control and other psychological characteristics. Generally externality is correlated with greater psychological distress on the pathology scales of the MMPI (Donovan & O'Leary, 1983; Rohsenow & O'Leary, 1978a). Low experienced control as measured by the Tiffany scale is associated with greater depression (Donovan & O'Leary, 1983). Externals are more likely to report drinking in the service of relating better interpersonally (to feel more important, to decrease shyness, to relax socially, and to overcome feelings of inferiority). Further, the externals on the experienced control measure suffer more severe drinking outcomes (O'Leary, Donovan, & O'Leary, 1978).

Externals and internals, although not differing in overall defensiveness, do differ in the style adopted in denying their faults. Externals rely on projection and blaming of others. Internals rely on isolation of affect, intellectualization, and rationalization (Donovan & O'Leary, 1983). Some have found that alcoholic internals are more likely to score highly on the Crowne Marlowe social desirability scale (Costello & Manders, 1974).

Locus of control for events in general has not been found to relate consistently with outcome. There have been several studies in which externals remained in aftercare for a longer period of time, but other studies suggest that externals are more likely to drop out of inpatient treatment programs. Most often patients become more internal in their orientation over the course of treatment (Donovan & O'Leary, 1983). These inconsistent results make it difficult to draw clear inferences as to whether internality for global events (although not control over ability to resist temptations to drink) is necessarily better and whether therapists should seek to promote the perception of internal control. Whereas treatment may increase internality, long-term AA exposure may not. Costello and Manders (1974) compared recently admitted alcoholics with recovering alcoholic counselors who had been sober for at least 3 years. The counselors were more external than were the new admissions.

Aside from the issue of which is better, is the emerging indication that a person's control orientation will predict his/her comfort level with particular approaches to treatment. Externals are more often willing to accept antabuse (Obitz, 1978). Those perceiving less control over their ability to resist pressures to drink are more willing to request help and more often accept the disease concept as opposed to the learned behavior explanation of alcoholism (Stafford, 1980). In a study in which alcoholics were given instruction in self-monitoring urges to drink, those scoring internally at the initiation of treatment enhanced to a greater extent their initial internal orientation and more often relied on the self-monitoring procedures (Kennedy, Gilbert, & Thoreson, 1978).

Summary. There have been mixed reports on whether alcoholics are more likely to be internals or externals. Major authorities in the field generally hold that alcoholics are more likely to be externals. Externality does not relate to treatment outcome. It is predictive of psychological ill health, drinking patterns, coping strategies, and those treatment approaches that will be viewed as more attractive.

Scales Which Are Elevated on the MMPI in Alcoholic Populations

A good deal of research has been conducted in alcoholic samples using the MMPI as an assessment device. Those scale elevations that have been observed, add to the knowledge about those traits or states that can be expected to be exhibited in groups of alcoholics.

Pathology Scale Elevations. Across studies the most likely scale from the MMPI to achieve elevation is scale 4, the psychopathic deviance scale (Graham & Strenger, 1988). Because this scale remains elevated well into sobriety, it has been inferred that this measure does not reflect the short-term consequences of heavy drinking. Graham and Strenger (1988) describe persons scoring high on scale 4 as hostile, irritable, antisocial, and rebellious toward authority figures. It has not gone unrecognized that some items on scale 4 ask directly about drinking or the sequale of drinking (I have used alcohol excessively; I have never been in trouble with the law; I have not lived the right kind of life). When these items are eliminated from scale 4, the scale no longer identifies the alcoholics (Mac-Andrew, 1978; MacAndrew & Geertsma 1963). Further, in comparing alcoholics with psychiatric inpatients, alcoholics have been found to score lower on scale 4 (MacAndrew, 1979a), although this is not always the case (MacAndrew & Geertsma, 1963; Rosen, 1960).

MacAndrew and Geertsma (1963) factor analyzed the responses of 200 male outpatient alcoholics to the items on scale 4. Five factors accounted for much of the variance in scale 4: Desurgency, Acceptance by others, Discontent with family situation, Social deviance, and Remorseful intropunitiveness. Mac-Andrew and Geertsma's (1963) factor analysis provides information as to personality structure in alcoholics. The analysis does not necessarily imply that alcoholics will be distinguished on these factor scales. In fact, this study found that alcoholics were differentiated from psychiatric patients on the social deviance and remorseful-intrapunitiveness factors only. Alcoholics scored in the more socially deviant and more remorseful directions. A similar analysis was conducted for female alcoholics in which a different factor structure was obtained (MacAndrew, 1978).

Possibly reflecting the dysphoria resulting from persistent heavy drinking, those scales from the MMPI tapping somatic complaints and distress are frequently elevated in alcoholic populations (Hypochondriasis, Depression, Hysteria, Paranoia, Psychathenia). Elevations on these scales attenuate given a significant period of sobriety (Conley, 1981). Consistent with the hypothesis that the distress scales reflect magnitude of alcohol consumption, the distress scales have been found to be a better correlates of the amount consumed during drinking periods than is the psychopathy scale (Nerviano et al., 1980; Whitelock, et al., 1971).

There is an additional finding which sheds further light on MMPI scale elevations. Alcoholics volunteering for treatment, the volunteering often being spurred by distress, more often display psychological distress profiles, whereas those who are court ordered more often display characterological (4/9) profiles (Nerviano et al., 1980).

Comment.   MMPI findings reinforce the expectation that alcoholics who have recently quit drinking or are continuing to drink will be depressed. The often encountered elevation on the psychopathic deviance scale seems to capitalize on those items which inquire about drinking. Only particular facets of personality measured by the Pd scale are elevated in alcoholic samples compared to psychiatric controls, viz., remorsefulness and social deviance.

TYPES OF ALCOHOLICS

Female Alcoholics

General Statistics.   It is estimated that approximately 20% of the alcoholic population in the United States is comprised of females (Rathod & Thomson, 1971; Schuckit & Morrissey, 1976). The ratio of male to female alcoholics will vary depending on the setting in which the alcoholics are identified. In community samples, the ratio is 1:5 (Helzer & Pryzbeck, 1988). In treatment centers the ratio has been estimated at 1:5. In medical settings, the ratio is much narrower. Men and women are equally likely to develop cirrhosis. In jailhouse and court settings, which employ a public disruption criteria for defining alcoholism, the ratio is 1:11. It is estimated that about 5% of the female population in the United States is alcoholic (Gomberg, 1980; Schuckit, 1986; Vaillant, 1983, p. 108).

In the general population, drinking habits of females are known to differ among the social classes. Among the lower class, higher rates of abstention are found among females but higher rates of heavy drinking are also found (Schuckit & Morrissey, 1976). An employed female is more likely to be a problem drinker than is a housewife (Benson & Wilsnack, 1983). Among young adults, college women display higher rates of heavy drinking than do their same age peers who are not seeking an education (Schuckit & Morrissey, 1976). These general population statistics imply that the drinking practices do vary according to social group.

It has been suggested that the differential in the incidence of alcoholism between the sexes is in part attributable to particular patterns of approved drinking for each sex. Whatever personal risk factors are causative in the development of alcoholism, drinking practices that are determined by one's reference group, will either foster expression or inhibit expression of personal risk factors. Sanctioned drinking practices for each sex do vary with social class. They also seem to be in a state of flux. Drunkenness in females meets with more disapproval than drunkenness in males, but the number of persons exhibiting the double standard is decreasing (Wilsnack, 1976). Given the same drinking behavior (heavy amount consumed per occasion, concern from relatives over drinking, drinking at unusual times, DWIs, intoxication, etc.) females are more likely to be labeled as problem drinkers than are males (Leavy & Dunlosky, 1989).

Before discussing the particular patterns of female alcoholism a discussion of primary vs. secondary alcoholism should be introduced. Primary alcoholics are those whose problematic drinking is not preceded by a another major psychiatric diagnosis. Secondary alcoholics are those alcoholics for whom problematic drinking was preceded by some other disorder. Those disorders that most frequently accompany or precede alcoholism are antisocial personality disorder and depression. There are major sex differences in terms of the percentage of secondary diagnosis and the type of primary diagnoses. Females are more likely to exhibit primary depression/secondary alcoholism. Males are more likely to exhibit primary sociopathy/secondary alcoholism. The percentage of secondary alcoholics and the type of secondary alcoholism will vary according to particular treatment settings. Correctional settings and public facilities are more likely to provide services to alcoholics with a dual diagnosis of antisocial personality disorder. Private treatment facilities are more likely to see primary alcoholics and alcoholics with a secondary or primary diagnosis of depression.

Patterns of Female Alcoholism

Female alcoholics present for treatment at the average age of 44, which is the average age of the male alcoholic. Whereas men more often experience the onset of heavy drinking in their 20s, women most often date their heavy drinking to age 32. These findings have inspired the hypothesis that female alcoholism is telescoped, that is women begin their abusive drinking at a later age but progress more rapidly, arriving at the necessity for treatment at the same time as their male counterparts (Benson & Wilsnack, 1983). In terms of symptomotology, female alcoholics less often report morning drinking, blackouts, or withdrawal symptoms. They are physiologically more vulnerable to the impact of heavy drinking. They are less likely to have run afowl of the law as a result of their drinking

(Beckman, 1975; Benson & Wilsnack, 1983; Gallant, 1986; Hill, 1984; Ross, 1989; Saunders, Davis, & Williams, 1981). Women score higher on measures of psychological distress compared to their male counterparts (Brooner, Templer, Svikis, Schmidt, & Monopolis, 1990).

The manner in which female alcoholics drink also differs from the usual male pattern. Whereas males often drink in public places with peers, older women are more likely to drink at home by themselves (Gomberg, 1980; Linasky, 1957). Whereas males endorse escape reasons for drinking, they also endorse social reasons. Women report escape drinking. They more exclusively endorse tension relief reasons for drinking (Gomberg, 1980). Female alcoholics, in contrast to male alcoholics, more often identify a specific stressful life event precipitant (death, child leaving home, divorce, etc.) to the onset of their abusive drinking (Benson & Wilsnack, 1983).

The inference that women exhibit a pattern of alcoholism which differs in its form from that of male alcoholism seems to be suggested. Schuckit and Morrissey (1976), however, caution against this interpretation. They point out the confounding of types of alcoholism with sex of the alcoholic. If male and female primary depression/secondary alcoholics are compared, the finding of shorter duration of heavy drinking prior to treatment presentation and the finding of more frequent specific precipitant to the onset of drinking disappears. In populations of primary sociopaths/secondary alcoholics in both sexes, the drinking is initiated at an early age. Further, social class among women alcoholics exerts an influence on the pattern of alcoholism. Whereas higher class female alcoholics exhibit a telescoped drinking history, lower class women alcoholics are less likely to have developed problems later in life (Cramer & Blacker, 1966).

Interpersonal Consequences of Drinking

Female alcoholics report more marital disruption and disharmony than do their male counterparts. They are more likely to be divorced (Gomberg, 1980; McCrady & Sher, 1983). They are more likely than their male counterparts to be married to another alcoholic, and this probability is increased on the second marriage relative to the first marriage (Lindbeck, 1972; Schuckit & Morrissey, 1976).

Differences in Seeking Treatment

There is some disagreement in the literature regarding whether female alcoholics less often seek treatment than do male alcoholics. Beckman and Amaro (1984), who have reviewed the literature, suggest that females are less likely to seek treatment. In a recent community survey, Helzer and Pryzbeck (1988) found that females were more likely to have sought treatment and to have discussed their drinking with a physician. Ross (1989) found no difference in the help seeking behavior between male and female alcoholics.

A review of the outcome literature, finds no support for differential outcome between males and females, although a limited survey suggests that treatment providers may expect worse outcomes for females than males (Vannicelli, 1984). A study by Dahlgren and Willander (1989) compared female alcoholics treated in an all female specialized treatment center to females treated in a traditional coeducational facility. Although there were a number of confounds in this study (more of the females in the specialized treatment group were living with a male; those in the specialized treatment unit were in treatment for a longer time), the results at 2 year follow-up found a higher rate of sobriety in the specialized treatment group.

Search for Distinct Etiology of Female Alcoholism

Although the case for heredity in alcoholism has been supported for males, the case has not been as thoroughly explored or demonstrated in females (see chapter on genetics). Whereas early theorists in alcoholism have explored heightened dependency needs and exaggerated power needs as psychological explanations for alcoholism (Miller, 1976), researchers focused on female alcoholism have cautioned that there is no reason to assume that the factors causing alcoholism in men are those that cause alcoholism in women. These researchers (see Wilsnack, 1984) have advanced the hypothesis that female alcoholism is developed in an attempt to cope with sex-role conflict. Several findings support this view.

Female alcoholics display high rates (higher than nonalcoholic women) of menstrual dysfunction and gynecological problems which precede the onset of their heavy drinking (Wilsnack, 1976). Further, they report that heaviest drinking occurs premenstrum (Belfer, Shader, Carroll, & Harmatz, 1971). Parker (1972) finds that female alcoholics, particularly spree drinkers, endorse a preference for masculine roles. Female alcoholics more often describe a domineering, cold mother and a warm, albeit frequently alcoholic father. According to theory, this positive view of father and negative view of mother suggests that the female alcoholic may have identified with the opposite sex parent creating a confused identity (Beckman, 1975; Belfer et al., 1971).

Wilsnack (1976) has suggested that women may drink in an attempt to exaggerate their femininity. She cites the finding that college women who report heavy drinking hold the expectation that they will act in a more feminine manner after drinking. Wilsnack (see Wilsnack, 1976, for discussion) has conducted research to explore whether drinking will result in enhanced femininity. For an actual pre–post test of the impact of alcohol on behavior, Wilsnack devised an unusual dependent measure of femininity. First, she examined the themes in response to TAT cards produced by women when they were and were not nursing. She found that when nursing, the themes of enjoying life for its own sake rather than future goal orientation predominated. She interpreted these themes as indicative of femininity and used this newly devised index as her dependent measure. Examining a female sample, she found that drinking did indeed increase the production of enjoying each moment for its own sake theme.

Comments on the Theory.   In our culture it is the case that drinking, at least traditionally, has been a male prerogative and is associated with macho behavior. Given the masculine connotation of the behavior, it is not surprising that women who are willing to engage in a masculine activity, are probably less traditionally feminine in other ways as well. This does not mean that ameliorating confused femininity is a motive for drinking, rather it is probably a prerequisite for drinking behavior, which is certainly a prerequisite to alcoholism. This could explain the finding of confused femininity being likely among alcoholic women than nonalcoholic women.

As others have recognized (Schuckit & Morrissey, 1976), the finding of enhanced familial disruption in the family of origin, with a domineering mother, and alcoholic but warm father, may all be attributable to having been raised in an alcoholic home. The social conditions could have predisposed daughters to alcoholism. Alternatively, the genetic background, a concomitant of social disruption in the family of origin could have caused alcoholism in the daughter. Both hypotheses are equally viable possibilities.

The hypothesis that drinking allows heightened femininity to emerge should be further explored. Wilsnak's choice of dependent measures to tap femininity can be questioned. An existential focus (concern with the moment rather as opposed to future goal orientation) would certainly be expected to emerge during the nursing experience. It might also be expected to emerge in fathers after the birth of a new baby. Such a philosophical shift however may not be more characteristic of one sex than the other. The fact that drinking allows philosophical concerns to emerge has been demonstrated in men (Kalin, McClelland, & Kahn, 1965). It would seem that Wilsnack demonstrated the same phenomenon in women.

The finding that women expect to be more feminine after imbibing is intriguing. Caution should be exercised however in moving from an expectation of how behavior will be affected by a drug, to positing a motivation for using the drug. Women expect alcohol to impair their performance also. The inference that women drink because they wish to display impaired performance requires proof of additional assumptions.

Summary

About 5% of females are alcoholic. The modal female pattern of alcoholism does differ from the modal male pattern. Problem drinking in women develops later in life, accelerates beyond a problem threshold more rapidly, and a stressful precipitant is more likely to be identified. Women are more frequently primary depressed/secondary alcoholics than are men. Some have questioned whether the etiological factors in women are the same as in men. The bottomline is not yet available. There is tentative suggestion that treatment specifically developed for women may result in better outcome.

Alcoholism in the Elderly

Drinking is less likely in persons over 65 (Schuckit & Miller, 1976) and alcoholism is less prevalent in older than younger individuals (Finney & Moos, 1984; McCrady & Sher, 1983). Using a criteria of loss of control over drinking, 6% of males between 61 and 70 and 2% of males over 70 can be categorized as alcoholic (Finney & Moos, 1984). Although the elderly are not as a group at risk for alcoholism, concern over the issue has emerged. The fact that older people are comprising a larger percentage of the population suggests that there will be more older alcoholics numerically, than there were previously. Unlike other age groups, female alcoholics outnumber male alcoholics three to one in populations over 65 (Rosin & Glatt, 1971). However, this finding must be evaluated in light of the fact that in samples of the elderly, women always outnumber the men. In community surveys, elderly male widowers display higher rates of heavy drinking than their female counterparts, suggesting that the risk factor for alcoholism is still greater for males than females even at advanced ages (Zimberg, 1974a).

The problems attributable to alcoholism are different in the elderly than in younger populations. Whereas the young display social problem, health problems are more likely to emerge in older populations (Schuckit & Miller, 1976). Increased health problems can clearly be expected given that the liver is less efficient and that the decreased volume of muscle tissue in the elderly will promote higher blood alcohol levels. Self-neglect, falls, excessive incontinence, and confusion are high probability complaints given a sample of geriatric alcoholics (Schuckit & Miller, 1976).

Zimberg (1974a) suggests that alcoholics over 65 can be differentiated into those whose alcoholism emerged at an earlier age vs. those who initiated their problematic drinking after the age of 50. Given a population of alcoholics over 65, the former will comprise roughly 66% of the group (Finney & Moos, 1984; Rosin & Glatt, 1971). Those elderly alcoholics whose drinking emerged after 50, can more often identify specific stressful events (retirement, death of a spouse, onset of a chronic debilitating illness) that preceded their heavy drinking (Rosin & Glatt, 1971). Finney and Moos (1984) have examined the population of elderly alcoholics to explore the issue of whether stress (certainly more likely to occur in aging populations) causes alcoholism. They conclude that by itself, stress does not cause alcoholism. However, given a combination of factors (conditions conducive to unrestrained behavior, a history of moderate social drinking, etc.) then stress can contribute to the risk.

Skid Row Derelicts

The existence of a skid row community has received acknowledgment by the sociological community (Feeney et al., 1955). This community does overlap with alcoholism, but is certainly not identical. It is generally estimated that only 5% of the alcoholics in the United States reside on skid row; further, only 5% of those on skid row are alcoholics (Feldman et al., 1975, p. 408; Wiseman, 1982), although more recent estimates from homeless shelters places the estimate between 22.9% to 62.9% if alcoholism is measured by a life time diagnosis. The distinguishing feature of those on skid row seems to be poverty. Most individuals are not regularly employed and if working, are engaged in day labor endeavors. Blumberg et al. (1971) observes that as a demographic area, skid row is dominated by symbols of heavy drinking, the detox center, and bars. Although other institutions (missions and Salvation Army) provide services to all types of destitute individuals.

A recent study in Los Angeles has attempted to identify characteristics of today's homeless alcoholics (Koegel & Burnam, 1988). Homeless alcoholics are distinguished from other alcoholics in that they are younger and more often Black. The trend toward a younger age is recent. In the past the alcoholic denizens of skid row had been older than other residents. The changing characteristics of homeless alcoholics reflect emerging societal trends of economic dislocation for the less educated and minority groups as well as deinstitutionalization of the chronically mentally ill.

Kogel and Burnam (1988) made additional observations regarding those on skid row. Homeless alcoholics (skid row) as contrasted with nonhomeless alcoholics are less well educated themselves and have parent's who are poorly educated. Fourteen and a half percent of homeless alcoholics in a Los Angeles sample were found to have a concurrent diagnosis of schizophrenia. In contrast to nonhomeless alcoholics, the homeless alcoholics drank more heavily, had experienced more severe and frequent withdrawal, and alcohol had interfered to a greater extent with their social functioning. Comparisons of new and old alcoholic homeless residents indicated that the drinking habits of the former were less severe than the latter. Although the denizens of skid row display alcohol problems prior to becoming residents, there is reason to believe that living conditions exacerbate the alcoholism.

There is a unique culture that has emerged in skid row and new arrivals are enculturated by older residents who provide information on availability of services and survival skills. The longer the individual resides on skid row the less likely that friendships outside the area will be maintained and the more likely that friendships within the community will be established (Blumberg et al., 1971). There is little sharing of information about former lives (Blumberg et al., 1971). There is strong evidence that skid row is a hostile environment in which to reside. One-third of residents report having been robbed or mugged in the prior year (Blumberg et al. 1971). It is common practice for money to be taken from intoxicated individuals. The hotels and bars in the area offer loans at usurious rates of interest. Information quickly spreads regarding the arrival of SSI checks.

About 25% of the residents self-describe themselves as members of skid row. In one study the terms nominated to describe oneself included "drunk, lush, wino, teetotaler, ex-con, mission stiff, homeguard, panhandler, vagrant, hobo, migratory worker, and retired worker (Blumberg et al., 1971).

Whereas the foregoing suggest that denizens of skid row acknowledge heavy drinking, Wiseman (1982) has concluded that drinking is not viewed as the major problem of life. The issue of drinking is overshadowed by more pressing concerns of finding food and shelter and avoiding exploitation. Indeed, hospitalization and jail may be viewed not as opportunities for changing one's life style but rather an answer to the more short-term problem of finding food and shelter. Skid row residents compared to problem drinkers do display lower self-esteem (Lovald & Neuwirth, 1968). However, they do not manifest guilt over their drinking (Lovald & Neuwirth, 1968). Perhaps the bad feelings of the skid row derelict represent shame rather than guilt. The essential difference between the two experiences is whether the internal attribution is stable or unstable. With guilt, one feels badly over an occurrence about which control could have been exercised. With shame, one feels badly but could not have acted otherwise.

Summary

Although only 5% of alcoholics reside on skid row, this group of alcoholics does constitute a unique segment of the alcoholic population. The problems of this group are special. They are confronted with the daily issue of locating food and shelter. They are constantly threatened by physical assault and exploitation. Treatment for this group requires special tailoring. The drinking in the lives of these individuals is not the primary concern as it is eclipsed by so many other life threatening conditions.

Bingers vs. Continuous Drinkers

One obvious way in which alcoholics differ from each other is in the heterogeneity of their drinking patterns. Two contrasting variations are binge drinkers vs. continuous drinkers. Bingers are those alcoholics who maintain abstinence for months or years and then consume large quantities continuously over a several day period. This binge pattern contrasts with alcoholics who are daily drinkers consuming roughly the same amount each day. Jellinek suggested that the binge pattern is a later stage development in the alcoholic progression. He also advanced a typology notion that distinguished a binge drinker, the epsilon type. Enough empirical data is now available to evaluate the ways in which binge drinkers might differ from other alcoholics. Some research contrasting in bingers with more regularly consuming alcoholics follows.

Walton (1968) classified inpatient alcoholics as loss of control types or inability to abstain types harkening back to Jellinek's distinction between gamma and delta alcoholics. The loss of control types were those who abstained for periods but became notably intoxicated during drinking episodes (bingers). The inability to abstain types were characterized by a regular pattern of daily drinking. The bingers and regular drinkers proved to be remarkably similar in terms of their personalities. The only personality dimension that succeeded in distinguishing the groups was the enhanced apprehension regarding the possibility of a careless indisgression, which was elevated among the loss of control types.

Schuckit, Rimmer, Reich, and Winokur (1971) compared bender alcoholics (defined as 48 hours of drinking concomitant with neglect of usual responsibilities) with others. The benders did not differ in family background. As a group they were older, with relatively more social and health problems. Similar findings were reported by Tomsovic (1974). Although Tomsovic's binge vs. continuous drinkers did not differ on age, the bingers had been drinking problematically for a longer period of time. They had had more experience with hospitalization and AA, and had been working to maintain sobriety for a longer period of time. Further, they reported having experienced more deleterious consequences from their drinking (blackouts, dts, trouble with the law, neuropathy, days missed on the job). Connors, Tarbox, and McLaughlin (1986) also contrasted binge pattern alcoholics with other alcoholics. Unlike Schuckit et al., Connors et al. found more frequent family history among the bingers. Further, Connors et al. replicated the finding of increased problem severity among the bingers.

Whereas the prior research contrasted bingers vs. alcoholics with other types of drinking patterns, some researchers have sought to determine which characteristics from a menu of characteristics would cluster together. Morey, Skinner, and Blashfield (1984) administered a host of instruments to alcoholics in treatment in order to identify typologies. Three types were discerned. One of these types was a binge type, characterized by the most extreme psychological distress, a binge pattern during which imbibing occurred in a solitary context, extreme physical dependence, and extreme social role maladaptation (divorce, job loss, etc.). Distinguished from the binge pattern was a daily drinker type. This second pattern was described by gregarious drinking and continuous daily drinking pattern marked by some physical dependence although not as severe as the binge type. Thus, Morey et al. were able to distinguish binge drinker alcoholics from those whose pattern is less irregular. Morey et al. differentiated an additional type as well. This type had not manifested extreme physical dependence or social role maladaptation. Compared to the binge type, this group had a shorter history of alcoholic drinking.

Some unusual findings are emerging from Jacobs and colleagues. These findings are detailed in the family section. In Jacob's studies, the daily drinker vs. the binge drinker keep emerging as distinct types. Jacob's data suggest that among the daily drinkers, alcohol improves the social functioning of the drinker and the mood of the spouse, where the opposite is the case for the bingers.

Comment. Several investigators have found that bingers have more protracted drinking histories than other types. The research just discussed evaluated drinking patterns at one point in time. Whether any given alcoholic exhibited another drinking pattern in the past, which was later replaced by binging, was not examined. However, the longer drinking history in the bingers is consistent with Jellinek's hypothesis that binges are an end stage finding. Binging seems to represent an adaptation to drinking associated with extreme deleterious consequences. It represents a compromise position, wherein the person most often seeks sobriety but occasional indiscretions punctuate the abstinent pattern. The high concentrations of alcohol consumed within a short window of time does seem to be associated with the more severe alcoholic sequela.

Primary Vs. Secondary Alcoholism

In one of the earliest attempts to subtype alcoholics, Knight (1937) applied the essential and reactive dichotomy, in vogue in his day for differentiating populations of schizophrenics, to alcoholics. Later, Schuckit and colleagues (Schuckit, 1980c; Schuckit, Pitts, Reich, King, & Winokur, 1969) suggested a similar dichotomy. Schuckit has been a strong exponent of the utility of differentiating alcoholics whose alcoholism has not been preceded by a prior psychiatric condition vs. those alcoholics whose problematic drinking may have developed in response to a prior major psychiatric diagnosis. Differentiating the primaries from the secondaries is useful in predicting course of the disease. Predictions for secondary alcoholics are more likely to follow the path of their primary disorder rather than the path of primary alcoholism.

In a sample of hospitalized alcoholics, 78% were found to exhibit primary alcoholism. The most frequently occurring types of secondary alcoholics are those in whom the primary disorder is antisocial personality and those in whom the primary disorder is depression (Schuckit, 1979). There are also some secondary alcoholics who are attempting to self-medicate the manic phase of Manic Depressive Illness (O'Sullivan, Whillans, Daly, Carroll, Clare, & Cooney, 1983).

Secondary alcoholics who are primary depressives represent about 5–10% of alcoholics presenting for treatment. Schuckit (1979) estimates that 20% of females and 5% of male alcoholics will be primary depressed. Although Powell et al. (1987) estimate the rate in males to be be 2–3% Primary depressive/secondary alcoholics have fewer alcoholic relatives than primary alcoholics. They have more depressed relatives than primary alcoholics. Depressives are more often divorced than primary alcoholics and display fewer health problems than primaries (Schuckit, 1985). Although primary depressive/secondary alcoholics may be attempting to self-medicate their conditions, the hypothesis that depression alone causes alcoholism does not follow. Only 5–10% of those displaying affective disorders are secondary alcoholics (Schuckit, 1986). Primary depressive/secondary alcoholics display better outcomes than do primary alcoholics and primary ASP/secondary alcoholics (Schuckit, 1985).

Ross, Glaser, and Germanson (1988) found that 47% of their alcoholic sample met the DSM-III criteria for ASP, although these authors did not differentiate according to whether alcoholic drinking had predated or postdated the occurrence of alcoholic drinking. Schuckit (1979) estimates the rate of primary ASP in a male sample of alcoholics to be 20% and 5% in a female sample of alcoholics. Secondary alcoholics who are primary ASPs exhibit less favorable outcomes than do the primaries. They develop their alcoholism earlier in life. They are more likely to have attempted suicide than are the primaries, and more likely to abuse drugs as well as alcohol. As a group, they are less well educated than primary alcoholics. In some samples they have been observed to drink more than do primary alcoholics (Schuckit, 1985), although in other samples late onsetters have been found to drink more (Schuckit, Rimmer, Reich, & Winokur, 1970). They display a higher rate of alcoholic relatives than primaries and depressed alcoholics, and also higher rates of familial ASP (Winokur study, cited by Schuckit, 1973).

MMPI Code Types

The MMPI has been used to investigate the personalities of alcoholics. There have been several ways in which it has been employed. Some have sought to identify those scales among the original 10 pathology scales on which alcoholics as a group achieve significant elevations. This research was discussed earlier. Others have begun with the assumption that alcoholics are probably a homogeneous group such that employing techniques that average across types will obscure extant typologies. Given this assumption, researchers have employed cluster analytic techniques to assist in identifying types of alcoholics. Some major findings from this endeavor are discussed here. Finally, MMPI items have also been used to develop specific scales that will distinguish alcoholic populations from psychiatric controls and from normals. The next topic, assessment devices for identifying alcoholics from others, discusses the MMPI scale used to identifying alcoholics.

Types of Alcoholics Identified Through Cluster Analysis

Blashfield (1985) published a review of studies that attempted to identify clusters of alcoholics employing the MMPI. In his analysis, Blashfield examined the data from 11 cluster analyses and employed meta-analytic statistics. He concluded that two profile types emerged. The first consists of a generally low profile with a peak elevation on scale 4 (psychopathic deviance). The second is typified by higher elevations on all scales with peak elevations on scales 2, 7, and 8 (Depression, Psychasthenia, and Schizophrenia).

Analyzing responses from an alcoholic sample, Goldstein and Linden (1969) reported that 4 distinct cluster types succeeded in describing 45% of alcoholics. These types have been used as typologies for later research. The first pattern is characterized by primary elevation on the psychopathy scale and secondary elevation on the depression scale. This scale type is the most frequent profile achieved by alcoholics (Clopton, 1978). Type II displays primary elevations on the depression, psychasthenia, and schizophrenia scales with secondary elevations on the psychopathy scale. Type II alcoholics drink more than Type I alcoholics (Graham & Strenger, 1988; Morey & Bashfield, 1981). Type III alcoholics achieve elevations on the psychopathy scale and either the depression or hypomania scale. Type IV alcoholics achieve elevation on psychopathy and hypomania scales. All scale types have been replicated by others (Graham & Strenger, 1988).

Donovan, Chaney, and O'Leary (1978) administered the MMPI and the Alcohol Use Inventory (AUI) to primary alcoholics in treatment at a VA hospital. The Alcohol Use Inventory is discussed later in this chapter. It provides information about the pattern of an alcoholic's behavior. By administering the MMPI and the AUI together, Donovan et al. (1978) were further able to differentiate empirical types. In their analysis, Donovan et al. differentiated alcoholics according to the Golden and Linden types. Correlating Golden and Linden types with the AUI scales, they found no differences in terms of usual setting for drinking (gregarious, social, or solitary); the pattern of drinking (sustained or binging), the use of alcohol to modify mood, or the quantity of alcohol consumed. The following differences were obtained: Type IIs were distinguished by reliance on drinking to enhance ability to relate interpersonally and to alleviate social anxiety. Type IIs more often perceived that alcohol would improve their intellectual functioning. Type IIs more often reported obsessions with alcohol and worry and guilt regarding their drinking. They more often had attempted to curtail their drinking often through reliance on external means. Further, Type IIs evidenced more severe physical, psychological, and social impairment attributable to drinking. In a similar study, Type Is and IIs were found to have experienced fewer drunk days during the 1 year follow-up period than had Type IIIs and IVs (O'Leary, Donovan, Chaney, & O'Leary, 1980).

It has been recognized that the profile types identified in alcoholic populations are not unique. Given enough persons, it was speculated that most MMPI types recognized in hospital populations will emerge for alcoholics as well (Apfeldorf & Hunley, 1985; Skinner, Jackson, & Hoffman, 1974). The recognition that alcoholics are probably as diverse as the general population is useful. Less often discussed in the literature is the recognition that a particular profile achieved by a heavy consumer may not imply the same things as it would in a nondrinker. For example, an elevated depression scale in a nondrinker most likely reflects a depressive person with all the implications for cognitive processing that this diagnosis implies. If an alcoholic achieves a elevated depression scale, a state of depression induced by heavy consumption is reflected. The personality structure may be quite different than the nondrinking person who achieves an elevated depression scale. Hence, scale implications are probably different for alcoholics than for others.

There have been attempts to relate typologies to other variables. Older alcoholics are more likely to display elevations on distress scales as opposed to elevations on 4 (Psychopathic Deviance) and 9 (Mania). In a middle-class treatment center, the 4/9s displayed more favorable treatment outcomes (abstinent at 12 months, improved social relationships, improved self-image) than did those displaying greater elevations on scales 2 (Depression) and 7 (Psychasthenia), which were assessed within a week of admission (Conley, 1981). Whereas the 4/9s displayed the better outcomes, their MMPI profiles changed less over the course of treatment than did those displaying greater psychological distress (Conley, 1981). The significance of the distress scales may be related to treatment outcome, through the variable of severity of alcoholism. Distress scales are correlated with amount consumed and more severe abuse (Whitelock, Overall, & Patrick, 1971). The more severe the alcoholism, usually the worse the prognosis on any given treatment occasion (see chapter 5 on outcome studies).

TESTS FOR IDENTIFYING ALCOHOLICS FROM OTHERS

MMPI Scales Constructed for the Identification of Alcoholics

MacAndrew (1983) has reviewed the efforts to discriminate populations of alcoholics from samples of normals or psychiatric controls using items from the MMPI. Early efforts yielded the Hampton, the Holmes, and the Hoyt and Sedlack scales. Only 7 items appeared on all three scales with the same scoring. These items were: (1) I have not lived the right kind of life; (2) I go to church almost every week; (3) I know who is responsible for most of my troubles; (4) I have used alcohol excessively; (5) I have never been in trouble with the law; (6) I have used alcohol moderately or not at all; (7) The only miracles I know of are simply tricks that people play on one another. Given the relative lack of item overlap among the scales, MacAndrew concluded that little intrinsic to core personality of alcoholics had been extracted by the scales. The Hampton scale (1953) correlates highly with the Welsh anxiety scale. The Hoyt/Sedlacek (1958) contains many Psychopathic Deviance scale items (Apfeldorf, 1978). In addition to the scale discussed by MacAndrew; Atsaides, Neuringer, and Davis (1977); Rich and Davis (1969), and Rosenberg (1972) have also published measures for identifying alcoholics using the MMPI.

Zager and Megargee (1981) employed the Hampton, Holmes, Hoyt/Sedlacek, MacAndrew, Rich and Davis, Rosenberg, Atsaides et al. MMPI scales as well as several drug abuse scales to assess a population of criminals. They found significant correlations between the Hoyt/Sedlacek and the Rosenberg; the MacAndrew and the Atsaides et al.; the MacAndrew and the Hampton, and the Hampton and the Atsaides et al. In this population, the Atsaides et al. scale alone was able to discriminate the alcohol abusing from the nonabusing among White inmates.

MacAndrew Scale

Perhaps the most robust of scales developed to identify alcoholics has been the MacAndrew scale (1965), a 51-item scale in which only 2 of the items directly ask about drinking. The MacAndrew scale has succeeded in differentiating alcoholics from normals and psychiatric patients. Across 16 investigations, true positive have averaged 85% with a range of 79 to 97.5% (MacAndrew, 1983). The false positive rate varies with the age of the population. In a college age sample, 28% of the sample unselected for drinking problems but possibly containing some potential or extant alcoholics, was labeled alcoholic by the MacAndrew (MacAndrew, 1979a). In older male samples of medical patients and general population, the MacAndrew labeled 38% of the sample alcoholic (Davis et al., 1987a). The internal consistency of the scale is rather low (.49 for male alcoholics) (Davis et al., 1987a).

In some populations the MacAndrew scale is a poor discriminator of alcoholism. Like alcoholics, drug abusers and gamblers achieve elevated MacAndrew scores (Graham & Strenger, 1988) as do heavy smokers (Leon, Kolotkin, & Korgeski, 1979). Criminally deviant also achieve high scores (MacAndrew, 1981a; Zager & Megargee, 1981). The scale does not differentiate as well in Black male samples (Graham & Strenger, 1988). The scale has been found to differentiate female alcoholics from female psychiatric patients, although a lower cutoff score is recommended for differentiating female alcoholics (Svanum, Levitt, & McAdoo, 1982). Recently, MacAndrew (1988) has published a more refined measure for discriminating female alcoholics.

There are several dimensions along which alcoholics are suggested to be better off by the MacAndrew. Alcoholics claim more social competence, have an easier time concentrating, and are more free of worry over sex matters (MacAndrew, 1967). They endorse items suggesting a penchant for risk taking and gambling. They also endorse items suggesting a fundamentalist interpretation of God and affirmation of deserving punishment for sins (MacAndrew, 1967). The MacAndrew scales correlates with the hypomania scale of the MMPI (scale 9), with the Wiggins hypomania scale, with the Wiggins authority conflict scale, and with the Wiggins manifest hostility scale. High negative correlations with the MMPI K scale and Welsh repression scale, suggest that high MacAndrews present themselves in a straight forward, nondefensive manner (Schwartz & Graham, 1979). MacAndrew (1981a) characterizes his scale as tapping a basic personality dimension of orientation toward positive reinforcement. Whereas some are motivated to avoid aversive consequences, alcoholics identified from the MacAndrew scale, are seekers of positive experiences.

The MacAndrew scale does not change appreciably with sobriety, suggesting that the instrument is assessing a stable trait (Graham & Strenger, 1988). The fact that in a longitudinal study (Hoffmann, Loper, & Kammeier, 1974) prealcoholics achieved elevated MacAndrew scores, suggests that the scale is not assessing the consequences of alcoholism (Graham & Strenger, 1988). Rather, if alcoholics have any one personality style, it is reflected in the MacAndrew.

Who Are the False Negatives?   Although the MacAndrew will identify about 85% of alcoholics, there are false negatives. MacÁndrew (1981a) labels these individuals as neurotic, depressed alcoholics. They cannot be distinguished off the MMPI from other psychiatric patients. The suggestion is that these alcoholics correspond to Schuckit's secondary alcoholic/primary depressives who develop their problem drinking as a coping mechanism for their primary depression which temporally precedes the alcoholism. They more often report a discrete precipitating event to the onset of their problematic drinking.

Factor Analyses.   There have been three factor analyses of the MacAndrew scale. In each, researchers conducted their analyses on different populations. MacAndrew (1967) factor analyzed the responses of male alcoholic outpatients. Schwartz and Graham (1979) conducted a factor analysis of the combined responses of populations of male alcoholic inpatients, male psychiatric inpatients, female alcoholic inpatients, and female psychiatric inpatients. Svanum and Hoffman (1982) factor analyzed the responses of male and female inpatient alcoholics. Some consistency in factor structures has been obtained.

Both Svanum and Hoffman (1982) and Schwartz and Graham (1979) derived a cognitive impairment factor. Svanum and Hoffman attributed MacAndrew's failure to identify this factor to an absence of cognitive impairment in a sample of outpatient alcoholics who can be expected to display less severe sequale resulting from alcohol intake. Interestingly, on the original MacAndrew scale the cognitive impairment items are scored in the direction of less impairment. However, on the cognitive impairment factors of Svanum and Hoffman and Schwartz and Graham, these items are scored in the direction of more impairment. This suggests that the meaning of the items changes in populations of inpatient alcoholics. In the inpatient sample, the cognitive impairment factor may be reflecting the consequences of drinking rather than a stable personality dimension.

All factor analyses have identified a school maladjustment factor, an interpersonal competence factor, and a risk taking factor. Svanum and Hoffman's analysis additionally found a fundamental religious orientation factor and a blackout/memory loss factor. Schwartz and Graham's fifth and sixth factors were moral indignation and exhibition/extroversion. MacAndrews (1967) factor structure contained 13 factors. In addition to the school maladjustment, risk taking, and interpersonal competence factors were ability to concentrate, lack of sexual preoccupation, freedom from parental control, identification with a female caregiver, endorsement of living the wrong kind of life, religiosity and guilt, self-responsibility for one's troubles, chronic deterioration, blackouts, and bodily complaints.

Robustness to Faking Good.   Otto et al. (1988) compared the responses of VA alcoholics and VA medical patients under instructions to hide shortcomings vs. standard instructions. The MacAndrew scores of subjects were significantly less elevated under the hide shortcoming instructions. However, the validity scales of the dissimulators were also elevated, making it possible to identify those faking good. Only 3 out of 40 dissimulators avoided detection by both the MacAndrew scale and the validity scale. The validity scales employed in the study consisted of decision rules combining the usual validity scales in addition to several specifically constructed scales. The Otto et al. study does suggest that when used in conjunction with validity scales, the MacAndrew is difficult to fake.

Other Measures for Identifying Alcoholics: MAST, CAGE, and Laboratory Tests

MAST.   The Michigan Alcoholism Screening Test (MAST) was developed by Selzer (1971). Selzer (1971) provides the following information. The MAST consists of 25 face valid items designed to discriminate alcoholics from normals. Most items either describe extreme drinking practices or establish the presence of deleterious results of extreme drinking. The test has been found to discriminate between hospitalized alcoholics and medical patients from an outpatient allergy clinic. Items are weighted according to their diagnostic utility. The most discriminating items being (Have you ever attended a meeting of AA? Have you ever gone to anyone for help about your drinking? Have you ever been in a hospital because of drinking?).

Selzer (1971) does indicate that alcoholics wishing to avoid detection can do so. He also reports that alcoholics instructed to fake good on the test, were still identified by test. In a sample of hospitalized alcoholics, internal consistency among the items was .93 (Skinner & Allen, 1983a). In a hospital sample the two items that discriminated best were "Have you ever had a drinking problem" and "When was your last drink? (scored positive if within the last 24 hours). Answers to the latter question identified 91.5% of the alcoholics (Cyr & Wartmen, 1988).

A shortened 10-item version of the MAST has been presented by Pokorny, Miller, and Kaplan (1972), which correlates .99 with the original version. The MAST has been modified such that self-administration is possible. The new version, the SMAST, is a 35-item questionnaire. Research examining the SMAST administered to a general population sample suggests that items regarding whether an individual labels his/her drinking as aberrant (Do you feel you are a normal drinker? Do friends or relatives think you are a normal drinker?) can be interpreted in more than one fashion. Many of the very light drinkers, probably consuming less than normative amounts, responded positively to these items (Harburg et al., 1988), which may explain the finding that in populations containing few alcoholics, the Brief MAST, SMAST, and MAST have been found to correlate negatively with an amount consumed per occasion measure (Lee & DeFrank, 1988). Harburg et al. (1988) suggest that leaving out the above 2 items creates a scale that correlates more highly with consumption measures.

Davis, Hurt, Morse, and O'Brien (1987b) administered the SMAST as well as a 9-item version of the SMAST to 1156 subjects (520 alcoholics and 636 controls). The researchers found that both versions of the SMAST identified 92.1% of the alcoholics while incorrectly classifying only 1.3% of controls.

In the Davis et al. study (1987b) two items correctly classified 80.9% of the alcoholics while falsely identifying only 3.6% of the controls. The items were "Do close relatives ever worry or complain about your drinking?" and "Have you ever felt the need to cut down on your drinking?" The Davis et al. findings were consistent with Harburg et al.'s (1988) findings. Items tapping family problems and help seeking best differentiated consumption levels per occasion, unsuccessfully attempting to quit, hangovers, and persons exhibiting dysphoria.

Another useful suggestion has been made by Lee and Frank (1988). If the investigator wishes to identify current heavy consumers, it has been suggested that a time frame for the MAST items be provided.

The CAGE.   The CAGE was developed to identify alcoholics in hospital populations. It has been reported to successfully distinguish those with alcohol problems in hospital samples (Ewing, 1984; King, 1986). The CAGE consists of 4 items: Have you ever felt you ought to cut down on your drinking? Have people annoyed you by criticizing your drinking? Have you ever felt bad or guilty about your drinking? Have you ever had a drink first thing in the morning to steady your nerves or get rid of a hangover? A positive response to 2 or more questions will classify an individual as alcoholic. In a hospital sample, all of the CAGE positives were drinking more than 8 drinks per day, although one-third of the CAGE negatives were drinking at this level. In a sample of health clinic attenders, the CAGE demonstrated a sensitivity of 84% and a specificity of 95% in identifying those consuming over 8 drinks per day (King, 1986). In a general population sample, it was found to correlate with mean corpuscular volume (Lee & DeFrank, 1988).

Mayfield, McLeod, and Hall (1974) found that the least sensitive item on the CAGE was "Have people annoyed you by criticizing your drinking? In their sample, 50% of the alcoholics failed to endorse this item. Ewing (1984) provided further information on false detection. He found that 9% of normals from a general hospital population indicated having considered cutting down on their drinking. Fifteen percent of normals reported having felt guilty over their drinking. None of the normals endorsed the item concerning criticism by others or morning drinking.

Laboratory Tests.   Given the predictable impact of alcohol on physiology, laboratory tests that identify heavy drinkers have been proffered. There are some positive findings in that blood test indices often covary with other measures of alcoholism, however, false negatives are rather high when blood test indices are employed to identify alcoholics. Some of the specific findings are now reported.

Mean corpuscular volume (MCV), an index of unusually large red blood cells, has been found to correlate with the CAGE and amount consumed per occasion. Across studies the range in correlation has been .25 to .44 (Lee & DeFrank, 1988). Gamma glutamyl transferase (GGT) is an index of liver cell damage. In a study by Bernadt et al. (1982) it failed to detect two-thirds of the excessive drinkers. When psychiatric diagnoses for alcoholism are employed, there are many false negatives on the GGT and MCV (Bernadt et al., 1984). Skinner, Holt, Schuller, Roy, and Israel (1984) also found that the number of false negatives on blood test indices (Mean corpuscular volume, Gamma glutamyl transferase, and high density lipoproteins) are rather high (60–70% false negatives) although true positives are also high (90%). Skinner et al. (1984) combined blood tests with a questionnaire assessing trauma, which increased the accuracy of prediction.

Watson et al. (1986) have reviewed the laboratory markers that have been employed to detect heavy alcohol consumption. Prior to the development of alcohol induced organ damage, changes in mean corpuscular volume (size of red blood cells), GGT, high density lipoproteins, and ferritin were not sensitive indices. Liver enzymes (alkaline phosphatase, AST, and GGT) will often be elevated in those who are daily drinkers but will not be sensitive markers of binge drinking. Promising measures include erythrocyte calcium, serum transferrin microheterogeneity abnormality, the serum activity of mitochondrial aspartate aminotransferase and its ratio with total aspartate aminotransferase activity.

Several discriminant analyses have been performed yielding indices for correctly classifying heavy consumers vs. moderate consumers. Discriminant functions have included serum iron values (which are elevated), blood urea nitrogen, creatine levels, as well as changes in immunoglobins (Watson et al., 1986).

Behrens et al. (1988) were able to identify 80% of a racially mixed sample of alcoholics by examining plasma elevations in carbohydrate-deficient transferrin, a glycoprotein produced by the liver. The urine also contains clues for heavy drinking. Roine et al. (1987) was able to correctly identify 68% of alcoholics and only falsely identify 3.9% of controls by examining elevations of urinary dolichol.

ASSESSMENT MEASURES TO ASSIST IN THE TREATMENT PROCESS

Comprehensive Drinking Profile

Miller and Marlatt (1984) have published the Comprehensive Drinking Profile through Psychological Assessment Resources. This instrument provides guidelines and questions for a structured interview as well as a system for scoring. The authors provide normative information from 103 outpatients in treatment at a university clinic. They caution that such patients represent a less severely effected population than might be encountered in other settings. The test provides assessment of dimensions of family history, social stability, drinking history, drinking pattern, alcohol-related life problems, alcohol dependence, topology of drinking behavior, reasons for drinking and positive expectations regarding the impact of alcohol, and motivation for treatment.

Intuition suggests that the dimensions assessed by the Comprehensive Drinking Profile are certainly relevant. Empirical support relating person variables to treatment modalities is lacking, however (see chapter on outcome studies). Such being the case, the results of assessment will not imply clear treatment strategies. Although the promise of improved treatment given tailoring of treatment to the individual has yet to be fulfilled, such extensive individual evaluation is useful on additional grounds. The instrument offers a stimulus for inducing the patient to think about his/her own behavior, which may prove to be a necessary step for enhancing motivation as well as successful behavioral change. The thoroughness of the assessment also may prove useful for future research endeavors, perhaps revealing which treatments best serve specific types of individuals.

Alcohol Use Inventory

The Alcohol Use Inventory consists of 147 multiple-choice items. The test was developed on subject samples of over 3000 patients and development included a series of factor analyses. The AUI items have yielded 16 factors, 5 second-order factors, and 1 third-order factor (Wanberg, Horn, & Foster, 1977). The AUI first-order factors were constructed to be relatively independent. Scales do not share items. The highest correlation between any two scales was .59 (obtained between scales 2 and 3). Internal consistency of the various scales ranged between .38 to .93 with most scales achieving a Kuder Richardson above .70. In an independent sample of alcoholics Skinner and Allen (1983a) report a median reliability of .72 for the 16 primary scales. Wanberg et al. (1977) report the following first order factors:

1. Drinking to improve sociability
2. Drinking to improve mental functioning
3. Gregarious vs. solitary drinking
4. Obsessive-compulsive drinking (e.g., hiding bottles, sneaking drinks, drinking during workday)
5. Continuous, sustained drinking-refers to daily, heavy drinking unpunctuated by sober hiatuses
6. Post drinking worry, fear, and guilt
7. Drinking to change mood
8. External support to stop drinking (refers to prior attendance at AA, having used disulfiram, tranquilizers, etc.)
9. Loss of behavior control when drinking (refers to blackouts, passing out, gulping drinks, exhibiting belligerence)
10. Social-role maladjustment (includes loss of job, being jailed for drunkenness, etc.)
11. Psychoperceptal withdrawal (includes alcohol hallucinosis, dts, etc.)
12. Psychophysical withdrawal (refers to convulsions, shakes, hangovers, etc.)
13. Nonalcoholic drug use
14. Quantity of alcohol used
15. Drinking followed marital problems (refers to attribution of drinking to marital troubles)
16. Drinking provoke marital problems

Second-order factors reflect correlations among the scales. Again, there is no item overlap among the factors. Five second-order factors were extracted.

A. Self-enhancement drinking reflects both social benefits, mental benefit drinking, drinking to change mood often in a gregarious drinking context

B. Obsessive, sustained drinking captures a sustained pattern in a person who ensures his/her supply by sneaking, planning, hiding bottle, etc.

C. Anxiety related to drinking reflects own concern as well as polarized feelings with regard to other's reactions to one's own drinking

D1. Alcoholic deterioration reflects total amount consumed, which is correlated with physical consequences, overt intoxicated behavior, and marital and occupational consequences

D2. Alcoholic deterioration of an adjunct variety reflecting endorsement of some disease model associated concepts (dry drunk, loss of control) as well as extreme behaviors or alterations in life structure to accommodate heavy drinking such as not sleeping during binges, drinking alcohol substitutes

A third-order factor of general alcoholism was also reported. This scale is comprised of items from all of the primary scales but is most closely associated with the two alcohol deterioration scales.

Wanberg et al. (1977) identified those factors that would predict sobriety at 6 month follow-up. Most predictive were the general alcoholism scale, the alcoholic deterioration scale (D1), and the social role maladaptation (10) scales. Also predictive were factors 6, 7, 8, 11, and 12 among the primary factors, and factors B, C, and D2 among the secondary factors.

Skinner and Allen (1983b) further examined the psychometric properties of the AUI in a population of alcoholics. They found inverse correlations between most of the primary scales and a social desirability scale, suggesting that those reporting extreme symptomotology are not concerned with creating a favorable impression. The AUI, particularly D1 scale and the General alcoholism scale were highly correlated with the MAST ($r = .72$; $r = .71$, respectively). Those scoring highly on the D1 scale showed more intellectual deterioration.

An additional factor analysis of the AUI along with several personality inventories, the MAST, and several other alcohol and drug interview schedules was presented by Skinner (1981). Four factors were extracted. The first was an alcohol dependence factor that encompassed loss of control, experience of withdrawal symptoms, social maladaptation, high quantity consumed per day, obsession over drinking, drinking to alter mood, seeking help for drinking. Persons scoring highly on this factor manifested more dysphoria and were less concerned about presenting a socially desirable picture. Factor II pertained to social and mental benefits from drinking. Persons scoring highly on this factor also manifested anxiety on personality measures. Scoring highly on factor II did not predict MAST scores nor did it predict alcohol dependence. Factor III captured marital problems encompassing both marital problem attributable to drinking and drinking attributable to marital problems. Persons scoring highly on this factor reported interpersonal aggression difficulties in other areas of their lives as well. Factor IV captured illicit drug use and suggested that illicit drug users tended to be gregarious as opposed to solitary drinkers. Further, the drug users reported drinking alcohol to enhance social functioning.

MEASURES ASSESSING SEVERITY OF PAST WITHDRAWAL

Alcohol Dependence Scale

Skinner and Allen (1982) reported the results of their development of a measure (Alcohol Dependence Scale) designed to assess the severity of alcohol dependence. They suggested that this measure might be employed to select candidates for control drinking vs. abstention goals. Refinement of the measure began with a scale from the Alcohol Use Inventory. This 29-item measure tapped such domains as (1) loss of behavioral control, which included blackouts and gulping drinks; (2) psychoperceptual withdrawal symptoms, which included hallucinations; (3) psychophysical withdrawal symptoms, which included hangovers and delirium tremens; and (4) obsessive-compulsive drinking, which included sneaking drinks and always having a bottle handy.

Skinner and Allen (1982) gave the Alcohol Dependence Scale to 225 alcoholics entering treatment. All appeared sober at assessment. Results supported the internal consistency of the measure (coefficient alpha = .92), suggesting that the scale assessed a core syndrome. The scale did correlate to a moderate degree with a social desirability scale which had also been administered. Correlation between the scale with the amount typically consumed by the alcoholic as well as social problems created by alcohol in the individual's life was noted.

A further evaluation of the Alcohol Dependence Scale was completed by Kivlahan et al. (1989) who administered the test to 268 VA alcoholics. The scale demonstrated good internal consistency (alpha = .85). It was related to the typical amount consumed prior to treatment, number of years of problem drinking prior to the present VA admission, and to the number of prior treatment occasions. It was modestly predictive of relapse in the months following treatment (r = .16). It did not predict aftercare attendance, program completion, or amount consumed during the follow-up interval.

SADQ (Severity of Alcohol Dependence Questionnaire)

Stockwell, Hodgson, Edwards, Taylor, and Rankin (1979) developed the Severity of Alcohol Dependence Questionnaire (SADQ). As originally presented this instrument was a 23-item questionnaire that was divided into the following sections: physical withdrawal (7 items querying about physical symptoms of withdrawal); affective withdrawal (7 items querying regarding mood during withdrawal); withdrawal relief (7 items asking about drinking to decrease withdrawal); typical daily consumption (6 items); and symptoms displayed "the morning after 2 days of heavy drinking following at least 4 weeks of abstention" (6 items asking about symptoms after a binge). In a subsequent paper, a new version of the original scale was evaluated. The second questionnaire contained only 20 items (Stockwell, Murphy, & Hodgson, 1983). Respondents were instructed to focus on their most recent period of heavy drinking, if this episode was also typical of their heavy drinking. Results of factor analysis extracted one general factor suggesting that the five domains from the original scale were highly intercorrelated. Test-retest reliabilities with 2-week intervals between test administrations was .85 (Stockwell et al. 1983). The measure corresponded with clinical ratings of alcohol dependence (Stockwell et al., 1979). The measure also correlated with typical amount consumed per day, subjective cravings, amount of medication administered during detoxification, and with pattern of typical drinking (Stockwell et al., 1983). Bingers and consistent daily drinkers achieved higher scores on the SADQ than did those who did not drink daily and were not characterized by extremely heavy protracted drinking (Stockwell et al., 1983).

MEASURES ASSESSING CURRENT WITHDRAWAL SYMPTOMATOLOGY

The Clinical Institute Withdrawal Assessment for Alcohol (CIWA-A)

The CIWA-A was developed at the Addiction Research Foundation in Toronto (Sullivan et al., 1989). Scale developers relied on prior work by Gross and colleagues who had provided description of alcohol withdrawal phenomenon. The scale consists of withdrawal dimensions rated as to degree of presence or absence. Withdrawal dimensions include: nausea/vomiting, tremor, paroxysmal sweats, anxiety, agitation, tactile disturbances, visual disturbances, headaches or fullness in head, orientation and clouding of sersorium. The scale has been employed by Wartenberg et al. (1990) to train physician's in assessing withdrawal severity. After training physicians decreased the number of patients given benzodiazepines for withdrawal (from 73% to 13%). Foy, March, and Drinkwater (1988) employed an earlier version of the CIWA to assess withdrawal severity in a hospital population. They established a cutoff score above which the risk for later severe withdrawal (hallucinations, seizures, or confusion) was increased. Patients, who were left unmedicated, scoring below the cutoff score were not found to develop severe withdrawal except in those cases in which another medical condition (head injury, septicaemia, shock, hypoxia, etc.) was also present.

Liskow et al. (1989) also relied on the work of Gross in developing a measure of withdrawal. They did their work prior to the publication of the CIWA-A, although they indicate that their measure is similar to the CIWA-A having similar roots. The scale measures 18 symptoms assessed along 3-point scales. The areas assessed are: eating disturbance, nausea/vomiting, tremors, sweating, sleep, nightmares, disorientation, hallucinations, delusions, quality of contact, agitation, temperature, pulse, convulsions, drowsiness, dysarthria, ataxia, nystagmus. The range of agreement among 3 raters ranged from 77–100%. The score correlated with the total amount of alcohol consumed in the 24-hour interval prior to admission. Older persons were rated as significantly higher on the scale. The scale score did correlate with the dosage of benzodiazepine prescribed by the physician.

MEASURES ASSESSING DRINKING
LOCUS OF CONTROL

Two measures of control over drinking behavior have been developed: the Drinking-Related Locus of Control Scale (DRIE) (Keyson & Janda, 1972) and the LOPD (Stafford, 1980).

DRIE

The DRIE contains 25 items presented in a forced choice format. Similar to the Rotter locus of control scale, each item consists of a pair of items, one reflecting internality and the other reflecting externality. Factor analysis of the DRIE has yielded 3 factors. Factor I contains items reflecting low expection in resisting social pressure to drink (It is impossible for me to resist drinking if I am at a party where others are drinking) or urges to drink in order to assuage negative mood (I feel powerless to prevent myself from drinking when I am anxious or unhappy). Factor II consists of expectations to succumb to drinking given stressful interpersonal events (Trouble at work or home drives me to drink; I get so upset over small arguments that they cause me to drink). Factor III accounts for less variance than the first two factors, consists of only 3 times, and appears to tap general control over sobriety (Without the right breaks one cannot stay sober; Staying sober depends mainly on things going right for you; Sometimes I cannot understand how people can control their drinking).

The DRIE has demonstrated good internal consistency (.77 for Kuder–Richardson) and reliability (unequal-length Spearman–Brown split-half reliability coefficient of .70) (Donovan & O'Leary, 1978). It is uncorrelated with measures of cognitive functioning. It does correlate significantly with the overall Rotter scale but not with Mirels sociopolitical subscale. It is correlated with the Beck depression inventory and several of the pathology scales off the MMPI. In terms of drinking measures, it does correlate with particular scales off the AUI suggesting that those scoring externally on the DRIE have drunk in a more sustained fashion, have previously utilized more outside resources to stop, have exhibited a greater degree of indiscreet behavior when drinking, have experienced more trauma during withdrawal, and have manifested greater deterioration attributable to drinking (Donovan & O'Leary, 1983).

LODP (Locus of Drinking Problem Scale)

The LODP includes 31 items in a forced choice format. These items were selected to represent perception of control over behavior when intoxicated and control of alcohol consumption. Measures of internal consistency are good ranging from .762 to .78. The LODP when factor analyzed yielded 3 factors which Stafford indicated were not easily conceptualized. They were therefore left unlabeled. Alcoholics in a public detox center scored significantly more externally

154

than did alcoholics in private hospital. Responses were found to correlate with the Rotter scale. Those alcoholics scoring more externally on the LODP had sought and received more treatment. Further, they were more likely to endorse a disease concept perspective rather than a social learning perspective (Stafford, 1980).

MEASURES FOR IDENTIFYING CHILDREN OF ALCOHOLICS

CAST

The CAST was developed to identify children of alcoholics among large groups of children. The Children of Alcoholics Screening Test (Jones, 1981) consists of 30 dichotomous items. An interitem reliability coefficient of .98 has been reported (Jones, 1982). All of the items have been found to discriminate between groups of children of clinically diagnosed alcoholics vs. children of normals at the .05 or less level.

COALES

The Children of Alcoholics Life-Events Schedule (COALES) (Roosa et al., 1988) was developed to assess the degree to which a child in an alcoholic family is experiencing stress. The measure contains 39 items which can be dichotomized into good and bad events. The internal consistency for the good items was .81 and .71 for the bad items. Good events and bad events subscales were independent. The test did correlate with children's level of depression (more bad events and fewer good events). Children of alcoholics achieved higher scores on the bad events measure and lower good events measure than age matched peers.

5 Outcome Research

This chapter informs the reader of some of the bottom lines that have emerged from the wealth of research conducted on outcome. Before consideration of treatment outcome findings, a discussion of the those features that distinguish the population of alcoholics who seek treatment from those who do not is presented. The first half of the chapter concerns itself with the general question of "Does it work?" The discussion of efficacy of treatment is approached from several different angles. Those studies in which advice is compared with extensive treatment are considered. Reviews of the outcome literature have provided estimates of the percentage of abstainers, control drinkers, and those who are definitely unimproved several years subsequent to treatment. By contrasting these percentages post treatment as compared to these same outcome categories among untreated samples of alcoholics, it becomes possible to generate conclusions about whether treatment works.

The latter half of the chapter explores more fine grained questions. Data pertaining to expected rate of drop out and the identifying features of drop outs are considered. Studies in which procedures were developed for attenuating attrition are discussed. Then, conclusions of what works better are explored. Particular outcome issues include: inpatient vs. outpatient, group vs. individual, duration of treatment, efficacy of behavioral treatment, coerced treatment vs. voluntary treatment, recovered-alcoholic therapists, which approaches do alcoholics prefer, meta analyses comparing aversion therapy with milieu or standard treatment packages, whether particular treatments work best for particular types of alcoholics, and efficacy of aftercare. As will be discussed, most researchers have concluded that patient characteristics are better predictors of outcome than is type of treatment received. The patient characteristics associated with particular outcomes are reviewed. A few questions that are indirectly related to outcome are also considered. For researchers endeavoring to conduct outcome studies, the issue of when outcome can be considered to be stable has been an important one. Some findings pertaining to this issue are examined. Patients are more likely to be allowed to remain in treatment and therapists are more likely to invest energy when the therapist believes the patient is motivated and when the therapist likes the patient. Data pertaining to patient characteristics that influence the therapist are explored. The issue of whether sobriety brings better functioning in other areas of life is examined. And finally, we discuss the impact of the Rand report on alcoholics.

AA ATTENDANCE AS TREATMENT

There have been many testimonials to the beneficial effects of AA attendance, but very little controlled research. There are only three random assignment, controlled studies in the literature. The first studies which attempted to objectively evaluate the impact of AA attendance were provided by Ditman and Crawford (1966) and Ditman et al. (1967). Both studies randomly assigned public inebriates to no treatment, outpatient treatment, or several meetings of AA (3 in the 1966 study and 5 in the 1967 study). Results of both studies failed to render support for AA efficacy. Since the degree of AA exposure was probably not adequate to allow a test of efficacy, definitive conclusions cannot be drawn from the two studies. An additional issue was examined in the Ditman et al. (1967) study. Those individuals who achieved success in AA were compared to those referred to AA who were not successful. The successful were distinguished by being older than 40, less well educated, and more likely to be solitary drinkers.

A study by Bradsma, Maultsby, and Welsh (1980) represents the best outcome evaluation of AA that has been published to date (Miller & Hester, 1980). These researchers were able to randomly assign 197 alcoholics, most of whom had been referred into treatment by the courts, into one of five treatments: insight therapy, rational behavior therapy conducted by a professional, rational behavior therapy conducted by a paraprofessional, AA attendance, or a control group which only received a list of community resources. (The community resources group, in fact, received almost no treatment from other agencies.) Drop out rates from all treatments were exceedingly high, although the rate for the AA group surpassed the other groups by a statistically significant degree (68% vs. 57%). In order for the data from a subject to be counted, the authors required that a subject assigned to a treatment complete 10 sessions of the respective therapy over a 210-day period. Data from 104 subjects met the criteria and were analyzed. The authors were able to make contact with 78% of completing subjects at follow-up, which occurred at 3, 6, and 12 months. The authors remarked that there was little consistency in the results. No particular approach was superior across all follow-up occasions and the significant findings did not consistently occur on any particular dependent variable. At no point in time, and on no variable was AA attendance found to be superior to the other approaches. At 6 months follow-up, those in the AA group had experienced more binging than the other groups, including the control group. Whereas the other treatment groups decreased on elevation of the Hysteria scale from the MMPI (a general index of somatization and distress) across time, persons assigned to AA increased.

There is a qualification in drawing conclusions from the Bradsma et al. study resulting from the way in which the authors analyzed their data. Unfortunately, they computed follow-up analyses only on treatment completers. Although random assignment was successful, more of those assigned to AA dropped out during the treatment interval. The authors' analyses suggested that the more severely alcoholic tended to remain in treatment. This suggests that the AA attendance group was left with individual alcoholics who had more severe alcohol problems. That is, self-selection of the more severe cases into treatment completion, stacked the deck against AA, which ended up with a higher percentage of severe cases than the other groups. Hence, a selection factor rather than the impact of AA attendance may have accounted for the worse outcomes for the AA group found on some measures (viz., binging and distress).

Whereas the three studies just discussed, were random assignment studies specifically designed to examine the efficacy of AA, others have examined correlational data. Of course, this type of research can never allow for a causal inference. Researchers have looked at AA attendance after a treatment program, to see if AA attendance posttreatment is associated with better outcome. Despite the probable confound of AA attendance and motivation, which could preclude assessment of efficacy, some interesting findings have accumulated. There is a suggestion that those former patients who self-select into AA are more likely to maintain sobriety. The Rand commission (Polich et al., 1981) assessed alcoholic patients at 18 months and at 4 years postdischarge. Those who were regularly attending AA at 18 months vs. those who were not, were more likely to be sober for at least 6 months immediately prior to the 4 year follow-up. In a second sample, Sanchez-Craig, Walker, and Bornet (cited by Ogborne & Bornet, 1982) found that following treatment, those attending AA reported more sober days at 18 months follow-up than those who did not attend. Others have reported similar findings (Belasco, 1971; Hoffman, Harrison, & Belille, 1983).

Some studies have not found an association between outcome and posttreatment AA affiliation. In a study by Edwards, Orford, Egert, Guthrie, Hawker, Hensman, Mitcheson, Oppenheimer, & Taylor (1977) neither attendance at AA or frequency of attendance was associated with outcome. Elal-Lawrence et al. (1987) found no difference in the percentage of AA attenders among the abstinent and the relapsed, although there was a lower percentage of AA attenders in the control drinking outcome group. Ogborne, Wiggins, and Shain (1980) examined outcome in a number of different halfway houses. They detected no difference in the mean duration of stay comparing halfway houses, which did and did not employ an AA orientation. A structured halfway house program, less likely to be found in houses where there was a strong AA orientation, was associated with increased length of stay among the less deteriorated.

A study by Bromet, Moos, Bliss, and Wuthmann (1977a) suggested that the association of AA attendance with outcome may vary as a function of population under study. Bromet et al. examined the association between AA affiliation and outcome as a function of orientation of the facility in which the patient had received treatment. The authors examined residual functioning, that is, they computed expectancies for a patients' posttreatment functioning based on socioeconomic status and the severity of pretreatment drinking. Results were the following. AA participation was associated with better residual functioning for patients who had been treated in a milieu orientation. Among patients who were treated in a facility offering aversion therapy, AA participation was associated with poorer functioning than would have been predicted on the basis of socioeconomic status and pretreatment drinking. According to the authors AA participation among those in aversion therapy treatment centers was associated with "worse residual functioning in alcohol consumption, physical impairment, and rehospitalization" (Bromet et al., 1977a, p. 838).

Additional studies have examined whether AA might work under specific conditions. Vaillant (1983, pp. 156–157) compared public clinic alcoholics who were and were not regular AA attenders. He dichotomized these public clinic alcoholics according to whether or not the alcoholic was a skid row, unemployed type. None of Vaillant's socially stable alcoholics, the group evincing the better outcomes, was a regular AA attender. Among the skid rowers, Vaillant found that the regular AA attenders achieved greater sobriety. Vaillant unfortunately did not report whether there was a confounding of halfway house residence and AA affiliation. There is reason to believe that skid row alcoholics might often reside in halfway houses. Halfway houses often mandate AA attendance for continued residence. Thus, halfway house residence might have been more prevalent among the AA attenders than the non-AA attenders. Since residence in a halfway house can be expected to increase sobriety, the confounded variable, viz., halfway house residence might have been the operative variable rather than AA attendance in the association with better outcome.

Gregson and Taylor (1977) have rendered findings pertinent to the issue of for which type of patient might AA be salutary. Among those normally functioning, as measured on cognitive impairment batteries, there was no relationship between AA attendance and sobriety. However, in the Gregson and Taylor total sample and among the cognitively impaired, AA attendance was associated with increased sobriety.

Sheeran (1988) published a study she believes is pertinent to evaluating outcome. She compared AA attenders who had sustained 2 years of abstention vs. AA attenders who had relapsed and thus failed to accrue 2 years of enduring abstention at the time of follow-up. The mean duration of AA involvement was 8.64 years in the successful group vs. 6.25 years in the relapsed group. The author suggested that her study supported AA's efficacy. Another interpretation is that on average, it will take the population of alcoholics which self-selects into AA, more than 6 years to reach a point where they can stay sober for 2 years. Sheeran did examine some other variables. She found no difference between the successful and nonsuccessful group on a dichotomous measure of frequency of meeting attendance and a dichotomous measure of meeting participation. The unsuccessful group, however, perceived themselves as less often reaching out and less often relying on their sponsors. Since self-assessment occurred subsequent to relapse, it is unclear whether the relapse caused the self-perception. Perhaps, after a slip, AA members decide that they are failing to reach out, even when before the fact of the relapse there is no difference between self-perceived reaching out of the group that will relapse and the group that will not. Although the Sheeran study may not address AA's efficacy, it does provide food for thought regarding the cognitive processes of AA members.

The discussion thus far has primarily referred to outcome variables of duration of sobriety. Other dependent variables can be examined. Such was the case in the Rand report (Polich et al., 1981) and the Sanchez-Craig, Walker, and Bornet (1983, cited by Ogborne and Bornet, 1982) studies. The Rand commission compared those who had been AA attenders at 18 months vs. those who had not been AA attenders at 18 months within the group who had been drinking during some point in the 6 months preceding the 4 year follow-up. The data suggested that given a relapse the AA attenders were more likely to be experiencing severe consequences from their drinking as well as symptoms of dependence. Sanchez-Craig and colleagues (discussed in Ogborne & Bornet, 1982), replicated this finding, reporting that the AA attenders who had relapsed displayed more severe physical consequences and more admissions to detox centers than those non-AA attenders who had relapsed. The implication was that for some reason AA attendance is associated with more severe, albeit less frequent relapse. The possibility that more severe relapse reflects the self-selection of the more extreme alcoholics into AA was addressed by Sanchez-Craig. There was no evidence that the findings in the Sanchez-Craig et al. study could be attributed to self-selection of the more severely alcoholic into AA. There were no differences between AA attenders and nonattenders on severity of alcoholism assessed at treatment intake. Self-selection could not account for the association between AA affiliation and severity of relapse. These findings led Ogborne and Bornet (1982) to suggest that AA may inculcate a self-fulfilling prophecy of greater debauchery which becomes activated given a slip.

Comment. The three controlled studies evaluating AA's efficacy have failed to produce support for a causal link between AA participation and positive outcome. It is the case that an association between AA attendance and positive outcome is found, although this probably reflects that the more highly motivated will more actively search for solutions and will more often succeed in their endeavors to stay sober. Some studies do suggest that the association between success and AA affiliation is more likely to be concentrated among those who are without economic resources and cognitive skills.

A causal connection between AA and better outcome has not been established. There is tentative suggestion of a causal connection between AA attendance and enhanced severity of relapse. AA may be a place where those assiduously seeking sobriety may congregate. The beliefs promoted in AA may, however, lead to a self-fulfilling prophecy of greater debauchery given a relapse.

What Percentage of Alcoholics Will Become AA Affiliates?

Tournier (1979) suggests that 5% of the alcoholics in America will attend AA. In a household survey conducted by Bailey, Haberman, and Alksne (1965), only 10 of the identified 133 alcoholics had ever attended an AA meeting. In Vaillant's (1983, p. 190) community sample not selected for having received treatment, 38% of those who were securely abstinent (those who were sober for over 3 years) had AA contact.

Others have determined the percentage of individuals who will maintain AA contact following treatment. Examining findings from a number of studies, Ogborne and Glaser (1981) report that only 20% of alcoholics ever regularly attend AA after treatment. Edwards, Hensman, Hawker, and Williamson, (1966) found that at 1 month postdischarge only 33% of patients retained AA contact. The figure fell to 13% by 1 year follow-up. By 2 year follow-up, regular AA attendance was found in only 14 of 78 patients (7%) by Vallance (1965). At 4 year follow-up, the Rand commission (Polich et al., 1981) found that of those patients who ever regularly attended AA (only 27% of treated individuals), only 39% of the 27% (10% of the total sample) were still continuing to attend. Higher reports are provided by patients treated at Hazelden, which given the treatment center's reputation as a strong AA advocate may draw a population particularly favorably disposed to AA. In a study of patients treated under the Minnesota (Hazelden) model, Hoffmann et al. (1987) report that at 6 month follow-up 50% were attending AA at least weekly whereas 25% were nonattenders.

Characteristics of AA Attenders

Surveys of AA members have yielded demographic characteristics as well as descriptors of the drinking patterns of AA affiliates. Leach (1973) reported that across 4 surveys, males accounted for between ⅔ to ¾ of membership. One half to three quarters of AA meeting attenders were between the ages of 33 to 49. Approximately a third of the sample was over 50. Most of the membership was middle class. Emrick (1987) reports that the percentage of women (now at 30%) and those under 31 (now at 18%) have increased in recent years.

Other studies have investigated additional variables. Persons having difficulty with their families and single individuals are more likely to affiliate (Gynther & Brilliant, 1967; Vannicelli, Gingerich, & Ryback, 1983). A London survey found that 82% had experienced withdrawal symptoms and 60% had been hospitalized (Edwards, Hensman, Hawker, & Williamson, 1966). O'Leary, Calsyn, Haddock, and Freeman (1980) found that persons who regularly attended AA vs. nonattenders had experienced greater severity of alcohol related sequale. Vaillant (1983) compared alcoholics who were AA members with alcoholics who were not AA members. Although the alcoholics were not differentiated on their DSM-III alcohol dependence scores, the AA attenders had accumulated more alcohol related problems than the nonattenders.

There have been studies comparing the personality characteristics of alcoholics who have and have not AA affiliated. Some have examined psychological distress. O'Leary, Calsyn, Haddock, and Freeman (1980a) at time of hospital admission to an alcoholism treatment program compared those who had attended a substantial number of AA meetings vs. those who had not. AA affiliates were more anxious than non-AA affiliating alcoholics. Although Hurlburt, Gade, and Fuqua (1984) found that AA affiliates with greater than 6 months of sobriety were less neurotic than non-AA alcoholics just completing treatment, the obtained differences might have been attributable to differential duration of sobriety.

AA members compared to alcoholic non-AA members are more likely to score highly on the California F-scale, a measure of authoritarianism (Canter, 1966) and on measures of tough-mindedness (Hurlburt et al., 1984). They are less likely to be cognitively complex (Fontana, Dowds, & Bethel, 1976; Reilly & Sugerman, 1967) and less well educated (Canter, 1966). They are more likely to be extroverted (Hurlburt et al., 1974; O'Leary, Calsyn, Haddock, & Freeman, 1980), more likely to exhibit affiliative and group dependency needs (Trice, 1959); and less likely to be socially ill at ease, isolated, or lonely (Mindlin, 1964). They are prone to guilt (O'Leary et al., 1980a; Trice, 1959); they are more likely to be religious (Gregson & Taylor, 1977) and to exhibit a greater disparity between their ideal and real selves than other alcoholics (Gynther & Brilliant, 1967). Professional alcohol counselors who are also AA members differ from non-AA professionals in terms of greater espousal of traditional values and encouragement of others to attend church (Ogborne & Glaser, 1981).

Vaillant (1983, p. 206) compared alcoholic AA members with nonmembers in his Boston sample. The AA members reported warmer childhoods and were more often Irish. Following those alcoholics who were advised to go to AA after treatment, Alford (1980) found that the women rather than the men were more likely to comply with treatment recommendation to maintain an AA connection.

In some studies AA members have been compared to the general population. Edwards et al. (1966) found that persons attending AA in London, undifferentiated as to duration of sobriety or AA membership, scored higher on the Eysenck neuroticism scale than the population norm. Kurtines, Ball, and Wood (1978) compared a sample of AA members who had at least 4 years of sobriety and a mean of 8.9 years of sobriety with a normal control group. All subjects were assessed on the California Personality Inventory. The AA members did not differ from the normals in terms of subjective sense of well being. Compared to normals, they were less socially mature, more socially detached, and functioned less well interpersonally.

Boscarino (1980) investigated those variables which predicted whether an individual would drop in and out of AA participation vs. establishing a stable relationship with AA. Those establishing a stable relationship were older, had been hospitalized fewer times for drinking, had experienced fewer problems related to drinking, were of higher SES, had experienced fewer slips while attending AA, and subscribed to the ideology espoused in AA.

Comment

The foregoing studies suggest that those with severe alcohol problems vs. those with less severe problems do search more earnestly for a solution, which will lead many to AA. Hence there will be the observed association between severity of problem and AA attendance. Only the Boscarino study examined stable protracted attendance. Here the variable of severity of alcohol problem was negatively associated with AA affiliation. The Boscarino study suggested that those with the less severe alcohol sequale were able to maintain consistent affiliation as opposed to dropping in and out.

The reviewed studies do suggest that cognitive variables (tough mindedness, authoritarian approach, religiosity) distinguish AA attenders from nonattenders. There is a suggestion that those who AA affiliate are gregarious enough to benefit from group affiliation. The finding that AA members are more likely to be single or unhappily married suggests that other avenues for social affiliation may be closed to AA members. It should be recognized that not all reviews of the literature conclude that AA members can be distinguished from their nonaffiliating counterparts. Emrick (1987) in his review of the same studies, concludes that AA members are not distinguished from non-AA members in terms of personality characteristics.

Although the outcome data on AA cannot justify a strong case for AAs efficacy in keeping people sober, Tournier (1979) has suggested that AA has a function other than keeping people sober. AA does offer a fraternity which provides social support and a sense of affiliation. Those persons for whom organizational affiliations, or group indentification, is attractive, should also find AA comfortable.

How Long Do AA Members Maintain Their Affiliation?

Edwards et al. (1966), surveying AA meetings in London, reported that the modal duration of AA membership represented at any given meeting was 6 months (21% of individuals). The mean duration of attendance was 48 months. Edwards et al. concluded that at any given meeting there will be a small but stable core of AA members with many transients who can be expected to drop out quickly.

Times have changed since 1966 when Edwards et al. accumulated statistics of the longevity of membership represented at any meeting. Given the burgeoning of new treatment programs all of which refer people to AA, the proportion of transients in attendance at any given AA meeting is probably higher today. Another factor that has changed recently is that courts are requiring AA attendance as a requirement of probation. As such, there will be a greater number of involuntary persons found at any given AA meeting today than in the past (Weisner & Room, 1984).

What Increases Attendance at AA?

Previous statistics suggest that not everyone will affiliate with AA. Edwards et al. (1977) found that advice from treatment providers to attend AA significantly increased membership. At 1 year follow-up, 24% of those advised to affiliate were attending at least once per month whereas 13% in the control group were so doing. Fink et al. (1985) found that those in "partial hospitalization" (day care) vs. inpatient treatment made greater use of AA during the follow-up interval.

Do AAs Stay Sober?

Rudy (1980) has hypothesized that AA is an organization of alcoholics who are experiencing difficulty in maintaining sobriety, i.e., AA selectively draws those alcoholics who continue to have difficulty in maintaining sobriety whereas those who do not have difficulty either drop out or never attend. It may be that those who accumulate a significant interval of sobriety leave AA whereas those who have difficulty staying sober retain their affiliation. Surveys of individuals in AA do suggest the patterns of sobriety that will be encountered in AA.

Empirical Findings.   Findings from a survey conducted by the General Service Board of AA were reported by Leach (1973). It was reported that 62.5% of male AAs who had been sober an unspecified length of time had been in AA 1 year prior to achieving reliable sobriety; 18.5% reported having been in AA up to

5 years, and 8.2% reported being in AA between 5 to 10 years before achieving reliable sobriety. Edwards et al. (1966) found that 57% of the AAs surveyed had slipped once since joining AA and 18% had slipped more than 5 times. Emrick (1987) concluded that between 40 to 50% of long-term AA affiliates accrue at least several years of sobriety while active in the AA program. In a New York survey of AA members with greater then 5 years of affiliation (clearly a select group), a positive association was found between frequency of AA attendance and frequency of relapse (Leach, 1973, p. 268). It would seem that AA members increase their meeting attendance when experiencing frequent relapse.

Statistics have been complied as to the percentages with long-term sobriety that can be expected at any AA meeting. Edwards et al. (1966) found that 42% of Londoner AAs attending meetings had been sober less than 6 months. Edwards et al. (1966) reported a 28.8 month mean duration of sobriety for AA attenders. Leach (1973) reported that across surveys of attenders at AA meetings, 38–42% will have been sober less than a year and 24–48% will have been sober between 1 and 5 years.

Bill C. (1965) examined the outcome over a protracted time interval for those persons (n = 393) who had attended at least 10 meetings of AA. He did not specify the time frame during which the 10 meetings were accrued. He also neglected to mention the follow-up period, although the title of the article suggested that 8 years may have elapsed. At last follow-up, 31% had attained at least a year of sobriety and were sober at last contact; 12% (N = 46) had been sober at least a year but had relapsed, of these, 14 were still attending AA; 9% were still in AA but had not accrued a year's sobriety; 38% had disappeared and could not be classified as to drinking outcome. The remainder of the sample was deceased or institutionalized.

Comment.   The data on percentages of AA participants who remain sober for varied periods of time does suggest a range of difficulty in achieving sobriety. If Bill C.'s estimate of 31% of AA affiliates achieve enduring sobriety can believed, this figure can be compared to Lemere's (1953) estimate of the percentage of untreated, non-AA affiliated alcoholics who can be expected to achieve enduring sobriety in the course of their lives. Bill C.'s estimate of 31% is about the same as the estimate from Lemere's sample (33%). Unfortunately, data allowing a comparison of whether persons in AA more quickly achieve enduring sobriety is unavailable. Hence, Ruby's hypothesis that AA is an organization of alcoholics who are having unusual difficulty in staying sober cannot be evaluated.

There has been no study allowing for inferences regarding whether greater numbers of people drop out of AA because they start drinking again or because they have achieved stable sobriety and no longer feel the exigence of AA affiliation. Such a study would require tracking persons who all began in AA over time and determining at which point the stably sober and the intermittently relapsing leave AA. Perhaps future research will address this issue.

Summary

Research pertinent to the issue of whether AA works has been scanty. Little support for efficacy has been adduced. If there is a salubrious effect, it is probably isolated among alcoholics who are worse off economically and cognitively. There is evidence suggesting that AA participation can make the occurrence of severe relapse given a slip more likely.

Beyond the issue of a causal connection between AA and sobriety, data are available suggesting the percentage of treated alcoholics who will AA affiliate and their personality characteristics. Only about 13% of treated alcoholics will maintain an enduring relationship. Those who are gregarious, better adjusted as children, but lacking in social support in their adult lives are more likely to seek solace in AA. Those who are more religious, authoritarian, and who eschew control drinking as a goal are more likely to remain in AA.

HOW DO PERSONS WHO SEEK TREATMENT DIFFER FROM THOSE WHO DO NOT?

Some investigators have sought to determine whether alcoholics who seek treatment differ from those who do not. This question has been examined in two populations: alcoholics in general and alcoholics whose problem drinking has remitted. The findings from these studies are important for several reasons. First, they confirm that alcoholics who seek treatment are definitely different from those who do not seek treatment. Thus a group of community alcoholics cannot be used as a control group against which outcome in a treated group is evaluated. Second, they provide insight into those factors that inspire alcoholics to change their behavior.

Comparisons of Those Seeking Help vs. Those Who Have Not Sought Help

In a community sample, Bailey, Haberman, and Alksne (1965) found that one-half of the alcoholics identified in their community survey had sought help. Mulford and Fitzgerald (1981b) compared the scores of groups of alcoholics presenting to 30 community alcoholism centers vs. alcoholics who had not sought treatment but were identified by clinicians. A greater percentage of those alcoholics in treatment scored above a cutoff criterion on a list of troubles attributable to drinking. Another study also found that greater severity of drinking makes help seeking more likely. Saunders, Wodak, and Williams (1985) identified a group of alcoholics presenting in a general clinic for treatment of liver disease. Greater severity of drinking was a feature distinguishing those who had sought prior help for their drinking.

Strug and Hyman (1981) compared patients in a detox center (who had never sought treatment), with patients in a rehabilitation center who had sought treatment. They found that those who had sought treatment had a more extensive social network, and also found that their social contacts encouraged treatment. By contrast, the social contacts of those in detox (who had not sought treatment) had encouraged drinking.

Hingson, Mangione, Meyers, and Scotch (1982) identified persons in a community sample who believed they had a drinking problem. Amount consumed was the major factor related to recognition of a drinking problem in the community sample. The researchers tracked their sample of self-identified problem drinkers over a 2-year period. For 42% of the self-diagnosed problem drinkers there was a 2-year lag time between the recognition of a problem and help seeking. (Unfortunately, Hingson et al. did not report whether those recognizing a problem took action on their own to ameliorate their problem prior to seeking treatment.) Those who had sought help by the second year, had most often done so within 2 weeks of making a decision. Help seeking was prompted in over 50% of the cases by some specific event (family argument, receipt of DWI, etc.) Those who sought help were differentiated from those who had not by the recognition of the deleterious impact of drinking on their lives (number of problems created by drinking which were recognized), by the perception of loss of control, and by self-labeling as alcoholic. Because the study was retrospective, it was unclear whether the identifying features reflected the impact of treatment or perceptions extant at the time that treatment was sought. It was noteworthy that there was no evidence that (1) differential access to treatment, (2) differential knowledge of treatment availability, or (3) differential belief in treatment efficacy was associated with seeking treatment.

Others have found that those experiencing greater psychological distress are more likely to seek help (Helzer & Pryzbeck, 1988; Weissman & Meyers, 1980). Those lower in self-esteem are more likely to seek help (Charalampous et al., 1976). Women have been found to more often seek assistance (Helzer & Pryzbeck, 1988), although there are inconsistent findings (Nathan & Skinstand, 1987).

Comparisons of Those Who Recover Through AA or Treatment vs. Those Who Recover Without AA or Treatment

It is clear that there are many people who have had severe drinking problems, who have never received professional help, and have not attended AA, and yet at some point have recovered in the sense that they are either maintaining abstinence, or controlling their drinking. Are they different in some specifiable ways from those former alcoholics who have recovered with the aid of treatment or AA attendance? There are a several studies making this comparison.

Vaillant (1983) tracked an inner city sample of men throughout their life times. From this sample he culled those alcoholics who had established secure abstinence (sobriety for 3 years in which a sober year was defined as not more than one occasion of intoxication during the year). Of the securely abstinent group, 38% had been active in AA and 20% had received treatment. Severity of alcoholism, as assessed by the number of accumulated symptoms, differentiated the group of those who sought help from those who did not. Those with more problems had more often sought help.

Another study (Saunders & Kershaw, 1979), examined remitted alcoholics identified in a community sample. (They were either control drinking or abstinent.) Those who recovered on their own vs. those who sought help differed from each other in the duration of their problematic drinking prior to remitting. Although both groups had experienced withdrawal symptoms, the duration of problem drinking was longer in the group that sought help. Interestingly, though perhaps not surprisingly, those who recovered on their own more often became control drinkers, while those who sought treatment more often became abstinent.

It does appear then, that as problems persist for a longer period of time, or as the problems become more severe, alcoholics are motivated to seek help. There is a contrary finding, however. A study by Goodwin, Crane, and Guze (1971) failed to detect differences in severity of drinking between those who recovered through treatment vs. those who recovered without treatment. In this study, failure to detect a difference was probably attributable to the extremely small N of the study. The notion that those with the more extreme alcoholism are more likely to achieve recovery through treatment has received some support. It is consistent both with common sense, and with the AA assumption that suffering brings people in for help.

Summary

Some studies have compared alcoholics, undifferentiated in terms of sobriety, who have and have not sought treatment. Other studies have examined alcoholics who achieved sobriety on their own vs. alcoholics who have achieved sobriety with treatment. Both types of comparisons support the notion that problems and distress created by drinking inspire alcoholics to seek treatment.

Whereas the studies comparing treated and untreated are consistent with the idea that "hitting bottom" as operationalized by the experience of distress moves people to treatment, the data also imply other pathways in the road to recovery. Those whose drinking problems remit outside of treatment, as a group, have experienced relatively mild distress. For this group, a change in behavior was inspired without hitting bottom.

DOES TREATMENT WORK?

How Should the Question of Whether Treatment Is Effective Be Asked?

The question of whether treatment works is a very complex one. It is instructive to first suggest one way in which the question should not be addressed. A study by Babor et al. (1988) found that regardless of drinking outcome measure selected at the 1 year follow-up, all patients are doing better at the end of treatment compared to their functioning at the time of entering treatment. Results from this study serve as a reminder that the best prediction for the outcome of patients entering treatment is that they will be doing better in the following year. Alcoholics can be expected to enter treatment at a time when the natural course of the disease is at a very low point. With or without treatment intervention, functioning can be expected to improve relative to the time when help seeking occurred. Outcome should never be assessed by pre/post comparisons.

In order to properly evaluate treatment efficacy, an untreated control group for purposes of comparison is a necessity. As suggested in the preceding section, those who self-select into treatment are the most severely alcoholic (Vaillant, 1983), so the comparisons of those who have and have not been treated will involve two different populations. The methodology for evaluating treatment is to randomly assign to treatment or no treatment, ensuring equivalence of the populations in each group. Despite the fact that for inferential purposes the comparison is not helpful, comparisons of life time outcomes for the treated and untreated alcoholics are available.

Studies in which alcoholics are observed over 20 years or life time intervals suggest that those in the treated group fail to display higher rates of sobriety than those in the untreated group. In Vaillant's (1983) study of 110 alcoholics raised in inner city Boston, 21/110 had achieved stable sobriety during the course of the study. The percentage of those receiving treatment did not differ between the group achieving stable sobriety and the group that failed to arrest their drinking. This raw comparison is not germane to treatment efficacy. Other more relevant data are available.

Before reviewing studies on treatment outcome, some additional preliminary comments on appropriate methodology are in order. The question of the duration of the follow-up interval is a relevant one. All studies on natural history of alcoholism tracking people over 20 year to life time periods suggest that spontaneous recovery rates are high, in the neighborhood of about one-third (Lemere, 1953; Vaillant, 1983). Such being the case, treatment effects may disappear if the control group is given a sufficient duration of time to realize the achievements obtained by the treated group. Perhaps the appropriate question is will treatment make an early recovery or even a period early recovery more likely. Perhaps the most appropriate yardstick for evaluating treatment is a 2-year window of time.

Of course, there will be those who argue that long-term status is the issue that matters. Recent investigators (Ewing & Rouse, 1976) caution that follow-up periods of 1 or 2 years are too short to be predictive of long-term status. This may well be the case, but short-term status is important as well. Treatment that induces greater abstinence or attenuated drinking during a 1- or 2-year-period following care, even if that individual reverts to totally degenerated drinking in subsequent years, is still delaying the deterioration of health, and offers some period of normal living. The importance of 2 years of recovery should not be discounted.

Given some of the considerations regarding the best methods for evaluating treatment, discussion now turns to specific findings. There have been a number of studies in which the control group in the study was a group of patients who were advised to quit drinking but offered no treatment to assist them. These studies addressing the issue of whether advice alone works as well as advice and treatment are reviewed first. The second section reports on the outcomes that can be expected given a 2 year follow-up time interval. Finally, the basic question of whether treatment is better than no treatment is asked again, and the results of some publications aggregating results from many treatment centers are examined.

Does Advice Alone Work?

Given the expense of treatment, the question of the minimal intervention necessary to achieve a salubrious outcome becomes relevant. A study by Patek and Hermos (1981) followed cirrhotic patients who successfully attenuated or quit drinking on the advice of their doctor. Over 60% had not sought treatment or AA. The Patek and Hermos study examined the successful and did not report the percentage of those that were unsuccessful, but it did suggest that even those with severe liver disease can recover without help. A study by Burnum (1974) suggested that only 8.6% of those persons who are not necessarily threatened by imminent death due to liver disease will abstain when told to by their physicians. In the Burnum study, those who responded to medical advice did so quickly. This rate of 8.6% is lower than the rate responding to doctor's advise to quit smoking or lose weight. If advice alone is sometimes effective, it becomes reasonable to ask whether added treatment will improve recovery rates.

Edwards, Orford, Egert, Guthrie, Hawker, Hensman, Mitcheson, Oppenheimer, & Taylor (1977) addressed this question by randomly assigning married male alcoholics to either a treatment group or an advice only session. In the treatment group, patients received outpatient therapy followed by inpatient therapy for 6 weeks if drinking did not remit. All were strongly encouraged to attend AA. In the advice group, a psychiatrist queried the patient regarding drinking habits, the patient was told that abstinence was the responsibility of the patient, and the patient was exhorted to maintain abstinence.

To evaluate outcome, patients and wives in both the advice and treatment groups were followed for 12 months. On drinking measures and subjective ratings of drinking problems, no differences between the groups were detected. In each group, two-thirds of the patients exhibited improvement relative to admission. Within the treatment group none of the associations between amount of treatment received and drinking variables were significant save for a significant relationship between visits with the general practitioner and the dichotomous variable of improved/unimproved drinking status. Those patients manifesting improvement most often attributed their success to better external circumstances rather than AA or treatment.

Follow-up data at 2 years on the Edwards et al. (1977) subjects were reported by Orford, Oppenheimer, and Edwards (1976). There was a caveat provided to the bottom line of the 1 year follow-up analysis. This report suggested that those with more severe drinking problems achieve better outcome with more treatment while the opposite is true for those with less severe drinking problems.

An additional study added support for the conclusion that those alcoholics who are truly deteriorated can benefit from treatment. Whereas Edwards et al. examined a sample with intact social support, Pittman and Tate (1969) investigated the effect of minimal vs. extensive treatment in a population with little social support. Pittman and Tate compared the efficacy of a 10-day detox program with a 3–6 week program coupled with provision of extensive, outpatient services. Patients were randomly assigned. The group receiving the more extensive treatment achieved higher rates of abstinence without relapse, higher rates of protracted periods of abstinence with occasional relapse, and higher rates of improved functioning in jobs, health, and social stability. All but one of the 19 individuals in the experimental group who achieved stable abstinence was a recipient of extensive outpatient social services.

Of course, the findings suggesting that extensive treatment is gratuitous have met with controversy. In commenting upon the results of the Orford et al. study, Kissen (1977) has suggested that the variable of social support may differentiate those who can benefit most from treatment. Kissen indicated that men with stable families and jobs might do very well without treatment, whereas treatment might be crucial for those lacking in such resources. The Pittman and Tate study lend support to Kissen's speculation.

There are several more studies in the literature comparing treatment to advise only groups. Chick et al. (1988) reported negative findings (no differences in various drinking criteria at 2 year follow-up) in comparing a minimal advice group, a group with advice and an intensive interview, and a treatment group. Unfortunately there were confounding factors in the study, for example many "advice only" patients also had extended contact with their physicians, and there were severity differences between the groups, so the conclusions, at least from this study, are suspect.

Another study that compares advice to treatment was provided by Chapman and Huygens (1988). Chapman and Huygens' sample concerned patients who had all been detoxed for 2 weeks and all of whom had intact social support systems. Following detox, patients received 6 weeks of inpatient therapy, or 6 weeks of outpatient therapy, or a 2-hour motivational interview. There was also a fourth group, which consisted of patients who refused treatment or dropped out. At 6 month follow-up, the results favored the outpatient group. At 18 month follow-up, the results favored the advice only group on drinking dependent variables. There were no differences between those refusing treatment and those receiving inpatient treatment.

Eriksen (1986) conducted yet another study contrasting the impact of extensive treatment with absence of treatment. Persons were detoxed and then remained on a waiting list for 4 weeks or, they were detoxed and then treated for 7 weeks as inpatients. Results were assessed at 4 week follow-up, which was 4 weeks after hospital discharge for the treated group and 4 weeks after being placed on the waiting list for the untreated group. This meant that the treated group was evaluated 11 weeks after initial contact, while the untreated group was evaluated 4 weeks after contact, a serious confounding factor. No differences emerged between groups, but the small sample and time confound makes this a difficult study to interpret.

Zimberg (1974b), with a low-SES sample of alcoholics, compared a 5-day per week comprehensive outpatient program with a 1-hour per week medication program which dispensed antabuse, anxiolytics, or antidepressants. No differences were detected in terms of abstinence during the latter half of the year long treatment.

Summary

In general, studies suggest that treatment may not add much, if anything, to advice. This conclusion seems particularly germane for those with less extreme drinking problems and those with intact support systems. There is some evidence that treatment may be better than just advice for those without good social support (Pittman & Tate, 1969). Those with more severe drinking problems may benefit from treatment, while some of those with less severe problems may be better off without it (Orford, et al. 1976). Inasmuch as the previously cited evidence suggests that those seeking treatment tend to have more severe problems, there may be a happy coincidence in the pattern of self-selection for treatment.

Expected Outcomes Following Treatment

The accumulation of numerous outcome studies in the literature does allow for the generation of reliable expectations for treatment outcome. These outcomes are relevant to relatively short intervals of time, viz., 2- to 4-years posttreatment. Some of the major studies and major review articles pertinent to this issue are now discussed.

The Rand report (Polich et al., 1981) offered 4-year outcome data on 758 patients who had been treated in government sponsored treatment programs. The original sample consisted of 758 patients. Fourteen-and a-half percent of the original sample died during the follow-up period. Eighty-five percent of the sample was contacted. Data waves were collected at 18 months, 2 years, and 4 years.

Polich et al. (1980) reported that 28% of the sample were in remission at both 18 months and 4 years, that is, they could be considered stably remitted. The authors differentiated types of remission. Thirteen percent of the subjects were considered abstinent at both 18 months and 4 years follow-up, although only 7% of the sample of 548 patients (the contacted patients) could be considered consistently abstinent throughout the 4-year period. Nine percent of the sample was control drinking at both 18 months and 4 years. Six percent of the sample had changed category of remission over the course of the study.

The Rand report has elicited legitimate criticisms (see Emrick & Stilson, 1977). Treatment facilities from which patients were selected may not have been representative of the 44 potential treatment centers. Although 85% of the sample was contacted at 4 year follow-up, the percentages contacted were lower at 6 and 18 months. In addition, the Rand report estimated as much as 15% underreporting of amount consumed at time of interview as validated against blood alcohol levels. Thus, the rate of control drinking may have been inflated. These considerations suggest that the rates of abstinence and control drinking represent upper limits on treatment success.

The Rand report findings can be compared to other evaluations of outcome. Emrick (1974, 1975), examining 271 outcome studies in his first review, and 384 in his second, provided some estimates of expected outcomes. At 6 month follow-up, the time at which Emrick suggests outcomes tend to stabilize, one-third of the patients can be expected to be abstinent with a single standard deviation confidence interval between 10.5% and 53.3%; $\frac{1}{20}$ can be expected to be control drinking; and $\frac{1}{3}$ can be expected to be unimproved with a confidence interval between 15.8 and 52.2%. (More succinctly, one-third abstinent, one-third unimproved, and 5% control drinking).

Costello (1975a, 1975b) reviewed 23 studies that reported a 2 year follow-up. Costello estimated expected outcomes at 1-year treatment follow-up for populations of derelicts and for more fortunate alcoholics. On average at 1 year follow-up, programs treating derelicts can expect to find that 0% will be dead, 60% will be relapsed, 12% will be abstinent or control drinking, and 28% will be lost to follow-up. Programs treating more affluent alcoholics can expect 1% to be deceased, 44% to be relapsed, 45% to be control drinking or abstinent, and 10% to be lost to follow-up. Costello indicates that the rates in the above categories remain approximately the same at 2 year follow-up.

The Rand report, Costello, and Emrick provide expectations of outcomes that can be expected to follow within the 2- to 4-year window of time following treatment. These outcomes can be contrasted with expected outcomes over the course of a 20 year to life time period. Although such a contrast is not relevant to the issue of treatment efficacy, such comparisons suggest how outcomes over a short interval of time will contrast with long term outcomes.

Control Drinking: Emrick's estimate of only 5% control drinking following treatment (measured at 6 months follow-up) is considerably lower than Lemere's lifetime estimate of 10% control drinking, and Vaillant's finding of 16% control drinking in his sample of inner city men followed for 20 years.

Abstinent: Emrick's estimate of 33% abstinence (6 months posttreatment) is the same as Lemere's finding of abstention in his sample of 500 alcoholics observed over the course of a lifetime; although other studies tracking over 15–20 year intervals have found lower rates of abstention (19% for Vaillant, 1983, 14.5% for McCabe, 1986).

Relapsed (Unimproved): Emrick estimates that 33% will be definitely relapsed at 6 months posttreatment. This estimate is lower than Lemere's (1953) life-time finding of 57% who never achieved recovery, and Vaillant's (1983) finding of 38% who do not achieve recovery within a 20-year time frame. Costello's (1975a, 1975b) 2 year follow-up after treatment is interesting in this context, since he differentiated derelicts from his middle-class sample. Among the middle class, 44% had relapsed, and 10% were lost to follow-up. Some portion of that lost group should probably be added to the 44%. This can be compared with his derelict sample estimating 60% relapsed and 28% lost to follow-up.

The contrasts of short-term follow-up intervals with long-term follow-up intervals suggest that the unimproved category increases slightly, abstention rates in the long run may be a little smaller than they are in the short run, and control drinking rates in the short run are a little smaller than they are over the course of a life time.

A Second Look at Evaluating Treatment Efficacy

The most appropriate way to evaluate treatment efficacy is with studies that allow for random assignment to treated and untreated groups. The question of the appropriate outcome measure must be addressed. Although follow-up intervals of long duration comparing patients who have been randomly assigned to treatment or no treatment groups are not available, the question of treatment efficacy over the short run has been addressed. Short-term outcome is the yardstick that has been employed to evaluate treatment programs.

Emrick (1975), summarizing over 384 outcome studies at 6 months posttreatment for the treated groups, concludes that treatment does work. He utilized a number of criteria, and found that the criterion of abstinence had only a minimal relationship to treatment whereas amount of drinking was clearly related to treatment. ". . . the findings suggest that alcoholics are, in a practical sense, as likely to stop drinking completely for 6 months or longer when they have no or minimal treatment as when they have more than minimal treatment. On the other hand, treatment seems to increase an alcoholic's chances of at least reducing his drinking problem" (pp. 97–98). He cautions that "these results must be taken with some reservation since very few minimal- and no-treatment data were involved and patient characteristics were not controlled" (p. 97).

Health Maintenance Organizations have collected statistics on the impact of alcohol treatment programs. These studies suggest that after participation in alcoholism treatment programs, visits to doctors in the health plan decrease for both the alcoholic and the alcoholic's family members. These findings offer indirect support for decreased drinking following treatment, and possibly for less family tension. The data provide direct evidence for improved health for alcoholics posttreatment. However, health plan statistics also show that alcoholic families were still exhibiting higher rates of outpatient services than nonalcoholic families at 2 year follow-up (NIAAA, 1984/1985).

In addition to providing estimates of life time outcomes for alcoholics, Vaillant (1983) provided estimates of short-term outcome as well. Vaillant (1983) estimates on the basis of studies reporting outcome on untreated samples that each year 2 to 3% of alcoholics will become abstinent and 1% will revert through control drinking. Vaillant's estimate of improvement rates for untreated samples can be contrasted with expected outcomes after treatment. The rates of improvement for treated samples in the previously cited studies do exceed Vaillant's estimates of spontaneous remission. Further, as previously indicated, it is known that those who select into treatment are differentiated by the greater severity of their alcoholism from the population who do not present for treatment. Hence, the difference in expected rates of improvement after therapy vs. Vaillant's estimate of improvement in untreated samples would probably have been even greater had Vaillant calculated his estimate of improvement without therapy on a population equivalent to the population which presents for treatment.

Given the results of Emrick's analysis and the results of studies in which treatment was compared to mere advice to quit drinking does suggest that, at least for the severe alcoholics, treatment does assist in recovery. For the relatively brief window of time following treatment, the treated group does exhibit better outcome than the nontreated group. Perhaps over the long run of a life time, the control group will catch up with the treated group. However, differences between the treated and untreated group for any 2-year period of time, should not be discounted as to their importance.

One final consideration in evaluating treatment efficacy must be stated. Controlled, random assignment studies are critical. A confounding variable in comparing treated alcoholics with untreated alcoholic samples is motivation. Even though alcoholics who self-select into treatment have more severe drinking problems than those who do not, they also desire recovery more. The motivation factor may be a major causal factor in determining outcome. The studies contrasting extensive treatment with advice only, fail to support treatment efficacy for the well off. For the less well off, treatment seems to exert a beneficial effect. Perhaps there is an additional group for whom treatment has an opportunity to improve on spontaneous events, viz., the unmotivated, coerced into treatment alcoholics.

In a subsequent section in this chapter, the question of differential treatment efficacy in voluntary vs. coerced samples is examined. The bottomline from empirical findings relevant to this question suggests that the coerced do as well as the voluntary. Perhaps treatment has an opportunity to positively influence the lives of the involuntary, initially unmotivated alcoholics who might not have considered recovery as an alternative had they not been coerced into treatment.

WHEN DO PATIENTS DROP OUT OF TREATMENT?

Any therapist who has ever worked with an alcoholic population is aware there will be a large number of window shoppers. Many alcoholics present for an intake but fail to follow through with treatment. For new therapists entering the field it is useful to have some realistic expectation of the percentage that will engage in treatment. Fortunately, such statistics are available.

There have been several reports estimating the percentage of persons dropping out of treatment after specified number of sessions. Rosenberg and Liftik (1976) reported that 33% of their largely blue collar patient sample did not return for a second visit. Baekeland, Lundwall, and Shanahan (1973) in a lower class sample found that 17.5% failed to return for a second visit. Smart and Gray (1978b) report that 12% of their sample failed to present for a second visit. These findings are consistent with prior reports indicating that about 33 to 75% of patients fail to attend more than four sessions (see also, Chafetz, Blane, Abram, Golner, Lacy, McCourt, Clark, & Myers, 1962; Kissen, Platz, & Su, 1970; Mayer & Myerson, 1971; Panepinto & Higgins, 1969). At the other end of the time dimension scale, between 10 to 38% of patients are active for 6 months (Baekeland et al., 1973; Rosenberg & Liftik, 1976; Smart & Gray, 1978b).

Patient Characteristics Associated with Early Drop Out?

Patients who fail to report for a second visit more often have alcoholic relatives, more often report for the initial intake appointment in an intoxicated state, have not showed for a prior intake appointment, are less likely to have maintained abstinence for any substantial period of time; and are more likely to live alone (Baekeland et al. 1973; Gertler et al., 1973). Baekeland et al. (1973) found that those engaging in treatment following the intake had more AA contact, whereas Gertler et al. (1973) found the opposite. Those who are admitted for treatment at off hours in an intoxicated state are more likely to leave AMA (against medical advice) (Beck et al., 1983). Those whose families (rather than the patients) have initiated treatment are less likely to remain in treatment (Noel et al., 1987). Younger patients, particularly those who exhibit additional pathology and a history of AMA exits from hospitals drop out more quickly (Beck et al., 1983; Leigh, Ogborne, Cleland, 1984; Miller, Pokorny, Valles, & Cleveland, 1970; Noel et al., 1987; Schofield, 1978; Welte, Hynes, Sokolow, Lyons, 1981b).

There have been inconsistent findings on whether depression is associated with dropout from treatment. Baekeland et al. (1973) found that those who failed to report to a second visit more often displayed depression and anxiety at the first appointment. Noel et al. (1987) also found that presence of depression unrelated to alcoholism, is associated with increased dropping out. MacMurray et al. (1987), however, found that those with higher Beck scores (a depression inventory) continued longer in treatment. MacMurray et al.'s study examined VA alcoholics, a group in which a large number of homeless might be expected. Since homelessness might be anticipated to covary with depression, the confound of homelessness might have accounted for the discrepant findings. Other variables have been examined with regard to treatment retention. Hostility is associated with higher dropout rates (Altman, Evenson, & Won Cho, 1978). The dependent as opposed to the counterdependent tend to persist in treatment longer (Blane & Meyers, 1964).

Those with positive attitudes toward drinking are more likely to be discharged for drinking from halfway houses (Krasnoff, 1976; Orford & Hawker, 1974). Equally unsurprising is the finding that patients who view treatment positively are less likely to leave early (Moos, Mehren, & Moos, 1978; Robson, Paulus, & Clarke, 1965).

Patients who are less socially stable (less stable residence patterns, lower pretreatment financial status, more extensive unemployment history, etc.) tend to leave treatment prematurely (Chapman & Huygens, 1988; Gertler, Raynes, & Harris, 1973; Leigh et al., 1984; Welte et al., 1981b). Persons with stable lives (a family and a job) remain in treatment longer (Rosenberg & Liftik, 1976; Wilkinson, Prado, Williams, & Schnadt, 1971). However, family desertion of the alcoholic has also been found to decrease dropout rates (Altman, Evenson, & Won Cho, 1978). Patients less adept at abstract reasoning leave treatment earlier (Erwin & Hunter, 1984). Men are more likely to leave AMA than women (Schofield, 1978). Patients whose spouse's report greater marital satisfaction are more likely to be retained in treatment (Noel et al., 1987).

Patients with high Pd (Psychopathic deviance) scales on the MMPI are more likely to leave prior to completion (Beck et al., 1983; Pekarik, Jones, & Blodgett, 1986). Those who score highly on the L (lie) scale of the MMPI, possibly reflecting a favorable impression management style, and those with a strong need for approval more often complete treatment (Krasnoff, 1976). Wright and Obitz (1984) found that patients who attributed more responsibility to themselves for hypothetical future events were less likely to drop out of treatment prior to completion.

The variable of severity of alcoholism has not been found to consistently relate to completion in treatment. Robson et al. (1965) found that patients with more severe drinking histories remain in treatment longer. In a sample of alcoholics who had volunteered for outpatient treatment, Skinner and Allen (1982) state that those who scored higher on an alcohol dependence scale were more likely to remain in treatment. Leigh et al. (1984) found that those with very low MAST scores (a measure of alcoholism) failed to return for a second visit after an intake session. Smart and Gray (1978b), using the dependent variable of retention in treatment, identified a curvilinear relationship between the dependent measure and the two predictor variables of duration of drinking problems and quality of life experiences. Those at the extreme ends of quality of life and alcoholism severity dropped out of treatment more quickly. It would seem that a certain degree of problem must be present to motivate continuation in treatment and change. However, if alcoholism is too severe and the condition of life has seriously deteriorated, then it may be impossible to envision the possibility of change.

A finding with some practical importance, is that of Leigh et al. (1984), who found that those with a scheduled delay of over 2 weeks between their intake and their second appointment were more likely to fail to return for a second appointment.

Enhance Retention Procedures in Therapy

Panepinto and Higgins (1969) have found that aggressive pursuit of patients does increase presentation for rehabilitation therapy after release from a detoxification unit, does increase the rate of presentation for second and subsequent visits at the rehabilitation unit, and does decrease the number of unscheduled appointments during the treatment period. Panepinto and Higgins achieved their results by immediately sending letters to all patients who no showed, rescheduling their appointments. Tarleton and Tarnower (1960) produced similar findings.

Panepinto et al. (1980) found that incorporating a group orientation to outpatient rehabilitation while patients were hospitalized for detoxification enhanced the rate of presentation for outpatient rehabilitation. Dolan (1975) and Gallant et al. (1973) used orientation groups after the intake interview thereby decreasing the wait time between intake and treatment. In both studies, the experimental groups manifested a higher retention rate.

Schroeder et al. (1982) found a shorter inpatient program vs. a longer inpatient program (comparison was 42 days to 112 days) resulted in fewer dropouts. Limiting the size of therapy groups also helped to diminish dropout rates.

According to Noel et al. (1987), patients assigned to marital rather than individual therapy were more likely to be retained in treatment. Rosenberg et al.

(1976) found that some therapist characteristics were associated with diminished dropout rates. Therapists who were older, who were female, and who were less socially assertive and less outgoing evidenced lower drop out rates among their patients. Milmoe et al. (1967) found that doctors who manifested some anxiety in general as assessed outside of the therapy context, were more successful in inducing alcoholics to engage in treatment.

In general psychotherapy populations, several procedures have been demonstrated to enhance retention in therapy. Hoehn-Saric, Frank, Imber, Nash, Stone, and Battle (1964) increased retention rates by providing explanation of the therapeutic process before therapy initiation. Sherman and Anderson (1987) employed an imagination procedure to increase retention in therapy. Clients who imagined and explained at the intake session their reasons for continuing in therapy for at least 4 sessions manifested less therapy dropout than those who did not engage in this imagination/explanation procedure.

Summary

Any therapist engaged in the treatment of alcoholism can expect to encounter high dropout rates. As many as a third of intakes will fail to engage in treatment. As the duration of therapy increases more dropouts will accrue. Some patients are more likely to drop out than others. A history of lack of dependability in general (no job stability, prior history of AMA exits from hospitals, high psychopathy scale on the MMPI) predicts a higher dropout rate. There is an optimal level of distress created by the alcoholic process which is associated with retention in therapy. Too little distress will decrease retention. Too much distress will also decrease retention. There are some things the therapist can do to increase therapy retention. Aggressive pursuit helps. Shortening the waiting period between intake and therapy engagement helps. Providing an explanation of the anticipated treatment helps. Engaging relatives in the treatment process and the therapist's being less focal and less talkative during the first treatment encounter also helps.

IS INPATIENT MORE EFFECTIVE THAN OUTPATIENT?

Edwards and Guthrie (1966; 1967) randomly assigned middle-class alcoholics to an average of 8.5 weeks of inpatient treatment or 7.7 weeks of weekly outpatient group sessions. No difference in treatment outcome was detected at 6 month or 1 year follow-up. McLachlan and Stein (1982) detected no difference between a day treatment program and an inpatient program. Chapman and Huygens (1988) failed to detect a difference in patients who had received inpatient vs. outpatient therapy at 18 months. A lack of difference has been reported in other studies as well (Fink et al., 1985; Longabaugh et al., 1983).

The Longabaugh study did find some outcome measures on which differences between inpatient and outpatient therapy were observed. Longabaugh, McCrady, Fink, Stout, McAuley, Doyle, and McNeil (1983) examined a group of patients who had been inpatient detoxified over an 8-day period. Following detoxification, patients were randomly assigned to the same 3-week program either provided on an outpatient or inpatient basis. At 6 month follow-up no differences were detected between the inpatient and outpatient versions of treatment on drinking variables, although marginally significant ($p = .07$) better outcome for the outpatient program was noted on spousal social role functioning, life satisfaction, and positive affect.

Others have examined whether particular types of patients might do better in inpatient therapy rather than outpatient therapy. A study by Meyer, Berman, and Rivers (1985) suggested that particular types of patients do better as inpatients. Meyer et al. collected data on 44 patients on drinking measures at 3 month follow-up. The more socially stable, the higher the socioeconomic class, and the less severe the alcoholism of the patient, was related to greater superiority of inpatient therapy. The less socially stable, the lower the socio-economic class, and the more severe the alcoholism of the patient, was related to greater superiority of outpatient therapy. The Meyer et al. study was a regression analysis in which the interaction term (type of patient X type of treatment) was tested for significance. No specific group mean comparisons were conducted. Further, patients were categorized according to their standing on a composite set of variables. Thus, it was impossible to determine which particular variable in the composite might have been most important in producing the results. The findings from the Meyer et al. study are somewhat counterintuitive and should be replicated with further delineation of the meaning before treatment implications are derived. They also contradict an earlier study by Kissen, Platz, and Su (1970) wherein the socially stable did better with outpatient therapy while the unstable did better as inpatients. The Meyer et al. findings are, however, consistent with a study by McLellan, Luborsky, Woody, O'Brien, and Druely (1983) in which those with more severe employment and family problems improved more in outpatient therapy. This latter study by McClellan et al. found several variables interacting. Among patients displaying a midrange severity of affective symptomotology, outpatient treatment worked better for those with more family support and fewer employment problems.

Summary

The studies comparing inpatient therapy with outpatient therapy fail to detect differences between the two approaches on drinking variables. The studies asking whether inpatient vs. outpatient might work better for particular types of patients have produced significant differences, although across studies little consistency has been found. The bottom line seems to be that there is little difference between inpatient and outpatient therapy in terms of outcome. In their review of the outcome literature, Miller and Hester (1986) suggested that in light of the lack of demonstrated differential efficacy, the cost effectiveness concerns dictate that outpatient treatment is better than inpatient treatment. Miller and Hester (1986) suggest that for those patients who have failed in outpatient treatment, inpatient might be tried.

DOES LENGTH OF TREATMENT EFFECT EFFICACY?

There have been reports in the literature addressing the question of whether longer vs. shorter duration of therapy produces better outcomes. The best approach for answering this question is to randomly assign patients at intake to a specified duration of treatment and then to compare the longer duration group with the shorter duration group. There are a number of such studies in the literature. Some publications addressing efficacy of length of treatment have not observed random assignment. Rather, there are a few studies in which outcome from treatment programs that were of short duration have been compared to outcome from treatment programs of longer duration. Of course, this type of strategy does not allow for random assignment and hence findings could reflect differences in the patient population rather than differences in the impact of length of treatment. A final approach to the question has correlated individual patient duration in treatment with individual patient outcome. Conclusions from this third approach are particularly difficult to draw. The investigators have not indicated whether a shorter duration in treatment reflects a patient's dropping out or whether the duration of treatment was planned. Nevertheless, all three types of strategies for addressing the question of whether length of treatment effects efficacy exist in the literature. Results from the three types of studies are reviewed.

Random Assignment Studies.   Several studies have failed to detect differential efficacy based on duration of inpatient treatment. Mosher, Davis, Mulligan, and Iber (1975) randomly assigned 200 alcoholics to 9 days or 30 days of inpatient treatment. At 3 and 6 month follow-up no difference between the groups could be detected. Willems, Letemendia, and Arroyave (1973a) failed to detect an association between patient groups randomly assigned to long (over 2 month) or short (1 month) duration of inpatient at 2 year follow-up evaluation, although the longer treatment group was slightly better at 1 year follow-up. Stein, Newton, and Bowman (1975) randomly assigned to short duration or longer duration of hospital treatment. No difference between those hospitalized for average of 9 days vs. those hospitalized for average of 82 days was observed at 13 month follow-up. Although Kish, Ellsworth, and Woody (1980) did not randomly assign patients to long and short duration of treatment, there probably was no systematic bias in assignment of patients to groups. The treatment center in which Kish et al. conducted their study decided to shorten the duration of treatment. Patients treated before the new policy were compared with patients treated after the policy. Kish, Ellsworth, and Woody (1980) found no difference at 6 month follow-up between completers of an 84- vs. a 60-day program on a dependent measure of amount of alcohol consumed during the follow-up interval. However those who had participated in the longer program were more often completely abstinent.

Although most of the random assignment studies have found no difference in drinking outcome between programs of long and short duration, there is some evidence that programs of longer duration will experience more dropouts. Walker, Donovan, Kivlahan, and O'Leary (1983) randomly assigned patients to a 2 week or a 7 week inpatient stay. They found no difference between the two treatment groups at follow-up, although the longer program exhibited a higher dropout rate. Page and Schaub (1979) randomly assigned patients to 3 or 5 weeks of inpatient treatment. Again no difference in outcome (at 6 months in this study) was detected. Among the psychologically well adjusted with good home situations, commitment to a 5 week inpatient program was difficult to secure.

Comparison of Short- and Long-term Treatment Programs Without Random Assignment.   Welte et al. (1981a) examined data from 17 different treatment programs in the state of New York. They compared outcomes from programs of long treatment duration (over 30 days) to outcomes from treatment programs of shorter duration (30 days or shorter). Longer treatment programs did produce greater abstinence at 3 and 8 month follow-up. The differential outcome was particularly pronounced for those of lower socioeconomic standing.

A study by Smart and Gray (1978a) addressed the question of relationship between planned treatment duration and outcome. The design of the study precluded random assignment. Smart and Grey observed outcomes for patients in various treatment centers which differed as to planned treatment duration. Smart and Grey matched patients on the variables of age, alcohol involvement at intake, physical health, motivation for treatment, social stability, and attitudes towards abstention. Sixty-six patients were selected who had received minimal treatment (defined as only one outpatient treatment contact). One hundred and thirty-three patients were selected who had received moderate treatment (defined as up to 6 months of treatment). Three hundred and eleven patients were selected who had received long-term treatment (defined as treatment over 6 months). At 1 year follow-up, when 70% of the selected patients were contacted, no differences were discerned among the groups on the dichotomous categories of improved/unimproved. However, there was a larger percentage of abstention in the two treated groups than in those receiving only one therapy visit. This study suggests that therapy worked better than no therapy, although duration of therapy did not produce a difference.

Studies that Correlate Duration in Treatment with Outcome Functioning.   A large outcome study by McLellan et al. (1982) and a large literature review by

Smart (1978b) concluded that longer duration of treatment is associated with better outcome. These studies did not differentiate as to whether the shorter duration reflected treatment dropout or planned shorter stay. Conclusions pertinent to whether longer duration of treatment is better from these two studies can therefore not be drawn. Some additional large-scale studies aggregating data from a number of treatment centers suffer from the same problem. These studies suggest that the correlation between duration in therapy and outcome may differ depending upon the type of treatment center. Because of the differential associations between duration of treatment and outcome as a function of type of treatment setting, they are interesting.

Finney, Moos, and Chan (1981) found a correlation between length of stay and 6 month follow-up functioning for residents at a halfway house, but not for those in a Salvation Army program or for patients in a milieu oriented program. Reviewing outcome data from 5 types of treatment programs Bromet et al. (1977b) found that longer stay in the hospital and the halfway house is associated with better outcome, although the reverse is true for aversion programs. Among skid row alcoholics, duration of residential treatment stay was not found to be associated with subsequent detox admissions by Ogborne and Clare (1979). In the Ogborne and Clare study, a short stay usually reflected discharge for drinking. In only 6% of the cases did staff approve of the premature discharge.

Summary

Those studies in which patients were randomly assigned to short or long duration of treatment constitute the best method for evaluating whether duration of treatment makes a difference in outcome. Random assignment studies have failed to detect differences in outcome between short duration and long duration programs, although programs of longer duration do experience higher drop out rates. Those studies, which did not randomly assign to condition, but rather compared short and long duration treatment programs have also failed to find differences in outcome, with the exception that in the Welte et al. (1981a) study longer duration improved outcome for those of lower socioeconomic standing.

Several reviews have correlated patient duration in treatment with outcome. When an association is found, it is the patients who remain in treatment the longest who produce the better outcomes, save for those in aversion therapy. The proper conclusion from these studies is probably that patients who drop out will do less well on outcome measures.

IS GROUP OR INDIVIDUAL A BETTER VEHICLE
FOR TREATMENT?

There has been very little evaluation of whether group therapy vs. individual therapy produces better outcomes. Most inpatient treatment programs provide a combination of both. Outpatient programs usually employ group therapy as the vehicle for treatment. A study by Smart (1978b) did attend to the issue of whether group therapy vs. individual therapy produces better outcomes. Although Smart (1978b) was unable to randomly assign patients to treatment, he found those who were assigned to group therapy exhibited the best outcome. Those patients who were attending both group and individual simultaneously did worse than those in either group or individual. Further work in this area should be conducted. If group therapy does produce better outcome, it is important to determine whether composition of the group (e.g., mixed socioeconomic status, mixed sexes) might make a difference.

EFFICACY OF BEHAVIORAL TREATMENTS

A complete review of behavior therapy for alcoholism is beyond the scope of this chapter. In this section, a few of the interesting findings pertaining the type of interventions which have been evaluated are discussed. Research discussed in other sections of this chapter has primarily evaluated treatment in which patients are sent to AA and are exposed to educational films. Behavior therapists have evaluated interventions that are not part of the standard package in most treatment centers across the country. In fact, Vaillant (1983, p. 192) has analogized behavior therapy to receiving heart transplant. Although such treatments may be theoretically efficacious, they require too much sophistication and expensive equipment to ever be offered to the masses. Whether Vaillant is correct is an empirical question. Some of the findings from behavioral studies are interesting and worthy of discussion.

Many have evaluated aversion therapy in which a shock is delivered contingent upon drinking any alcohol or contingent upon achieving a high blood alcohol level. Some efficacy for such procedures has been demonstrated (Hamburg, 1975). In a study by Cannon, Baker, and Wehl (1981) treating alcoholics in a VA hospital, it was found that emetic aversion was superior to shock aversion. In fact, the shock aversion group displayed a worse outcome than the no behavior therapy control group. Adding relaxation training to aversion therapy has been found to produce even higher rates of improvement (Blake cited by Hamburg, 1975). Hunt and Azrin (1973) and Arzin (1976) compared a broad spectrum community environment behavioral approach with a standard state hospital approach. The standard state hospital approach comprises AA and education. The behavioral approach added components to the standard state hospital program. The behavior approach added (1) assignment of a buddy who would encourage sobriety during the aftercare interval, (2) assistance in obtaining employment, (3) a social interaction group, (4) family counseling, (5) help in building a sober friendship circle, and (6) therapist assistance with legal and financial problems. Outcome data favored the broad spectrum behavioral approach at 2 year follow-up on drinking variables, increased employment, and social functioning. Van

Hasselt, Hersen, and Milliones (1978) reviewed studies evaluating social skills training for alcoholics. Most of the results were promising, although many of the reviewed studies lacked a control group.

In the Patton State Hospital study (1978b), the Sobells compared standard state hospital abstinence oriented AA approach with a behavioral approach for control drinking. The behavioral approach included (1) aversion therapy contingent upon gulping drinks and ordering excessive quantities of alcohol; (2) training in refusing drinking; and (3) exposure to videotapes of drunken comportment. At 1 year follow-up, the behavioral approach group manifested superior results on number of relapsed days and number of abstinent days compared to the control group. This particular study has invited scathing criticism. The majority of the behavioral treated patients were not found to be control drinking at later follow-up (Pendery et al., 1982). Unfortunately, the critics of the study did not provide follow-up data on control patients thus precluding meaningful evaluations as to efficacy or the deleterious impact of treatment.

Comment. A variety of behavioral approaches have been applied to alcoholism. Evaluation of behavior therapy has consisted of comparing behavioral therapy to standard hospital therapy, rather than an untreated control group. Significant difference have been found in favor of behavior therapy at follow-up intervals of 1 to 2 years (Hunt & Azrin, 1973; Sobell & Sobell, 1978b). Whether these differences will remain evident given longer follow-up intervals is unknown. These findings have suggested that differential efficacy is achieved among those patients who are willing to participate in behavioral therapy programs. The lack of a randomly assigned, no treatment control has precluded a statement about whether one or both treatments are doing less better than those not receiving treatment. The demonstrations of efficacy for behavioral therapy can be faulted for failing to control for therapist attention to the patient and staff enthusiasm. Any new therapy probably engenders a better placebo effect. Whether the efficacy demonstrated for behavior therapy is attributable to the specific method or therapist enthusiasm cannot be determined.

WHICH APPROACHES DO ALCOHOLICS PREFER?

Patient preference for particular treatments of any disorder is an important consideration. It is reasonable to assume that if a patient is more subjectively satisfied with the treatment, he/she will be more likely to continue with treatment and perhaps derive more benefits. There have been a few investigations into what alcoholics report are their preferences as to type of treatment.

Knox (1971) surveyed 200 VA alcoholics who had listened to an orientation lecture enumerating the various approaches to treating alcoholism. These alcoholics were asked to list those interventions they believed might ameliorate their alcoholism. The top listings were individual therapy with a psychiatrist or psychologist, lectures, and discussions. Asked what had helped them, the top choices were having spoken with other alcoholics, talking to a former alcoholic counselor, regular group therapy, AA, and movies on the topic of alcoholism. In another investigation examining patient preference, Obitz (1975) found that alcoholics preferred Albert Ellis to Carl Rogers when shown tapes of each therapist.

Other investigations have found that particular types of patients prefer particular types of therapy. In a sample of lower SES alcoholics, those scoring higher on authoritarian scale and those with dual diagnoses preferred lectures to approaches in which self-disclosure was required (Canter, 1966, 1971).

DO FORMER ALCOHOLICS IN THE ROLE OF COUNSELOR PRODUCE MORE FAVORABLE OUTCOMES?

With the advent of increased funding for treatment of alcoholism in the 1970s, paraprofessional recovering alcoholics without professional degrees have been inducted into the treatment of alcoholism. There has been concern to evaluate whether these alcoholic paraprofessionals produce outcomes that are equal in quality to the outcomes of those who are not alcoholic. Findings from a few studies are available. All of these studies have compared alcoholic, paraprofessionals with nonalcoholic paraprofessionals rather than professionally trained individuals.

Rosenberg et al. (1976) failed to find any difference in dropout rates among those treated by former alcoholic counselors and nonalcoholic counselors who did not hold professional degrees.   In this study, treatment retention and not efficacy was evaluated. Covner (1969) compared professional evaluation of the competency of volunteer counselors who were and were not alcoholic themselves. No difference was detected between the counseling skills of the former alcoholics vs. the nonalcoholic, counselors. Argeriou and Manohar (1978) found in a population of DWI offenders, that recovering alcohol counselors achieved higher rates of acceptance of problems assessed at termination of counseling and higher levels of abstention in referrals who were under 35, although no differences were detected among older patients. Of the three nonalcoholic counselors, only one held a professional degree (a master's degree in rehab counseling). These three studies suggested relatively equivalent outcome for alcoholic vs. nonalcoholic treatment providers.

In recent times, the burden of proof has shifted to the nonalcoholic therapist. There is a study that addressed whether alcoholics would be more willing to accept a recovering alcoholic in the role of therapist than a therapist who does not hold this qualification. Kirk, Best, and Irwin (1986) showed a videotape of a counseling session to alcoholics in treatment. In one condition the counselor was purported to be a recovering alcoholic while in the other no information was provided. The status of the counselor produced no impact on the perceived empathy of the counselor.

Those few studies comparing recovering alcoholics in the role of counselor with nonalcoholic counselors have not demonstrated major differences in outcome. Perhaps the difference between recovering alcoholic vs. professional is not the relevant variable. It may be that belief in the disease concept and traditional approach is the relevant variable along which differences in outcome might emerge. This empirical question should be evaluated in future research.

DOES FORCED TREATMENT WORK?

In recent years the number of individuals sent into alcoholism treatment by the courts has increased. Employers also refer alcoholics into treatment and loss of job can be the consequence for failure to attend. Forced treatment constitutes a significant departure from the manner in which treatment was once provided. The question of whether forced treatment can work has been addressed.

Before outcome can be considered, let us examine whether coercion is sufficient to bring alcoholics into treatment. Rosenberg and Liftik (1976) compared patients who were court referred after DWIs with voluntary patients at the same treatment center. Each group was comprised of working class persons with stable families. Court order did increase attendance. Further, 16% of the coerced patients remained in treatment 6 months later after the court order expired. Decreased dropout rates in the court ordered DWI group compared to voluntary patients was also found by Hoffmann et al. (1987). Whereas there is evidence that court coercion will increase attendance, family pressure may exert less influence on behavior. Noel et al. (1987) found that those pressured into treatment by their families vs. those who were not evidenced early dropouts from the program.

Outcome studies have compared coerced patients with noncoerced patients in the same program. As will be seen, the impact of coerced treatment varies depending on whether the alcoholic has an intact life or is a skid row denizen. Most studies have found that coerced patients who have jobs and a family do as well as voluntary patients. At 6 month follow-up, Hoffman et al. (1987) detected no differences in abstention or AA use between the DWI referrals (the coerced group) and other patients in the same treatment program. Smart (1974) compared employed alcoholics who were referred by their employees with alcoholics who had self-referred. At 12 month follow-up, there were no significant differences between the groups on drinking dependent variables. Dubourg (1969) failed to find a difference on outcome measures between those presenting for treatment under duress and those who volunteered. Chapman and Huygens (1988) found that at 18 month follow-up, those who had entered treatment under pressure from family members or employer had slightly better outcomes than those who did not report such pressure.

Although most studies either find no difference or better outcome for the coerced group within an economically stable population, there are a few contrary findings. Gillis and Keet (1969) note that those entering treatment under duress vs. voluntary patients evidenced worse outcome at 3 year follow-up. McLachlan and Stein (1982) found less abstention at 1 year follow-up among employer referred patients than among voluntary referred patients. Although the former group was less often abstinent, many had decreased their absenteeism from work, such that their employers considered them to be successes.

The prior research has compared coerced patients with voluntary patients in the same treatment program. There is a study that evaluated coerced treatment on ex-convicts. Here, the control group consisted of ex-convicts who were not mandated into treatment. Gallant, Faulkner, Stoy, Bishop, and Langdon (1967) examined the effect of treatment on ex-convicts as a condition of parole. Those who were mandated into 6 months treatment vs. those who were not treated displayed a nonsignificant trend toward increased abstinence and less criminal recidivism. Four of the nine mandated patients elected to continue therapy for an additional 6 months after the court mandate had expired.

Whereas the prior research has investigated the impact of coerced treatment on employed persons, others (Ditman, Crawford, Forgy, Moskowitz, & Mac-Andrew, 1967; Gallant, Bishop, Mouledoux, Faulkner, Brisolara, & Swanson, 1973; Mindlin, 1960) have examined the effect of mandated treatment on public inebriates. The studies examining impact on skid row individuals have found that court ordered treatment has little impact. Apparently, threat only works for those individuals who have something to lose. Lemere, O'Hallern, and Maxwell's (1958) study supported this view. Those coming to treatment under threat of loss of job or marriage manifested favorable recovery rates. Those presenting after loss had occurred manifested worse outcomes than others.

For those coerced individuals who do improve with treatment, the perception of coercion dissipates (Freedberg & Johnston, 1978). Although this decrease in perceived coercion may reflect an actual decrease in pressure, it is significant that alcoholics are able to recognize this decrease in external pressure. The picture seems to be that if the alcoholic can be engaged in treatment, somewhere in the treatment process sufficient motivation is acquired for success. Given time in treatment, alcoholics forced into therapy do feel that their recoveries are volitional.

DIFFERENTIAL EFFICACY AS A FUNCTION OF TYPE OF TREATMENT

Several large outcome studies have examined a broad range of treatment facilities and addressed the question of whether particular treatments are more effective than others. This endeavor has been hindered by the fact that different types of patients do self-select into particular forms of treatment. The indigent more often appear in halfway houses or Salvation Army facilities. Private hospitals and residential treatment centers more often attract more socially stable, financially self-sufficient individuals (Bromet et al., 1977b; Smart et al., 1969).

Bromet et al. (1977b) assessed 6-month outcomes in a halfway house, a Salvation Army residential program, a hospital program for the indigent, a milieu program drawing a more stable population, and an aversion treatment program also drawing a stable population. They controlled for the effect of SES by using as their dependent variable deviations from predictions based on patient characteristics assessed at intake. Patient characteristics included SES, marriage, and drinking variables (quantity/frequency; symptomotology). Bromet et al. report that differences in treatment modality did account for between 1.5 to 3.8% of the variance in explaining outcome on drinking measures, psychological functioning measures, and vocational measures. The aversion therapy and the milieu therapy programs produced the best outcomes. Patients in the aversion therapy program were functioning better on drinking variables although their social and psychological functioning was worse than prediction. Patients from the milieu program were functioning better in all arenas.

The milieu program examined by Bromet et al. differed from the other program in that it involved heavy participation by the patient. There are several other studies that suggest that actively involving patients in the process improves outcome. Stinson, Smith, Amidjaya, and Kaplan (1979) randomly assigned patients to a staff intensive or a peer directed 4- to 6-week inpatient experience. The staff directed program had a higher staff to patient ratio and involved both employers and family. Aftercare planning was initiated early in treatment in this program. Medications, individual counseling, family therapy, group therapy, role playing, education, AA meeting, and vocational counseling were included. The peer treatment program had a low patient to staff ratio. In the peer treatment program, patients participated in ward government, wherein patients could request staff consultation, but staff participation was not built into the treatment. At 18 month follow-up, results favored the peer directed program on drinking variables, although there were no differences between the groups on social functioning variables.

Galanter, Castaneda, and Salamon (1987) results also favored patient directed therapy. These researchers compared a patient directed program to staff directed program for a patient sample of largely Black and Hispanic alcoholics. The patient directed program achieved a higher patient retention rate during transition to an aftercare program. No differences at 1 year follow-up on drinking variables or AA use were detected, although the self-help group was performing better on social functioning.

Others have failed to detect differences in outcome when comparing particular treatments. McCance and McCance (1969) randomly assigned patients to aversion therapy, or group therapy. No differences were detected at follow-up. Some have found that therapist behavior has an effect on outcome. Among patients in a treatment program to teach control drinking, therapist accurate empathy is associated with better treatment outcome (Miller, Taylor, & West, 1980). Valle (1981) found that patients, in a standard treatment program, who rated their therapists highly on the Truax triad (empathy, genuineness, unconditional regard for the client) displayed lower rates of relapse and a diminished dropout rate.

Dependent Variables on Which Different Types of Treatment Produce Differential Outcomes

Whereas little difference in efficacy has been demonstrated among treatment programs, treatment programs vary in their impact on thinking processes. Maisto et al. (1988) examined attributions for relapse episodes among male alcoholics and their spouses who had participated in a behavioral marital therapy treatment program, male alcoholics who had participated in a couples interactional marital treatment program, and male alcoholics who had participated in traditional treatment wherein both AA and antabuse were encouraged. Relapse occurrence and duration in treatment did not differ among the groups, whereas attributions for relapse did differ. Those involved in the couples treatment more often attributed their relapses to interactions with their spouses. Those receiving traditional treatment attributed relapses to cravings and urges. The groups did not differ in their stated reasons for curtailing relapses. Approximately 39% in each group mentioned self-control as the reason.

DO DIFFERENT TREATMENTS WORK BEST FOR DIFFERENT PEOPLE?

Pattison, Coe, and Rhodes (1969) have advanced the notion that particular individuals may achieve better outcomes in particular types of treatment centers. It is a well-documented finding that particular treatment centers do draw from particular populations (Costello, 1975b; Finney & Moos, 1986; Pattison et al., 1969). Aversion treatment centers are privately run and quite expensive and therefore recruit a more stable and affluent population. Halfway houses attract the homeless, often without jobs. The modal form of treatment available, the traditional model, has been applied to the broadest range of clients. There have been few studies investigating whether particular types of people achieve better outcomes in particular treatment orientations.

Most meta analyses of treatments have failed to discern a differential effect of treatment among patient groups. Smart (1978a), whose patients were not randomly assigned to treatment facility examined the impact of 7 different treatment programs. None of the interactions between type of treatment and type of patient was significant. Finney and Moos (1986), in a similar meta analysis, failed to find statistical support for the idea that particular types of patients would achieve better outcomes in particular types of treatments.

McLachlan (1974) found that better outcomes were achieved when patients differing on levels of cognitive complexity were matched to therapist with the same level of cognitive complexity. An early study by Kissen, Platz, and Su (1970) in which random assignment was achieved, suggested that the psychologically sophisticated do better with a psychological approach whereas the less sophisticated respond best to drug therapy. Specifically, those more intelligent and field independent improved more in psychotherapy whether provided on an inpatient or outpatient basis, whereas the less intelligent, more field dependent improved more with drug therapy.

A recent study by Kadden et al. (1989) differentiated patients who were low on the socialization scale of the California Personality inventory, patients who displayed a high degree of psychological distress, and patients who were cognitively impaired. They randomly assigned patients to either a coping skills, a structured aftercare group, or an aftercare group that focused on interpersonal issues among the group members. The interpersonal issues group produced better outcomes among those who were cognitively impaired and those who were high on the socialization scale. The coping skill group produced better outcomes among those scoring low on the socialization scale (i.e., those who were more sociopathic) and those who were psychologically distressed.

Summary

For the most part no particular treatment has been demonstrated as strongly superior to other forms of treatment. There is suggestion that greater patient involvement and greater patient self-direction results in better outcome. Therapist empathy enhances treatment efficacy. For patients who are cognitively impaired, approaches that require a great deal of processing of cognitive material should be avoided. Those who are sociopathic benefit from skills training.

AFTERCARE

What Percentage Will Participate in Aftercare?

The high dropout rates that are to be expected in alcoholism treatment have already been discussed. The transition from a packaged treatment program to aftercare during which therapy is usually provided once per week, constitutes a point at which many will fail to return. Researchers have provided data on the percentages that can be expected to drop out in the transition to aftercare.

In examining the transition from inpatient treatment to outpatient aftercare, Pokorny, Miller, Kanas, and Valles (1973) found that 66% of their 122 patients came to aftercare, 38% came to between 1 to 3 sessions, and 28% attended over 3 sessions. Pratt, Linn, Carmichael, and Webb (1977) found that one-third of their 90 VA patients who had attended an 8-week inpatient program attended at least 1 aftercare session. Only 9% attended over 4 sessions. In Booth et al.'s

(1984) sample of patients who had completed a 6-week inpatient program, 27/37 came to at least 1 aftercare session. The mean number of aftercare sessions attended was 3.

Is Aftercare Participation Related to Outcome?

There have been studies in which as association between outcome and aftercare attendance has not been detected (Dubourg, 1969; Gibbins & Armstrong, 1957; Kish, Ellsworth, & Woody, 1980). Others have found that those who attend aftercare display better outcome during the follow-up periods than those who do not (Booth et al., 1984; Bromet & Moos, 1979; Costello, 1980; Costello, Baillargeon, Biever, & Bennett, 1980; Gillis & Keet, 1969; Intagliata, 1976; Moore & Ramseur, 1959; Ornstein & Cherepon, 1985; Pokorny et al., 1973; Ritson, 1969; Walcott & Straus, 1952). The studies finding a positive association do not allow for a causal statement. The obtained association may reflect the fact that motivation causes both better outcome and aftercare attendance, rather than aftercare attendance causing improved outcome. Walker, Donovan, Kivlahan, and O'Leary (1983) found that those completing an agreed upon aftercare program were more successful than those who failed to complete the program. Aftercare completion predicted outcome after the effects of pretreatment functioning were statistically controlled. Others have found that duration of aftercare attendance rather than number of sessions attended is more strongly correlated with outcome (Gilbert, 1988; Walker et al., 1983).

There have been few studies that can allow for a causal statement about the impact of aftercare. These studies employed random assignment. A study by Gilbert (1988) investigated methods for increasing aftercare attendance randomly assigning patients to a group that would be heavily induced to come to aftercare vs. a group following standard protocol. The procedures (later reviewed) were successful in increasing aftercare attendance. However, there was no evidence that the groups in which aftercare attendance had been increased, differed on drinking outcome. McLatchie and Lomp (1988) randomly assigned patients to mandatory aftercare, aftercare which was on a voluntary basis, or a group in which aftercare was not available. Although aftercare participation did differ among the groups, (such that those for whom aftercare participation was presented as a mandatory extension of the inpatient program more often participated), differences at 3 and 12 month aftercare relapse did not differ among the groups. These studies employing random assignment offer no support for the idea that aftercare causes a better outcome.

When a correlation between aftercare and better outcome (as was found in the Gilbert, 1988, study) is found it could reflect several causal associations. One possible causal association is that those patients who are more enthused will come to aftercare and stay sober. A second possible causal association is that patients who comply with treatment recommendations to attend aftercare or anything else are likely to stay sober. McLatchie and Lomp (1988) found that those patients who complied with their counselors recommendations, even when the recommendations did not include aftercare attendance, were more likely to stay sober than those who did not. Those who voluntarily attended aftercare exhibited fewer relapses than did those who were noncompliant, but were not as successful as the group who were selected for compliance with counselor recommendations. Apparently, compliance is a personality factor that augurs well for future positive outcome.

Is Leaving Aftercare Always a Bad Sign?

There are studies suggesting that people who are doing well drop out of treatment. Vannicelli (1978) conducted a cross lag panel analysis on the relationship between aftercare attendance and outcome during the first 3 months postdischarge and then during the third through sixth month post discharge. She found a positive correlation between attendance during the first 3 months and sobriety. There was a negative correlation between aftercare attendance and outcome during the second 3-month interval. Elal-Lawrence et al. (1987) discovered a similar pattern. Those who were relapsing throughout the follow-up period attended aftercare sporadically. The successful attended aftercare consistently immediately following program discharge, but then dropped out.

Patient Characteristics of Those Who Attend Aftercare

Some attempts to identify patient characteristics that are associated with aftercare attendance have occurred. Pratt et al. (1977) found those patients who preceived the inpatient therapy as allowing for more autonomy as assessed by the Moos ward atmosphere scale were more likely to present for aftercare. The variable of patient stability of residence has not been found to consistently relate to aftercare attendance. Pratt et al. (1977) found that those attending aftercare were more likely to be living away from home. Intagliata (1976) observed positive associations between aftercare attendance and stability in living situation. Pokorny, Miller, Kanas, and Valles (1973) found that aftercare attenders were more likely to be married and to have stable work histories. Costello (1980) failed to detect a relationship between stability assessed at intake and aftercare attendance or between ward adjustment and aftercare attendance.

Pokorny et al. (1973) found no difference on drinking severity at intake between aftercare attenders and nonattenders.

What Procedures Enhance Retention in Aftercare?

Contracting does increase the rate of aftercare attendance (Ossip-Klein et al., 1984; Powell & Viamontes, 1974). Provision of medication of any type is associated with increased aftercare attendance (Powell & Viamontes, 1974). Gilbert (1988) compared methods designed to increase aftercare attendance following 4 to 5 weeks of inpatient VA alcoholism treatment. Provision of individual therapy in a location of the patients choosing along with active pursuit when the patient missed an appointment, increased the number of sessions attended and increased the percentage of patients who completed a year of aftercare. When therapists reverted at 6 months to providing aftercare in the usual manner (individual sessions at the hospital without pursuit following failed appointments), attendance rates reverted to control levels. Aheles et al. (1983) and Ossip-Klein et al. (1984) increased aftercare attendance by providing patients with calenders at discharge on which their appointments were designated. Ahles et al. (1983) also found that when significant others agreed to reinforce aftercare attendance, absenteeism from aftercare decreased. Intagliata (1976) demonstrated that biweekly phone calls expressing concern and encouraging aftercare attendance would increase aftercare attendance during a 3 month follow-up interval subsequent to a 6- to 8-week inpatient program.

Summary

Studies suggest that at least a third of the patients attending a treatment program will fail to transition to aftercare. Aggressive pursuit with phone calls and letters, along with calender reminders and family encouragement can increase aftercare attendance. There is little evidence that aftercare attendance causes better outcome. The association between attendance and better outcome when found, probably reflects greater enthusiasm and greater compliance. Enthusiasm and compliance may be the causal mechanisms for increasing sobriety. There is some evidence that after about 3 months, the patients who are having less trouble staying sober will drop out of aftercare. Hence, leaving treatment is not necessarily an ominous sign.

PATIENT VARIABLES PREDICTING SUCCESS

Most reviewers of the research have concluded that patient variables are more powerful predictors of success than are treatment variables (Bromet, Moos, Bliss, & Wuthmann, 1977a; Polich et al., 1981). Bromet et al. (1977a) who examined outcome at 6- to 8-month follow-up, found that 15 to 33% of the variance was predicted by pretreatment functioning.

Social Stability and Socioeconomic Standing

The strongest predictors of success are socioeconomic status (Bromet et al., 1977a; Gibbs & Flanagan, 1977; Gillis & Keet, 1969; Trice, Roman, & Belasco,

1969) and being married at intake (Bromet et al., 1977a; Davies, Sheperd, & Myers, 1956; Pokorny, Miller, & Cleveland, 1968; Ornstein & Cherepon, 1985). Leading a more stable life as evidenced by fewer arrests and stable work history is associated with better outcome (Costello, 1980; Davies et al., 1956; Gibbs & Flanagan, 1977; Kendall & Stanton, 1966; McCance & McCance, 1969; Orford, Oppenheimer & Edwards, 1976; Ornstein & Cherepon, 1985; Selzer & Holloway, 1957; Trice et al., 1969; Walcott & Straus, 1952). Being on disability predicts treatment failure (Chapman & Huygens, 1988). Higher income predicts success (Chapman & Huygens, 1988).

Whereas the preceding studies examined short follow-up intervals, Vaillant (1983 pp. 155–171) reports results of a follow-up interval of 8 years in a sample of public clinic treated alcoholics. By 8 year follow-up, social stability at intake, employment at intake, and living with spouse at intake continued to predict better outcome. However, education was not predictive. In the Vaillant (1983) report, rates of stable abstention were compared in a group of blue collar alcoholics who were raised in inner city Boston with a group of college educated alcoholics. The rates of stable remission did not vary in the two alcoholic samples.

Summary.   Social stability and more economic advantages are clearly associated with better outcome prognosis. Vaillant's comparison of the college educated with the blue collar suggest there is a point at which an increase in income will level off in terms of adding to better outcome. The real differences are probably between those who do and do not have a job, a home, and a family.

Age

Inconsistent relationships between outcome and age have emerged in the literature. Orford (1973) failed to detect a relationship between age and outcome. Walcott and Straus (1952) and Chapman & Huygens (1988) found that younger patients are less likely to be relapsed. In some studies older patients have better outcomes (Bateman & Petersen, 1971; Fawcett et al., 1984; Hoff & McKeown, 1953; Litman, Eiser, Rawson, & Oppenheim, 1979a; Lundwall & Baekland, 1971; Ornstein & Cherepon, 1985; Rathod et al., 1966; Selzer & Holloway, 1957) and are more likely to become abstinent (Chapman & Huygens, 1988; Helzer et al., 1985). Wolff and Holland (1964) found that those over 45 more often were abstinent at follow-up. Whereas older persons are more likely to remit through abstention, younger persons will display higher rates of control drinking (Vogler et al., 1977).

There are theoretical reasons suggesting that age will be inconsistently related to outcome. In chapter 1, studies in which individuals who were exhibiting problem drinking, who became asymptomatic drinkers in their midtwenties were reviewed (e.g., Fillmore 1974, 1975). It is probably the case, that in some subcultures norms pertinent to the young will pressure problem drinking. As young problem drinkers age, another set of norms will obtain, and they will become asymptomatic drinkers. If many of these social norm-induced problem drinkers constitute the bulk of younger alcoholics in a particular treatment center, then their positive outcomes are expected on the basis of a change in age-related norms. These individuals probably were not primary alcoholics and should improve with graduation to a category in which norms related to older people apply. This is a theoretical explanation for why young alcoholics can be expected to produce favorable outcomes. On the other hand, it is known that severity of alcoholism during the lifetime is associated with younger age of onset of drinking problems. If a particular sample of young alcoholics at a particular treatment center were heavily comprised of younger, early onset, sociopathic, family history positive alcoholics, then very poor outcomes would be found for the young.

Sociopathy

Patients with lower Psychopathic Deviate scores on the MMPI and without personality disorders display superior treatment outcomes (Davies et al., 1956; Porkorny, Miller, & Cleveland, 1968; Rathod et al., 1966; Rounsaville et al., 1987; Trice et al., 1969). Whereas such findings obtain in studies with 1- or 2-year follow-up intervals, there is reason to believe that long-term studies will not detect a relationship. In Vaillant's (1983) study in which alcoholics (most of whom were never in treatment) were tracked over several decades, sociopathy was unrelated to outcome. Although sociopathy was not predictive of stable abstinence in the inner city, untreated sample, sociopaths were more likely to become institutionalized or die (p. 169). Further, they were less likely to become control drinkers (p. 170).

Whereas sociopathy is a negative predictor in general, if a middle-class population is observed, then those scoring highly on the psychopathic deviate and mania scales of the MMPI are found to do better than others at follow-up (Conley, 1981). Zivich (1981) found that impulsive types as assessed by the Personality Research Form displayed relatively good outcomes, although Zivich thought that perhaps the extremely impulsive may have dropped out of treatment prior to assessment.

Depression

The bottom lines on how depression relates to outcome will vary according to whether the depressed are compared to those with a personality disorder or those without additional diagnoses. Some studies have found that patients who are more depressed at intake are less likely to be improved at follow-up than those without psychiatric diagnoses (Lundwall & Baekeland, 1971; McLellan et al., 1983; Thurstin et al., 1986). Other studies have not detected an association between intake depression and outcome. Freed, Riley, and Ornstein (1977) found that intake Profile of Mood States responses did not distinguish those who were successful and unsuccessful at follow-up. However, higher hostility scores on the POMs at discharge was related to lack of success at follow-up. Schuckit (1986) failed to find any relationship between intake depression and number of days abstention during the follow-up interval. Pottenger et al. (1978) found higher relapse rates among those whose depression persisted throughout the 1 year follow-up interval.

If those who are depressed at intake are compared to those who are sociopathic, depression at intake predicts better outcome. In their review of the literature, Gibbs and Flanagan (1977), who may have been comparing the psychoneurotically depressed with those who were sociopathic, found better outcome for the depressed. Hedberg et al. (1971) found that the depressed/ distressed at intake are functioning better at follow-up than are the antisocial personalities.

Rounsaville et al. (1987) found that depression was differentially associated with outcome for males and females. For males, depression, whether the depression onset was concomitant with heavy drinking or whether it predated alcoholism, predicted worse outcome even after covarying drinking severity. For women, depression predicted better outcome compared to those who were not depressed or those who were sociopathic.

There are theoretical reasons for hypothesizing inconsistent relationship between outcome and depression. If depression is measured at intake, it will reflect the pharmacological impact of the amount of alcohol consumed. Hence, it will be a correlate of alcoholism severity, which itself predicts worse outcome. However, depression can also reflect a primary depression/secondary alcoholism status.

Schuckit (1979) has been a proponent of distinguishing primary alcoholics from primary depression/secondary alcoholics. Primary despressives are those for whom depression predated alcoholism or for whom there have been 3-month intervals of depression during periods of sobriety. Schuckit (1986) found that primary depressives have better outcomes than primary alcoholics.

A certain amount of depression probably reflects dissatisfaction with drinking and hence represents a correlate of motivation. Consistent with this view, Shaw et al. (1975) found in a population of young alcoholics (mean age 35), that less depression predicted increased treatment dropout.

There are two studies in the literature that examined whether different variables will predict outcome among persons at various levels of depression. Both studies (McLellan, Luborsky, Woody, O'Brien, & Druley 1983; Svanum & McAdoo, 1989) found that the severely depressed produced the worst outcomes. They did find some complex interactions, however. The basic findings are reviewed.

McLellan et al. (1983) divided 879 patients into three groups (low, medium, and high) based on the severity of psychiatric symptoms (most of them symptoms of affective and anxiety disorders) at intake. The low symptom group improved most at 6 month follow-up and did so regardless of the treatment provided. The high group displayed the worst outcomes especially when the patient was older. Duration of treatment did not matter for this group. In those displaying midrange symptoms, the older patients, those with more previous treatment, those with increased family and legal problems improved the least. Greater length of treatment in this group was associated with better outcome; those with severe employment and family problems improved less in outpatient therapy than inpatient.

Svanum and McAdoo (1989) found that those with elevated MMPI profiles (indicating a large number of psychiatric symptoms) at intake exhibited poorer outcomes. In this study the MMPI profile elevations were correlated with greater severity of withdrawal symptoms. MMPI elevations at intake did not predict MMPI elevations during the follow-up interval.

Svanum and McAdoo had a second objective for their study—to determine if different factors were associated with better outcome at distinct levels of intake MMPI profile elevation. They explored their question by examining relapse predictors in the group with high intake MMPI elevations and the group with low intake MMPI elevations. Different factors were related to outcome in each of the groups. For the normal profile group, the predictors of success were: more exercise during the aftercare interval, greater satisfaction with posttreatment living arrangements, stability in work arrangements, lower SES, absence of alcohol related financial problems, a higher level of drug use at intake, a greater number of family alcohol related problems at intake. For the elevated MMPI profile group, the predictors of success were: less psychiatric turmoil during the follow-up interval, developing nondrinking friend, a change in work situation during follow-up interval, taking antabuse, living in a family situation, diminished belief in one's ability to control alcohol and drug use, increasing severity of withdrawal assessed at intake, and diminished severity of alcohol related legal problems at intake.

Others have examined personality traits often associated with depression. The more gregarious (Trice et al., 1969) and those who have established relationships with others (Kendell & Stanton, 1966) have been found to display better posttreatment outcomes. Costello (1980), however, failed to detect a relationship between ward adjustment during inpatient treatment and outcome. Patients with higher MMPI K scores, possibly reflecting ego strength, display better outcomes (Thurstin et al., 1986). Zivich (1981) found that schizoid alcoholics displayed particularly poor outcomes.

Treatment Dropouts

Some studies failed to detect a difference in outcome between treatment dropouts vs. those who complete treatment (Chapman & Huygens, 1988). Other studies have found that those discharged or dropping out of treatment display poorer outcomes (Elal-Lawrence et al., 1987; Fitzgerald, Pasewark, & Clark, 1971; Ornstein & Cherepon, 1985; McWilliams & Brown, 1977).

Perception of Treatment and Degree of Enthusiasm Manifested While in Treatment

Patients who participate in more activities regardless of the length of time in treatment produce better outcomes (Bromet et al., 1977a; Gillis & Keet, 1969; Moos, Mehren, & Moos, 1978). Patients who view their treatment programs positively and who work harder at improvement have better outcomes (Rathod, Gregory, Blows, & Thomas, 1966). Bromet et al. (1977a) report that patient participation variables accounted for between 1–20% of the variance in predicting outcome in the various treatment centers. Patients who violate rules and refuse antabuse display worse outcomes at follow-up (McWilliams & Brown, 1977).

Drinking While in Treatment

Those who drink while in treatment display poor outcomes (McWilliams & Brown, 1977; Rathod et al., 1966; Skolada et al., 1975). Those who are discharged prematurely for disciplinary reasons are more often found in the relapsed category at follow-up (Elal-Lawrence, 1987). In experimental drinking programs, those who opt to drink and who display an enhanced autonomic reaction to drinking have poorer outcomes (Alterman, Gottheil, Gellens, Thornton, 1977; Cannon, Baker, Gino, & Nathan, 1986; Pomerleau et al., 1983). Patients holding the expectation that alcohol will relieve their tensions display less favorable outcomes (Brown, 1985). Miller, Hernsen, Eisler, and Elkins (1974) found that those patients who worked harder in an operant paradigm for alcohol and who rated the taste as more pleasing evidenced less recovery.

Severity of Alcoholism

Fewer prior hospitalizations for treatment of alcoholism and a relatively lower degree of physical problems created by drinking are associated with better outcome (Bill C., 1965; Bromet et al., 1977a; Davies et al., 1956; Orford, 1973; Ornstein & Cherepon, 1985; Rosenberg, 1983). There is an inconsistent finding. Gillis and Keet (1969) found that those with more prior alcohol treatment admissions evidenced better outcomes. The findings regarding presence of absence of withdrawal have not been consistent. Litman et al. (1979a) show that more severe withdrawal predicted less relapse. Willems, Letemendia, and Arroyave (1973a) found that a history of delirium tremens predicted more relapse.

Whereas prior hospitalizations are often associated with treatment failure, prior attempts to stay sober are predictive of better posttreatment outcome. Mulford (1977) states that more attempts to quit drinking was a correlate of treatment success. Ornstein and Cherepon (1985) found that more pretreatment abstention predicted better outcome. Haberman (1966) asserts that sobriety at follow-up was predicted by prior attendance at AA and prior periods of protracted abstention. Chapman and Huygens (1988) found that more previous abstention was related to improvement at 18 month follow-up.

In terms of style of drinking, McCabe (1986) found in a study assessing alcoholics 16 years after treatment that the binge drinkers at intake were less likely to be improved than the steady state drinkers.

The findings relating outcome with duration of problem drinking have been inconsistent. This is probably to be expected since duration of problem drinking is correlated with age of the patient. There are contradictory theoretical predictions for how age should relate to outcome. These contradictions are related to the findings examining the association between duration of alcoholism and outcome as well.

Some have shown that a longer history of alcoholism predicts success (Lundwall & Baekeland, 1971; Trice et al., 1969; Vogler et al., 1977). Rathod et al. (1966), who defined success only in terms of abstinence, found that a longer history of excessive drinking among the older alcoholics but not the younger predicted success. Selzer and Holloway (1957), however, found in a group of older alcoholics that younger age of problem drinking onset predicted poorer outcome. Those who are first treated for alcoholism after the age of 45, display better outcome (Chapman & Huygens, 1988). Others have found that longer duration of excessive drinking is predictive of treatment failure (Davies et al., 1956; Kendall & Stanton, 1966; Orford, 1973) or have failed to detect a relationship (Ornstein & Cherepon, 1985; Selzer & Holloway, 1957).

Vogler et al. (1975) state that heavier consumption prior to treatment predicted treatment failure. Alford (1980) detected a curvilinear relationship between amount of alcohol consumption and treatment outcome. Those consuming between 100–200 oz. of whiskey per week displayed the best outcome, better than those consuming less or more than this amount. Those consuming over 200 oz. per week displayed the worse outcomes. A curvilinear relationship was suggested for duration of alcohol problems as well. Those who had manifested problem drinking for less than 10 years had the highest percentage in the success category, followed by the group displaying the problem for over 35 years. The group manifesting problems between 11–34 years displayed success rates that were midway between the two other groups.

In his sample of public clinic alcoholics followed for 8 years, Vaillant (1983, p. 155) found that many variables which predicted success in the short run, failed to predict long-range response. At 8 year follow-up, physiological dependence on alcohol, age of onset of alcoholism, age of admission, adolescent alcohol abuse, history of previous abstention, family history status, no longer differentiated the successful from the relapsed.

Cognitive Capacity

Most reviewers of the research conclude that the cognitively impaired alcoholics evidence less favorable treatment outcomes (Abbot & Gregson, 1981; Donovan et al., 1987; Gibbs & Flanagan, 1977; Miller & Hester, 1980, p. 97; Walker, Donovan, Kivlahan, & O'Leary, 1983). They are more likely to drop out of treatment prior to program completion (Donovan et al., 1987, p. 342). They are less likely to be employed at follow-up time (Donovan et al., 1987, p. 352).

Internal vs. External Locus of Control

Internal–external locus of control has not been found to relate in a consistent manner to treatment outcome (Donovan & O'Leary, 1983). There is some suggestion that patients do become more internal with regard to life outcomes in general and ability to resist pressures to drink over the course of treatment (Donovan & O'Leary, 1983), although paradoxically, recovering alcoholics employed as alcoholism counselors score more externally than do alcoholics who are first entering treatment (Costello & Manders, 1974). There is also suggestion that externals remain in aftercare for a longer period of time than do internals (Donovan & O'Leary, 1983). Although this latter finding might be extended to imply that externals should produce better outcomes, it should be recalled that aftercare dropout does not necessarily reflect treatment failure. As a general rule of thumb, participation in aftercare is associated with success, however Vannicelli's (1978) findings suggest that after 3 months, the successful leave treatment whereas those who are making a difficult adjustment remain. Rather than having implications for outcome, the finding of extended aftercare participation among the externals may reflect a particularly good fit between patient orientation and modality of treatment offered.

Sex

In a study by Chapman and Huygens (1988), women displayed better outcomes than men. Vannicelli (1984) reviewing the literature concluded there are no differences between men and women in outcome.

Events Occurring During the Follow-up Interval

Moos, Finney, and Chan (1981) found that relapse was predicted by the number of stressful life events experienced by the patient during the follow-up interval.

Tucker, Vuchinich, and Harris (1985) state that negative events associated with an area in which drinking had depleted the individuals resources were particularly likely to precipitate relapse.

Discussion and Summary

Cronkite and Moos (1978) have suggested that variables predicting outcome can be grouped into classes or blocks of variables. Categories include (1) patient characteristics (SES, stability of work and social relations, drinking history); (2) treatment variables; (3) patient participation and perception of treatment variables; (4) environmental stresses encountered after discharge; and (5) availability and quality of social support subsequent to discharge. Determining the relative importance of each of these influences on outcome has been difficult owing to the covariation among the variables. Cronkite and Moos contend that the relative unimportance of treatment variables in contrast to the strong influence of patient variables on treatment outcome may be an artifact of researchers standard procedure of entering patient variables first into regression analyses. Such procedures mask the importance of program variables. Cronkite and Moos advocate path analysis as a mechanism for untangling the confusion created by the covariation of variables.

In their 1978 path analysis, Cronkite and Moos concluded that patient socioeconomic status best predicted occupational functioning posttreatment. Participation in treatment and perception of treatment, however, predicted amount of alcohol consumed during the follow-up interval.

Studies examining patient variable predicting treatment success provide obscure bottom lines in many areas. Severity of alcoholism, which can be operationalized in so many different ways, does not relate in a consistent manner. Further, Alford (1980) has detected a curvilinear relationship using operationalizations of duration of problem drinking and typical amount consumed.

Personality factors, such as sociopathy and depression, have produced inconsistent findings as well. Much of the inconsistency is probably due to the fact that the same personality trait will reflect different things depending on the population. For example, the presence of depression can reflect a primary condition of depression, it can reflect dissatisfaction with one's drinking, or it can reflect withdrawal distress. An elevated psychopathy scale in a middle-class population does not have the same significance as it does in a skid row sample. Added to the confusion in trying to predict outcome from personality variables are the results of long-term studies. Vaillant (1983) has found that personality predictors (e.g., sociopathy) of failure in the short run (a 2-year window of time after any particular treatment attempt) will no longer be predictive over a 20-year time frame.

There are consistent findings that emerge from the investigations of patient variable predicting outcome. The strongest predictors of success are having a stable job and an intact family. Patients who view the therapeutic experience more positively and participate more actively in treatment do better. A relatively stress free existence following treatment makes drinking relapse less likely.

HOW STABLE ARE OUTCOME CATEGORIES?

Clinicians will want to know how long to follow a patient after it appears that the patient has achieved a meaningful sobriety. The questions of "when is the patient out of the woods?" and "how long should a patient who is doing well continue to participate in aftercare?" are of practical importance. For researchers who conduct investigations of outcome, the issue of stability of outcome is also very important. Such being the case, it is not surprising that researchers have collected data on the issue of outcome stability. Findings from these investigations are reviewed next.

Emrick (1975), citing data from many articles, concluded that although individual patients may indeed change their status at any point in time, group statistics seem to stabilize around 6 months. Movement from recovery to relapse is as likely as movement from relapse to recovery. Those who are in the moderate drinking category are less stable than the totally relapsed. With the exception of a study by Gottheil et al. (1982), abstinence also seems to be a stable category. Bottom lines from specific studies provide further information.

Gottheil et al. (1982) found that 26% of his sample of 156 were in the relapsed categories across all follow-up periods (6, 12, and 24 months); 26% of the sample were consistently in the moderate drinking categories across all follow-up periods; 8% were in the consistently abstinent category across all follow-up periods. The remainder of the sample fluctuated across categories with movement from a remitted category to a relapse category being as likely as movement from a relapsed category to a remitted category.

The Gottheil et al. data are consistent with the Rand report (Polich et al., 1981), which concluded that percentages of individuals in each outcome category are stable after 1 year follow-up. Forty-two percent of the Rand report sample remained in the same outcome category from 18 months to 4 years. Although there was change for some individuals, change from recovered to crapulous drinking was as likely as change from crapulous drinking to recovered. The findings of Chapman and Huygens lend confidence to the idea that outcome categories are fairly consistent. Chapman and Huygens (1988) followed-up at 6 and 18 months. Between 3 to 8% of each outcome category had switched categories at the second follow-up.

Rychtarik et al. (1987) had an unusually long follow-up interval. They found that abstention or uncontrolled drinking outcome for the period of 7 through 12 months predicted the 6-month interval prior to 5- to 6-years follow-up. Moderate drinking was not a reliable predictor for the future. Watson and Pucel (1985) were concerned to identify the point in time at which outcome stabilizes, concluding that stabilization occurs at 2 to 3 months, although prediction during the first month is not as accurate. Those who are control drinking during the first 9 months of follow-up are frequently changed to the relapsed category at later follow-up. However, those who maintain control drinking beyond 9 months, are likely to exhibit stable patterns.

Studies have been consistent in reporting that abstention and crapulous drinking is more stable than is the moderate (control) drinking. Control drinking seems to be the category in which the greatest instability emerges. This is a particular problem for treatment programs in which the goal is control drinking. Miller and Baca (1983) report on outcome stability for individuals after participation in a control drinking program. In a sample of 69 subjects available for follow-up, at 2 years 81% were in the same category as they had been at treatment termination. Eighty-five percent were in the same category at 3- to 6-months as they had been at treatment termination, and 89% were in the same category at 1 year. Ewing and Rouse (1976) have cautioned that a 2-year period will not be long enough to make predictions about lifetime recovery. Persons who are control drinking for 2 years may not be able to do so for decades.

In terms of long-term stability it is important to specify the interval of time about which predictions are being made. In Lemere's (1953) sample, 8% sustained abstention for 3 years and then relapsed.

DOES THE ARREST OF ALCOHOLISM CORRELATE WITH IMPROVEMENT IN OTHER AREAS

Pattison, Coe, and Rhodes (1969) have cautioned the treatment community against the knee-jerk assumption that abstinence will redound in improved functioning in other life areas or, conversely, that abstinence will not produce deterioration in other life areas. The critical test for such a hypothesis is addressed by those studies in which a correlation is computed between amount of drinking and indices of particular problems. Another test of the hypothesis is provided by comparison of groups of abstinent, controlled drinking, and problematic drinking on indices of life function.

Numerous outcome studies have found greater improvement in other life areas among the abstinent or controlled drinkers than among those who continue to drink heavily (Alford, 1980; Chapman & Huygens, 1988; Fink et al., 1985; Gillis & Keet, 1969; Gottheil et al., 1982; Pokorny, Miller, & Cleveland, 1968; Rathod et al., 1966; Selzer & Holloway, 1957; Skolada, Alterman, Cornelison, Gottheil, 1975; Vaillant, 1983, p. 213). Costello et al. (1980) found that drinking success was related to all other areas of improved functioning. Highest correlations were observed between drinking and interpersonal relations, whereas drinking status correlated lowest with engagement in recreational activities. Emrick's (1974) meta analysis across 271 studies concluded that there is a positive association between drinking outcome (improved) and functioning in other life areas.

It is an oft reported finding that alcoholics first entering into treatment will score in the depressed range on assessment instruments. This depression remits by the second week of treatment (Overall et al., 1985). Vaillant's (1983) compared a sample of men who had been abstinent from alcohol for over 3 years to a normal control group. No differences in psychological functioning could be detected. It can be inferred that refraining from heavy drinking allows the depression induced by heavy consumption to ameliorate.

Other studies with regard to improvement in psychological functioning post-treatment suggest that a cessation of heavy drinking is the necessary adjustment. If comparisons are made between those who are abstinent at follow-up and those who are control drinking at follow-up, no differences in psychological functioning are observed. Both groups are better than the unremitted group, however (Polich, Armor, & Braiker, 1980). It would seem that the important category in terms of psychological and social functioning is whether the individual is drinking heavily vs. either being abstinent or being a controlled drinker. Some studies have found high rates of disturbance among the abstinent (see review by Miller & Caddy, 1977) or have failed to detect better functioning among the abstinent compared to pretreatment functioning (Hill & Blane, 1967; Moore & Ramseur, 1959; Pattison et al., 1969). In a study by Gerard et al. (1962) 54% of the abstinent were overtly disturbed. These studies suggest that abstinence per se will not guarantee better functioning.

Other statistical analyses have supported some independence of drinking outcome and social functioning outcome. In a study by Babor et al. (1988) a factor analysis of outcome variables did produce separate factors for drinking variables and social/psychological functioning variables. Drinking outcome and social/psychological functioning do constitute separate, distinct dimensions. However, in the Babor et al. study the two factors were significantly correlated ($r = .39$).

The bottom line seems to be that recovery, be it through control drinking or abstention, more often than not will ramify positively through other areas of life. Some studies have failed to detect difference between pre–post functioning among those who are sober. Because alcoholics vary enormously in terms of the areas of their lives impacted by their drinking, and some alcoholics are only affected in terms of health but not social functioning, a failure to witness gains in the social life areas should not be surprising.

WHICH PATIENT CHARACTERISTICS CREATE THERAPIST PERCEPTION OF PATIENT MOTIVATION?

It is known that the subjective judgments of clinicians regarding patient's prognosis are influenced by a variety of patient characteristics. Only some of these characteristics have been demonstrated empirically to be linked to outcome. Inasmuch as therapist enthusiasm and hope, may itself be related to outcome, it is important for clinicians to be aware of those factors that can influence their perceptions.

Research suggests that therapists view patients who are compliant and accepting, who are dependent, and who are more psychologically distressed as more motivated for sobriety (Miller, 1985). Some traits that lead to a judgment of greater motivation themselves predict better treatment outcome. Some traits do not. Although compliance is predictive of less relapse (McLatchie & Lomp, 1988), patients with better ego strength (a negative correlate of dependency) (Thurstin et al., 1986) exhibit less relapse. Hence, it is well to remember that therapist's judgments about who are the best candidates for sobriety may not always correspond to empirical findings.

Related to therapist's perceptions of client motivation are the phenomenon of therapist's liking for the client and their recommendation that the client continue with therapy. O'Leary, Donovan, Chaney, and O'Leary (1979) have found that if the staff liked the patient, the staff was more likely to recommend that the patient continue with treatment. Additional therapist-subjective judgment variables also related to recommendation to continue treatment. Therapist's perception of clients greater knowledge of current events, therapist's perception of client's better moral standards, and therapist's perception of client's good social adjustment predicted recommendations for continued treatment. Staff recommendation of continued treatment participation were predicted by 4 out of 40 assessment measures completed by the patient: (1) higher educational level; (2) a greater need for others to initiate close, intimate relationships; (3) higher ego strength; and (4) a higher level of defensiveness as assessed by the K scale of the MMPI.

THE IMPACT OF THE RAND REPORT

Given the stir produced by the Rand report, it is fortunate that data were collected regarding its impact on alcoholics. The Rand report suggested that many alcoholics treated in AA oriented programs went on to achieve control drinking. Hingson, Scotch, and Goldman (1977) assessed the impact of the Rand report 6 months after its findings were publicized in major newspapers. Awareness of the report followed dispersion pattern of other information, i.e., educated persons were more likely to be aware of the report. Severity of drinking problem did not increase the likelihood that an individual would be aware of the report. Twenty-three percent of Boston area residents were cognizant of the report as were 23% of alcoholic patients. Of the 23%, two-thirds stated they believed the findings (ability to control drink) were probably peculiar to some but not all alcoholics. Most did not believe the findings were relevant to them. That is, they did not feel they had received a mandate to control drink. Only 5/244 reported that they had been effected by the report.

References

Abbott, M. W., & Gregson, R. A. M. (1981). Cognitive dysfunction in the prediction of relapse in alcoholics. *Journal of Studies on Alcohol, 42,* 230–243.

Ahles, T. A., Schlundt, D. G., Prue, D. M., & Rychtarik, R. G. (1983). Impact of aftercare treatment on the maintenance of treatment success in abusive drinkers. *Addictive Behaviors, 8,* 53–58.

Alcoholics Anonymous: The story of how many thousands of men and women have recovered from alcoholism. (1976). New York: Alcoholics Anonymous.

Alcoholics Anonymous World Service Inc. (1985). *Twelve Steps and Twelve Traditions.* New York: Alcoholics Anonymous.

Alden, L. E. (1988). Behavioral self-management controlled-drinking strategies in a context of secondary prevention. *Journal of Consulting and Clinical Psychology, 56,* 280–286.

Alford, G. S. (1980). Alcoholics Anonymous: An empirical outcome study. *Addictive Behavior, 5,* 359–370.

Alterman, A. I., Gottheil, E., Gellens, H. K., & Thornton, C. C. (1977). Relationship between drinking behavior of alcoholics in a drinking-decision treatment program and treatment outcome. In P. E. Nathan, G. A. Marlatt, & T. Loberg (Eds.), *Alcoholism: New directions in behavioral research and treatment* (pp. 211–234). New York: Plenum Press.

Altman, H., Evenson, R., & Won Chon, D. (1978). Predicting length of stay by patients hospitalized for alcoholism or drug dependence. *Journal of Studies on Alcohol, 39,* 197–201.

Andersson, T., & Magnusson, D. (1988). Drinking habits and alcohol abuse among young men: A prospective longitudinal study. *Journal of Studies on Alcohol, 49,* 245–252.

Annis, H. H. (1979). Self-report reliability of skid-row alcoholics. *British Journal of Psychiatry, 34,* 459–465.

Apfeldorf, M. (1978). Alcoholism scales of the MMPI: Contributions and future directions. *International Journal of the Addictions, 13,* 17–53.

Apfeldorf, M., & Hunley, P. J. (1985). Two MMPI approaches for identifying alcoholics: Evaluation and implications for further research. *International Journal of the Addictions, 20,* 1361–1398.

Argeriou, M., & Manohar, V. (1978). Relative effectiveness of nonalcoholics and recovered alcoholics as counselors. *Journal of Studies on Alcohol, 39,* 793–799.

Ashley, M. J., le Riche, W. H., Olin, J. S., Hatcher, J., Kornaczewski, A., Schmidt, W., & Rankin, J. G. (1978). 'Mixed' (drug abusing and pure alcoholics: A socio-medical comparison. *British Journal of Addiction, 73,* 19–34.

Asp, D. R. (1977). Effects of alcoholics' expectation of a drink. *Journal of Studies on Alcohol, 38,* 1790–1795.

Atsaides, J. P., Neuringer, C., & Davis, K. L. (1977). Development of an institutionalized chronic alcoholic scale. *Journal of Consulting and Clinical Psychology, 45,* 645–653.

Ayers, J., Ruff, C. F., & Templer, D. T. (1976). Alcoholism, cigarette smoking, coffee drinking and extraversion. *Journal of Studies on Alcohol, 37,* 983–985.

Azrin, N. H. (1976). Improvements in the community-reinforcement approach to alcoholism. *Behavior Research and Therapy, 14,* 339–348.

Babor, T. F., Dolinsky, Z., Rousaville, B., & Jaffee, J. (1988). Unitary versus multidimensional models of alcoholism treatment outcome: An empirical study. *Journal of Studies on Alcohol, 49,* 167–177.

Babor, T. F., Stephens, R. S., & Marlatt, G. A. (1987). Verbal report methods in clinical research on alcoholism: Response bias and its minimization. *Journal of Studies on Alcohol, 48,* 410–424.

Baekeland, F., Lundwall, L., & Shanahan, T. J. (1973). Correlates of patient attrition in the outpatient treatment of alcoholism. *Journal of Nervous and Mental Disease, 157,* 99–107.

Baer, J. S., & Lichtenstein, E. (1988). Classification and prediction of smoking relapse episodes: An exploration of individual differences. *Journal of Consulting an Clinical Psychology, 56,* 104–110.

Bailey, M. B., Haberman, P. W., & Alksne, H. (1965). The epidemiology of alcoholism in an urban residential area. *Quarterly Journal of Studies on Alcohol, 26,* 19–40.

Bailey, M. B., Haberman, P. W., & Sheinberg, J. (1966). Identifying alcoholics in population surveys: A report on reliability. *Journal of Studies on Alcohol, 27,* 300–315.

Bailey, M. B., & Stewart, J. (1967). Normal drinking by persons reporting previous problem drinking. *Quarterly Journal of Studies on Alcohol, 28,* 305–315.

Baker, T. B., Udin, H., & Vogler, R. E. (1975). The effects of videotaped modeling and self-confrontation on the drinking behavior of alcoholics. *International Journal of Addictions, 10,* 779–793.

Bandura, A., Adams, N. E., & Beyer, J. (1977). Cognitive processes mediating behavior change. *Journal of Personality and Social Psychology, 35,* 125–139.

Baron, R. A., & Byrne, D. (1981). *Social Psychology: Understanding human interaction.* Boston: Allyn and Bacon.

Barr, H. L., Antes, D., Ottenberg, D. J., & Rosen, A. (1984). Mortality of treated alcoholics and drug addicts: The benefits of abstinence. *Journal of Studies on Alcohol, 45,* 440–452.

Bateman, N. I., & Petersen, D. M. (1971). Variables related to outcome of treatment for hospitalized alcoholics. *International Journal of Addictions, 64,* 2115–224.

Battjes, R. J. (1988). Smoking as an issue in alcohol and drug abuse treatment. *Addictive Behaviors, 13,* 225–230.

Bauman, D. J., Obitz, F. W., & Reich, J. W. (1982). Attribution theory: A fit with substance abuse problems. *International Journal of Addictions, 17,* 295–303.

Baumohl, J., & Room, R. (1987). Inebrity, doctors and the state: Alcoholism treatment institutions before 1940. In M. Galanter (Ed.), *Recent developments in alcoholism* (pp. 125–174, Vol. 5). New York: Plenum Press.

Beck, N. C., Skekim, W., Fraps, C., Borgmeyer, A., & Witt, A. (1983). Prediction of discharges against medical advice from an alcohol and drug misuse treatment program. *Journal of Studies on Alcohol, 44,* 171–180.

Beck, A. T., Steer, R. A., & Trexler, L. D. (1989). Alcohol abuse and eventual suicide: A 5- to 10-year prospective study of alcohol-abusing suicide attempters. *Journal of Studies on Alcohol, 50,* 202–209.

Beckman, L. J. (1975). Women alcoholics: A review of social and psychological studies. *Journal of Studies on Alcohol, 36,* 797–824.

Beckman, L. J., & Amaro, H. (1984). Patterns of women's use of alcohol treatment agencies. In S. C. Wilsnak & L. J. Beckman (Eds.), *Alcohol problems in women: Antecedents, consequences, and interventions* (pp. 319–348). New York: Guilford Press.

Behar, D., Winokur, G., & Berg, C. J. (1984). Depression in the abstinent alcoholic. *American Journal of Psychiatry, 141,* 1105–1107.

Behrens, U. J., Worner, T. M., Braly, L. F., Schaffner, F., & Lieber, C. S. (1988). Carbohydrate-deficient transferrin, a marker for chronic alcohol consumption in different ethnic populations. *Alcoholism: Clinical and Experimental Research, 12,* 427–432.

Belasco, J. A. (1971). The criterion question revisited. *British Journal of Addiction, 66,* 39–44.

Belenko, S. (1979). Alcohol abuse by heroin addicts: Review of research findings and issues. *International Journal of Addictions, 14,* 965–975.

Belfer, M. L., Shader, R. I., Carroll, M., & Harmatz, J. S. (1971). Alcoholism in women. *Archives of General Psychiatry, 25,* 540–544.

Bellack, A. S., Rozensky, R., & Schwartz, J. (1974). A comparison of two forms of self-monitoring in a behavioral weight reduction program. *Behavior Therapy, 5,* 523–530.

Bem, D. J. (1972). Self-perception theory. In L. Berkowitz (Ed.), *Advances in experimental social psychology* (pp. 2–61, Vol. 6). New York: Academic Press.

Benson, C. S., & Wilsnack, S. C. (1983). Gender differences in alcoholic personality characteristics and life experiences. In W. M. Cox (Ed.), *Identifying and measuring alcoholic personality characteristics* (pp. 53–72). San Francisco: Jossey-Bass.

Berg, N. L. (1971). Effects of alcohol intoxication on self-concept: Studies of alcoholics and controls in laboratory conditions. *Quarterly Journal of Studies on Alcohol, 32,* 442–453.

Berg, G., Laberg, J. C., Skutle, A., & Ohman, A. (1981). Instructed versus pharmacological effects of alcohol in alcoholics and social drinkers. *Behavior, Research, & Therapy, 19,* 55–66.

Berglund, M. (1984). Suicide in alcoholism: A prospective study of 88 suicides: I. The multidimensional diagnosis at first admission. *Archives of General Psychiatry, 41,* 888–891.

Bernadt, M. W., Mumford, J., Taylor, C., Smith, B., & Murray, R. M. (1982). Comparison of questionnaire and laboratory tests in the detection of excessive drinking and alcoholism. *Lancet, 1,* 325–328.

Best, J. A. (1975). Tailoring smoking withdrawal procedures to personality and motivational differences. *Journal of Consulting and Clinical Psychology, 43,* 1–8.

Bigelow, G., Liebson, I., & Griffiths, R. (1974). Alcoholic drinking: Suppression by a brief time-out procedure. *Behavior Research and Therapy, 12,* 107–115.

Bill, C. (1965). The growth and effectiveness of Alcoholics Anonymous in a southwestern city, 1945–1962. *Quarterly Journal of Studies on Alcohol, 26,* 279–284.

Blakey, R., & Baker, R. (1980). An exposure approach to alcohol abuse. *Behavior Research and Therapy, 18,* 319–325.

Blane, H. T., & Meyers, W. R. (1964). Social class and establishment of treatment relations by alcoholics. *Journal of Clinical Psychology, 20,* 287–290.

Blashfield, R. K. (1985). Meta-cluster-analysis on MMPI studies of alcoholics. *Bulletin of the Society of Psychologists in Addictive Behaviors, 4,* 29–40.

Blittner, M., Goldberg, J., & Merbaum, M. (1978). Cognitive self-control factors in the reduction of smoking behavior. *Behavior Therapy, 9,* 553–561.

Blum, T. C., Roman, P. M., & Bennett, N. (1989). Public images of alcoholism: Data from a Georgia survey. *Journal of Studies on Alcohol, 50,* 5–14.

Blumberg, L. (1977). The ideology of therapeutic social movement: Alcoholics Anonymous. *Journal of Studies on Alcohol, 38,* 2122–2143.

Blumberg, L. U., Shipley, T. E., & Moor, J. O. (1971). The skid row man and the skid row status community: With perspectives on their future. *Quarterly Journal of Alcohol, 32,* 909–941.

Booth, P. G., Dale, B., & Ansari, J. (1984). Problem drinkers' goal choice and treatment outcome: A preliminary study. *Addictive Behaviors, 9,* 357–364.

Boscarino, J. (1980). Factors related to "stable" and "unstable" affiliation with Alcoholics Anonymous. *International Journal of the Addictions, 15,* 839–848.

Bower, G. H. (1981). Mood and memory. *American Psychologist, 36,* 129–148.

Brandsma, J. M., Maultsby, M. C., & Welsh, R. J. (1980). *The outpatient treatment of alcoholism: A review and comparative study.* Baltimore, MD: University Park.

Brehm, S. S., & Brehm, J. W. (1981). *Psychological Reactance: A theory of freedom and control.* New York: Academic Press.

Brenner, B. (1967). Alcoholism and fatal accidents. *Quarterly Journal of Studies on Alcohol, 28,* 517–528.

Brickman, P., Rabinowitz, V. C., Karuza, J., Coates, D., Cohn, E., & Kidder, L. (1982). Models of helping and coping. *American Psychologist, 37,* 368–384.

Brissett, D., Laundergan, J. C., Kammeier, M. L., & Biele, M. (1980). Drinkers and nondrinkers at three and a half years after treatment: Attitudes and growth. *Journal of Studies on Alcohol, 41,* 945–952.

Bromet, E., & Moos, R. (1976). Sex and marital status in relation to the characteristics of alcoholics. *Journal of Studies on Alcohol, 37,* 1302–1312.

Bromet, E. J., & Moos, R. (1979). Prognosis of alcoholic patients: Comparisons of abstainers and moderate drinkers. *British Journal of Addictions, 74,* 183–188.

Bromet, E., Moos, R., Bliss, F., & Wuthmann, C. (1977a). Posttreatment functioning of alcoholic patients: Its relation to program participation. *Journal of Consulting and Clinical Psychology, 45,* 829–842.

Bromet, E., Moos, R., Wuthmann, C., & Bliss, F. (1977b). Treatment experiences of alcoholic patients: An analysis of five residential alcoholism programs. *International Journal of Addictions, 12,* 953–958.

Brooner, R. K., Templer, D., Svikis, D. S., Schmidt, C., & Monopolis, S. (1990). Dimensions of alcoholism: A multivariate analysis. *Journal of Studies on Alcohol, 51,* 77–81.

Brown, R. A., & Williams, R. J. (1975). Internal and external cues relating to fluid intake in obese and alcoholic persons. *Journal of Abnormal Psychology, 84,* 512–519.

Brown, S. A. (1985). Reinforcement expectancies and alcoholism treatment outcome after a one-year follow-up. *Journal of Studies on Alcohol, 46,* 304–308.

Brown, S. A., Goldman, M. S., & Christiansen, B. A. (1985). Do alcohol expectancies mediate drinking patterns in adults? *Journal of Consulting and Clinical Psychology, 53,* 512–519.

Brown, S. A., Goldman, M. S., Inn, A., & Anderson, L. R. (1980). Expectations of reinforcement from alcohol: Their domain and relation to drinking patterns. *Journal of Consulting and Clinical Psychology, 48,* 419–426.

Brown, S. A., & Schuckit, M. A. (1988). Changes in depression among abstinent alcoholics. *Journal of Studies on Alcohol, 49,* 412–417.

Brownell, K. D., Marlatt, G. A., Lichtenstein, E., & Wilson, G. T. (1986). Understanding and preventing relapse. *American Psychologist, 41,* 765–782.

Burish, T. G., Maisto, S. A., Cooper, A. M., & Sobell, M. B. (1981). Effects of voluntary short-term abstinence from alcohol on subsequent drinking patterns of college students. *Journal of Studies on Alcohol, 42,* 1013–1020.

Burling, T. A., Reilly, P. M., Moltzen, J. O., & Ziff, D. C. (1989). Self-efficacy and relapse among inpatient drug and alcohol abusers: A predictor of outcome. *Journal of Studies on Alcohol, 50,* 354–360.

Burnum, J. F. (1974). Outlook for treating patients with self-destructive habits. *Annals of Internal Medicine, 81,* 387–393.

Caddy, G. R., Addington, H. J., & Perkins, D. (1978). Individualized behavior therapy for alcoholics: A third year independent double-blind follow-up. *Behavior Research and Therapy, 16,* 345–362.

Cadoret, R. J., Troughton, E., O'Gorman, T. W., & Heywood, E. (1986). An adoption study of genetic and environmental factors in drug abuse. *Archives of General Psychiatry, 43,* 1131–1136.

Caetano, R. (1987). Public opinions about alcoholism and its treatment. *Journal of Studies on Alcohol, 48,* 153–160.

Cahalan, D., Cisin, I. H., & Crossley, H. M. (1969). American drinking practices. *Monographs of Rutgers Center of Alcohol Studies.* Number 6.

Cahalan, D., & Room, R. (1972). Problem drinking among American men aged 21–59. *American Journal of Public Health, 62,* 1473–1482.

Campbell, J. D., & Fairey, P. J. (1985). Effects of self-esteem, hypothetical explanations, and verbalizations of expectancies on future performance. *Journal of Personality and Social Psychology, 48,* 1097–1111.

Cannon, D. S., Baker, T. B., Gino, A., & Nathan, P. E. (1986). Alcohol-aversion therapy: Relation between strength of aversion and abstinence. *Journal of Consulting and Clinical Psychology, 54,* 825–830.

Cannon, D. S., Baker, T. B., & Ward, N. O. (1977). Characteristics of volunteers for a controlled drinking training program. *Journal of Studies on Alcohol, 38,* 1799–1803.

Cannon, D. S., Baker, T. B., & Wehl, C. K. (1981). Emetic and electric shock alcohol aversion therapy: Six- and twelve-month follow-up. *Journal of Consulting and Clinical Psychology, 49,* 360–368.

Canter, F. M. (1966). Personality factors related to participation in treatment by hospitalized male alcoholics. *Journal of Clinical Psychology, 22,* 114–116.

Canter, F. M. (1971). Authoritarian attitudes, degree of pathology and preference for structured versus unstructured psychotherapy in hospitalized mental patients. *Psychological Reports, 28,* 231–234.

Carroll, L. J., Yates, B. T., & Gray, J. J. (1980). Predicting obesity reduction in behavioral and nonbehavioral therapy from client characteristics: The self-evaluation measure. *Behavior Therapy, 11,* 189–197.

Carver, C. S., Blaney, P. H., & Scheier, M. F. (1979). Reassertion and giving up: The interactive role of self-directed attention and outcome expectancy. *Journal of Personality and Social Psychology, 37,* 1859–1870.

Chafetz, M. E., Blane, H. T., Abram, H. S., Golner, J., Lacy, E., McCourt, W. F., Clark, E., & Meyers, W. (1962). Establishing treatment relations with alcoholics. *Journal of Nervous and Mental Disease, 134,* 395–409.

Chambliss, C., & Murray, E. J. (1979). Cognitive procedures for smoking reduction: Symptom attribution versus efficacy attribution. *Cognitive Therapy and Research, 3,* 91–95.

Champlin, S. M., & Karoly, P. (1975). Role of conflict negotiation in self-management of study time: A preliminary investigation. *Psychological Reports, 37,* 724–726.

Chandler, B. C., Parsons, O. A., & Vega, A. (1975). Autonomic functioning in alcoholics: A study of heart rate and skin conductance. *Journal of Studies on Alcohol, 36,* 566–577.

Chaney, E. F., O'Leary, M. R., & Marlatt, G. A. (1978). Skill training with alcoholics. *Journal of Consulting and Clinical Psychology, 46,* 1092–1104.

Chaney, E. F., Roszell, D. K., & Cummings, C. (1982). Relapse in opiate addicts: A behavioral analysis. *Addictive Behaviors, 7,* 291–297.

Chapman, P. L. H., & Huygens, I. (1988). An evaluation of three treatment programmes for alcoholism: An experimental study with 6- and 18-month follow-ups. *British Journal of Addictions, 83,* 67–81.

Charalampous, K. D., Ford, B. K., & Skinner, T. J. (1976). Self-esteem in alcoholics and non-alcoholics. *Journal of Studies on Alcohol, 37,* 990–994.

Chick, J. (1980a). Alcohol dependence: Methodological issues in its measurement; Reliability of the criteria. *British Journal of Addiction, 75,* 175–186.

Chick, J. (1980b). Is there a unidimensional alcohol dependence syndrome? *British Journal of Addiction, 75,* 265–280.

Chick, J., Ritson, B., Connaughton, J., Stewart, A., & Chick, J. (1988). Advice versus extended treatment for alcoholism: A controlled study. *British Journal of Addiction, 83,* 159–170.

Choquette, K. F., Hesselbrock, M. N., & Babor, T. F. (1985). Discriminative control of alcoholics' drinking by the drinking situation. *Journal of Studies on Alcohol, 46,* 412–415.

Christiansen, B. A., Goldman, M. S., & Inn, A. (1982). Development of alcohol-related expectancies in adolescents: Separating pharmacological from social-learning influences. *Journal of Consulting and Clinical Psychology, 50,* 336–344.

Cialdini, R. B. (1984). *Influence.* New York: Morrow.

Ciraulo, D. A., Sands, B. R., & Shader, R. I. (1988). Critical review of liability for benzodiazepine abuse among alcoholics. *American Journal of Psychiatry, 145,* 1501–1506.

Clark, W. (1966). Operational definitions of drinking problems and associated prevalence rates. *Quarterly Journal of Studies on Alcohol, 27,* 648–668.

Clark, W. B. (1976). Loss of control, heavy drinking, and drinking problems in a longitudinal study. *Journal of Studies on Alcohol, 37,* 1256–1290.

Clopton, J. R. (1978). Alcoholism and the MMPI: A review. *Journal of Studies on Alcohol, 39,* 1540–1558.

Condiotte, M. M., & Lichtenstein, E. (1981). Self-efficacy and relapse in smoking cessation programs. *Journal of Consulting and Clinical Psychology, 49,* 648–658.

Conley, J. J. (1981). An MMPI typology of male alcoholics: Admission, discharge, and outcome comparisons. *Journal of Personality Assessment, 45,* 33–39.

Connors, G. J., Tarbox, A. R., & McLaughlin, E. J. (1986). Contrasting binge and continuous drinkers using demographic and drinking history variables. *Alcohol and Alcoholism, 21,* 105–110.

Cooper, A. M., Sobell, M. B., Maisto, S. A., & Sobell, L. C. (1980). Criterion intervals for pretreatment drinking measures in treatment evaluation. *Journal of Studies on Alcohol, 41,* 1186–1195.

Costello, R. M. (1975a). Alcoholism treatment and evaluation: In search of methods. *International Journal of Addictions, 10,* 251–275.

Costello, R. M. (1975b). Alcoholism treatment and evaluation: In search of methods II. Collation of two-year follow-up studies. *International Journal of Addictions, 10,* 857–867.

Costello, R. M. (1980). Alcoholism aftercare and outcome: Cross-lagged panel and path analyses. *British Journal of Addiction, 75,* 49–53.

Costello, R. M., Baillargeon, J. G., Biever, P., & Bennett, R. (1980). Therapeutic community treatment for alcohol abusers: A one-year multivariate outcome evaluation. *International Journal of Addictions, 15,* 215–232.

Costello, R. M., & Manders, K. R. (1974). Locus of control and alcoholism. *British Journal of Addictions, 69,* 11–17.

Covner, B. J. (1969). Screening volunteer alcoholism counselors. *Quarterly Journal of Studies on Alcohol, 30,* 420–425.

Cox, W. M., & Klinger, E. (1988). A motivational model of alcohol abuse. *Journal of Abnormal Psychology, 97,* 168–180.

Cramer, M. J., & Blacker, E. (1966). Social class and drinking experience of female drunkenness offenders. *Journal of Health and Human Behavior, 7,* 276–283.

Critchlow, B. (1985). The blame in the bottle: Attributions about drunken behavior. *Personality and Social Psychology Bulletin, 11,* 258–274.

Cronkite, R. C., & Moos, R. H. (1978). Evaluating alcoholism treatment programs: An integrated approach. *Journal of Consulting and Clinical Psychology, 46,* 1105–1119.

Curlee, J. (1970). A comparison of male and female patients at an alcoholism treatment center. *Journal of Psychology, 74,* 239–247.

Curry, S. G., & Marlatt, G. A. (1987). Building self-confidence, self-efficacy, and self-control. In W. M. Cox (Ed.), *Treatment and prevention of alcohol problems* (pp. 117–137). Orlando, FL: Academic Press.

Cutter, H. S. G., Schwaab, E. L., & Nathan, P. E. (1970). Effects of alcohol on its utility for alcoholics and nonalcoholics. *Quarterly Journal of Studies on Alcohol, 31,* 369–378.

Cyr, M. G., & Wartman, S. A. (1988). The effectiveness of routine screening questions in the detection of alcoholism. *Journal of the American Medical Association, 259,* 51–54.

Czarnecki, D. M., Russell, M., Cooper, M. L., & Salter, D. (1990). Five-year reliability of self-reported alcohol consumption. *Journal of Studies on Alcohol, 51,* 68–76.

Dahlgren, L., & Willander, A. (1989). Are special treatment facilities for female alcoholics needed? A controlled 2-year follow-up study from a specialized female unit (EWA) versus a mixed male/female treatment facility. *Alcoholism: Clinical and Experimental Research, 13,* 499–504.

Davies, D. L. (1962). Normal drinking in recovered alcohol addicts. *Quarterly Journal of Studies on Alcohol, 23,* 94–104.

Davies, D. L., Shepherd, M., & Myers, E. (1956). The two-years' prognosis of 50 alcohol addicts after treatment in hospital. *Quarterly Journal of Studies on Alcohol, 17,* 485–502.

Davis, L. J., Colligan, R. C., Morse, R. M., & Offord, K. P. (1987a). Validity of the MacAndrew scale in a general medical population. *Journal of Studies on Alcohol, 48,* 202–206.

Davis, L. J., Hurt, R. D., Morse, R. M., & O'Brien, P. C. (1987b). Discriminant analysis of the self-administered alcoholism screening test. *Alcoholism: Clinical and Experimental Research, 11,* 269–273.

DiClemente, C. C. (1981). Self-efficacy and smoking cessation maintenance: A preliminary report. *Cognitive Therapy and Research, 5,* 175–187.

Ditman, K. S., & Crawford, G. G. (1966). The use of court probation in the management of the alcohol addict. *American Journal of Psychiatry, 122,* 757–762.

Ditman, K. S., Crawford, G. G., Forgy, E. W., Moskowitz, H., & MacAndrew, C. (1967). A controlled experiment on the use of court probation for drunk arrests. *American Journal of Psychiatry, 124,* 160–163.

Dolan, L. P. (1975). An intake group in the alcoholism outpatient clinic. *Journal of Studies on Alcohol, 36,* 996–999.

Donovan, D. M., Chaney, E. F., & O'Leary, M. R. (1978). Alcoholic MMPI subtypes: Relationship to drinking styles, benefits, and consequences. *Journal of Nervous and Mental Disease, 166,* 553–561.

Donovan, J. E., Jessor, R., & Jessor, L. (1983). Problem drinking in adolescence and young adulthood: A follow-up study. *Journal of Studies on Alcohol, 44,* 109–137.

Donovan, D. M., & O'Leary, M. R. (1978). The drinking-related locus of control scale: Reliability, factor structure, and validity. *Journal of Studies on Alcohol, 39,* 759–784.

Donovan, D. M., & O'Leary, M. R. (1983). Control orientation, drinking behavior, and alcoholism. In H. M. Lefcourt (Ed.), *Research with the locus of control construct: Developments and social problems* (pp. 107–153, Vol 2). New York: Academic Press.

Donovan, D. M., Walker, R. D., & Kivlahan, D. R. (1987). Recovery and remediation of neuropsychological functions: Implications for alcoholism rehabilitation process and outcome. In O. A. Parsons, N. Butters, & P. E. Nathan (Eds.), *Neuropsychology of alcoholism: Implications for diagnosis and treatment* (pp. 339–360). New York: Guilford.

Drew, L. R. H. (1968). Alcoholism as a self-limiting disease. *Quarterly Journal of Studies on Alcohol, 29,* 956–967.

Dubourg, G. O. (1969). After-care for alcoholics—A follow-up study. *British Journal of Addiction, 64,* 155–165.

Duffy, J. C., & Waterton, J. J. (1984). Under-reporting of alcohol consumption in sample surveys: The effect of computer interviewing in fieldwork. *British Journal of Addictions, 79,* 303–308.

Dweck, C. S. (1975). The role of expectations and attributions in the alleviation of learned helplessness. *Journal of Personality and Social Psychology, 31,* 674–685.

Eastman, C., & Norris, H. (1982). Alcohol dependence, relapse and self-identity. *Journal of Studies on Alcohol, 43,* 1214–1231.

Edwards, G. (1985). A later follow-up of a classic case series: D. L. Davies's 1962 report and its significance for the present. *Journal of Studies on Alcohol, 46,* 181–190.

Edwards, G., & Guthrie, S. (1966). A comparison on inpatient and outpatient treatment of alcohol dependence. *Lancet, 1,* 467–468.

Edwards, G., & Guthrie, S. (1967). A controlled trial of inpatient and outpatient treatment of alcohol dependency. *Lancet, 1,* 555–560.

Edwards, G., Hensman, C., Hawker, A., & Williamson, V. (1966). Who goes to Alcoholics Anonymous? *Lancet, 2,* 382–384.

Edwards, G., Hensman, C., & Peto, J. (1973). Drinking in a London suburb: Reinterview of a subsample and assessment of response consistency. *Quarterly Journal of Studies on Alcohol, 34,* 1244–1254.

Edwards, G., Orford, J., Egert, S., Guthrie, S., Hawker, A., Hensman, C., Mitcheson, M., Oppenheimer, E., & Taylor, C. (1977). Alcoholism" A controlled trial of "treatment" and "advice". *Journal of Studies on Alcohol, 38,* 1004–1031.

Elal-Lawrence, G., Slade, P. D., & Dewey, M. E. (1987). Treatment and follow-up variables discriminating abstainers, controlled drinkers, and relapses. *Journal of Studies on Alcohol, 48,* 39–46.

Elliot, E. S., & Dweck, C. S. (1988). Goals: An approach to motivation and achievement. *Journal of Personality and Social Psychology, 54,* 5–12.

Emrick, C. D. (1974). A review of psychologically oriented treatment of alcoholism. I. The use and interrelationships of outcome criteria and drinking behavior following treatment. *Quarterly Journal of Studies on Alcohol, 35,* 523–549.

Emrick, C. D. (1975). A review of psychologically oriented treatment of alcoholism: II. The relative effectiveness of different treatment approaches and the effectiveness of treatment versus no treatment. *Journal of Studies on Alcohol, 36,* 88–108.

Emrick, C. D. (1987). Alcoholics Anonymous: Affiliation processes and effectiveness of treatment. *Alcoholism: Clinical and Experimental Research, 11,* 416–423.

Emrick, C. D., & Stilson, D. W. (1977). The "Rand Report": Some Comments and a response. *Journal of Studies on Alcohol, 38,* 152–163.

Engle, K. B., & Williams, T. K. (1972). Effect of an ounce of vodka on alcoholics' desire for alcohol. *Quarterly Journal of Studies on Alcohol, 33,* 1099–1105.

Eriksen, L. (1986). The effect of waiting for inpatient alcoholism treatment after detoxification. An experimental comparison between inpatient treatment and advice only. *Addictive Behaviors, 11,* 389–398.

Erwin, J. E., & Hunter, J. J. (1984). Prediction of attrition in alcoholic aftercare by scores on the embedded figures tests and two Piagetian Tasks. *Journal of Consulting and Clinical Psychology, 52,* 354–358.

Evans, R. I., Rozelle, R. M., Mittelmark, M. B., Hansen, W. B., Bane, A. L., & Havis, J. (1978). Deterring the onset of smoking in children: Knowledge of immediate physiological effects and coping with peer pressure, media pressure, and parent modeling. *Journal of Applied Social Psychology, 8,* 126–135.

Ewing, J. A. (1984). Detecting alcoholism: The CAGE questionnaire. *Journal of the American Medical Association, 252,* 1905–1907.

Ewing, J. A., & Rouse, B. A. (1976). Failure of an experimental treatment program to inculcate controlled drinking in alcoholics. *British Journal of Addiction, 71,* 123–134.

Faraj, B. A., Camp, V., Davis, D. C., Lenton, J. D., & Kutner, M. (1989). Elevation of plasma salsolinol sulfate in chronic alcoholics as compared to nonalcoholics. *Alcoholism: Clinical and Experimental Research, 13,* 155–163.

Farber, P. D., Khavari, K. A., & Douglass, F. M. (1980). A factor analytic study of reasons for drinking: Empirical validation of positive and negative reinforcement dimensions. *Journal of Consulting and Clinical Psychology, 48,* 780–781.

Fawcett, J., Clark, D. C., Gibbons, R. D., Aagesen, C. A., Pisani, V. D., Tilkin, J. M., Sellers, D., & Stutzman, D. (1984). Evaluation of lithium therapy for alcoholism. *Journal of Clinical Psychology, 45,* 494–499.

Fazio, R. H., Effrein, E. A., & Falender, V. J. (1981). Self perception following social interaction. *Journal of Personality and Social Psychology, 41,* 232–242.

Fazio, R. H., Zanna, M. R., & Cooper, J. (1977). Dissonance and self-perception: An integrative view of each theory's proper domain of application. *Journal of Experimental Social Psychology, 13,* 464–479.

Feeney, F. E., Mindlin, D. F., Minear, V. H., & Short, E. E. (1955). The challenge of the skid row alcoholic: A social, psychological and psychiatric comparison of chronically jailed alcoholics and cooperative alcoholic clinic patients. *Journal of Studies on Alcohol, 16,* 465–477.

Feldman, D. J., Pattison, E. M., Sobell, L. C., Graham, T., & Sobell, M. B. (1975). Outpatient alcohol detoxification: Initial findings on 564 patients. *American Journal of Psychiatry, 132,* 407–412.

Festinger, L., Riecken, H. W., & Schachter, S. (1956). *When Prophecy fails,* Minneapolis: University of Minnesota Press.

Fillmore, K. M. (1974). Drinking and problem drinking in early adulthood and middle age: An exploratory 20-year follow-up study. *Quarterly Journal of Studies on Alcohol, 35,* 819–840.

Fillmore, K. M. (1975). Relationships between specific drinking problems in early adulthood and middle age: An exploratory 20-year follow-up study. *Journal of Studies on Alcohol, 36,* 882–907.

Fingarette, H. (1988). *Heavy drinking: The myth of alcoholism as a disease.* Berkeley: University of California Press.

Fink, E. B., Longabaugh, R., McCrady, B. M., Stout, R. L., Beattie, M., Ruggieri-Authelet, A., & McNeil, D. (1985). Effectiveness of alcoholism treatment in partial versus inpatient settings: Twenty-four month outcomes. *Addictive Behaviors, 10,* 235–248.

Finney, J. W., & Moos, R. H. (1981). Characteristics and prognoses of alcoholics who become moderate drinkers and abstainers after treatment. *Journal of Studies on Alcohol, 42,* 94–105.

Finney, J. W., & Moos, R. H. (1984). Life stressors and problem drinking among older adults. In M. Galanter (Ed.), *Recent developments in alcoholism* (pp. 267–288, Vol 2). New York: Plenum Press.

Finney, J. W., & Moos, R. H. (1986). Matching patients with treatments: Conceptual and methodological issues. *Journal of Studies on Alcohol, 47,* 122–133.

Finney, J. W., Moos, R. H., & Chan, D. A. (1981). Length of stay and program component effects in the treatment of alcoholism: A comparison of two techniques for process analysis. *Journal of Consulting and Clinical Psychology, 49,* 120–131.

Fisher, J. D., & Farina, A. (1979). Consequences of beliefs about the nature of mental disorders. *Journal of Abnormal Psychology, 88,* 320–327.

Fitzgerald, B. J., Pasewark, R. A., & Clark, R. (1971). Four-year follow-up of alcoholics treated at a rural state hospital. *Quarterly Journal of Studies on Alcohol, 32,* 636–642.

Flaherty, J. A., McGuire, H. T., & Gatski, R. L. (1955). The psychodynamics of the "dry drunk." *American Journal of Psychiatry, 112,* 460–464.

Folkman, S., & Lazarus, R. S. (1988). Coping as a mediator of emotion. *Journal of Personality and Social Psychology, 54,* 466–475.

Fontana, A. F., Dowds, B. N., & Bethel, M. H. (1976). A. A. and group therapy for alcoholics: An application of the word hypotheses scale. *Journal of Studies on Alcohol, 37,* 675–682.

Foy, A., March, S., & Drinkwater, V. (1988). Use of an objective clinical scale in the assessment and management of alcohol withdrawal in a large general hospital. *Alcoholism: Clinical and Experimental Research, 12,* 360–364.

Frank, J. D. (1974). *Persuasion and healing: A comparative study of psychotherapy.* New York: Schochen Books.

Freed, E. X. (1970). Alcoholism and manic-depressive disorders: Some perspectives. *Quarterly Journal of Studies on Alcohol, 31*, 62–89.

Freed, E. X. (1973). Drug abuse by alcoholics: A review. *International Journal of Addictions, 8*, 451–473.

Freed, E. X., Riley, E. P., & Ornstein, P. (1977). Assessment of alcoholics' moods at the beginning and end of a hospital treatment program. *Journal of Clinical Psychology, 33*, 887–894.

Freedberg, E. J., & Johnston, W. E. (1978). Effects of various sources of coercion on outcome of treatment of alcoholism. *Psychological Reports, 43*, 1271–1278.

Freedberg, E. J., & Johnston, W. E. (1980). Validity and reliability of alcoholics' self-reports of use of alcohol submitted before and after treatment. *Psychological Reports, 46*, 999–1005.

Freedman, J. L. (1965). Long-term behavioral consequences of cognitive dissonance. *Journal of Experimental Social Psychology, 1*, 145–155.

Fuller, R. K., Lee, K. K., & Gordis, E. (1988). Validity of self-report in alcoholism research: Results of a Veteran's Administration cooperative study. *Alcoholism: Clinical and Experimental Research, 12*, 201–205.

Galanter, M., Castaneda, R., & Salamon, I. (1987). Institutional self-help therapy for alcoholism: Clinical outcome. *Alcoholism: Clinical and Experimental Research, 11*, 424–429.

Gallant, D. M. (1986). The female alcoholic: Early onset of brain damage. *Alcoholism: Clinical and Experimental Research, 11*, 190–191.

Gallant, D. M., Bishop, M. P., Mouledoux, A., Faulkner, M. A., Brisolara, A., & Swanson, W. A. (1973). The revolving-door alcoholic: An impasse in the treatment of the chronic alcoholic. *Archives of General Psychiatry, 28*, 633–635.

Gallant, D. M., Faulkner, M., Stoy, B., Bishop, M. P., & Langdon, D. (1967). Enforced clinic treatment of paroled criminal alcoholics: A pilot evaluation. *Quarterly Journal of Studies on Alcohol, 29*, 77–83.

Gerard, D. L., Saenger, G., & Wile, R. (1962). The abstinent alcoholic. *Archives of General Psychiatry, 6*, 83–95.

Gertler, R., Raynes, A. E., & Harris, N. (1973). Assessment of attendance and outcome at an outpatient alcoholism clinic. *Quarterly Studies on Alcohol, 34*, 955–959.

Gibbins, R. J., & Armstrong, J. D. (1957). Effects of clinical treatment on behavior of alcoholic patients: An exploratory methodological investigation. *Quarterly Journal of Studies on Alcohol, 18*, 429–450.

Gibbs, L., & Flanagan, J. (1977). Prognostic indicators of alcoholism treatment outcome. *International Journal of Addictions, 12*, 1097–1141.

Gilbert, F. S. (1988). The effect of type of aftercare follow-up on treatment outcome among alcoholics. *Journal of Studies on Alcohol, 49*, 149–159.

Gillis, L. S., & Keet, M. (1969). Prognostic factors in treatment results in hospitalized alcoholics. *Quarterly Journal of Studies on Alcohol, 30*, 426–437.

Gitlow, S. (1973). Alcoholism: A disease. In P. Bourne & R. Fox (Eds.), *Alcoholism: Progress and treatment* (pp. 1–9). New York: Academic Press.

Glasgow, R. E., Klesges, R. C., Mizes, J. S., & Pechacek, T. F. (1985). Quitting smoking: Strategies used and variables associated with success in a stop-smoking contest. *Journal of Consulting and Clinical Psychology, 53*, 905–912.

Goldstein, S. G., & Linden, J. D. (1969). Multivariate classification of alcoholics by means of the MMPI. *Journal of Abnormal Psychology, 74*, 661–669.

Gomberg, L. E. (1980). *Women and alcohol—1980*. National Council on Alcohol, New York.

Goodwin, D. W. (1973). Alcohol in suicide and homicide. *Quarterly Journal of Studies on Alcohol, 34*, 144–156.

Goodwin, D. W., Crane, J. B., & Guze, S. B. (1969a). Alcoholic "blackouts": A review and clinical study of 100 alcoholics. *American Journal of Psychiatry, 126*, 191–198.

Goodwin, D. W., Crane, J. B., & Guze, S. B. (1969b). Phenomenological aspects of the alcoholic "blackout". *British Journal of Psychiatry, 115*, 1033–1038.

Goodwin, D. W., Crane, J. B., & Guze, S. B. (1971). Felons who drink: An 8-year follow-up. *Quarterly Journal of Studies on Alcohol, 32,* 136–147.

Goodwin, D. W., Davis, D. H., & Robins, L. N. (1975). Drinking amid abundant illicit drugs. *Archives of General Psychiatry, 32,* 230–233.

Goodwin, D. W., Powell, B., & Stern, J. (1971). Behavioral tolerance to alcohol in moderate drinkers. *American Journal of Psychiatry, 127,* 1651–1653.

Gordon, R. M. (1976). Effects of volunteering and responsibility on the perceived value and effectiveness of a clinical treatment. *Journal of Consulting and Clinical Psychology, 44,* 799–801.

Gorski, T. T., & Miller, M. (1982). *Counseling for relapse prevention.* Independence, MO: Independence Press.

Gottheil, E., Corbett, L. O., Grasberger, J. C., & Cornelison, F. S. (1972a). Fixed interval drinking decisions: I. A research and treatment model. *Quarterly Journal of Studies on Alcohol, 33,* 311–324.

Gottheil, E., Murphy, B. F., Skoloda, T. E., & Corbett, L. O. (1972b). Fixed interval drinking decisions: II. Drinking and discomfort in 25 alcoholics. *Quarterly Journal of Studies on Alcohol, 32,* 325–340.

Gottheil, E., Thornton, C. C., Skoloda, T. E., & Alterman, A. I. (1982). Follow-up of abstinent and nonabstinent alcoholics. *American Journal of Psychiatry, 139,* 560–565.

Graham, J. R., & Strenger, V. E. (1988). MMPI characteristics of alcoholics: A review. *Journal of Consulting and Clinical Psychology, 56,* 197–205.

Gregory, W. L., Cialdini, R. B., & Carpenter, K. M. (1982). Self-relevant scenarios as mediators of likelihood estimates and compliance: Does imagining make it so? *Journal of Personality and Social Psychology, 43,* 89–99.

Gregson, R. A. M., & Taylor, G. M. (1977). Prediction of relapse in men alcoholics. *Journal of Studies on Alcohol, 38,* 1749–1759.

Greiner, J. M., & Karoly, P. (1976). Effects of self-control training on study activity and academic performance: An analysis of self-monitoring, self-reward, and systematic-planning components. *Journal of Counseling Psychology, 23,* 495–502.

Guze, S. B., & Goodwin, D. W. (1972). Consistency of drinking history and diagnosis of alcoholism. *Quarterly Journal of Studies on Alcohol, 33,* 111–116.

Guze, S. B., Tuason, V. B., Stewart, M. A., & Picken, B. (1963). The drinking history: A comparison of reports by subjects and relatives. *Quarterly Journal of Studies on Alcohol, 24,* 249–260.

Gynther, M. D., & Brilliant, P. J. (1967). Marital status, readmission to hospital, and intrapersonal and interpersonal perceptions of alcoholics. *Quarterly Journal of Studies on Alcohol, 28,* 52–58.

Haberman, P. W. (1966). Factors related to increased sobriety in group psychotherapy with alcoholics. *Journal of Clinical Psychology, 22,* 229–235.

Hall, S. M., Havassy, B. E., & Wasserman, D. A. (1990). Commitment to abstinence and acute stress in relapse to alcohol, opiates, and nicotine. *Journal of Consulting and Clinical Psychology, 58,* 175–181.

Halisch, F., & Heckhausen, H. (1977). Search for feedback information and effort regulation during task performance. *Journal of Personality and Social Psychology, 35,* 724–733.

Hamburg, S. (1975). Behavior therapy in alcoholism: A critical review of broad-spectrum approaches. *Journal of Studies on Alcohol, 36,* 69–87.

Hamm, J. E., Major, L. F., & Brown, G. L. (1979). The quantitative measurement of depression and anxiety in male alcoholics. *American Journal of Psychiatry, 136,* 580–582.

Hampton, P. J. (1953). A psychometric study of drinkers: The development of a personality questionnaire for drinkers. *Genetic Psychology Monograph, 48,* 55–115.

Harackiewicz, J. M., Sansone, C., Blair, L. W., Epstein, J. A., & Manderlink, G. (1987). Attributional process in behavior change and maintenance: Smoking cessation and continued abstinence. *Journal of Consulting and Clinical Psychology, 55,* 372–378.

Harburg, E., Gunn, R., Gleiberman, L., Roeper, P., DiFranceisco, W., & Caplan, R. (1988). Using the short Michigan Alcoholism Screening Test to study social drinkers: Tecumseh, Michigan. *Journal of Studies on Alcohol, 49,* 522–531.

Hasin, D. S., Grant, B. F., & Endicott, J. (1988). Severity of alcohol dependence and social/occupational problems: relationship to clinical and familial history. *Alcoholism: Clinical and Experimental Research, 12,* 660–664.

Heather, N., & Robertson, I. (1981). *Controlled drinking,* London: Methuen.

Heather, N., Rollnick, S., & Winton, M. (1983). A comparison of objective and subjective measures of alcohol dependence as predictors of relapse following treatment. *British Journal of Clinical Psychology, 22,* 11–17.

Hedberg, A. G., Campbell, L. M., Weeks, S. R., & Powell, J. A. (1971). The use of the MMPI (Mini–multi) to predict alcoholics' response to a behavioral treatment program. *Journal of Clinical Psychology, 31,* 271–274.

Heilburn, A. B., & Schwartz, H. L. (1980). Self-esteem and self-reinforcement in men alcoholics. *Journal of Studies on Alcohol, 41,* 1134–1141.

Heilburn, A. B., Tarbox, A. R., & Madison, J. K. (1979). Cognitive structure and behavioral regulation in alcoholics. *Journal of Studies on Alcohol, 40,* 387–399.

Hellvuo, K., Kiianmaa, K., Juhakoski, A., & Kim, C. (1987). Intoxicating effects of lorazepam and barbital in rat lines selected for differential sensitivity to ethanol. *Psychopharmacology, 91,* 263–267.

Helzer, J. E., & Pryzbeck, T. R. (1988). The co-occurrence of alcoholism with other psychiatric disorders in the general population and its impact on treatment. *Journal of Studies on Alcohol, 49,* 219–224.

Helzer, J. E., Robins, L. N., Taylor, J. R., Carey, K., Miller, R. H., Combs-Orme, T., & Farmer, A. (1985). The extent of long-term moderate drinking among alcoholics discharged from medical and psychiatric treatment facilities. *New England Journal of Medicine, 321,* 1678–1682.

Hermos, J. A., Locastro, J. S., Glynn, R. J., Bouchard, G. R., & DeLabry, L. O. (1988). Predictors of reduction and cessation of drinking in community-dwelling men: Results from the normative aging study. *Journal of Studies on Alcohol, 49,* 363–368.

Hershon, H. I. (1977). Alcohol withdrawal symptoms and drinking behavior. *Journal of Studies on Alcohol, 38,* 953–970.

Hesselbrock, M., Hesselbrock, V., Syzmanski, K., & Weidenman, M. (1988). Suicide attempts and alcoholism. *Journal of Studies on Alcohol, 49,* 436–442.

Higginbotham, H. N., West, S. G., & Forsyth, D. R. (1988). *Psychotherapy and behavior change: Social, cultural, and methodological perspectives.* New York: Pergamon Press.

Hill, S. Y. (1984). Vulnerability to the biochemical consequences of alcoholism and alcohol-related problems among women. In S. C. Wilsnak & L. J. Beckman (Eds.), *Alcohol problems in women: Antecedents, consequences, and interventions* (pp. 121–154). New York: Guilford Press.

Hill, M. J., & Blane, H. T. (1967). Evaluation of psychotherapy with alcoholics: A critical review. *Quarterly Journal of Studies on Alcohol, 28,* 76–104.

Hilton, M. E. (1987). The presence of alcohol in four social situations: Survey results for 1964 and 1984. *International Journal of Addictions, 22,* 487–495.

Hingson, R., Mangione, T., Meyer, A., & Scotch, N. (1982). Seeking help for drinking problems: A study in the Boston metropolitan area. *Journal of Studies on Alcohol, 43,* 273–288.

Hingson, R., Scotch, N., & Goldman, E. (1977). Impact of the "Rand Report" on alcoholics, treatment personnel and Boston residents. *Journal of Studies on Alcohol, 38,* 2065–2076.

Hodgson, R., Rankin, H., & Stockwell, T. (1979). Alcohol dependence and the priming effect. *Behavior Research and Therapy, 17,* 379–387.

Hoehn-Saric, R., Frank, J., Imber, S., Nash, E., Stone, A., & Battle, C. (1964). Systematic preparation of patients for psychotherapy: I. Effects on therapy behavior and outcome. *Journal of Psychiatric Research, 2,* 267–281.

Hoff, E. C., & McKeown, C. E. (1953). An evaluation of the use of tetraethylthiuram disulfide in the treatment of 560 cases of alcohol addiction. *American Journal of Psychiatry, 109,* 670–673.

Hoffmann, H., Loper, R. G., & Kammeier, M. L. (1974). Identifying future alcoholics with MMPI alcoholism scales. *Quarterly Journal of Studies on Alcohol, 35*, 490–498.

Hoffmann, N. G., Harrison, P. A., & Belille, C. A. (1983). Alcoholics Anonymous after treatment: Attendance and abstinence. *International Journal of Addictions, 18*, 311–318.

Hoffmann, N. G., Ninonuevo, F., Mozey, J., & Luxenberg, M. G. (1987). Comparison of court-referred DWI arrests with other outpatients in substance abuse treatment. *Journal of Studies on Alcohol, 48*, 591–594.

Horan, J. J., Baker, S. B., Hoffman, A. M., & Shute, R. E. (1975). Weight loss through variations in the coverant control paradigm. *Journal of Consulting and Clinical Psychology, 43*, 68–72.

Hore, B. D. (1971). Life events and alcoholic relapse. *British Journal of Addictions, 66*, 83–88.

Hoyt, M. F., & Janis, I. L. (1975). Increasing adherence to a stressful decision via a motivational balance sheet procedure: A field experiment. *Journal of Personality and Social Psychology, 31*, 833–839.

Hoyt, D. P., & Sedlacek, G. M. (1958). Differentiating alcoholics from normals and abnormals with the MMPI. *Journal of Clinical Psychology, 14*, 69–74.

Hull, J. G., Young, R. D., & Jouriles, E. (1986). Applications of self-awareness model of alcohol consumption: Predicting patterns of use and abuse. *Journal of Personality and Social Psychology, 51*, 790–796.

Hunt, G. M., & Azrin, N. H. (1973). A community-reinforcement approach to alcoholism. *Behavior, Research and Therapy, 11*, 91–104.

Hurlburt, G., Gade, E., & Fuqua, D. (1984). Personality differences between Alcoholics Anonymous members and nonmembers. *Journal of Studies on Alcohol, 45*, 170–171.

Hyman, M. M. (1976). Alcoholics 15 years later. *Annals New York Academy of Sciences, 273*, 613–623.

Intagliata, J. (1976). A telephone follow-up procedure for increasing the effectiveness of a treatment program for alcoholics. *Journal of Studies on Alcohol, 37*, 1330–1335.

Israel, A. C., & Saccone, A. J. (1979). Follow-up of effects of choice of mediator and target of reinforcement on weight loss. *Behavior Therapy, 10*, 260–265.

Istvan, J., & Matarazzo, J. D. (1984). Tobacco, alcohol, and caffeine use: A review of their interrelationships. *Psychological Bulletin, 955*, 301–326.

Jackson, J. K. (1957). The definition and measurement of alcoholism. H-techniques scales of preoccupation with alcohol and psychological involvement. *Quarterly Journal of Studies on Alcohol, 18*, 240–262.

Janis, I. L. (1983). The role of social support in adherence to stressful decisions. *American Psychologists, 38*, 143–160.

Jellinek, E. M. (1946). Phase in the drinking history of alcoholics: An analysis of a survey conducted by the official organ of Alcoholics Anonymous. *Quarterly Journal of Studies on Alcohol, 7*, 1–88.

Jellinek, E. M. (1952). Phases of alcohol addiction. *Quarterly Journal of Studies on Alcohol, 13*, 673–684.

Jellinek, E. M. (1960). *The disease concept of alcoholism.* New Brunswick, NJ: Hillhouse Press.

Johnson, V. (1980). *I'll quit tommorrow.* New York: Harper & Row.

Johnson, V. E. (1986). *Intervention: How to help someone who doesn't want help.* Minneapolis: Johnson Institute Books.

Jones, J. W. (1981). *The children of alcoholics screening test.* Des Plaines, IL: Family Recovery Press.

Jones, J. W. (1982). *Preliminary test manual: The children of alcoholics screening test.* Chicago: Family Recovery Press.

Kadden, R. M., Cooney, N. L., Getter, H., & Litt, M. D. (1989). Matching alcoholics to coping skills or interactional therapies: Posttreatment results. *Journal of Consulting and Clinical Psychology, 57*, 698–704.

Kalb, M., & Popper, M. S. (1976). The future of alcohology: Craft or science? *American Journal of Psychiatry, 133,* 641–645.

Kalin, R., McClelland, D. C., & Kahn, M. (1965). The effects of male social drinking on fantasy. *Journal of Personality and Social Psychology, 1,* 441–452.

Kanfer, F. H., & Grimm, L. G. (1978). Freedom of choice and behavioral change. *Journal of Consulting and Clinical Psychology, 46,* 873–878.

Kaplan, R. F., Cooney, N. L., Baker, L. H., Gillespie, R. A., Meyer, R. E., & Pomerleau, O. F. (1985). Reactivity to alcohol-related cues: Physiological and subjective responses in alcoholics and nonproblem drinkers. *Journal of Studies on Alcohol, 46,* 267–272.

Kaplan, R. F., Meyer, R. E., & Stroebel, C. F. (1983). Alcohol dependence and responsivity to an ethanol stimulus as predictors of alcohol consumption. *British Journal of Addictions, 78,* 259–267.

Kaplan, R. F., Meyer, R. E., & Virgilio, L. M. (1984). Physiological reactivity to alcohol cues and the awareness of an alcohol effect in a double-blind placebo design. *British Journal of Addiction, 79,* 439–442.

Keller, M. (1972a). On the loss of control phenomenon in alcoholism. *British Journal of Addiction, 67,* 153–166.

Keller, M. (1972b). The oddities of alcoholics. *Quarterly Journal of Studies on Alcohol, 33,* 1147–1148.

Kendell, R. E. (1965). Normal drinking by former alcohol addicts. *Quarterly Journal of Studies on Alcohol, 26,* 247–257.

Kendell, R. E., & Stanton, M. C. (1966). The fate of untreated alcoholics. *Quarterly Journal of Studies on Alcohol, 27,* 30–41.

Kennedy, R. W., Gilbert, G. S., & Thoreson, R. (1978). A self-control program for drinking antecedents: The role of self-monitoring and control orientation. *Journal of Clinical Psychology, 34,* 238–243.

Keyson, M., & Janda, L. (1972). *The drinking-related locus of control scale.* Phoenix, AZ: Saint Lukes Hospital.

King, M. (1986). At risk drinking among general practice attenders: Prevalence, characteristics, and alcohol-related problems. *British Journal of Psychiatry, 148,* 533–540.

Kinney, J., & Leaton, G. (1982). *Understanding alcohol.* New York: Mosby Medical Library.

Kirk, W. G., Best, J. B., & Irwin, P. (1986). The perception of empathy in alcoholism counselors. *Journal of Studies on Alcohol, 47,* 82–84.

Kirschenbaum, D. S., Humphrey, L. L., & Malett, S. D. (1981). Specificity of planning in adult self-control: An applied investigation. *Journal of Personality and Social Psychology, 40,* 941–950.

Kirschenbaum, D. S., & Tomarken, A. J. (1982). On facting the generalization problem: The study of self-regulatory failure. *Advances in Cognitive Behavioral Research and Therapy* (pp. 119–199, Vol. 1). New York: Academic Press.

Kirschenbaum, D. S., Tomarken, A. J., & Ordman, A. M. (1982). Specificity of planning and choice applied to adult self-control. *Journal of Personality and Social Psychology, 42,* 576–585.

Kish, G. B., Ellsworth, R. B., & Woody, M. M. (1980). Effectiveness of an 84-day and a 60-day alcoholism treatment program. *Journal of Studies on Alcohol, 41,* 81–85.

Kissen, B. (1977). Comments on Alcoholism: A controlled trial of 'treatment' and 'advice'. *Journal of Studies on Alcohol, 38,* 1804–1829.

Kissen, B., Platz, A., & Su, W. H. (1970). Social and psychological factors in the treatment of chronic alcoholism. *Journal of Psychiatric Research, 8,* 13–27.

Kissen, B., Schenker, V., & Schenker, A. (1959). The acute effects of ethyl alcohol and chlorpromazine on certain physiological functions in alcoholics. *Journal of Studies on Alcohol, 20,* 480–492.

Kivlahan, D. R., Sher, K. J., & Donovan, D. M. (1989). The Alcohol Dependence Scale: A validation study among inpatient alcoholics. *Journal of Studies on Alcohol, 50,* 170–175.

Klinger, E. (1987). Imagery and logotherapeutic techniques in psychotherapy: Clinical experiences and promise for application to alcohol problems. In W. M. Cox (Ed.), *Treatment and prevention of alcohol problems: A resource manual* (pp. 139–156). New York: Academic Press.

Knight, R. P. (1937). The psychodynamics of chronic alcoholism. *Journal of Nervous and Mental Disease, 86*, 538–548.

Knott, V. J., & Bulmer, D. R. (1985). Effects of repetitive high intensity stimulation on electrodermal responsivity in male alcoholics and normal controls. *Addictive Behaviors, 10*, 181–185.

Knox, W. J. (1971). Attitudes of psychiatrists and psychologists toward alcoholism. *American Journal of Psychiatry, 127*, 1675–1683.

Koegel, P., & Burnam, M. A. (1988). Alcoholism among homeless adults in the inner city of Los Angeles. *Archives of General Psychiatry, 45*, 1011–1018.

Kolb, D., & Gunderson, E. K. E. (1980). Comparison of alcohol abusers who abused other drugs with those who did not. *Naval Health Research Center*. ADA 079132.

Krasnoff, A. (1976). Differences between alcoholics who complete or withdraw from treatment. *Journal of Studies on Alcohol, 37*, 1666–1671.

Kuhl, J. (1981). Motivational and functional helplessness: The moderating effects of state versus action orientation. *Journal of Personality and Social Psychology, 40*, 155–170.

Kurtines, W. M., Ball, L. R., & Wood, G. H. (1978). Personality characteristics of long-term recovered alcoholics: A comparative analysis. *Journal of Consulting and Clinical Psychology, 46*, 971–977.

Leach, B. (1973). Does Alcoholics Anonymous really work? In P. G. Bourne & R. Fox (Eds.), *Alcoholism: Progress in research and treatment*. New York: Academic Press.

Leavy, R. L., & Dunlosky, J. T. (1989). Undergraduate student and faculty perceptions of problem drinking. *Journal of Studies on Alcohol, 50*, 101–107.

Lee, D. J., & DeFrank, R. S. (1988). Interrelationships among self-reported alcohol intake, physiological indices and alcoholism screening measures. *Journal of Studies on Alcohol, 49*, 532–537.

Leigh, B. C. (1989). In search of the seven dwarves: Issues of measurement and meaning in alcohol expectancy research. *Psychological Bulletin, 105*, 361–374.

Leigh, G., Ogborne, A. C., & Cleland, P. (1984). Factors associated with patient dropout from an outpatient alcoholism treatment service. *Journal of Studies on Alcohol, 45*, 359–362.

Lemere, F. (1953). What happens to alcoholics. *American Journal of Psychiatry, 109*, 674–676.

Lemere, F., O'Hallaren, P., & Maxwell, M. A. (1958). Motivation in the treatment of alcoholism. *Quarterly Journal of Studies on Alcohol, 19*, 428–431.

Lemmens, P., Knibbe, R. A., & Tan, F. (1988). Weekly recall and diary estimates of alcohol consumption in a general population survey. *Journal of Studies on Alcohol, 49*, 131–135.

Leon, G. R., Kolotkin, R., & Korgeski, G. (1979). MacAndrew addiction scale and other MMPI characteristics associated with obesity, anorexia, and smoking behavior. *Addictive Behaviors, 4*, 401–407.

Leonard, K., Dunn, N. J., & Jacob, T. (1983). Drinking problems of alcoholics: Correspondence between self and spouse reports. *Addictive Behaviors, 8*, 369–373.

Lepper, M. R., Greene, D., & Nisbett, R. E. (1973). Undermining children's intrinsic interest with extrinsic reward: A test of the overjustification hypothesis. *Journal of Personality and Social Psychology, 28*, 129–137.

Levenson, R. W., Oyama, O. N., & Meek, P. S. (1987). Greater reinforcement from alcohol for those at risk: Parental risk and sex. *Journal of Abnormal Psychology, 96*, 242–253.

Leventhal, H. (1971). Fear appeals and persuasion: The differentiation of a motivational construct. *American Journal of Public Health, 61*, 1208–1224.

Lewis, C. E., Croughan, J. L., Whitman, B. Y., & Miller, J. P. (1983a). Association of alcoholism and antisocial personality in a narcotic-dependent population: The Lexington addicts. *Psychiatry Research, 10*, 31–46.

Lewis, C. E., Rice, J., & Helzer, J. E. (1983b). Diagnostic interactions: Alcoholism and antisocial personality. *Journal of Nervous and Mental Disease, 171*, 105–113.

Lichtenstein, E. (1982). The smoking problem: A behavioral perspective. *Journal of Consulting and Clinical Psychology, 50,* 804–819.

Linansky, E. S. (1957). Alcoholism in women; social and psychological concomitants. I: Social history data. *Quarterly Journal of Studies on Alcohol, 18,* 588–623.

Lindbeck, V. L. (1972). The woman alcoholic: A review of the literature. *International Journal of Addictions, 7,* 567–580.

Linsky, A. S., Colby, J. P., & Strauss, M. A. (1986). Drinking norms and alcohol-related problems in the United States. *Journal of Studies on Alcohol, 47,* 384–393.

Liskow, B. I., Rinck, C., Campbell, J., & DeSouza, C. (1989). Alcohol withdrawal in the elderly. *Journal of Studies on Alcohol, 50,* 414–421.

Litman, G. K., Eiser, J. R., Rawson, N. S. B., & Oppenheim, A. N. (1979a). Differences in relapse precipitants and coping behaviour between alcohol relapsers and survivors. *Behavior, Research and Therapy, 17,* 89–94.

Litman, G. K., Eiser, J. R., & Taylor, C. (1979b). Dependence, relapse, and extinction: A theoretical critique and a behavioral examination. *Journal of Clinical Psychology, 35,* 192–199.

Litman, G. K., Stapleton, J., Oppenheim, A. N, & Peleg, M. (1983). An instrument for measuring coping behaviours in hospitalized alcoholics: Implications for relapse prevention treatment. *British Journal of Addiction, 78,* 269–278.

Longabaugh, R., McCrady, B., Fink, E., Stout, R., McAuley, T., Doyle, C., & McNeil, D. (1983). Cost effectiveness of alcoholism treatment in partial vs. inpatient settings. *Journal of Studies on Alcohol, 44,* 1049–1071.

Lovald, K., & Neuwirth, G. (1968). Exposed and shielded drinking: Drinking as role behavior and some consequences for social control and self-concept. *Archives of General Psychiatry, 19,* 95–103.

Lovallo, W., Parsons, O. A., & Holloway, F. A. (1973). Autonomic arousal in normal, alcoholic, and brain-damaged subjects as measured by the plethysmograph response to cold pressor stimulation. *Psychophysiology, 10,* 166–176.

Lowe, J. B., Windsor, R. A., Adams, B., Morris, J., & Reese, Y. (1986). Use of a bogus pipeline method to increase accuracy of self-reported alcohol consumption among pregnant women. *Journal of Studies on Alcohol, 47,* 173–175.

Lucas, R. W., Mullin, P. J., Luna, C. B. X., & McInroy, D. C. (1977). Psychiatrists and a computer as interrogators of patients with alcohol-related illness: A comparison. *British Journal of Psychiatry, 131,* 160–167.

Ludwig, A. M. (1972). On and off the wagon: Reasons for drinking and abstaining by alcoholics. *Quarterly Journal of Studies on Alcohol, 33,* 91–96.

Ludwig, A. M. (1986). Pavlov's "bells" and alcohol craving. *Addictive Behaviors, 11,* 87–92.

Ludwig, A. M., & Stark, L. H. (1974). Alcohol craving. Subjective and situational aspects. *Quarterly Journal of Studies on Alcohol, 35,* 899–905.

Ludwig, A. M., & Wikler, A. (1974). "Craving" and relapse to drink. *Quarterly Journal of Studies on Alcohol, 35,* 108–130.

Ludwig, A. M., Wikler, A., & Stark, L. H. (1974). The first drink: Psychological aspects of craving. *Archives of General Psychiatry, 30,* 539–547.

Lundwall, L., & Baekeland, F. (1971). Disulfiram treatment of alcoholism: A review. *Journal of Nervous and Mental Disease, 153,* 381–394.

MacAndrew, C. (1965). The differentiation of male alcoholic outpatients from nonalcoholic psychiatric outpatients by means of the MMPI. *Quarterly Journal of Studies on Alcohol, 26,* 238–246.

MacAndrew, C. (1967). Self-reports of male alcoholics: A dimensional analysis of certain differences from nonalcoholic male psychiatric outpatients. *Quarterly Journal of Studies on Alcohol, 28,* 43–51.

MacAndrew, C. (1978). Women alcoholics' responses to scale 4 of the MMPI. *Journal of Studies on Alcohol, 39,* 1841–1854.

MacAndrew, C. (1979a). On the possibility of the psychometric detection of persons who are prone to the abuse of alcohol and other substances. *Addictive Behaviors, 4,* 11–20.

MacAndrew, C. (1979b). A retrospective study of drunkenness-associated changes in the self-depictions of a large sample of male outpatient alcoholics. *Addictive Behaviors, 4,* 373–381.

MacAndrew, C. (1981a). What the MAC Scale tells us about men alcoholics: An interpretative review. *Journal of Studies on Alcohol, 42,* 604–625.

MacAndrew, C. (1983). Alcoholic personality or personalities: Scale and profile data from the MMPI. In W. M. Cox (Ed.), *Identifying and measuring alcoholic personality characteristics* (pp. 73–86). San Francisco: Jossey-Bass.

MacAndrew, C. (1988). Differences in the self-depictions of female alcoholics and psychiatric outpatients: Towards a depiction of the modal female alcoholic. *Journal of Studies on Alcohol, 49,* 71–77.

MacAndrew, C., & Garfinkel, H. (1962). A consideration of changes attributed to intoxication as common-sense reasons for getting drunk. *Quarterly Journal of Studies on Alcohol, 23,* 252–266.

MacAndrew, C., & Geertsma, R. H. (1963). An analysis of responses of alcoholics to Scale 4 of the MMPI. *Quarterly Journal of Studies on Alcohol, 241,* 23–28.

MacMurray, J. P., Nessman, D. G., Haviland, M. G., & Anderson, D. L. (1987). Depressive symptoms and persistence in treatment for alcohol dependence. *Journal of Studies on Alcohol, 48,* 277–280.

Maisto, S. A., Lauerman, R., & Adesso, V. J. (1977). A comparison of two experimental studies of the role of cognitive factors in alcoholics' drinking. *Journal of Studies on Alcohol, 38,* 145–149.

Maisto, S. A., O'Farrell, T. J., Connors, G. J., McKay, J., & Pelcovits, M. (1988). Alcoholics' attributions of factors affective their relapse to drinking and reasons for terminating relapse episodes. *Addictive Behaviors, 13,* 79–82.

Maisto, S. A., Sobell, L. C., & Sobell, M. B. (1979). Comparison of alcoholics' self-reports of drinking behavior with reports of collateral informants. *Journal of Consulting and Clinical Psychology, 47,* 106–112.

Maisto, S. A., Sobell, M. B., & Sobell, L. C. (1980). Predictors of treatment outcome for alcoholics treated by individualized behavior therapy. *Addictive Behaviors, 5,* 259–264.

Malatesta, V. J., Sutker, P. B., & Treiber, F. A. (1981). Sensation seeking and chronic public drunkenness. *Journal of Consulting and Clinical Psychology, 49,* 292–294.

Maletzky, B. M., & Klotter, J. (1974). Smoking and alcoholism. *American Journal of Psychiatry, 131,* 445–447.

Mann, M. (1950). *Primer on Alcoholism.* New York: Rinehart.

Marlatt, G. A. (1985a). Relapse prevention: Theoretical rationale and overview of the model. In G. A. Marlatt & J. R. Gordon (Eds.), *Relapse prevention: Maintenance strategies in the treatment of addictive behaviors* (pp. 3–70). New York: Guilford Press.

Marlatt, G. A. (1985b). Situational determinants of relapse and skill-training interventions. In G. A. Marlatt & J. R. Gordon (Eds.), *Relapse prevention: Maintenance strategies in the treatment of addictive behaviors* (pp. 71–127). New York: Guilford Press.

Marlatt, G. A. (1985c). Cognitive factors in the relapse process. In G. A. Marlatt & J. R. Gordon (Eds.), *Relapse Prevention: Maintenance strategies in the treatment of addictive behaviors* (pp. 128–200). New York: Guilford Press.

Marlatt, G. A. (1985d). Cognitive assessment and intervention procedures for relapse prevention. In G. A. Marlatt & J. R. Gordon (Eds.), *Relapse Prevention: Maintenance strategies in the treatment of addictive behaviors* (pp. 201–279). New York: Guilford Press.

Marlatt, G. A. (1985e). Lifestyle modification. In G. A. Marlatt & J. R. Gordon (Eds.), *Relapse prevention: Maintenance strategies in the treatment of addictive behaviors* (pp. 280–348). New York: Guilford Press.

Marlatt, G. A., Demming, B., & Reid, J. B. (1973). Loss of control drinking in alcoholics: An experimental analogue. *Journal of Abnormal Psychology, 81,* 233–241.

Mathew, R. J., Claghorn, J. L., & Largen, J. (1979). Craving for alcohol in sober alcoholics. *American Journal of Psychiatry, 136,* 603–606.

Mayer, J., & Myerson, D. J. (1970). Characteristics of outpatient alcoholics in relation to change in drinking, work, and marital status during treatment. *Quarterly Journal of Studies on Alcohol, 31,* 889–897.

Mayer, J., & Myerson, D. J. (1971). Outpatient treatment of alcoholics: Effects of status, stability, and nature of treatment. *Quarterly Journal of Studies on Alcohol, 32,* 620–627.

Mayfield, D., McLeod, G., & Hall, P. (1974). The CAGE questionnaire: Validation of a new alcoholism screening instrument. *American Journal of Psychiatry, 131,* 1121–1123.

Mayfield, D. G., & Montgomery, D. (1972). Alcoholism, alcohol intoxication, and suicide attempts. *Archives of General Psychiatry, 27,* 349–353.

McCabe, R. J. R. (1986). Alcohol-dependent individuals sixteen years on. *Alcohol and Alcoholism, 21,* 85–91.

McCance, C., & McCance, P. F. (1969). Alcoholism in north-east Scotland: Its treatment and outcome. *British Journal of Psychiatry, 115,* 189–198.

McCrady, B. S., & Sher, K. J. (1983). Alcoholism treatment approaches: Patient variables, treatment variables. In B. Tabakoff, P. B. Sutker, & C. L. Randall (Eds.), *Medical and social aspects of alcohol abuse* (pp. 309–374). New York: Plenum Press.

McIntyre, T. D., & Alpern, H. P. (1985). Reinterpretation of the literature indicates differential sensitivities of long-sleep and short-sleep mice are not specific to alcohol. *Psychopharmacology, 87,* 379–389.

McIntyre, K. O., Lichtenstein, E., & Mermelstein, R. J. (1983). Self-efficacy and relapse in smoking cessation: A replication and extension. *Journal of Consulting and Clinical Psychology, 51,* 632–633.

McLachlan, J. F. C. (1974). Therapy strategies, personality orientation, and recovery from alcoholism. *Canadian Psychiatric Association Journal, 19,* 25–30.

McLachlan, J. F. C., & Stein, R. L. (1982). Evaluation of a day clinic for alcoholics. *Journal of Studies on Alcohol, 43,* 261–272.

McLatchie, B. H., & Lomp, K. G. E. (1988). An experimental investigation of the influence of aftercare on alcoholic relapse. *British Journal of Addiction, 83,* 1045–1054.

McLellan, A. T., Luborsky, L., O'Brien, C. P., Woody, G. E., & Druley, K. A. (1982). Is treatment for substance abuse effective? *Journal of the American Medical Association, 247,* 1423–1428.

McLellan, A. T., Luborsky, L., Woody, G. E., O'Brien, C. P., & Druley, K. A. (1983). Predicting response to alcohol and drug abuse treatments. *Archives of General Psychiatry, 40,* 620–625.

McNamee, H. B., Mello, N. K., & Mendelson, J. H. (1968). Experimental analysis of drinking patterns of alcoholics: Concurrent psychiatric observations. *American Journal of Psychiatry, 124,* 1063–1069.

McWilliams, J., & Brown, C. C. (1977). Treatment termination variables, MMPI scores and frequencies of relapse in alcoholics. *Journal of Studies on Alcohol, 38,* 477–486.

Mellinger, G. D., Balter, M. B., Manheimer, D. I., Cisin, I. H., & Parry, H. J. (1978). Psychic distress, life crisis, and use of psychotherapeutic medications. *Archives of General Psychiatry, 35,* 1045–1052.

Mellinger, G. D., Balter, M. B., & Uhlenhuth, E. H. (1984). Prevalence and correlates of the long-term regular use of anxiolytics. *Journal of the American Medical Association, 251,* 375–379.

Mello, N. K., & Mendelson, J. H. (1971). A quantitative analysis of drinking patterns in alcoholics. *Archives of General Psychiatry, 25,* 527–539.

Mendelson, J. H., Miller, K. D., Mello, N. K., Pratt, H., & Schmitz, R. (1982). Hospital treatment of alcoholism: A profile of middle income Americans. *Alcoholism: Clinical and Experimental Research, 6,* 377–383.

Mermelstein, R., Lichtenstein, E., & McIntyre, K. (1983). Partner support and relapse in smoking-cessation programs. *Journal of Consulting and Clinical Psychology, 51,* 465–466.

Merry, J. (1966). The "loss of control" myth. *Lancet, 1,* 1257–1258.

Meyer, J., Berman, J., & Rivers, P. C. (1985). Dispositional assessment with alcoholics. *International Journal of the Addictions, 20,* 1463–1478.

Midanik, L. (1982). The validity of self-reported alcohol consumption and alcohol problems: A literature review. *British Journal of Addiction, 77,* 357–382.

Midanik, L. T. (1988). Validity of self-reported alcohol use: A literature review and assessment. *British Journal of Addiction, 83,* 1019–1031.

Mikulincer, M., & Nizan, B. (1988). Causal attribution, cognitive interference, and the generalization of learned helplessness. *Journal of Personality and Social Psychology, 55,* 470–478.

Miller, W. R. (1976). Alcoholism scales and objective assessment methods: A review. *Psychological Bulletin, 33,* 649–674.

Miller, W. R. (1985). Motivation for treatment: A review with special emphasis on alcoholism. *Psychological Bulletin, 98,* 84–107.

Miller, W. R. (1989). Increasing motivation for change. In R. K. Hester & W. R. Miller (Eds.), *Handbook of alcoholism treatment approaches,* (pp. 67–80). New York: Pergamon Press.

Miller, W. R., & Baca, L. M. (1983). Two-year follow-up of bibliotherapy and therapist-directed controlled drinking training for problem drinkers. *Behavior Therapy, 14,* 441–448.

Miller, W. R., & Caddy, G. R. (1977). Abstinence and controlled drinking in the treatment of problem drinkers. *Journal of Studies on Alcohol, 38,* 986–1003.

Miller, P. M., Hersen, M., Eisler, R. M., & Elkin, T. E. (1974). A retrospective analysis of alcohol consumption on laboratory tasks as related to therapeutic outcome. *Behavior Research and Therapy, 12,* 73–76.

Miller, P. M., Hersen, M., Eisler, R. M., & Hilsman, G. (1974). Effects of social stress on operant drinking of alcoholics and social drinkers. *Behavior Research and Therapy, 12,* 67–72.

Miller, W. R., & Hester, R. K. (1980). Treating the problem drinker: Modern approaches. In W. R. Miller (Ed.), *The addictive behaviors: Treatment of alcoholism, drug abuse, smoking, and obesity* (pp. 3–141). Oxford: Pergamon Press.

Miller, W. R., & Hester, R. K. (1986). Inpatient alcoholism treatment: Who benefits. *American Psychologist, 41,* 794–805.

Miller, W. R., & Joyce, M. A. (1979). Prediction of abstinence, controlled drinking, and heavy drinking outcomes following behavioral self-control training. *Journal of Consulting and Clinical Psychology, 47,* 773–775.

Miller, W. R., & Marlatt, G. A. (1984). *Comprehensive Drinking Profile.* Odessa, FL: Psychological Assessment Resources.

Miller, W. R., & Munoz, R. F. (1976). *How to control your drinking.* Englewood Cliffs, NJ: Prentice-Hall.

Miller, B. A., Pokorny, A. D., Valles, J., & Cleveland, S. E. (1970). Biased sampling in alcoholism treatment research. *Quarterly Journal of Studies on Alcohol, 31,* 230–231.

Miller, W. R., Sovereign, R. G., & Krege, B. (1988). Motivational interviewing with problem drinkers: II. The drinker's check-up as a prevention technique. *Behavioral Psychotherapy, 16,* 251–268.

Miller, W. R., Taylor, C. A., & West, J. C. (1980). Focused versus broad-spectrum behavior therapy for problem drinkers. *Journal of Consulting and Clinical Psychology, 48,* 590–601.

Milmoe, S., Rosenthal, R., Blane, H. T., Chafetz, M. E., & Wolf, I. (1967). The doctor's voice: Postdictor of successful referral of alcoholic patients. *Journal of Abnormal Psychology, 72,* 78–84.

Mindlin, D. F. (1960). Evaluation of therapy for alcoholics in a workhouse setting. *Quarterly Journal of Studies on Alcohol, 21,* 90–112.

Mindlin, D. F. (1964). Attitudes toward alcoholism and toward self: Differences between three alcoholic groups. *Quarterly Journal of Studies on Alcohol, 25,* 136–141.

Mischel, W., & Mischel, H. N. (1976). A cognitive social-learning approach to morality and self-regulation. In T. Lickona (Ed.), *Moral development and behavior,* New York: Holt, Rinehart, & Winston.

Moberg, D. P., Krause, W. K., & Klein, P. E. (1982). Posttreatment drinking behavior among inpatients from an industrial alcoholism program. *International Journal of the Addictions, 17,* 549–567.

Monti, P. M., Binkoff, J. A., Abrams, D. B., Zwick, W. R., Nirenberg, T. D., & Liepman, M. R. (1987). Reactivity of alcoholics and nonalcoholics to drinking cues. *Journal of Abnormal Psychology, 96,* 122–126.

Moore, R. A., & Murphy, T. C. (1961). Denial of alcoholism as an obstacle to recovery. *Quarterly Journal of Studies on Alcohol, 22,* 597–609.

Moore, R. A., & Ramseur, F. (1960). Effects of psychotherapy in an open-ward hospital on patients with alcoholism. *Quarterly Journal of Studies on Alcohol, 21,* 233–252.

Moos, R. H., Finney, J. W., & Chan, D. A. (1981). The process of recovery from alcoholism: I. Comparing alcoholic patients with matched community controls. *Journal of Studies on Alcohol, 42,* 383–402.

Moos, R. H., Mehren, B., & Moos, B. S. (1978). Evaluation of a Salvation Army alcoholism treatment program. *Journal of Studies on Alcohol, 39,* 1267–1275.

Morey, L. C., & Blashfield, R. K. (1981). Empirical classifications of alcoholism. *Journal of Studies on Alcohol, 42,* 925–937.

Morey, L. C., Skinner, H. A., & Blashfield, R. K. (1984). A typology of alcohol abusers: Correlates and implications. *Journal of Abnormal Psychology, 93,* 408–417.

Morrow-Tlucak, M., Ernhart, C. B., Sokol, R. J., Martier, S., & Ager, J. (1989). Underreporting of alcohol use in pregnancy: Relationship to alcohol problem history. *Alcoholism: Clinical and Experimental Research, 13,* 399–401.

Mosher, V., Davis, J., Mulligan, D., & Iber, F. L. (1975). Comparison of outcome in a 9-day and 30-day alcoholism treatment program. *Journal of Studies on Alcohol, 36,* 1277–1281.

Mulford, H. A. (1977). Stages in the alcoholic process: Toward a cumulative, nonsequential index. *Quarterly Journal of Studies on Alcohol, 38,* 563–583.

Mulford, H. A. (1979). Treating alcoholism versus accelerating the natural recovery process; a cost-benefit comparison. *Journal of Studies on Alcohol, 40,* 505–513.

Mulford, H. A., & Fitzgerald, J. L. (1981a). Untitled. *Journal of Studies on Alcohol, 42,* 362–367.

Mulford, H. A., & Fitzgerald, J. L. (1981b). On the validity of the research diagnostic criteria, the Feighner criteria, and the DSM-III for diagnosing alcoholics. *Journal of Nervous and Mental Disease, 169,* 654–658.

Mulford, H. A., & Miller, D. E. (1964). Measuring public acceptance of the alcoholic as a sick person. *Quarterly Journal of Studies on Alcohol, 25,* 314–323.

Murphy, G. E., & Robins, E. (1967). Social factors in suicide. *Journal of the American Medical Association, 199,* 303–308.

Nakamura, M. M., Overall, J. E., & Hollister, L. E. (1983). Factors effecting outcome of depression in alcoholics. *Alcoholism: Clinical and Experimental Research, 7,* 188–193.

Nathan, P. E., & O'Brien, J. S. (1971). An experimental analysis of the behavior of alcoholics and nonalcoholics during prolonged experimental drinking: A necessary precursor of behavior therapy? *Behavior Therapy, 2,* 455–476.

Nathan, P. E., & Skinstad, A. H. (1987). Outcomes of treatment for alcohol problems: Current methods, problems, and results. *Journal of Consulting and Clinical Psychology, 55,* 332–340.

National Council on Alcoholism, Criteria Committee. (1972). Criteria for the diagnosis of alcoholism. *American Journal of Psychiatry, 129,* 127–135.

National Institute on Alcohol Abuse and Alcoholism. (1984/1985). Cost and utilization of alcoholism treatment under health insurance: A review of three studies. *Alcohol Health & Research World, 9,* 45–53.

Nerviano, V. J., McCarty, D., & McCarty, S. M. (1980). MMPI profile patterns of men alcoholics in two contrasting settings. *Journal of Studies on Alcohol, 41,* 1143–1152.

Newlin, D. B. (1985). The antagonistic placebo response to alcohol cues. *Alcoholism: Clinical and Experimental Research, 9,* 411–416.

Niaura, R. S., Rohsenow, D. J., Binkoff, J. A., Monti, P. M., Pedraza, M., & Abrams, D. B. (1988). Relevance of cue reactivity to understanding alcohol and smoking relapse. *Journal of Abnormal Psychology, 97,* 133–152.

Nicholls, P., Edwards, G., & Kyle, E. (1974). Alcoholics admitted to four hospitals in England. II. General and cause-specific mortality. *Quarterly Journal of Studies on Alcohol, 35,* 841–855.

Noel, N. E., McCrady, B. S., Stout, R. L., & Fisher-Nelson, H. (1987). Prediction of attrition from an outpatient alcoholism treatment program for couples. *Journal of Studies on Alcohol, 48,* 229–235.

Nordstrom, G., & Berglund, M. (1987). A prospective study of successful long-term adjustment in alcohol dependence: Social drinking vs. abstinence. *Journal of Studies on Alcohol, 48,* 95–103.

Obitz, F. W. (1975). Alcoholic's perceptions of selected counseling techniques. *British Journal of Addiction, 70,* 187–191.

Obitz, F. W. (1978). Control orientation and disulfiram. *Journal of Studies on Alcohol, 39,* 12997–1298.

Ogborne, A. C., & Bornet, A. (1982). Abstinence and abusive drinking among affiliates of Alcoholics Anonymous: Are these the only alternatives? *Addictive Behaviors, 7,* 199–202.

Ogborne, A. C., & Clare, G. (1979). A note on the interface between a residential alcoholism rehabilitation centre and detoxification centres. *British Journal of Addiction, 74,* 283–287.

Ogborne, A. C., & Glaser, F. B. (1981). Characteristics of affiliates of Alcoholics Anonymous: A review of the literature. *Journal of Studies on Alcohol, 42,* 661–675.

Ogborne, A. C., & Kapur, B. M. (1987). Drug use among a sample of males admitted to an alcohol detoxification center. *Alcoholism: Clinical and Experimental Research, 11,* 183–185.

Ogborne, A. C., Wiggins, I., & Shain, M. (1980). Variations in staff characteristics, programs and recruitment practices among halfway houses for problem drinkers. *British Journal of Addiction, 75,* 393–403.

Ojesjo, L. (1981). Long-term outcome in alcohol abuse and alcoholism among males in the Lundby general population, Sweden. *British Journal of Addiction, 76,* 391–400.

Ojehagen, A., & Berglund, M. (1986). Early and late improvement in a two-year out-patient alcoholic treatment programme. Acta *Psychiatrica Scandanavia, 74,* 129–136.

Ojehagen, A., & Berglund, M. (1989). Changes in drinking goals in a two-year out-patient alcoholic treatment program. *Addictive Behaviors, 14,* 1–10.

Ojehagen, A., Skjaerris, A., & Berglund, M. (1988). Prediction of posttreatment drinking outcome in a 2-year out-patient treatment program: A follow-up study. *Alcoholism: Clinical and Experimental Research, 12,* 46–51.

Okulitch, P., & Marlatt, G. A. (1972). Effects of varied extinction conditions with alcoholics and social drinkers. *Journal of Abnormal Psychology, 72,* 205–211.

O'Leary, M. R., Calsyn, D. A., Haddock, D. L., & Freeman, C. W. (1980a). Differential alcohol use patterns and personality traits among three Alcoholics Anonymous attendance level groups: Further considerations of the affiliation profile. *Drug and Alcohol Dependence, 5,* 135–144.

O'Leary, M. R., Donovan, D. M., Chaney, E. F., & O'Leary, D. E. (1979). Interpersonal attractiveness and clinical decisions in alcoholism treatment. *American Journal of Psychiatry, 136,* 618–622.

O'Leary, M. R., Donovan, D. M., Chaney, E. F., & O'Leary, D. E. (1980b). Relationship of alcoholic personality subtypes to treatment follow-up measures. *Journal of Nervous and Mental Disease, 168,* 475–480.

O'Leary, M. R., Donovan, D. M., & O'Leary, D. E. (1978). Drinking patterns of alcoholic subtypes differing in levels of perceived and experienced control. *Journal of Studies on Alcohol, 39,* 1499–1505.

Orford, J. (1973). A comparison of alcoholics whose drinking is totally uncontrolled and those whose drinking is mainly controlled. *Behavior Research and Therapy, 11,* 565–576.

Orford, J., & Hawker, A. (1974). An investigation of an alcoholism rehabilitation halfway house: II. The complex question of client motivation. *British Journal of Addiction, 69*, 315–323.

Orford, J., & Keddie, A. (1985). Gender differences in the functions and effects of moderate and excessive drinking. *British Journal of Clinical Psychology, 24*, 265–279.

Orford, J., & Keddie, A. (1986). Abstinence or controlled drinking in clinical practice: Indications at initial assessment. *Addictive Behaviors, 11*, 71–86.

Orford, J., Oppenheimer, E., & Edwards, G. (1976). Abstinence or control: The outcome for excessive drinkers two years after consultation. *Behavior, Research, and Therapy, 14*, 409–418.

Orford, J., Oppenheimer, E., Egert, S., Hensman, C., & Guthrie, S. (1976). The cohesiveness of alcoholism-complicated marriages and its influence on treatment outcome. *British Journal of Addiction, 128*, 318–339.

Ornstein, P., Cherepon, J. A. (1985). Demographic variables as predictors of alcoholism treatment outcome. *Journal of Studies on Alcohol, 46*, 425–432.

Orrego, H., Blendis, L. M., Blake, J. E., Kapur, B. M., & Israel, Y. (1979). Reliability of assessment of alcohol intake based on personal interviews in a liver clinic. *Lancet, 2*, 1354–1356.

O'Sullivan, K., Whillans, P., Daly, M., Carroll, B., Clare, A., & Cooney, J. (1983). A comparison of alcoholics with and without coexisting affective disorder. *British Journal of Psychiatry, 143*, 133–138.

Ossip-Klein, D. J., Vanlandingham, W., Prue, D. M., & Rychtarik, R. G. (1984). Increasing attendance at alcohol aftercare using calendar prompts and home based contracting. *Addictive Behaviors, 9*, 85–89.

Otto, R. K., Lang, A. R., Megargee, E. I., & Rosenblatt, A. I. (1988). Ability of alcoholics to escape detection by the MMPI. *Journal of Consulting and Clinical Psychology, 56*, 452–457.

Overall, J. E., Reilly, E. L., Kelley, J. T., & Holister, L. E. (1985). Persistence of depression in detoxified alcoholics. *Alcoholism: Clinical and Experimental Research, 9*, 331–333.

Pachman, J. S., Foy, D. W., & Erd, M. V. (1978). Goal choice of alcoholics: A comparison of those who choose total abstinence and those who choose responsible control drinking. *Journal of Clinical Psychology, 34*, 781–783.

Page, R. D., & Schaub, L. H. (1979). Efficacy of a three- versus a five-week alcohol treatment program. International *Journal of the Addiction, 14*, 697–714.

Panepinto, W., Galanter, M. Bender, S. H., & Strochlic, M. (1980). Alcoholics' transition from ward to clinic: Group orientation improves retention. *Journal of Studies on Alcohol, 41*, 940–945.

Panepinto, W. C., & Higgins, M. J. (1969). Keeping alcoholics in treatment: Effective follow-through procedures. *Quarterly Journal of Studies on Alcohol, 30*, 414–419.

Paredes, A., Gregory, D., Rundell, O. H., & Williams, H. L. (1979). Drinking behavior, remission, and relapse: The Rand report revisited. *Alcoholism: Clinical and Experimental Research, 3*, 3–10.

Paredes, A., Ludwig, K. D., Hassenfeld, I. N., & Cornelison, F. S. (1969). A clinical study of alcoholics using audiovisual self-image feedback. *Journal of Nervous and Mental Disease, 148*, 449–456.

Park, P. (1973). Developmental ordering of experiences in alcoholism. *Quarterly Journal of Studies on Alcohol, 34*, 473–488.

Park, P., & Whitehead, P. C. (1973). Developmental sequence and dimensions of alcoholism. *Quarterly Journal of Studies on Alcohol, 34*, 887–904.

Parker, F. B. (1972). Sex-role adjustment in women alcoholics. *Quarterly Journal of Studies on Alcohol, 33*, 647–657.

Parsons, O. A., Tarter, R. E., & Edelberg, R. (1972). Altered motor control in chronic alcoholics. *Journal of Abnormal Psychology, 80*, 308–314.

Patek, A. J. Jr., & Hermos, J. A. (1981). Recovery from alcoholism in cirrohotic patients. A study of 45 cases. *American Journal of Medicine, 70,* 783–785.

Pattison, E. M., Coe, R., & Rhodes, R. J. (1969). Evaluation of alcoholism treatment: A comparison of three facilities. *Archives of General Psychiatry, 20,* 478–488.

Pattison, E. M., Sobell, M. B., & Sobell, L. C. (1977). *Emerging concepts of alcohol dependence.* New York: Springer.

Pekarik, G., Jones, D. L., & Blodgett, C. (1986). Personality and demographic characteristics of dropouts and completers in a nonhospital residential alcohol treatment program. *International Journal of the Addictions, 21,* 131–137.

Pell, S., & D'Alonzo, C. A. (1973). A five year mortality study of alcoholics. *Journal of Occupational Medicine, 15,* 120–125.

Pendery, M. L., Maltzman, I. M., & West, L. J. (1982). Controlled drinking by alcoholics? New findings and a reevaluation of a major affirmative study. *Science, 2,* 169–174.

Penick, E. C., Powell, B. J., Liskow, B. I., Jackson, J. O., & Nickel, E. J. (1988). The stability of coexisting psychiatric syndromes in alcoholic men after one year. *Journal of Studies on Alcohol, 49,* 395–405.

Perri, M. G., Richards, C. S., & Schultheis, K. R. (1977). Behavioral self-control and smoking reduction: A study of self-initiated attempts to reduce smoking. *Behavior Therapy, 8,* 360–365.

Pfrang, H., & Schenk, J. (1985/1986). Controlled drinkers in comparison to abstinents and relapsed drinkers with regard to attitudes and social adjustment. *International Journal of the Addictions, 20,* 1793–1802.

Plant, M. A. (1979). Occupations, drinking patterns and alcohol-related problems: Conclusions from a follow-up study. *British Journal of Addiction, 74,* 267–273.

Pittman, D. J., & Tate, R. L. (1969). A comparison of two treatment programs for alcoholics. *Quarterly Journal of Studies on Alcohol, 30,* 888–899.

Pokorny, A. D., Kanas, T., & Overall, J. E. (1981). Order of appearance of alcoholic symptoms. *Alcoholism: Clinical and Experimental Research, 5,* 216–220.

Pokorny, A. D., Miller, B. A., & Cleveland, S. E. (1968). Response to treatment of alcoholism: A follow-up study. *Quarterly Journal of Studies on Alcohol, 29,* 364–381.

Pokorny, A. D., Miller, B. A., Kanas, T. E., & Valles, J. (1971). Dimensions of alcoholism. *Quarterly Journal of Studies on Alcohol, 32,* 699–705.

Pokorny, A. D., Miller, B. A., Kanas, T., & Valles, J. (1973). Effectiveness of extended aftercare in the treatment of alcoholism. *Quarterly Journal of Studies on Alcohol, 34,* 435–443.

Pokorny, A. D., Miller, B. A., & Kaplan, H. B. (1972). The brief Mast: A shortened version of the Michigan Alcoholism Screening Test. *American Journal of Psychiatry, 129,* 342–345.

Polich, J. M. (1982). The validity of self-reports in alcoholism research. *Addictive Behaviors, 7,* 123–132.

Polich, J. M., Armor, D. J., & Braiker, H. B. (1980). Patterns of alcoholism over four years. *Journal of Studies on Alcohol, 41,* 397–416.

Polich, J. M., Armor, D. J., & Braiker, H. B. (1981). *The course of alcoholism: Four years after treatment.* New York: Wiley.

Pomerleau, O. F., Adkins, D., Pertschuk, M. (1978). Predictors of outcome and recidivism in smoking cessation treatment. *Addictive Behaviors, 3,* 65–70.

Pomerleau, O. F., Fertig, J., Baker, L., & Cooney, N. (1983). Reactivity to alcohol cues in alcoholics and non-alcoholics: Implications for a stimulus control analysis of drinking. *Addictive Behaviors, 8,* 1–10.

Popham, R. E., & Schmidt, W. (1976). Some factors affecting the likelihood of moderate drinking by treated alcoholics. *Alcoholism: Clinical and Experimental Research, 7,* 188–193.

Pottenger, M., McKernon, J., Patrie, E. C., Weissman, M. M., Ruben, H. L., & Newberry, P. (1978). The frequency and persistence of depressive symptoms in the alcohol abuser. *Journal of Nervous and Mental Disease, 166,* 562–570.

Powell, B. J., Read, M. R., Penick, E. C., Miller, N. S., & Bingham, S. F. (1987). Primary and secondary depression in alcoholic men: An important distinction. *Journal of Clinical Psychiatry,* *48,* 98–101.

Powell, B. J., & Viamontes, J. (1974). Factors affecting attendance at an alcoholic day hospital. *British Journal of Addiction, 69,* 339–342.

Pratt, T. C., Linn, M. W., Carmichael, J. S., & Webb, N. L. (1977). The alcoholics' perception of the ward as a predictor of aftercare attendance. *Journal of Clinical Psychology, 33,* 915–918.

Prochaska, J. O., & DiClemente, C. C. (1983). Stages and processes of self-change of smoking: Toward an integrative model of change. *Journal of Consulting and Clinical Psychology, 51,* 390–395.

Rathod, N. H., Gregory, E., Blows, D., & Thomas, G. H. (1966). A two-year follow-up study of alcoholic patients. *British Journal of Psychiatry, 112,* 638–692.

Rathod, N. H., & Thomson, I. G. (1971). Women alcoholics: A critical review. *Journal of Studies on Alcohol, 32,* 45–52.

Reich, L. H., Davies, R. K., & Himmelhoch, J. M. (1974). Excessive alcohol use in manic-depressive illness. *American Journal of Psychiatry, 131,* 83–86.

Reilly, D. H., & Sugerman, S. (1967). Conceptual complexity and psychological differentiation in alcoholics. *Journal of Nervous and Mental Disease, 144,* 14–17.

Rich, C., & Davis, H. (1969). Concurrent validity of MMPI alcoholism scales. *Journal of Clinical Psychology, 25,* 425–426.

Richardson, D. C., & Campbell, J. L. (1978). Alcohol and wife abuse: The effect of alcohol on attributions of blame for wife abuse. *Personality and Social Psychology Bulletin, 6,* 51–56.

Rist, F., & Watzl, H. (1983). Self assessment of relapse risk and assertiveness in relation to treatment outcome of female alcoholics. *Addictive Behaviors, 8,* 121–127.

Ritson, B. (1969). Involvement in treatment and its relation to outcome amongst alcoholics. *British Journal of Addiction, 64,* 23–29.

Ritson, E. B., & Plant, M. A. (1977). The interaction between alcohol and other forms of drug taking. In M. M. Glatt (Ed.), *Drug dependence: Current problems and issues.* Baltimore, MD: University Park Press.

Robson, R. A. H., Paulus, I., & Clarke, G. G. (1965). An evaluation of the effect of a clinic treatment program on the rehabilitation of alcoholic patients. *Quarterly Journal of Studies on Alcohol, 26,* 264–278.

Rodin, M. B. (1981). Alcoholism as a folk disease: The paradox of beliefs and choice of therapy in an urban American community. *Journal of Studies on Alcohol, 42,* 821–835.

Rogers, R. W., & Mewborn, C. R. (1976). Fear appeals and attitude change: Effects of a threat's noxiousness, probability of occurrence, and the efficacy of coping responses. *Journal of Personality of Social Psychology, 34,* 54–61.

Rogers, R. W., & Thistlethwaite, D. L. (1970). Effects of fear arousal and reassurance on attitude change. *Journal of Personality and Social Psychology, 15,* 227–233.

Rohsenow, D. J. (1983). Alcoholics' perceptions of control. In W. M. Cox (Ed.), *Identifying and measuring alcoholic personality characteristics* (pp. 36–52). San Francisco: Jossey-Bass.

Rohsenow, D. J., & O'Leary, M. R. (1978a). Locus of control research on alcoholic populations: A review. I. Development, scales and treatment. *International Journal of Addictions, 18,* 55–78.

Rohsenow, D. J., & O'Leary, M. R. (1978b). Locus of control research on alcoholic populations: A review. II. Relationship to other measures. *International Journal of Addictions, 13,* 213–226.

Roine, R. P., Turpeinen, U., Ylikahri, R., & Salaspuro, M. (1987). Urinary dolichol—A new marker for alcoholism. *Alcoholism: Clinical and Experimental Research, 11,* 525–527.

Roman, P. M. (1988). Growth and transformation in workplace alcoholism programming. In M. Galanter (Ed.), *Recent developments in alcoholism* (pp. 132–159, Vol. 6). New York: Plenum Press.

Room, R. (1989). Alcoholism and Alcoholics Anonymous in U.S. films, 1945–1962: The party ends for the "wet generations". *Journal of Studies on Alcohol, 50,* 368–383.

Roosa, M. W., Sandler, I. N., Gehring, M., Beals, J., & Cappo, L. (1988). The children of alcoholics life-events schedule: A stress scale for children of alcohol-abusing parents. *Journal of Studies on Alcohol, 49,* 422–429.

Rosen, A. C. (1960). A comparative study of alcoholic and psychiatric patients with the MMPI. *Quarterly Journal of Studies on Alcohol, 21,* 253–266.

Rosenbaum, M., & Smira, K. B. A. (1986). Cognitive and personality factors in the delay of gratification of hemodialysis patients. *Journal of Personality and Social Psychology, 51,* 357–364.

Rosenberg, C. M. (1974). Drug maintenance in the outpatient treatment of chronic alcoholism. *Archives of General Psychiatry, 30,* 373–377.

Rosenberg, C. M., Gerrein, J. R., Manohar, V., & Liftik, J. (1976). Evaluation of training of alcoholism counselors. *Journal of Studies on Alcohol, 37,* 1236–1246.

Rosenberg, C. M., & Liftik, J. (1976). Use of coercion in the outpatient treatment of alcoholism. *Journal of Studies on Alcohol, 37,* 58–65.

Rosenberg, H. (1983). Relapsed versus non-relapsed alcohol abusers: Coping skills, life events, and social support. *Addictive Behaviors, 8,* 183–186.

Rosenberg, N. (1972). MMPI alcoholism scales. *Journal of Clinical Psychology, 28,* 515–522.

Rosin, A. J., & Glatt, M. M. (1971). Alcohol excess in the elderly. *Quarterly Journal of Studies on Alcohol, 32,* 53–59.

Ross, H. (1989). Alcohol and drug abuse in treated alcoholics: A comparison of men and women. *Alcoholism: Clinical and Experimental Research, 13,* 810–816.

Ross, H. E., Glaser, F. B., & Germanson, T. (1988). The prevalence of psychiatric disorders in patients with alcohol and other drug problems. *Archives of General Psychiatry, 45,* 1023–1031.

Rossi, J. J., Stach, A., & Bardley, N. J. (1963). Effects of treatment of male alcoholics in a mental hospital: A follow-up study. *Quarterly Journal of Studies on Alcohol, 24,* 91–108.

Rothstein, E., Cobble, J. C., & Sampson, N. (1976). Chlordiazepoxide: Long-term use in alcoholism. *Annals of New York Academy of Sciences, 273,* 381–384.

Rounsaville, B. J., Dolinsky, Z. S., Babor, T. F., & Meyer, R. E. (1987). Psychopathology as a predictor of treatment outcome in alcoholics. *Archives of General Psychiatry, 44,* 505–513.

Rounsaville, B. J., Spitzer, R. L., & Williams, J. B. W. (1986). Proposed changes in DSM-III substance abuse disorders: Description and rationale. *American Journal of Psychiatry, 143, 4,* 463–468.

Rousaville, B. J., Weissman, M. M., & Kleber, H. D. (1982). The significance of alcoholism in treated opiate addicts. *Journal of Nervous and Mental Disease, 170,* 479–488.

Rozensky, R. H., & Bellack, A. S. (1976). Individual differences in self-reinforcement style and performance in self- and therapist-controlled weight reduction program. *Behavior Research and Therapy, 14,* 357–364.

Rubin, L. S., Gottheil, E., Roberts, A., Alterman, A. I., & Holstine, J. (1977). Effects of stress on autonomic reactivity in alcoholics: pupillometric studies. *Journal of Studies on Alcohol, 38,* 2036–2048.

Rubin, L. S., Gottheil, E., Roberts, A., Alterman, A. I., & Holstine, J. (1978). Autonomic nervous system concomitants of short-term abstinence in alcoholics; pupillometic studies. II. *Journal of Studies on Alcohol, 39,* 1895–1907.

Rudy, D. R. (1980). Slipping and sobriety: The functions of drinking in Alcoholics Anonymous. *Journal of Studies on Alcohol, 41,* 727–732.

Rule, B. G., & Phillips, D. (1973). Responsibility versus illness models of alcoholism: Effects on attitudes toward an alcoholic. *Quarterly Journal of Studies on Alcohol, 34,* 489–495.

Russel, D., & McAuley, E. (1986). Causal attributions, causal dimensions, and affective reactions to success and failure. *Journal of Personality and Social Psychology, 50,* 1174–1185.

Russell, M., & Coviello, D. (1988). Heavy drinking and regular psychoactive drug use among gynecological outpatients. *Alcoholism: Clinical and Experimental Research, 12,* 400–406.

Rychtarik, R. G., Foy, D. W., Scott, T., Lokey, L., & Prue, D. M. (1987). Five-six-year follow-up of broad-spectrum behavioral treatment for alcoholism: Effects of training controlled drinking skills. *Journal of Consulting and Clinical Psychology, 55,* 106–108.

Sanchez-Craig, M. (1980). Random assignment to abstinence or controlled drinking in a cognitive-behavioral program: Short-term effects on drinking behavior. *Addictive Behavior, 5,* 35–39.

Sanchez-Craig, M. (1986). How much is too much? Estimates of hazardous drinking based on clients' self-reports. *British Journal of Addiction, 81,* 251–256.

Sanchez-Craig, M., Annis, H. M., Bornet, A. R., & MacDonald, K. R. (1984). Random assignment to abstinence and controlled drinking: Evaluation of a cognitive-behavioral program for problem drinkers. *Journal of Consulting and Clinical Psychology, 52,* 390–403.

Sanchez-Craig, M., Wilkinson, D. A., & Walker, K. (1987). Theory and methods for secondary prevention of alcohol problems: A cognitively based approach. In W. M. Cox (Ed.), *Treatment and prevention of alcohol problems* (pp. 287–331). New York: Academic Press.

Sannibale, C. (1989). A prospective study of treatment outcome with a group of male problem drinkers. *Journal of Studies on Alcohol, 50,* 236–244.

Saunders, J. B., Davis, M., & Williams, R. (1981). Do women develop alcoholic liver disease more readily than men? *British Medical Journal, 282,* 1140–1143.

Saunders, J. B., Wodak, A. D., & Williams, R. (1985). Past experience of advice and treatment for drinking problems of patients with alcoholic liver disease. *British Journal of Addiction, 80,* 51–56.

Saunders, W. M., & Kershaw, P. W. (1979). Spontaneous remission from alcoholism—A community study. *British Journal of Addiction, 74,* 251–265.

Schachter, S. (1982). Recidivism and self-cure of smoking and obesity. *American Psychologist, 37,* 436–444.

Schaefer, H. H., Sobell, M. B., & Mills, K. C. (1971). Some sobering data on the use of self-confrontation with alcoholics. *Behavior Therapy, 2,* 28–39.

Schaefer, H. H., Sobell, M. B., & Sobell, L. C. (1972). Twelve month follow-up of hospitalized alcoholics given self-confrontation experiences by videotape. *Behavior Therapy, 3,* 283–285.

Scheier, M. F., & Carver, C. S. (1977). Self-focused attention and the experience of emotion: Attraction, repulsion, elation, and depression. *Journal of Personality and Social Psychology, 35,* 625–636.

Scheier, M. F., Weintraub, J. K., & Carver, C. S. (1986). Coping with stress: Divergent strategies of optimists and pessimists. *Journal of Personality and Social Psychology, 51,* 1257–1264.

Schofield, L. J. (1978). Internal-external control and withdrawal AMA from an alcohol rehabilitation program. *Journal of Clinical Psychology, 34,* 571–573.

Schroeder, D. J., Bowen, W. T., & Twemlow, S. W. (1982). Factors related to patient attrition from alcoholism treatment programs. *International Journal of Addictions, 17,* 463–472.

Schuckit, M. A. (1973). Alcoholism and sociopathy-diagnostic confusion. *Quarterly Journal of Studies on Alcohol, 34,* 157–164.

Schuckit, M. A. (1979). *Drug and alcohol abuse: A clinical guide.* New York: Plenum Press.

Schuckit, M. A. (1980). Biological markers: Metabolism and acute reactions to alcohol in sons of alcoholics. *Pharmacology, Biochemistry, & Behavior, 13,* 9–16.

Schuckit, M. A. (1985). The clinical implications of primary diagnostic groups among alcoholics. *Archives of General Psychiatry, 42,* 1043–1049.

Schuckit, M. A. (1986). Genetic and clinical implications of alcoholism and affective disorder. *American Journal of Psychiatry, 143,* 140–147.

Schuckit, M. A., Gunderson, E. K. E., Heckman, N. A., & Kolb, D. (1976). Family history as a predictor of alcoholism in U.S. Navy personnel. *Journal of Studies on Alcohol, 37,* 1678–1685.

Schuckit, M. A., & Miller, P. L. (1976). Alcoholism in elderly men: A survey of a general medical ward. *Annals of the New York Academy of Sciences, 273,* 558–571.

Schuckit, M. A., & Morrissey, E. R. (1976). Alcoholism in women: Some clinical and social perspectives with an emphasis on possible subtypes. In M. Greenblatt & M. Schuckit (Eds.), *Alcoholism problems in women and children* (pp. 5–36). New York: Grune & Stratton.

Schuckit, M., Pitts, F. N., Reich, T., King, L. J., & Winokur, G. (1969). Alcoholism: I. Two types of alcoholism in women. *Archives of General Psychiatry, 20,* 301–306.

Schuckit, M., Rimmer, J., Reich, T., & Winokur, G. (1970). Alcoholism: Antisocial traits in male alcoholics. *British Journal of Psychiatry, 117,* 575–576.

Schuckit, M., Rimmer, J., Reich, T., & Winokur, G. (1971). The bender alcoholic. *British Journal of Addiction, 118,* 183–184.

Schuckit, M. A., & Russell, J. W. (1983). Clinical importance of age at first drink in a group of young men. *American Journal of Psychiatry, 140,* 1221–1223.

Schwartz, M. F., & Graham, J. R. (1979). Construct validity of the MacAndrew alcoholism scale. *Journal of Consulting and Clinical Psychology, 47,* 1090–1095.

Selzer, M. L. (1971). The Michigan alcoholism screening test: The quest for a new diagnostic instrument. *American Journal of Psychiatry, 127,* 1653–1658.

Selzer, M. L., & Holloway, W. H. (1957). A follow-up of alcoholics committed to a state hospital. *Quarterly Journal of Studies on Alcohol, 18,* 98–120.

Shaw, J. A., Donley, P., Morgan, D. W., & Robinson, J. A. (1975). Treatment of depression in alcoholics. *American Journal of Psychiatry, 132,* 641–644.

Sheeren, M. (1988). The relationship between relapse and involvement in Alcoholics Anonymous. *Journal of Studies on Alcohol, 49,* 104–106.

Sherman, R. T., & Anderson, C. A. (1987). Decreasing premature termination from psychotherapy. *Journal of Social and Clinical Psychology, 5,* 298–312.

Sherman, S. J., Skov, R. B., Hervitz, E. F., & Stock, C. B. (1981). The effects of explaining hypothetical future events: From possibility to probability to actuality and beyond. *Journal of Experimental Social Psychology, 17,* 142–158.

Shiffman, S. (1982). Relapse following smoking cessation: A situational analysis. *Journal of Consulting and Clinical Psychology, 50,* 71–86.

Shiffman, S. (1984). Coping with temptations to smoke. *Journal of Consulting and Clinical Psychology, 52,* 261–267.

Skinner, H. A. (1981). Primary syndromes of alcohol abuse: Their measurement and correlates. *British Journal of Addictions, 76,* 63–76.

Skinner, H. A., & Allen, B. A. (1982). Alcohol dependence syndrome: Measurement and validation. *Journal of Abnormal Psychology, 91,* 199–209.

Skinner, H. A., & Allen, B. A. (1983a). Differential assessment of alcoholism: Evaluation of the Alcohol Use Inventory. *Journal of Studies on Alcohol, 44,* 852–862.

Skinner, H. A., & Allen, B. A. (1983b). Does the computer make a difference? Computerized versus face-to-face versus self-report assessment of alcohol, drug, and tobacco use. *Journal of Consulting and Clinical Psychology, 51,* 267–275.

Skinner, H. A., Glaser, F. B., & Annis, H. M. (1982). Crossing the threshold: Factors in self-identification as an alcoholic. *British Journal of Addiction, 77,* 51–64.

Skinner, H. A., Holt, S., Schuller, R., Roy, J., Israel, Y. (1984). Identification of alcohol abuse using laboratory tests and a history of trauma. *Annals of Internal Medicine, 101,* 847–851.

Skinner, H. A., Jackson, D. N., & Hoffman, H. (1974). Alcoholic personality types: Identification and correlates. *Journal of Psychology, 83,* 658–666.

Skoloda, T. E., Alterman, A. I., Cornelison, F. S., & Gottheil, E. (1975). Treatment outcome in a drinking-decision program. *Journal of Studies on Alcohol, 36,* 365–380.

Smart, R. G. (1974). Employed alcoholics treated voluntarily and under constructive coercision: A follow-up study. *Quarterly Journal of Studies on Alcohol, 35,* 196–209.

Smart, R. G. (1975/1976). Spontaneous recovery in alcoholics: A review and analysis of the available research. *Drug and Alcohol Dependence, 1,* 277–285.

Smart, R. G. (1978a). Characteristics of alcoholics who drink socially after treatment. *Alcoholism: Clinical and Experimental Research, 2,* 49–51.

Smart, R. G. (1978b). Do some alcoholics do better in some types of treatment than others? *Drug and Alcohol Dependence, 3*, 65–75.

Smart, R. G., & Gray, G. (1978a). Minimal, moderate, and long-term treatment for alcoholism. *British Journal of Addiction, 73*, 35–38.

Smart, R. G., & Gray, G. (1978b). Multiple predictors of dropout from alcoholism treatment. *Archives of General Psychiatry, 35*, 363–367.

Smart, R. G., Schmidt, W., & Moss, M. K. (1969). Social class as a determinant of the type and duration of therapy received by alcoholics. *International Journal of Addictions, 4*, 543–556.

Snyder, C. R., & Higgins, R. L. (1988). Excuses: Their effective role in negotiation of reality. *Psychological Bulletin, 104*, 23–25.

Sobell, L. C., & Sobell, M. B. (1975a). Drunkenness, A "special circumstance" in crimes of violence: Sometimes. *International Journal of the Addictions, 10*, 869–882.

Sobell, M. B., & Sobell, L. C. (1976). Second year treatment outcome of alcoholics treated by individualized behavior therapy: Results. *Behavior Research and Therapy, 14*, 195–215.

Sobell, L. C., & Sobell, M. B. (1978a). Validity of self-reports in three populations of alcoholics. *Journal of Consulting and Clinical Psychology, 46*, 901–907.

Sobell, M. B., & Sobell, L. C. (1978b). *Behavioral treatment of alcohol problems.* New York: Plenum Press.

Sobell, L., & Sobell, M. (1981). Effects of three interview factors on the validity of alcohol abusers' self-reports. *American Journal of Drug and Alcohol Abuse, 8*, 225–237.

Sobell, L. C., Maisto, S. A., Sobell, M. B., & Cooper, A. M. (1979). Reliability of alcohol abusers' self-reports of drinking behavior. *Behavior Research and Therapy, 17*, 157–160.

Sobell, M. B., Sobell, L. C., & Samuels, F. H. (1974). Validity of self-reports of alcohol-related arrests by alcoholics. *Quarterly Journal of Studies on Alcohol, 35*, 276–280.

Sobell, M. B., Sobell, L. C., & VanderSpek, R. (1979). Relationships among clinical judgement, self-report, and breath-analysis measures of intoxication in alcoholics. *Journal of Consulting and Clinical Psychology, 47*, 204–206.

Stafford, R. A. (1980). Alcoholics' perception of the internal–external locus of their drinking problem. *Journal of Studies on Alcohol, 41*, 300–309.

Steele, C. M. (1975). Name-calling and compliance. *Journal of Personality and Social Psychology, 31*, 361–369.

Steele, C. M., & Liu, T. J. (1983). Dissonance processes as self-affirmation. *Journal of Personality and Social Psychology, 45*, 5–19.

Steele, C. M., Southwick, L. L., & Critchlow, B. (1981). Dissonance and alcohol: Drinking your troubles away. *Journal of Personality and Social Psychology, 41*, 831–846.

Steenbarger, B. N., & Aderman, D. (1979). Objective self-awareness as a nonaversive state: Effect of anticipating discrepancy reduction. *Journal of Personality, 47*, 330–339.

Stein, L. I., Newton, J. R., & Bowman, R. S. (1975). Duration of hospitalization for alcoholism. *Archives of General Psychiatry, 32*, 247–253.

Sterne, M. W., & Pittman, D. J. (1965). The concept of motivation: A source of institutional and professional blockage in the treatment of alcoholics. *Quarterly Journal of Studies of Alcohol, 26*, 41–57.

Stinson, D. J., Smith, W. G., Amidjaya, I., & Kaplan, J. M. (1979). Systems of care and treatment outcomes for alcoholic patients. *Archives of General Psychiatry, 36*, 535–539.

Stockwell, T., Hodgson, R., Edwards, G., Taylor, C., & Rankin, H. (1979). The development of a questionnaire to measure severity of alcohol dependence. *British Journal of Addiction, 74*, 79–87.

Stockwell, T. R., Hodgson, R. J., Rankin, H. J., & Taylor, C. (1982). Alcohol dependence, beliefs, and the priming effect. *Behavior Research and Therapy, 20*, 513–522.

Stockwell, T., Murphy, D., & Hodgson, R. (1983). The severity of alcohol dependence questionnaire: Its use, reliability and validity. *British Journal of Addiction, 78*, 145–155.

Strack, S., Carver, C. S., & Blaney, P. H. (1987). Predicting successful completion of an aftercare program following treatment for alcoholism: The role of dispositional optimism. *Journal of Personality and Social Psychology, 53,* 579–584.

Streissguth, A. P., Martin, D. C., & Buffington, V. E. (1976). Test-retest reliability of three scales derived from a quantity-frequency-variability assessment of self-reported alcohol consumption. *Annals New York Academy of Sciences, 273,* 458–496.

Strentz, T., & Auerbach, S. M. (1988). Adjustment to the stress of stimulated captivity: Effects of emotion-focused versus problem-focused preparation on hostages differing in locus of control. *Journal of Personality and Social Psychology, 55,* 652–660.

Strug, D. L., & Hyman, M. M. (1981). Social networks of alcoholics. *Journal of Studies on Alcohol, 42,* 855–884.

Sullivan, J. T., Sykora, K., Schneiderman, J., Naranjo, C. A., & Sellers, E. M. (1989). Assessment of alcohol withdrawal: The revised clinical institute withdrawal assessment for alcohol scale (CIWA-Ar). *British Journal of Addiction, 84,* 1353–1357.

Summers, T. (1970). Validity of alcoholics' self-reported drinking history. *Quarterly Journal of Studies on Alcohol, 31,* 972–974.

Sussman, S., Rychtarik, R. G., Mueser, K., Glynn, S., & Prue, D. M. (1986). Ecological relevance of memory tests and the prediction of relapse in alcohol. *Journal of Studies on Alcohol, 47,* 305–310.

Svanum, S., & Hoffman, R. G. (1982). The factor structure of the MacAndrew Alcoholism scale. *Addictive Behaviors, 7,* 195–198.

Svanum, S., Levitt, E. E., & McAdoo, G. (1982). Differentiating male and female alcoholics from psychiatric outpatients: The MacAndrew and Rosenberg alcoholism scales. *Journal of Personality Assessment, 46,* 81–84.

Svanum, S., & McAdoo, Wm. G. (1989). Predicting rapid relapse following treatment for chemical dependence: A matched-subjects design. *Journal of Consulting and Clinical Psychology, 57,* 222–226.

Swann, W. B., & Hill, C. A. (1982). When our identities are mistaken: Reaffirming self-conceptions through interaction. *Journal of Personality and Social Psychology, 43,* 59–66.

Tamerin, J. S., Weiner, S., & Mendelson, J. H. (1970). Alcoholics' expectancies during intoxication. *American Journal of Psychiatry, 126,* 1697–1704.

Tamkin, A. S., Carson, M. F., Nixon, D. H., & Hyer, L. A. (1987). A comparison among some measures of depression in male alcoholics. *Journal of Studies on Alcohol, 48,* 176–178.

Tarleton, G. H., & Tarnower, S. M. (1960). The use of letters as part of the psychotherapeutic relationship: Experience in a clinic for alcoholism. *Quarterly Journal of Studies on Alcohol, 21,* 82–89.

Tarter, R. E., Alterman, A. I., & Edwards, K. L. (1985). Vulnerability to alcoholism in men: A behavior-genetic perspective. *Journal of Studies on Alcohol, 46,* 329–356.

Tarter, R. E., Arria, A. M., Moos, H., Edwards, N. J., & Van Thiel, D. H. (1987). DSM-III criteria for alcohol abuse: Associations with alcohol consumption behavior. *Alcoholism: Clinical and Experimental Research, 11,* 541–543.

Thompson, W. D., Orvaschel, H., Prusoff, B. A., & Kidd, K. K. (1982). An evaluation of the family history method for ascertaining psychiatric disorders. *Archives of General Psychiatry, 39,* 53–58.

Thoreson, R. W., & Budd, F. C. (1987). Self-help groups and other group procedures for treating alcohol problems: A resource manual. W. M. Cox (Ed.), *Treatment and prevention of alcohol problems: A resource manual* (pp. 157–181). New York: Academic Press.

Thurstin, A. H., Alfano, A. M., & Sherer, M. (1986). Pretreatment MMPI profiles of A. A. members and nonmembers. *Journal of Studies on Alcohol, 47,* 468–471.

Tiebout, H. M. (1953). Surrender versus compliance in therapy: With special reference to alcoholism. *Quarterly Journal of Studies on Alcohol, 14,* 58–68.

Tomsovic, M. (1974). "Binge" and continuous drinkers: Characteristics and treatment follow-up. *Quarterly Journal of Studies on Alcohol, 35,* 558–564.

Tournier, R. E. (1979). Alcoholics Anonymous as treatment and as ideology. *Journal of Studies on Alcohol, 40*, 230–239.

Trice, H. H. (1959). The affiliation motive and readiness to join Alcoholics Anonymous. *Quarterly Journal of Studies on Alcohol, 20*, 313–320.

Trice, H. M., & Beyer, J. M. (1984). Work-related outcomes of the constructive-confrontation strategy in a job-based alcoholism program. *Journal of Studies on Alcohol, 45*, 393–404.

Trice, H. M., Roman, P. M., & Belasco, J. A. (1969). Selection for treatment: A poredictive evaluation of an alcoholism treatment regimen. *International Journal of the Addictions, 4*, 303–317.

Trice, H. M., & Sonnenstuhl, W. J. (1988). Constructive Confrontation and other referral processes. In M. Gallant (Ed.), *Recent developments in alcoholism* (pp. 160–171, Vol. 6). New York: Plenum Press.

Trice, H. M., & Wahl, J. R. (1958). A rank order analysis of the symptoms of alcoholism. *Quarterly Journal of Studies on Alcohol, 19*, 636–648.

Tuchfeld, B. S. (1981). Spontaneous remission in alcoholics: Empirical observations and theoretical implications. *Journal of Studies on Alcohol, 42*, 626–641.

Tucker, J. A., Vuchinich, R. E., & Harris, C. V. (1985). Determinants of substance abuse relapse. In M. Galizio & S. A. Maisto (Eds.), *Determinants of substance abuse: Biological, psychological, and environmental factors* (pp. 383–421). New York: Plenum Press.

Tversky, A., & Kahnemen, D. (1974). Judgements under uncertainty: Heuristics and biases. *Science, 185*, 1124–1131.

Twentyman, C. T., Greenwald, D. P., Greenwald, M. A., Kloss, J. D., Kovaleski, M. E., & Zibung-Hoffman, P. (1982). An assessment of social skill deficits in alcoholics. *Behavioral Assessment, 4*, 317–326.

Vaillant, G. E. (1983). *The natural history of alcoholism: Causes, patterns, and paths to recovery.* Cambridge, MA: Harvard University Press.

Vallance, M. (1965). Alcoholism: A two-year follow-up study of patients admitted to the psychiatric department of a general hospital. *British Journal of Addiction, 111*, 348–356.

Valle, S. K. (1981). Interpersonal functioning of alcoholism counselors and treatment outcome. *Journal of Studies on Alcohol, 42*, 783–790.

Van Hasselt, V. B., Hersen, M., & Milliones, J. (1978). Social skills training for alcoholics and drug addicts: A review. *Addictive Behaviors, 3*, 221–223.

Vanderpool, J. A. (1969). Alcoholism and the self-concept. *Quarterly Journal of Studies on Alcohol, 30*, 59–77.

Vannicelli, M. (1978). Impact of aftercare in the treatment of alcoholics: A cross-lagged panel analysis. *Journal of Studies on Alcohol, 39*, 18755–1886.

Vannicelli, M. (1984). Barriers to treatment of alcoholic women. *Substance and Alcohol Actions/Misuse, 5*, 29–37.

Vannicelli, M., Gingerich, S., & Ryback, R. (1983). Family problems related to the treatment and outcome of alcoholic patients. *British Journal of Addiction, 78*, 193–204.

Vogel-Sprott, M., & Banks, R. K. (1965). The effect of delayed punishment on an immediately rewarded response in alcoholics and nonalcoholics. *Behavior Research and Therapy, 3*, 69–73.

Vogler, R. E., Compton, J. V., & Weissbach, T. A. (1975). Integrated behavior change techniques for alcoholism. *Journal of Consulting and Clinical Psychology, 43*, 233–243.

Vogler, R. E., Weissbach, T. A., & Compton, J. V. (1977). Learning techniques for alcohol abuse. *Behavior Research and Therapy, 15*, 31–38.

von Knorring, L. (1976). Visual averaged evoked responses in patients suffering from alcoholism. *Neuropsychology, 2*, 233–238.

von Knorring, L., Oreland, L., & von Knorring, A. L. (1987). Personality traits and platelet MAO activity in alcohol and drug abusing teenage boys. *Acta Psychiatrica Scandanavia, 75*, 307–314.

von Knorring, L., Palm, U., & Andersson, H. E. (1985). Relationship between treatment outcomes and subtype of alcoholism in men. *Journal of Studies on Alcohol, 46*, 388–391.

Vuchinich, R. E., & Tucker, J. A. (1988). Contributions from behavioral theories of choice to an analysis of alcohol abuse. *Journal of Abnormal Psychology, 97,* 181–195.

Vuchinich, R. E., Tucker, J. A., Bordini, E., & Sullwold, A. F. (1981). Attributions of causality for drinking behavior made by alcoholics and normal drinkers. *Drug and Alcohol Dependence, 8,* 201–206.

Walcott, E. P., & Straus, R. (1952). Use of hospital facility in conjunction with outpatient clinics in the treatment of alcoholics. *Quarterly Journal of Studies on Alcohol, 13,* 60–77.

Walker, R. D., Donovan, D. M., Kivlahan, D. R., & O'Leary, M. R. (1983). Length of stay, neuropsychological performance, and aftercare: Influences on alcohol treatment outcome. *Journal of Consulting and Clinical Psychiatry, 51,* 900–911.

Walton, H. J. (1968). Personality as a determinant of the form of alcoholism. *British Journal of Psychiatry, 114,* 761–766.

Walton, R. G. (1972). Smoking and alcoholism: A brief report. *American Journal of Psychiatry, 128,* 1455–1456.

Wanberg, K. W., Horn, J. L., & Foster, F. M. (1977). A differential assessment model of alcoholism; the scales of the Alcohol Use Inventory. *Journal of Studies on Alcohol, 38,* 512–543.

Wartenberg, A. A., Nirenberg, T. D., Liepman, M. R., Silvia, L. Y., Begin, A. M., & Monti, P. M. (1990). Detoxification of alcoholics: Improving care by symptom-triggered sedation. *Alcoholism: Clinical and Experimental Research, 14,* 71–75.

Watson, C. G., Jacobs, L., Pucel, J., Tilleskjor, C., Hoodecheck, E. (1984a). The relationship of beliefs about controlled drinking to recidivism in alcoholic men. *Journal of Studies on Alcohol, 45,* 172–175.

Watson, C. G., & Pucel, J. (1985). Consistency of posttreatment alcoholic's drinking patterns. *Journal of Consulting and Clinical Psychiatry, 53,* 679–683.

Watson, C. G., Tilleskjor, C., Hoodecheck-Schow, E. A., Pucel, J., & Jacobs, L. (1984b). Do alcoholics give valid self-reports? *Journal of Studies on Alcohol, 45,* 344–354.

Watson, R. R., Mohs, M. M., Eskelson, C., Sampliner, R. E., & Hartmann, B. (1986). Identification of alcohol abuse and alcoholism with biological parameters. *Alcoholism: Clinical and Experimental Research, 10,* 364–385.

Weiner, B. (1972). *Theories of motivation: From mechanism to cognition.* Chicago: Rand McNally.

Weingartner, H., & Faillace, L. A. (1971). Verbal learning in alcoholic patients. *Journal of Nervous and Mental Disease, 153,* 407–416.

Weingold, H. P., Lachin, J. M., Bell, H., & Coxe, R. C. (1968). Depression as a symptom of alcoholism: Search for a phenomenon. *Journal of Abnormal Psychology, 73,* 195–197.

Weisner, C., & Room, R. (1984). Financing and ideology in alcohol treatment. *Social Problems, 32,* 167–184.

Weissman, M. M., & Myers, J. K. (1980). Clinical depression in alcoholism. *American Journal of Psychiatry, 137,* 372–373.

Weissman, M. M., Myers, J. K., & Harding, P. S. (1980). Prevalence and psychiatric heterogeneity of alcoholism in a United States urban community. *Journal of Studies on Alcohol, 41,* 672–681.

Welte, J., Hynes, G., Sokolow, L., & Lyons, J. P. (1981a). Effect of length of stay in inpatient alcoholism treatment on outcome. *Journal of Studies on Alcohol, 42,* 483–491.

Welte, J., Hynes, G., Sokolow, L., & Lyons, J. P. (1981b). Comparison of clients completing inpatient alcoholism treatment with clients who left prematurely. *Alcoholism: Clinical and Experimental Research, 5,* 393–399.

Whitelock, P. R., Overall, J. E., & Patrick, J. H. (1971). Personality patterns and alcohol abuse in a state hospital population. *Journal of Abnormal Psychology, 78,* 9–16.

Wilkinson, A. E., Prado, W. M., Williams, W. O., & Schnadt, F. W. (1971). Psychological test characteristics and length of stay in alcoholism treatment. *Quarterly Journal of Studies on Alcohol, 32,* 60–65.

Willems, P. J. A., Letemendia, F. J. J., & Arroyave, F. (1973a). A two-year follow-up study comparing short with long stay in in-patient treatment of alcoholics. *British Journal of Psychiatry, 122,* 637–648.

Willems, P. J. A., Letemendia, F. J. J., & Arroyave, F. (1973b). A categorization for the assessment of prognosis and outcome in the treatment of alcoholism. *British Journal of Psychiatry, 122*, 649–654.

Willis, K. A., Wehler, R., & Rush, W. A. (1979). MacAndrew scale scores in smoking and nonsmoking alcoholics. *Journal of Studies on Alcohol, 40*, 906–907.

Wilsnack, S. C. (1976). The impact of sex roles on women's alcohol use and abuse. In M. Greenblatt & M. Schuckit (Eds.), *Alcoholism problems in women and children* (pp. 37–64). New York: Grune & Stratton.

Wilsnack, S. C. (1984). Drinking, sexuality, and sexual dysfunction in women. In S. C. Wilsnack & L. J. Beckman (Eds.), *Alcohol problems in women: Antecedents, consequences, and interventions* (pp. 189–228). New York: Guilford Press.

Wise, R. A. (1988). The neurobiology of craving: Implications for the understanding and treatment of addiction. *Journal of Abnormal Psychology, 97*, 118–132.

Wiseman, J. P. (1982). Skid row alcoholics: Treatment, survival, and escape. In M. Patterson & E. Kaufman (Eds.), *Encyclopedic Handbook of Alcoholism* (pp. 946–953). New York: Gradner Press.

Wolff, S., & Holland, L. (1964). A questionnaire follow-up of alcoholic patients. *Quarterly Journal of Studies on Alcohol, 25*, 108–118.

Woodruff, R. A., Guze, S. B., Clayton, P. J., & Carr, D. (1973). Alcoholism and depression. *Archives of General Psychiatry, 28*, 97–100.

World Health Organization. (1952). Expert Committee on Mental Health. Alcoholism Subcommittee; second report (WHO Technical Report Serial No. 48). Geneva: [No. 5543].

Wright, M. H., & Obitz, F. W. (1984). Alcoholics' and nonalcoholics' attributions of control of future life events. *Journal of Studies on Alcohol, 45*, 138–143.

Wright, K. D., & Scott, T. B. (1978). The relationship of wive's treatment to the drinking status of alcoholics. *Journal of Studies on Alcohol, 39*, 1577–1581.

Yung, L., Gordis, E., & Holt, J. (1983). Dietary choices and likelihood of abstinence among alcoholic patients in an outpatient clinic. *Drug and Alcohol Dependence, 12*, 355–362.

Zager, L. D., & Megargee, E. I. (1981). Seven MMPI alcohol and drug abuse scales: An empirical investigation of their interrelationships, convergent and discriminant validity, and degree of racial bias. *Journal of Personality and Social Psychology, 40*, 532–544.

Zimberg, S. (1974a). The elderly alcoholic. *Genetologist, 14*, 221–227.

Zimberg, S. (1974b). Evaluation of alcoholism treatment in Harlem. *Quarterly Journal of Studies on Alcohol, 35*, 550–557.

Zivich, J. M. (1981). Alcoholic subtypes and treatment effectiveness. *Journal of Consulting and Clinical Psychology, 49*, 72–780.

THE FAMILY (CHARACTERISTICS AND TREATMENT)

INTRODUCTION TO THE SECTION

In considering the topic of alcoholism in the family many focuses suggest themselves. The question of how events in the family influence the evolution of the alcoholic drinking is an issue that has received attention from many frames of reference. Those who believe that alcoholism is not caused by the family, often hold the companion assumption that daily family events can stimulate perturbations in the drinking pattern, and that the family can create conditions that will precipitate recovery. Further, most frames of reference incorporate the belief that once recovery ensues particular conditions in the family can either make relapses more or less likely.

Focusing on family members for their own sake has also received a good deal of recent attention. The topic has been divided into spouses of alcoholics, children of alcoholics either still in the family system or as independent adults, and then the family interaction pattern or, otherwise stated, the family environment. The obvious question has been are there unique features of alcoholic family members and if so what are they. Explaining the origin of the characteristic features has also stimulated interest and empirically derived answers.

Therapeutic interventions for family treatment have developed. Treatment can be divided according to their purpose. Some interventions are designed to utilize the family to encourage the alcoholic's initiation of recovery. Some are geared toward making relapse in the alcoholic less likely and increasing the duration of the alcoholic's retention in treatment. Other interventions have as their purpose enhancing the mental health of the family member, regardless of the impact on the drinker. Techniques designed to treat the family relationship or the interaction pattern that manifests among family members have also been developed.

The first chapter in this section discusses ideas that have developed through the clinical observations of those working in traditionally oriented treatment centers. As will be recalled from the chapter on traditional treatment of alcoholism, the prototypes for these treatment centers were Hazelden and the Johnson Institute. These treatment centers incorporated the ideas espoused in the AA and Al-Anon literature. Others (Sharon Wegscheider, Claudia Black, Janet Woitiz, and Terry Gorski) have made original contributions that add to but do not contradict the Al-Anon beliefs. An entire system of belief has developed about family functioning, the impact of family functioning on promoting or mitigating against recovery, the characteristics of spouses and children, and proper treatment interventions. Although self-consciousness in delineating the purpose of treatment interventions is usually not manifested, the goals of enhancing the mental health of family members, of promoting initiation of treatment for by the drinker, and of decreasing the probability of relapse once an abstinence goal is embraced by the drinker have all received comment in the traditional literature. The traditional beliefs and approach to treatment are discussed in Chapter 6.

Chapter 7 examines the empirical literature. Scholars and clinicians, many of them unfamiliar with AA and Al-Anon concepts, have developed another literature. Early writings on the topics of family members of alcoholics contained the clinical observations of social workers and psychiatrists who were charged with the task of providing services to wives of alcoholics. A clinical lore developed. Later, these early assumptions were challenged by empirical investigation. Newer research has been of two types. With the rise in popularity of the traditional doctrine, some have tested hypotheses derived from traditional doctrine. Others have taken a less theoretically based approach. Rather than beginning with a hypotheses generated from a particular frame of reference, measurement of all kinds of characteristics has occurred in an attempt to construct some profile of what might be true of family members of alcoholics. Chapter 7 discusses these empirical literatures.

Chapter 8 concerns treatment. It is divided into treatments for the mental health of the family members, treatments to promote initiation of recovery in the drinker and to decrease the probability of relapse in the drinker, and treatment for the family system. Each section begins with a discussion of those treatment packages on which data pertinent to outcome have been generated. Unfortunately, outcome data are scanty. Since this is the case, some suggestions for ways to promote salubrious outcomes are proffered. In proffering suggestions I have sought to target problems that the empirical literature suggests are likely to be present. Further, I have looked to empirical social psychological literature addressing the question of what might be an optimal response given uncontrollable trauma or victimization. The chapter provides some specific interventions and suggestions for areas to address in treatment and how to do it.

6

Traditional Perspectives Concerning the Family

SPOUSES OF ALCOHOLICS

The Big Book of AA contains two chapters written about wives. Al-Anon has its own literature. Sharon Wegscheider (1981, 1985), and Claudia Black (1982), Terry Gorski and Marlene Miller (1982), clinicians who have embraced the Al-Anon and AA perspective have contributed descriptive generalizations regarding spouses. Vern Johnson in *I'll Quit Tomorrow* (1980) has also addressed the issue. These sources were used in developing the following statement of the traditional position. My personal exposure gained in the course of working in traditional settings has been drawn upon to make clear how the written recommendations are carried out in practice.

Traditionally, authors have primarily provided description of the behaviors of wives, rather than husbands of alcoholics. This focus on female spouses is not unique to the traditional school. Most family literature assumes a male alcoholic and a female spouse. This assumption is made because the large majority of spouses in treatment are wives, and because the bulk of clinical observation has concerned wives and not husbands. In this text, in the chapter on personality characteristics, a section is devoted to female alcoholism and includes what little general information is available about husbands of alcoholics.

For the most part, contributors to the literature of the traditional school have been aware of the positions espoused by others from the school, and have been supportive of each other's opinions. There are some disagreements however. One discrepant issue is whether all spouses of alcoholics, or just some spouses of alcoholics, are dysfunctional. Gorski (workshop presentation, 1984) cautions that not all spouses of alcoholics will develop pathology. He reserves the term codependent for those who do respond dysfunctionally. Johnson (1980, p. 94) includes all wives of alcoholics in the pathological category, viewing them as "dry drunks—a sort of mirror image of the alcoholic." According to Johnson, "The nonalcoholic or even abstemious spouse will show almost all of the symptoms of the disease except the physical deterioration caused by ethel alcohol." This assumption of parallel spouse behavior is proferred by many in the traditional school. Wives of alcoholics are said to be addicted to intoxicant emotions. They become addicted to worrying and obsessing over the alcoholic's behavior (Budenz, 1981).

The concept of enabling is the linch pin in understanding the traditionalist perspective on the spouse. They describe enablers as persons who intervene to keep the alcoholic from experiencing the natural consequences of the disease. Enablers may call in sick for the alcoholic, may make excuses for his behavior, may arrange for release from jail, and may purchase alcohol. They also assume role responsibilities that have been abrogated by the alcoholic. They completely take over the parenting, budgeting, and financial responsibilities, and decision making (Wegsheider, 1981).

As the drinking produces more and more aversive consequences for the family, a characteristic response from the spouse (say the traditionalists) is an attempt to control the drinking. Attempts to control through nagging, throwing out liquor, extracting promises to quit, threatening, and pleading are common (Al-Anon, 1984, pp. 6–12). Life for the spouse as for the alcoholic increasingly centers around the drinking. They become preoccupied with the comings and goings of the alcoholic. They are vigilant to watch for signs of clandestine drinking. Since the alcoholic does not respond to the exhortations and attempts to extract compliance, spouses end up feeling inadequate when their efforts prove unsuccessful. Eventually, they become too apathetic to believe in the possibility of change (Al-Anon, 1984, p. 14). They develop an angry facade overlaying a deep sense of hurt and inadequacy (Wegscheider, 1981). Often, they may blame themselves for the drinking, harboring the notion that if they were different, the alcoholic would not drink (Wegscheider, 1981).

Drinking distorts the spouse's relationships with the children as well. Lacking a nuptial companion, wives may direct their attention toward their children. They may feel responsible for regulating the relationship between the children and the alcoholic parent, intervening in altercations between the two sides. If children have positive feelings toward the alcoholic parent, the spouse may feel betrayed (Al-Anon, 1984).

In the process of assuming responsibility, spouses develop a sense of self-righteousness, arrogance, self-pity, and martyrdom (Al-Anon, 1984, pp. 14–15). Due to their overextension resulting from their need to control and from their many obligations, they often feel overwhelmed and desperate. Frequently they manifest hypochondriacal complaints. They may neglect their appearance. Their perpetual focus on the alcoholic diverts from the more productive focus of considering what they are doing with their lives (Wegscheider, 1981).

Many spouses will fear embarrassment should the community recognize the magnitude of the drinking problem. Rather than risk embarrassment, spouses isolate themselves from friends and relatives. They may deny the severity of the problem to themselves and others. They invoke a no-talk rule in the family. The magical belief, that if we do not talk about it it will not hurt, prevails. Rather than helping, the denial and isolation exacerbates the sense of burden and precludes development of social support.

The traditional literature takes an ambivalent stance on the issue of whether spouses are responsible for the alcoholic's drinking. Whereas the doctrine of powerlessness over the drinking is repetitively pronounced and guilt is discouraged, there are specific ways in which the spouse is viewed as implicated in the process of alcoholism. Although no responsibility for the initiation of disease process is implied, responsibility for problem maintenance, relapse, and inducing the alcoholic to seek treatment is replete in the literature. The concept of enabling includes the idea that enabling behavior prevents the alcoholic from hitting bottom, the crucial factor in precipitating rehabilitation. Wegscheider speaks directly to the issue. According to Wegscheider (1981, p. 173). "They [family members] do not understand that his illness could only grow as the family system allowed it to happen."

Responsibility for what happens to the alcoholic is implied in other ways as well. After sobriety is established spouses can make a relapse more probable by creating resentment in their spouse. ("Never forget that resentment is a deadly hazard to an alcoholic," AA, 1976, p. 117; "The slightest sign of fear or intolerance may lessen your husband's chance of recovery," AA, 1976, p. 120). Further, it is implied that joining Al-Anon and fostering the right home environment can enhance the chances of sobriety, "even the most stubborn refusal to seek help may change once the family's attitude has changed," (Al-Anon, 1984, p. 7).

Advice Given to Spouses of Alcoholics.   Anyone who attends an Al-Anon meeting, who participates in traditional treatment, or who reads the Al-Anon literature will be apprised of the characteristics which are believed to be manifested by spouses. Part of the treatment in treatment programs involves didactic presentation of these ideas. Patients are usually not asked whether they can recognize a particular trait in themselves, such as enabling behavior, rather, they are asked how they manifested the trait. Failure to recognize the concept in one's daily living is interpreted as denial.

Although advice is sometimes discouraged at Al-Anon meetings, advice abounds in the Al-Anon literature. Therapists from the traditional school do believe in offering specific directives. Above all spouses are directed to stop enabling. It is explained that enabling prevents the alcoholic from hitting bottom and allows the disease to progress. Spouses are enjoined from buying liquor, from participating in the repair process required after the alcoholic has failed to meet obligations, and from performing more than their equitable share of the work in the family.

The attitude of detachment from the drinking is recommended. Behaviorally, detachment means that spouses should cease efforts to control the alcoholic (nagging, cajoling, pleading, extracting promises). They should never argue with the intoxicated alcoholic. They should realize they are powerless over alcohol and turn the problem over to God, realizing that God does not burden people beyond their capacity to cope (Al-Anon, 1984, p. 28).

According to the Big Book (AA, 1976, p. 111), "The first principle of success is that you should never be angry. Even though your husband becomes unbearable and you have to leave him temporarily, you should, if you can, go without rancor. Patience and good temper are most necessary." Johnson has a somewhat different approach to spouse's anger. Johnson (1980) takes a firm stand against repression of negative emotions in the spouse and interprets Al-Anon as not advancing this position. Johnson believes that the dissipation of negative emotions will occur as the spouse begins to realize that she too has faults and she could have been the one with the disease herself.

Traditionalists have recognized that emotional detachment becomes easier if one is objectively independent. Spouses are encouraged to become more independent. They are directed to insulate themselves (detach) from the alcoholic, desensitizing themselves from the emotional impact of the verbal abuse and financial impact of the alcoholic's irresponsible behavior. They are to develop support systems outside the family.

Spouses should inform the alcoholic that the family is seeking treatment, display literature in conspicuous places, and encourage the alcoholic, when in a sober state, to also participate in treatment. Spouses should schedule and proceed with family activities despite the alcoholic's behavior. Whereas Al-Anon recommends participation in group discussion (the group is comprised of spouses), Twelve Step philosophy also suggests that nothing be revealed about the behavior of the alcoholic which the alcoholic would object to having discussed (AA, 1976, p. 125). The Al-Anon member should focus on his/her own behavioral response to the situation.

Al-Anon is clear in stating that the Al-Anon fellowship's goal is not to reform the alcoholic, but rather to bring hope and a better way of life to family members. Al-Anons (Al-Anon members) are instructed not to ask God for the alcoholic's recovery but rather for improvements in themselves. The objective is to become optimistic, cheerful, and serene regardless of what is happening. Spouses are directed to maintain hope, to be unfearful, and to put up a good front ("We are happiest when, in spite of discouragement, we put up a good home front", (Al-Anon, 1984, p. 112).

Al-Anon advises that spouses direct their attention to themselves. The same 12 steps that are recommended for the alcoholic are also recommended for the spouse. The spouses need to take a searching moral inventory. ("Many adjustments must be made in our transition from person 'wronged' to that of person who may have been wrong," (Al-Anon, 1984, p. 111). Spouses are directed in traditional treatment to abandon self-pity and self-righteousness in order to forgive (Johnson, 1980).

The treatment community is split in terms of those characteristics that spouses are directed to assess. Johnson and the Al-Anon literature focus spouses on those wrongs they have committed (e.g., We try to realize how he may have suffered from our martyr-like attitude, our criticism and nagging, Al-Anon, 1984, p. 47). Black (1982) and Wegscheider (1981) direct spouses to assess their more sympathetic qualities (e.g., trying to control areas over which one has no control; feeling guilty for the drinking; being overwhelmed and hurt). Black and Wegscheider recommend against assigning moral blame to any family member while advocating compassion toward the alcoholic. In contrasting the positions, it would seem that differences in focus could make a divorce outcome less likely in the Johnson model, and more likely in the Black and Wegscheider model.

In the Al-Anon book, the bulk of examples are of spouses who have opted to remain with the alcoholic. Al-Anon definitely presents staying as a viable option. In the AA literature there is also recognition that leaving is an option under some conditions. ("We realize some men are thoroughly bad intentioned, that no amount of patience will make any difference", AA, 1976, p. 108).

Al-Anon offers specific recommendations for those whose spouses are recovering. Spouses are cautioned not to resent the fact that AA has succeeded where they have failed. Devotion to the fellowship of Al-Anon will supplant resentment of the time spent in AA by the recovering alcoholic. Interfering in the recovery process by removing temptations to drink is discouraged (AA, 1976, pp. 120–121). Bringing up past resentments are enjoined lest a relapse be precipitated (AA, 1976, p. 115). Spouses are admonished against controlling and directing, which it is implied reflects the spouse's sense of life without a cause now that the alcoholic is recovering (Al-Anon, 1984, p. 89). Working through the need for exclusive control is recommended. The alcoholic should be allowed to resume a responsible, decision-making role in the family (Al-Anon, 1984, p. 15).

CHILDREN OF ALCOHOLICS

There has been an emerging emphasis on the need to treat the problems incurred by children of alcoholics. Rather than assuming that children of alcoholics will display the same dysfunctions as other children, albeit with higher incidence rates, the traditional school has fostered the view that children of alcoholics will manifest their own characteristic dysfunction. Treatment methods specific to children of alcoholics are recommended.

Sharon Wegscheider (1981, 1985) and Claudia Black (1982) have proferred a system of roles which they believe capture the behavior of the children who grow up in alcoholic homes. Both individuals based their categorical systems on clinical experience. The roles are assumed to be functional in the short term. However, roles are usually rigidly adhered to, limiting an individual's ability to spontaneously respond and leaving specific emotional needs unfulfilled. Treatment is directed toward helping children of alcoholics expand their range of coping choices. In addition to the roles, Janet Woitiz (1983), who clearly states that her attributions about children of alcoholics are not based on empirical research, has offered a list of characteristics descriptive of all children of alcoholics to which ameliorative efforts should be addressed.

Claudia Black's Assumptions about Children of Alcoholics

According to Black (1982), a common historical experience has fostered the following tendencies and behaviors. All children have participated in the denial process. Talking about the alcoholism within the family or with outsiders was taboo. Rationalizing and minimizing the drinking assisted in the pretense. Children of alcoholics have learned not to discern or label emotions. They are isolated from their feelings. Learning to trust was impossible in the familial context, hence a lack of trust in others is observed in children of alcoholics. However, exaggerated dependence on others is also characteristic. A sense of choice or control is lacking. Fear, guilt, isolation, and depression are accompanying features. In addition to shared characteristics, children of alcoholics can usually be described by one of the following composite attributional constructs: the responsible person, the adjuster, the placater, or the acting out child. Each role has its own cluster of characteristics.

The responsible person construct refers to the executive in the family who assumes responsibility for instrumental tasks. Because the spouse is too preoccupied with the alcoholic's drinking, the responsible child steps in making sure that the meals are prepared, that siblings' homework is finished, and the day-to-day business is dispatched. Responsible children are overly controlling of themselves and vigilant in controlling others. They are rigid and lacking in spontaneity. They are numb to feelings while secretly fearing loss of control of their feelings. They do not know how to have fun. They set obtainable goals and lead structured lives.

The placater is the emotional leader in the family. Sensitivity to the feelings of others is the hallmark feature. Placaters work to make other family members feel better. They intervene to resolve interpersonal problems among others. Despite the acute sensitivity to the emotions of others, placaters are obtuse and unreactive to their own emotional processes. Placaters never appear disappointed by anything, they do not display preferences, they are forever apologizing.

Adjusters are those who have arrived, through passivity and withdrawal, at a certain degree of comfort despite being buffeted about by events. Adjusters always remain unperturbed regardless of what is occurring. They acquiesce rather than taking corrective action, never wishing to assume a focal position. They react to rather than anticipate and direct future events. To observers they appear detached and unemotional, perhaps selfish. They may spend time away from the family. As adults they avoid responsibility and may select mates who create a chaotic environment recreating the environment of the family of origin.

Acting out children displace their emotions into antisocial behavior, which draws negative behavior from others. In terms of the function performed for the family system, the antisocial behavior helps to distract the family from focus on the alcoholic. Acting out children are more likely than those playing other roles to develop alcoholism at an early age.

Wegscheider's Assumptions about Children of Alcoholics

Sharon Wegscheider (1981, 1985), a student of Virginia Satir's, has proffered another categorical system of roles. Her system includes 4 roles: hero child, mascot, lost child, and scapegoat. Her theorizing reflects the family systems influence and Satir's specific thinking regarding emotions. Each role is assumed to fulfill a function for the larger family system. Overt, observable emotions are believed to mask hidden emotions.

Achievements outside the family identifies the hero child. The hero child's achievements provide a sense of worth for the family. In addition to achievement in the external world, the hero child adjustment subserves functions within the internal family environment as well. Feeling responsible for everything that happens in the family, the hero assumes executive as well as socioemotional leadership (functions performed by Black's placator and responsible one). In terms of inner emotions, the hero child is similar to the adult enabler. Like the enabler, the hero child's most predominant emotional response is anger, which masks hurt, a sense of inadequacy, and guilt redounding from the inability to stop the drinking. As adults, heroes are rigid, controlling, perfectionistic, prone to hypochondriasis, critical, and compelled to overwork and overachieve. Hero children focus on external goals in order to avoid focusing on themselves.

There are two versions of the mascot. The mascot can be cute and clowning, largely irrelevant and trivial. The mascot can also be hyperactive and fidgeting, distracting by accidently knocking things over or constantly chattering. The mascot's function is to provide distraction and tension relief for the family, be it humorous or annoying. The mascot prevailing emotion is a diffuse sense of fear attributable to living in an uncontrollable, but ominous, environment. The inner emotion is masked by frivolity or antagonistic behavior.

The scapegoat is roughly equivalent to Black's acting out child. Scapegoats intentionally get into trouble outside the home. They identify with an external peer group. They are often defiant, sullen, and unwilling to communicate with the family. Like the other roles, the family is distracted from the alcoholic's behavior by the diversion provided by the scapegoat.

Withdrawal from social activity is the salient feature of the lost child. Lost children attract little attention, be it negative or positive. In terms of their internal life, lost children generally blame themselves for not fitting in. A pervasive sense of worthlessness is accepted with resignation devoid of anger. Behaviorally, lost children may seek gratification in food. If attention is drawn to them, it is most likely to be for illness or enuresis. Relief from worry or responsibility is the contribution of the lost child to the family system.

TREATMENT FOR CHILDREN

As in all traditional treatment for alcoholism, much of the therapeutic contact with children is spent conveying the belief system which treatment providers hold to be true. Traditionalist do offer specific directives as well as suggesting particular philosophical stances with which to view the events in the family. Beyond these cognitive strategies, Wegscheider and Black, both of whom have backgrounds in other therapeutic schools, also view catharsis and self-disclosure as integral to the therapeutic process. The catharsis and self-disclosure often occur in a group context, which may allow for the creation of a subjective sense of social support for the group participants. Some of the specific advice as well as specific techniques for promoting catharsis and self-disclosure are delineated in the following section.

Advice given to children of alcoholics: Black (1982) offers specific advice for children who live with a nonrecovering alcoholic. The codependent (i.e., the spouse) should expand the family's social support system so that other adults can assume responsibility for instrumental tasks. Provisions should be made for assignment of those tasks that are likely to be neglected by the drinking alcoholic to other adults. The family should insulate itself from the impact of the alcoholic's drinking. For example, children should have a quarter to call a grandparent rather than ride in a car with an intoxicated parent. The spouse should take responsibility for the children's discipline so the child does not learn to take advantage of a drinking alcoholic who might be vulnerable to manipulation by the children. If violence or sexual abuse is a possibility, the family should seek shelter. The alcoholic should be informed of the family's contingency plans, although if this information is likely to elicit violence then no disclosure is advised.

The traditionalists offer a perspective for explaining the alcoholism. Children should be imbued with the view that alcoholism is a disease. The concept connotes that the alcoholic loves the family but lacks the ability to behave in a responsible, loving manner. Blackouts and mood changes should be discussed so that children properly attribute these phenomenon to the alcoholism. The emotional impact of events occurring as a result of the alcoholic's drinking should be openly discussed. Children should be warned about relapse and should be cautioned against assuming that sobriety will resolve all the problems in the family.

Black proffers specific treatment directives for children manifesting particular roles. Responsible children should list activities that will be fun for them and they should participate in these activities. Adjusters should practice listing opportunities for expressing choices as well as enumerating those options they have chosen not to exercise. Placaters should practice refraining from comforting others and should focus on their own emotional responses.

Techniques for Eliciting Catharsis and Self-Disclosure

Black relies on sentence completion type exercises as a means of priming emotions. Children of alcoholics are directed to recall those emotions their parents displayed under particular conditions and those emotions they themselves displayed or may have been suppressing. Black has published workbooks of these sentence completion exercises which are often utilized in group contexts. These sentences stimulate self-reflection upon one's emotional behavior. After completing sentence completion type exercises, each group member discloses their responses to other members of the group.

Wegscheider's (1981, p. 164) approach for family members is directed toward the goal of insight (accepting the therapist's frame of reference), and emotional expression, particularly for those emotions that are masked by the family member's usual emotional posture ("those emotions which are behind the wall"). Similar to Satir's view, the therapist's primary tools are caring, listening, acceptance, and creation of an atmosphere in which salubrious processes will occur rather than reliance upon specific techniques (1981, p. 170). Wegscheider does rely on the specific techniques of family sculpting and psychodrama. These techniques provide a static understanding of family dynamics. In contrast to other family therapists (e.g., Minuchin) who observe, comment upon, and alter spontaneous patterned processes in the family as they play out in the session, Wegscheider dramatizes prototypic scenes capturing the major elements of many repetitive prior interactions.

Wegscheider does believe that emotions need to be experienced rather than talked about in the session. In her 1985 book, she advocates gestalt techniques and psychodrama as mechanisms for eliciting emotional expression. Wegscheider believes that persons most often come to treatment wearing emotional masks. The mask is a chronic posture or habitual emotional response which camouflages underlying feelings. The therapeutic goal is to experience and feel the real, camouflaged emotions. Other than by referring to theory, which specifies which emotions are the mask and which are behind the mask, Wegscheider fails to explicate how the therapist is to decipher the true feeling from the facade.

In addition to family sculpting, gestalt, psychodrama, and lectures, Wegscheider advocates providing persons with descriptive feedback. She educates family members about the masked emotions which are assumed to underlie each of their roles. Wegscheider believes in the therapeutic value of affirmations (healthy self-statements) and instructs group members to chant these statements to particular individuals in the group.

ADULT CHILDREN OF

The therapeutic community has witnessed the development of "Adult Child of" as a diagnostic template. The traditional school recommends that ACAs form support groups. Through participation with those sharing a common background, a sense of belonging that may have been lacking in the past is achieved. In the support group meetings, Janet Woititz's speculations regarding characteristics of ACAs are presented as truths. In her book, Woititz (1983) went beyond the offering of 13 descriptive traits. Woititz offers plausible explanations, often invoking the notion of lack of good modeling, as to why these characteristics might have developed given the childhood context. Further, she offers suggestions for changing these attributes. The Woititz list of attributes as well as the suggested mechanisms for change are presented below:

1. ACAs guess at what is normal. Not having been raised in a healthy, functional environment, ACAs aspire to a standard of normal. But, they only have vague information about alternative ways to live. They try to emulate healthy behavior with only a approximate sense of what healthy might encompass. The solution is to change from a normative scale, comparing self to others, and to switch to an internal standard, asking what is functional. The realization that most characteristics can be good or bad depending on context will provide release from the constant scrutiny of whether one's behavior measures up to the normal.

2. ACAs have difficulty following a project through from beginning to end. The solution is to break the project down to realizable pieces and to select projects that can be accomplished in a realistic amount of time.

3. ACAs lie when it would be just as easy to tell the truth. The solution is to

self-monitor, discriminating when lying occurs and committing to a short-term goal of avoiding untruths, not forever but for a brief time frame.

4. ACAs judge themselves without mercy. The solution is to monitor positive behavior; be alert for complements from others; develop a relativistic view of all traits and to determine whether one is getting something out of viewing one's self in a negative manner (e.g., sympathy from other people or the familiar comfort of being miserable).

5. ACAs have difficulty having fun. The solution is to identify and participate in fun activities, surrounding self with individuals who are accustomed to enjoyment and allocating time which is unstructured.

6. ACAs take themselves very seriously. The solution is to self-disclose to a friend and to realize that one is more than what one does for a living. Further, leisure time should be allocated.

7. ACAs have difficulty with intimate relationships (defined as the lack of reciprocal self-disclosure as well as exaggerated fear of abandonment). The solution is to assess relationships according to the degree to which particular characteristics are reflected (vulnerability, understanding, empathy, compassion, respect, trust, acceptance, honesty, communication, compatibility, personal integrity, consideration). This assessment should promote better choices. To attenuate fear of abandonment, the recommendation is that intimates develop pacts. Intimates should agree to reassurance each other during the course of discussion of disagreements.

8. Having been overly sensitized by their childhood experiences, ACAs overreact to changes over which they have no control. The solution is to be aware of overreacting, to understand that one's overreactions are a function of one's history, and to experiment with deliberate disruptions of routine.

9. ACAs constantly seek approval and affirmation. The solution is to identify persons whom one can trust and who will offer support, encouragement, and approval; to conduct a daily assessment of the prior 24 hours recalling instances of positive behavior; to orient toward developing skills in those areas where there are deficiencies; and to make dispositional attributions for success and external attributions for failure.

10. ACAs usually feel that they are different from other people. The solution is to engage in reciprocal self-disclosure so that the universality of most traits becomes apparent. Realizing that a sense of belonging is generally a function of acceptance of group norms and that one has a choice over this acceptance provides direction for how to belong.

11. ACAs are super responsible or super irresponsible. The origin of distortions in responsibility derives from perfectionistic standards which are responded to with either giving up or trying hard. The solution, for the super responsible, is to begin to assess overcommitments and cut back. The irresponsible should select small goals and overcome the fear of success.

12. ACAs are extremely loyal even in the face of evidence that loyalty is unwarranted. The solution is to realistically assess what one is getting out of particular relationships. If the scales are unbalanced, one should explore what one might be deriving from a relationship (e.g., sense of superiority, fear of being alone, avoiding guilt for leaving).

13. ACAs are impulsive. They lock themselves into a course of action without giving serious consideration to alternative behaviors or possible consequences. This impulsivity leads to confusion, self-loathing, and loss of control over the environment. In addition, they spend an excessive amount of energy cleaning up the mess. The solution is to give oneself time to think through decisions before committing, fantasize future ramifications, consider impact of decisions on other people, and consider alternative solutions to each course of action.

SOME COMMENTS ON THE STEREOTYPES AND ASSUMPTIONS OF TRADITIONAL FAMILY TREATMENT

The several versions of treatment for children of alcoholics and spouses whether proferred by Wegsheider, Black, Johnson, or Woititz do share common elements. The writings of all authors are perfused with melodramatic vignettes of life in an alcoholic family. Children are always presented as pathetic victims. In most versions of traditional treatment a stereotypic view of the spouse, children, and alcoholic is presented. Each family member has his/her own list of characteristics. For those who are avid treatment participants, a habit is established whereby the behavior of any particular family member is attributed to his/her stereotype. (For example, "My husband must have done that because he is a typical alcoholic perfectionist.") In group sessions, family members are often referred to as "the alcoholic" or "the codependent" rather than by name. Whether such stereotyping has a salubrious impact on family relationships has not yet been evaluated.

In most traditional treatment centers spouses, and children of, are strongly encouraged to receive treatment. The admonitions that unless treatment is received a spouse will sabotage the alcoholic's sobriety or marry a second alcoholic and the child of will either marry an alcoholic or become alcoholic are explicitly stated. All traditionalist believe that becoming an alcoholic or marrying an alcoholic is caused in some way by distortions attributable to one's family of origin experience. The distortions can be corrected through insight, building self-esteem, and catharsis.

Traditionalists have varied in their objectives for including family members in treatment. Johnson and Al-Anon seem to emphasize the objective of enhancing the alcoholic's chance for sobriety. Wegscheider, Black, and Woititz place emphasis on treatment of family members for their own sake. Enhancing family cohesion has not been a major focus for any of the traditionalists.

All traditional experts have recommended that ACAs, spouses, and children form support groups. The purpose of the support group is to identify and acquire a sense of belonging which may not have been previously experienced. Of course, a sense of belonging could be achieved through participation in many types of group endeavors. The impact of identifying oneself as an ACA, Al-Anon, or codependent, rather than, for example, a member of an encounter group, has yet to be evaluated.

SUMMARY AND DISCUSSION

In this chapter the traditional doctrine of beliefs regarding spouses and children of alcoholics has been presented. In Chapter 7 the empirical research identifying traits of family members is reviewed. Those beliefs that have and have not been supported are differentiated.

There has been very little evaluation of traditional therapy for family members. In the final chapter in this section, the outcome research is reviewed. Unfortunately, most of the outcome research has evaluated therapeutic packages. Within each package, less traditional methods have been incorporated as well as methods based on traditional beliefs. Such confounding of the treatment variable renders it impossible to generate conclusions as to efficacy of traditional methods.

When outcome research is lacking, a second strategy for developing an approach based on empirical findings is available. This strategy is to examine the findings from research exploring human behavior and malleability in general. With regard to family members of alcoholics, a relevant question is what does the research community know about responses to uncontrollable trauma. Under the assumption that being a member of family with an alcoholic parent might qualify as a long-term traumatic experience, in Chapter 7, on treatment, this literature is reviewed. Specific recommendations for treatment based on this literature, is offered.

7

Empirical Findings on Family Characteristics

In this chapter the several bodies of empirical literature regarding the behavior and characteristics of family members are reviewed. The chapter begins with the topic of spouses. Next the characteristics of children of alcoholics are discussed. The literature on children in this chapter primarily focuses on behaviors that are more likely to be responses to the interpersonal environment, rather than genetically or physically determined traits. The reader is referred to the section on genetics in the second volume for discussion of what characteristics might be inherited. The last topic in this chapter concerns the interpersonal environment in alcoholic homes—how alcoholics view their spouses and how spouses view their alcoholic husbands, how family members view their homes, and finally, studies in which families have been observed as they interact both while drinking and while sober. Questions running through each of the literatures are (a) what particular features characterize families of alcoholics, (b) do these features reflect a unique response or rather a general response to stress, (c) are there some alcoholic families who do not display these characteristics, and (d) do problems in the family abate given recovery in the alcoholic.

HYPOTHESES AND EMPIRICAL RESEARCH ON THE CHARACTERISTICS OF WIVES OF ALCOHOLICS

The traditional literature was primarily developed by persons employed in settings in which AA philosophy and tenets provided the foundation for treatment. There is another preexperimental study containing the clinical observations of social workers and psychiatrists who did not begin with the set of assumptions made by the traditionalists. This clinical literature provided hypotheses that were later tested empirically. This material is further described in Edwards, Harvey, and Whitehead (1973). The position of this early clinical literature is labeled the disturbed personality hypothesis.

The view advanced in this early literature offered by social workers and psychiatrists characterized the spouse as overtly domineering, aggressive, and hostile. These features were believed to mask fears of inadequacy. Early thinking suggested that wives of alcoholics had experienced childhood trauma, often with an overly domineering mother. As a result of this distorted upbringing, wives required a distorted family of procreation in order to feel adequate. They therefore gravitated to inadequate men. They selected a husband who was poorly functioning in order to assume a superior role. Rather than risk relinquishing the superior ground, the wife would sabotage all efforts toward the husband's recovery. Should the husband manage to recover somehow, the wife would follow one of two paths. Either she would decompensate due to a lack of a mechanism for feeling superior, or she would leave the marriage and seek a second union in which she could again assume the superior role (i.e., marry another alcoholic).

Whalen (1953), relying on clinical observations, advanced a typology. She observed variation in the response of the wives she treated. "Suffering Susan" chose a husband who obliged her in making her miserable so that she could satisfy her masochistic needs. "Controlling Catherine" chose a weak, sniffling husband to satisfy her need to dominate. "Wavering Winnifred" craved gratitude and thus chose a husband who needed her desperately. "Punitive Polly" needed to control and punish and chose a husband who would tolerate emasculation.

Whalen's prototypes have captured the variations on the theme seen in the broader preempirical clinical literature. The clinical descriptions of others can be categorized into one or another of Whalen's types. This is also true of the AA traditionalists. However, the AA traditionalists do vary in terms of which Whalen prototype they emphasize or consider to be most typical. Claudia Black and Sharon Wegscheider more often depict "Suffering Susan" and "Wavering Winnifred." The Al-Anon literature and Vern Johnson more often offer portraits of "Controlling Catherine" and "Punitive Polly." Whalen should be credited for her rich clinical description.

In counterpoint to the disturbed personality view of wives of alcoholics of early clinicians was the view of sociologist Joan Jackson, who developed her hypotheses based on observations at numerous Al-Anon meetings. Jackson (1954) proposed the social stress hypothesis to account for any aberrant personality findings among the wives of alcoholics. According to Jackson's view, the distinctive behavior of the wives of alcoholics reflected a response to stress. The deviance that redounded, which is characteristic of the specific type of stress is differentiated from a general stress reaction, developed in response to the alcoholic husband's drinking. It represented an attempt to stabilize the family situation and to prevent shame and ostracism in the community. According to Jackson, as a group, wives of alcoholics did not display deviance before the development of the husband's alcoholism. Wives did not select alcoholic mates, and for the modal alcoholic family, there was no indication that the husband was alcoholic prior to the marriage. Should the alcoholic achieve sobriety, the wife's deviant functioning was predicted to attenuate.

In the course of proffering her social stress hypothesis, Jackson (1954), hypothesized stages through which the alcoholic family would evolve. The coping mechanisms of the family were believed to change as the alcoholism progressed. Jackson suggested that in the initial stages of alcoholic drinking, the wife's self-esteem would diminish as a result of the inadequacy of her attempts to stop the alcoholic from drinking. Jackson believed that the wife would take over the responsibilities in the family, excluding the alcoholic and relying on him for less and less. Eventually, the alcoholic would assume the status of petulant child who could still annoy but no longer cause great pain. As the wife assumed greater responsibility, her self-esteem would increase and her pathology would abate. Sometimes divorce would ensue following this type of detachment from the alcoholic.

The views of other contributors to the early professional literature vs. the views of Joan Jackson, did offer testable hypotheses. Both views suggested that wives of alcoholics would vary from wives of normal individuals. Both suggested that wives would differ from wives of those experiencing other stressors. Early clinical lore vs. Joan Jackson differed as to whether the wife selected the husband for his aberrant behavior, that is whether the alcoholism was apparent at the onset of the relationship. They differed as to whether the wife came from a traumatic family of origin. They differed on whether the wife would decompensate or flourish given the husband's recovery and as to whether she would seek a second union with an alcoholic husband.

Empirical Findings on Specific Traits of the Wives of Alcoholics

In the empirical literature, some investigators have conducted research from an atheoretical perspective asking the basic question of how wives of alcoholics differ from other wives. A number of investigators have compared wives of wet alcoholics to wives of normals or wives of depressed persons on the MMPI. Corder, Hendricks, and Corder (1964), Kogan and Jackson (1965b), Kogan, Fordyce and Jackson (1963), Rae and Forbes (1966) have all found that wives of alcoholics obtain higher scores on MMPI pathology scales than to normals. Bailey, Haberman, and Alksne (1962) found a higher percentage of wives of wet alcoholics compared to control wives scoring above a predetermined cutting score on a symptomatology measure. Orford (1976) found wives to be more neurotic than normals on the Eysenck's measure. Steinglass (1981a) found that wives of alcoholics were less symptomatic on a symptom checklist than psychiatric outpatient samples albeit more symptomatic than normals. It should be noted that family members of alcoholics reflect what may be stress on additional indices as well. Family members make more frequent visits to the doctor and have received more diagnoses for physical complaints than normal control samples (Roberts & Brent, 1982). These findings all support the view of more pathology in the wives of alcoholics. There are some findings that temper conclusions, however. Despite mean group differences, only 50% of Kogan et al.'s (1963) sample (n = 50) and 42% of Tarter's (1976) sample (n = 38) achieved elevations on an MMPI clinical scale.

There is further support for the view that not all wives of alcoholics will be symptomatic. Steinglass (1981a) found a correlation between wife's endorsement of symptoms off a checklist and the husband's self-assessed severity of his alcoholism. Symptoms were more heavily associated with social–behavioral consequences from drinking than they were to amount of alcohol consumed by the husband.

In characterizing the MMPI profiles of wives of alcoholics, some have sought to differentiate types. Rae and Forbes (1966) found that those wives of alcoholics who achieved elevated scales on the MMPI could be categorized into two groups: those who were anxious and depressed (elevations on the Depression, Psychathenia, and Hysteria scales) and those who achieved elevations on the Pd (Psychopathic Deviance) scale. Wives with high Pd scores are more likely to be married to men whose drinking had resulted in job losses (Rae, 1972).

There have been attempts to assess whether the wives of alcoholics view themselves in a characteristic, although not necessarily aberrant manner. Kogan and Jackson (1963a, 1963b) and Drewrey and Rae (1969) both found that wives of alcoholics were more likely to describe themselves in stereotypically feminine terms. Orford et al. (1976) recruiting a sample of wives of hospitalized alcoholics, found that these wives perceived themselves, irrespective of whether their husbands were drinking, as more passive, submissive, and wanting to be led. Gynther and Brilliant (1967) found that spouses of alcoholics viewed themselves as less dominant than other women and more ineffectual. Orford (1976) found that wives were less extroverted than normals on the Eysenck's measure.

Whereas the above findings suggest that wives may view themselves as demure and ineffectual, data on husband's views of wives provides a different picture. Gynther and Brilliant (1967) and Gynther, Presher, and McDonald (1959) found that husband viewed their wives as dominant, responsible, and managerial. Orford (1976) found husbands perceived wives as more dominant than wives perceived themselves. Orford et al. (1977) reported that 23% of their sample recalled wife domination from the beginning of the marriage. Paradoxically, in the Gynther and Brilliant (1967) study, husbands expressed a desire for wives to increase their domination.

Other research suggests that wife dominance may be peculiar to particular types of alcoholic families. Lemert (1962), finding a high incidence of wife dominance, noted that dominance is particularly pronounced among the wives of alcoholics whose alcoholism is severe and in whom alcoholism was prevalent from the beginning of the marriage. Deniker, DeSavgy, and Ropert (1964) found that undisputed (both spouses agree) and early onset wife dominance is peculiar to those marriages in which the alcoholic suffers social consequences but not those in which only physical symptoms are observed. Rae and Drewrey (1972) state that both husband and wife view a high Pd scoring wife as exhibiting masculine characteristics. Low Pd scoring wives are similar to controls.

The literature on assortative mating of alcoholics suggests that 12% of the wives of alcoholics are themselves alcoholic and that 34% of the husbands of alcoholic wives are alcoholic. These statistics suggest that assortative mating does occur for alcoholics of both sexes (Jacob & Bremer, 1986). According to Hall, Hesselbrock, and Stabenau's (1983b) findings, abstinent women do marry heavy drinkers, but the converse is seldom true. Assortative mating involving sociopathic and/or alcoholic males married to female hysterics, sociopaths, and/or alcoholics has been noted (Guze, Goodwin, & Crane, 1970; Woerner & Guze, 1968).

If wives of alcoholics are compared to wives of normals, social class differences will be found (deBlois & Stewart, 1983). This finding probably reflects the association between drinking habits and SES (socioeconomic status). Compared to wives married to normal drinking males, the wives of alcoholics, as a group, will be less well educated and more likely to be employed at unskilled jobs (deBlois & Stewart, 1983).

Coping Styles of Wives

Whereas the foregoing research examined traits of wives of alcoholics, other researchers have attempted to characterize the manner or manners in which wives have attempted to cope with their husband's excessive alcohol consumption. Consistent with traditional speculation, Lemert (1960) found that most spouses had attempted to control their husband's drinking. Orford and Guthrie (1968) factor analyzed the responses to a menu of coping behaviors that had been endorsed by spouses. Five factors emerged: attack, withdrawal, protection, acting-out, and safeguarding family interests. James and Goldman (1971) attempted to determine which factors would be differentially employed at various stages. Results suggested that coping mechanisms failed to cluster into sequential stages. Rather, all coping increased as drinking become more severe. The failure of specific coping mechanisms to be more characteristic of families in which alcoholism had only recently emerged vs. families in which alcoholism had persisted for a substantial duration, was corroborated by Lemert (1960). This finding contradicted Jackson's (1954) contention that there are progressive changes in response to an alcoholic spouse.

Orford, Guthrie, Nicholls, Oppenheimer, Egert, and Hensman (1975) suggested that coping in general and particular coping mechanisms were associated with specific occurrences in the family environment. More coping emerged when the drinking was intense. Further, aggregate coping was related to greater hardship in the marriage, increased neuroticism in the wife, and lower SES of the family (level at treatment intake, not the highest level ever achieved.) In the James and Goldman (1971) study, it was found that wives with violent husbands were more likely to respond with quarreling, violence, anger and helplessness, pretending to be drunk themselves, locking husband out of the house, and seeking a separation. Moos and Moos (1984) found that in those alcoholic families where there are more frequent arguments and less agreement between the perceptions of family members, avoidance was more likely to be employed as a coping mechanism.

Family of Origin of the Wives of Alcoholics

Kogan and Jackson (1965a) compared a sample of Al-Anons married to wet alcoholics with a control group. In terms of frequency of deviant childhood experiences, no differences between the two groups were detected; however, Al-Anons more often recalled a combination of inadequate mothering and childhood unhappiness. Within the Al-Anon sample, Al-Anons who recalled childhood happiness were less psychologically stressed by familial interpersonal conflict and were less likely to experience familial conflict.

There is support for the hypothesis that the wives of alcoholics, more often than what would be expected on the basis of chance, do come from families in which there was parental alcoholism. James and Goldman (1971) recruited 85 wives of alcoholics from a family service agency. They found that 22% of wives had alcoholic fathers, 4% of wives had alcoholic mothers, and 19% of wives had alcoholic brothers. In Stabenau and Hesselbrock (1983) samples of spouses (144 wives and 94 husbands), 30% of wives and 42% of husbands reported alcoholism in the immediate or extended family of origin. Combining the two small samples of Macdonald's (1956) and Nici (1979), approximately 20% of the wives of alcoholics labeled their fathers as alcoholic.

Some have attempted to address the question of association between parental alcoholism and spousal alcoholism by selecting a sample of ACAs (adult child of alcoholic) and then measuring the rate of reported spousal alcoholism. Black, Bucky, and Wilder–Padilla (1986) began with a sample of ACAs and compared them to a normal control sample. The ACAs reported a higher incidence of marriage to alcoholics. This particular study can be questioned for the manner in which the ACAs were recruited, however. All subjects had responded to adds in the magazines subscribed to by ACA Twelve Step meeting attenders. It seems plausible that the threshold for labeling a spouse alcoholic may be lower in this group than would be the case in a normal sample or even a sample of ACAs who were not frequent attenders of ACA meetings.

It may be that dysfunctional families of origin are particular to specific types of alcoholic families. Deniker et al. (1964) classified wives according to whether their husbands evidenced problems due to drinking in social and job arenas vs. those who were free of problems in terms of social consequence but were experiencing physical problems related to the drinking. Wives whose alcoholic husbands were aberrant socially manifested greater incidence of dysfunctional families of origin whereas those with exclusively physical problems did not differ from the control group.

There is some support for a disturbed childhood personality predicting remaining in a marriage in which verbal abuse toward self and children is occurring. O'Farrel, Harrison, and Cutter (1981) found that childhood shyness as opposed to gregariousness predicted remaining in a negative marital relationship. Shyness itself was not a correlate of an alcoholic family of origin or economic privation as a child. Having suffered a chaotic family of origin environment was not significantly related to the likelihood of divorce given hard times in the marital relationship. The direction of the nonsignificant correlation suggested that those with chaotic childhoods were more likely to seek a divorce given hard times, however.

Some Cautions on Conclusions.   The research exploring whether wives of alcoholics more often come from families in which there was parental alcoholism, suggests a positive association. This association cannot, however, confirm the hypothesis that something about the parental alcoholism created an attraction to alcoholic males. The association may merely reflect cultural influences. It is known that particular culture groups have higher incidences of alcoholism. An alcoholic has a higher probability of belonging to such a high risk for alcoholism culture. A daughter of an alcoholic is more likely to grow up in and remain in a high risk culture and so would be more likely to encounter others from the same culture, who would in turn be more likely to develop alcoholism.

The finding that wives of alcoholics report more dysfunction in their families of origin than do control populations, should also be viewed with caution. The variable of dysfunction in the family of origin was assessed via the self-report of the wife. It may be that the recall of stressed out individuals, as would be expected among wives of alcoholics, tends toward bleaker recollections. Perhaps their assessment of more dysfunction in their family of origin reflects their depressed mood, rather than objective situations in their families of origin.

Do Wives Select Alcoholic Husbands?

A linch pin assumption in the disturbed personality theory of wives is that wives chose an alcoholic husband, i.e., the alcoholism was obvious during the courtship. Pertinent data is available. Seventy-eight percent of the wives in James and Goldman's (1971) sample (N = 85) had married their husbands prior to any indication that the husband would become alcoholic. In other samples there is more support for the disturbed personality hypothesis. 53.9% of Lemert's (1960) sample of 112 and 14 out of 26 in Rae and Forbes (1966) sample, and 80% of Gorman and Rooney's (1979) sample of 123 had married their alcoholic husbands after the drinking had been established. Some differentiation as to the personality characteristics of those choosing to marry an active alcoholic have been distinguished. Lemert (1960) found that those wives who could be construed as having selected an alcoholic husband were more likely to be domineering. Rae (1972) found that those who married extant alcoholics were more likely to be high scorers on the Pd (Psychopathic Deviance) scale and were less likely to be supportive of recovery.

What Happens to the Spouse If Sobriety Ensues: Decompensation, No Change, or Recovery?

Joan Jackson predicted that wives of recovering alcoholics would become less distressed when sobriety ensued. The decompensation axiom of the disturbed personality hypothesis predicted enhanced deterioration in the wives of alcoholics given recovery. What would the data say? Most data are against the decompensation hypothesis. When husbands sober up, rather than decompensating the stress level of wives improves (Bailey et al., 1962; Billings & Moos, 1983; Haberman, 1964; Paolino, McCrady, & Kogan, 1978; Steinglass, 1979). Zweben (1986) and Billings and Moos (1983) find a positive correlation between amount of drinking by the relapsing alcoholic and wives discomfort.

Wives of dry alcoholics have not been found to differ from a control group on measures of mood, physical symptoms, and drinking (Bailey et al., 1962; Billings & Moos, 1983; Kogan & Jackson, 1965b). Although wives of dry alcoholics have not been found to differ significantly from controls, the wives no longer living with a wet alcoholic have been found to achieve means midway between the means of the control wives and the wives of wet alcoholics (Bailey et al., 1962; Kogan & Jackson, 1965b). These findings suggest that lack of statistical power may have resulted in Type II errors in studies in which differences between wives no longer living with wet alcoholics and controls were not detected. The possibility of residual trouble in many of the wives no longer living with wet alcoholics or the presence of some poorly functioning individuals amid the majority of healthy functioning individuals cannot be readily dismissed.

There is a study in which worse functioning in the wives of sober alcoholics was noted. Macdonald (1956) selected women in a mental hospital and found that among those who were married to alcoholics, there was an association between the wife's onset of mental illness and the husband's abstinence. Although this data might be consistent with the decompensation hypothesis, it is also possible that alcoholics in this study attenuated their drinking when burdened with major family obligations. Thus, wives deteriorated and then husband's sobered up, rather than the reverse.

A particular group of wives has been identified whose symptomatology does not remit given abstinence in the alcoholics. High Pd scoring wives are less likely to display improved functioning given abstention in the alcoholic (Rae, 1972).

Are Divorced Wives of Alcoholics More Likely to Marry a Second Alcoholic?

Little data are available regarding second marriages of wives of alcoholics. A study by Nici (1979) looked at a sample of women married for the second time. These women were categorized into those married to alcoholics vs. those married to normals. No difference was detected on the variable of "first husband alcoholic" between those presently married to an alcoholic vs. those presently married to a nonaberrant drinker. This particular study suggested no association.

Characteristics of Wives Predicting Recovery in Alcoholic Husbands

There have been studies in which wives of alcoholics who recover posttreatment have been compared to wives of alcoholics who exhibited relapse after treatment. These studies identify those features of wives of alcoholics that are less likely to discourage recovery. Further, they shed light on the issue of the profile of the wife of an alcoholic whose disturbed personality might not tolerate recovery in her spouse. If there is a category of wife of an alcoholic who fits the disturbed personality concept, her husband would be less likely to recover since his recovery would precipitate his wife's psychological decompensation or abandonment of the marriage.

Generally, wives of recovering alcoholics display better general coping skills. Considering alternatives, putting events in perspective, and disclosing to friends are more often represented in the coping repertoire of wives of the recovering. Heavy reliance on displacement, avoidance of thoughts about the stressful event, or the avoidance of the stressful event per se were more often relied upon by the relapsed alcoholics and their wives. In terms of the relationship between coping skills and other areas of psychological functioning, better coping skills were associated with good mood and higher self-esteem (Billings & Moos, 1983).

Alcoholics married to wives scoring high on the Pd scale are more likely to relapse (Rae, 1972), although general neuroticism in the wife is not related to treatment outcome (Orford et al., 1975). Improved treatment outcome operationalized as less posthospitalization relapse, has been found among couples in which the wives displayed greater trust assessed at intake by a primary communication inventory and a conjugal life questionnaire (Cadogan, 1973).

More overall coping in the wife, possibly an index or correlate of severity of the drinking, predicts negative outcome (Orford et al., 1975). Specific coping mechanisms are also related to better outcome. Orford et al. (1975) found that wives of unrecovered alcoholics had endorsed the following coping mechanisms at intake: avoidance, sexual withdrawal, fearful withdrawal, and taking special action (e.g., making special arrangements about finances). Those wives whose husbands exhibited good recovery had hidden bottles, made rules about not drinking in the house, gone out to fetch their husbands, made husband jealous, fought with husband when he was drunk, gotten drunk themselves, and gone out and had a good time alone. Schaffer and Tyler's (1979) survey duplicated some of these findings. Strong disapproval of the drinking (throwing out liquor and not making the husband comfortable as he drank) predicted sobriety. Pretending everything was ok also predicted recovery. Threats of divorce were associated with poor recovery.

A Pattern in the Findings

Early in this chapter two points of view were contrasted: the disturbed personality and the stress hypothesis (Joan Jackson). It was stated that the two points of view offered testable hypotheses. The empirical literature does shed light on these contrasting views, if a distinction is made between two populations. Those wives with low Pd scores seem to better fit Joan Jackson's stress hypothesis. This group did not choose alcoholic husbands as there was no indication of pathology during the courtship. The pathology displayed by these wives conforms to the picture of a general response to stress (elevations on MMPI stress scales). When the alcoholic's drinking remits, this group of wives gets better.

In contrast to the low Pd scoring wives, those wives who are high Pd scorers fit the disturbed personality hypothesis. They marry alcoholics whose drinking was obvious from the beginning of the relationship. Their pathology and personalities are distinctive (viz., they are likely to dominate their husbands) rather than exhibiting behaviors that are part of a generalized stress response. Should their spouses recover, which is less likely for husbands of high Pd scoring wives, their pathology fails to remit.

Some Cautions on Conclusions Regarding Wife's Behavior as a Causal Mechanism in Husband's Recovery.   On considering the findings on the association between coping responses to drinking and treatment outcome, there is a temptation to leap to the conclusion that particular coping mechanisms in the wife might cause recovery in the alcoholic. Orford et al. (1975) caution against a causal interpretation from the findings. The coping behavior of the wife may be another index of severity of alcoholism which is itself a predictor of outcome. All the data are correlational. Nevertheless, the number of enabling behaviors of the wives of alcoholics that are on the good outcome list is striking. These behaviors apparently do not greatly jeopardize the chances for recovery.

CHARACTERISTICS OF CHILDREN

As detailed in Chapter 5 of Volume II, the children of alcoholics are more likely to experience migraine headaches; to be low MAO (the enzyme which breaks down serotonin and catecholamines); to exhibit hyperactivity; to be delinquent; to be sensation seeking and high scorers on the MacAndrew scale; and to display cognitive and scholastic deficiencies. The predominant view is that these factors may be attributable to genetic events.

In addition to the physiological differences attributable to genetics, the physiological impact of having had a mother who drank through gestation can be profound. The effects of fetal alcohol syndrome (FAS) were presented in Chapter 8 of Volume II and therefore are not repeated here. Also discussed in Chapter 8 of Volume II were some recent findings from the rodent literature regarding the impact on the rat pup of heavy drinking by the father rat who impregnated the female rat. (Rat pups sired by heavy drinking males are lower in birth weight and are more lethargic.) It is likely that some differences found between family history positives (FHP)s and control children are attributable to underlying degrees of FAS or physical events mediated through the sperm. In addition to FAS and the impact of the sperm of heavy consuming fathers, el-Guebaly and Offord (1979) have noted that mothers who experience severe stress during gestation, such as might occur when one is married to a wet alcoholic, produce offspring who manifest emotional disturbance. Thus, there are predictable effects attributable to the intrauterine environment of mothers experiencing severe stress. Children of alcoholics also experience more head trauma and birth trauma than do other children (Tarter et al., 1984). All of these physiological traumas will no doubt be reflected on measures of erratic emotions, hyperactivity, and cognitive deficits.

Unfortunately it is difficult to determine which characteristics in a given population are attributable to environment and which are attributable to physical events. There is some overlap between the material reviewed in this chapter and the material reviewed in the section on genetics. Nevertheless a differentiation between physically mediated traits and traits due to the psychological impact of the environment was attempted. Having previously reviewed the genetic, intrauterine, and other biological bases of the characteristics of FHP children, this chapter reviews environmental contributions.

Behavioral and Emotional Problems of FHP Children

A number of studies have compared children of alcoholics with control group children on dependent variable, which may reflect environment rather than genetic or intrauterine influences. Haberman (1966) found increased temper tantrums and fighting in FHPs as compared with children of ulcer patients. Whitfield (1980) reported increased enuresis. Jacob and Leonard (1986) found that FHP children scored more deviantly on the Auchenbach, a parental self-report measure of behavioral problems. El-Guebaly and Offord (1979) found that 24% of FHP were high scorers on the Rutter parental questionnaire of childhood problems. A high percentage of school problems, less hard work, more absenteeism, more school expulsion, and decreased high school graduation has been noted (Chafetz, Blane, & Hill, 1971, Hughes, 1977; Kammeier, 1971; Miller & Jang, 1977). Ervin, Little, Streissguth, and Beck (1984) also found lower academic achievement. Werner (1986) found that FHP children evidenced more delinquency. Werner's sample included a large number of welfare mothers and welfare status may be a moderator variable that may preclude generalization to other FHP samples.

The above findings document more behavioral problems and less achievement among children of alcoholics. Children of alcoholics are also more likely to suffer from emotional-type problems. Children of nonrecovered alcoholics, particularly those with alcoholic mothers, have been found to display lower self-esteem (Hughes, 1977; Miller, & Jang, 1977; Kammeier, 1971; McLachlan cited by Jacob, Favorini, Meisel, & Anderson, 1978; O'Gorman, 1976), and lower self-confidence (Cork, 1969). They display higher dysphoria, more physical symptoms (Billings & Moos, 1983; Hughes, 1977), and higher externality (O'Gorman, 1976; Prewett et al., 1981). Steinhausen, Gobel, and Nestler (1984) found that children of alcoholic moms displayed emotional problems whereas the children of alcoholic fathers displayed conduct problems.

Emotional and Marital Problems of FHP Adults

Studies of adult children of alcoholics, unassessed as to whether or not their alcoholic parent had recovered, have appeared in the literature. Bennett et al. (1988) found lower self-esteem, more dysphoria, and physical symptoms among FHP (family history positives). Berkowitz and Perkins (1988) found that college age daughters of alcoholic fathers but not alcoholic mothers displayed lower self-esteem. Sons did not differ from the control group on self-esteem but were higher on autonomy. Clair and Genest (1987), examining a college age population, failed to detect self-esteem differences between FHP and controls but did find increased depression proneness among FHPs. Benson and Heller (1987) found enhanced neurosis and psychopathy among FHP daughters. These studies, then, do suggest more emotional distress among adult children of alcoholics.

Examining coping styles, Clair and Genest (1987) found that FHPs more often employed avoidant strategies to problems, viz., drinking, smoking, and sleeping more when confronted with a problem. They relied more on emotion focused coping behavior rather than problem focused coping behaviors. Although they did not differ from controls in terms of emotional social support received during adolescence, they had received less informational social support. In terms of which coping style resulted in better outcome, emotion focused coping, but not problem solution coping, predicted depression and lower self-esteem in the sample.

Employing a methodology which better separates the effects of nature and nurture, Goodwin, Schulsinger, Knop, Mednick, and Guze (1977) and Goodwin, Schulsinger, Moller, Hermansen, Winokur, and Guze (1974) compared family history positives who had been raised at home vs. family history positives who had been adopted out. Those males raised at home were more often single (never married) and they more often recalled school phobias and childhood disobedience than their adopted out brothers. Goodwin et al. (1974), reported that FHP males raised at home less often recalled a domineering mother. The females who had been raised at home displayed higher rates of depression than their sisters who had been adopted out (Goodwin et al., 1977).

Parker and Harford (1988) looking at FHPs vs. controls, reported findings consistent with Goodwin et al. and others. They found that FHP daughters displayed higher rates of depression. Both sexes displayed higher rates of marital conflict. In males, marital conflict was associated with the offsprings' own drinking. In females, the increased marital conflict and depression were particular to the nonproblem drinkers. A study by Beardslee, Son, and Vaillant (1986) was consistent with the confinement of greater mental health problems among those with their own drinking problems.

In a longitudinal study of sons of alcoholics selected for a lack of childhood delinquency problems, Drake and Vaillant (1988) identified childhood precursors to adult onset personality disorders. (The authors did not specify the particular personality disorders.) The predictors of adult onset personality disorders were a chaotic childhood environment, a bad relationship between the child and his mother, low IQ, and feelings of inadequacy as a child. The authors remarked upon the fact that predictors of personality disorders in FHPs were very similar to predictors in the larger population of FHNs (Family History Negatives).

Are the Characteristics of Children of Alcoholics a General Response to Stress?

There has been speculation that the impact of being brought up in an alcoholic home constitutes a stress similar to other stresses. This has been tested in a relatively weak way. That is, an attempt has been made to show a lack of difference between children of alcoholics and children from other stressful backgrounds, or from backgrounds that include pathology of a different sort in the parents. An absence of difference between FHP populations and children exposed to a hardship of a different sort bolster the view that the effects of alcoholism in parents does constitute a stress although a nonspecific one. It is a weak form of support, but the evidence is fairly consistent.

When FHPs are compared to children who have experienced stress due to other causes, differences from other children are rarely detected. Jacob and Leonard (1986) found no differences between children of depressed and children of alcoholics on most scales of the Auchenbach. Specific to the FHPs, however, was the finding of increased delinquency. Chafetz et al. (1971) failed to detect more school problems in alcoholic children vs. children who had experienced parental divorce. El-Guebaly and Offord (1979) compared FHP with children of depressed and children of schizophrenics. On none of the dependent measures (a medical history including school disturbances, Rutter's parental questionnaire, and a behavioral checklist) were differences found. El-Guebaly and Offord (1979) commented that in their sample of FHPs, 24% of the FHP produced scores in the deviant range on the Rutter measure. This 24% incidence of scorers in the deviant range on the Rutter did not, however, surpass the incidence of deviant scorers expected in samples selected from poor neighborhoods. Examining adults, Benson and Heller (1987) compared daughters of alcoholics to daughters of mentally ill fathers. The FHP daughters were not distinguishable from daughters of the depressed on a number of variables tested, although they were less depressed than the daughters of the depressed sample.

What about Life with an Alcoholic Parent Produces Troubled Behavior?

Previous data support the perspective that alcoholism is a stressor that impacts family members in much the same way as other stressors. There is also support for the corollary hypothesis: Alcoholism per se has little deleterious impact but rather achieves its effect through creation of environmental trauma. Support for this view comes from the following. When intact families of alcoholics who have not experienced great economic hardship are selected, the children have been found to function as well as controls. Kammeier (1971), who selected children of alcoholics attending a middle class parochial school, failed to detect differences in terms of aberrant school behavior (acting out, social withdrawal) from control children. Jacob and Leonard (1986), recruiting their families through the newspaper and selecting homes in which the father was drinking but had not sought treatment, found that 87% of the FHPs were functioning in the normal range on the parental responses to the Auchenbach Child Behavior Checklist. Heller, Sher, and Benson (1982) caution against the conclusion that FHP will necessarily display problems that exceed those of other children.

There are further data bolstering the view that problems in FHPs are associated with the occurrence of particular aspects of the family of origin. Billings and Moos (1983), examining a sample of FHPs, report a significant negative correlation between measures of family cohesion and children's physical symptomology. Jacob and Leonard (1986) report that childhood pathology is confined to the group in which the father's drinking is creating disruption and in which there is pathology in the mother. Wilson and Orford (1978) find that parental violence is a moderator variable influencing childhood dysfunction among FHPs. Benson and Heller (1987) remark that pathology in their FHP daughters seemed confined to those who had experienced parental conflict, poor peer relationships, and poor relationships with parents. Moos and Billings (1982) have identified similar factors in the family situation that negatively affect children's adjustment. These factor include parental anxiety and depression, parent's reliance on avoidance coping, occurrence of undesirable life changes, little family cohesion, and the presence of family conflict.

The list of deleterious conditions that could produce pathology and for which children of alcoholics are at greater risk is long. Children of alcoholics are more likely to be from divorced families and to have moved more frequently than other children (Black, Buckey, Wilder–Padilla, 1986; Chafetz et al., 1971; Miller & Jang, 1977; Nylander, 1960; Schulsinger et al., 1986). They are more likely to perceive problems in their families (Miller & Jang, 1977). Sixty percent of Booz–Allen and Hamilton's (1974) sample had observed parental conflict. Werner (1986) found that FHPs had received little emotional support and little educational stimulation. Children of wet alcoholics rate their family environment less positively (more tense, moody, less secure, less warm, etc.) (Callan & Jackson, 1986; O'Gorman, 1976).

The link between alcoholism and child abuse is assumed by many. Supporting data exist (e.g., Booz-Allen & Hamilton, 1974). Samples selected for child abuse sometimes evidence elevated rates of alcohol abuse. In their review of relevant literature, however, Combs-Orme and Rimmer (1981) concluded that proof of association was insufficient.

Wilson and Orford (1978) have averred the position that alcoholism be viewed as a diverse syndrome and that the particular variety of alcoholism in the family will determine the impact on family members. They suggest the following critical variables: whether the mother or father is alcoholic; whether the alcoholic becomes visibly intoxicated; whether the parent drinks away from the home; whether there is violence in the family; whether economic hardship is created by the drinking; whether parental conflict ensues; the mood of the alcoholic and spouse; whether the child is witness to the parental conflict; whether the spouse is burdened by added responsibility and enlists the support of the child in fulfilling the responsibility; the degree to which family rituals and routine functioning are intact; the degree to which the alcoholism is apparent and therefore is stigmatizing, which will vary as a function of the child's age; and the duration of the drinking problem. In addition to assessing whether particular characteristics are present, coping resources may moderate the impact of any particular drinking related stressor. Resources include the child's reliance on nurturing relatives or neighbors; the child's identification with siblings or friends; the child's cognitive coping skills.

There has been little research isolating factors that might insulate children from the stressors in an alcoholic home. Several researchers have found that girls emerge less affected than boys (el-Guebaly & Offord, 1979: Werner, 1986). Young children escape the stigma of having an alcoholic parent due to their social naivete (Wilson & Offord, 1978). A Polish study found that in those homes in which the child had a close relationship with the nonalcoholic mother, rather than displaying deficits, children did particularly well in school (el-Guebaly & Offord, 1977). When the parents in the alcoholic home display good coping skills children exhibit less dysfunction (Moos & Moos, 1984).

All of these findings caution against any global stereotyping of children of alcoholics. Statistically, they are an at risk population. However, risk status changes dramatically as a function of the presence or absence of particular hardships in the family that are associated with alcoholism.

Might the Good Functioning Reflect Being a Hero Child?

When confronted with data indicating a lack of pathology in populations of FHPs in which the father's drinking has not created hardship, a traditional treatment provider might argue that many children have become hero children. These children do not manifest problems that the community will identify, but nevertheless they suffer with their compulsion to achieve. There are data on the issue. Manning, Balson, and Xenakis (1986) evaluated whether FHP were more likely than FHNs to be Type As, a construct capturing high drive and ambition. Type As overlap the construct of hero child. Manning et al.'s data failed to support the hero child hypothesis. The children of alcoholics did not differ from the control group on the overall type A measure or on a subscale tapping competition. FHPs did, however, score more highly on a subscale tapping impatience and aggression. This study then failed to suggest that being a hero child is more likely to be represented in families of alcoholics than in other families. Findings from another study may also be germane. Possibly consistent with increased incidence of hero child types, is the previously mentioned finding from the Polish study in which FHPs who displayed a close relationship with their mothers more often excelled in school. However, conclusions from this study regarding the promotion of "hero child" traits in FHPs is unwarranted. A control group for assessing the impact of a close relationship with a mother amongst children from nonalcoholic families is required before concluding that an alcoholic environment is particularly conducive to the development of children who excel.

Support for Traditionalist Roles

There has been little attempt to validate the claims of traditionalist theorists that children of alcoholics adopt specific roles. To the clinician, the roles may appear valid because all FHPs can be classified as fitting one or another role. What the clinician may fail to realize is that the roles are so broadly encompassing, any human being could be similarly categorized. Rhodes' study (1984) represents an attempt to evaluate whether Black's roles were more likely to be represented among children of alcoholics than among normals. Rhodes used the CAST (see Chapter 4, Volume I) to classify adolescents in public school as children of alcoholics. She developed her own measures of each of the five roles suggested by Claudia Black. Those classified as children of alcoholics by the CAST achieved a higher mean score than other children only on the role of acting out child. Differences on the other four roles were not achieved.

The Hypothesis that FHP Will Carry On the Family Alcoholic Tradition

A central belief in traditional programs is that being raised in an alcoholic home will increase the probability of becoming alcoholic. Attempts to separate the influences of genetics from the impact of the environment have occurred. Goodwin et al. (1974) did not find a statistically significant difference in the incidence of alcoholism among FHP children raised at home compared to those children who had been adopted away. In fact, in the sample, the incidence of alcoholism was lower among those raised at home (17% vs. 25%). Further, there was no relationship between duration of exposure to active drinking in a parent and alcoholism in the FHP. Cloninger, Bohman, and Sigvardsson (1981) found that adoptees raised by an alcoholic adoptive parent were not more inclined to become alcoholic themselves. Again, the difference in the sample was in the other direction (13% vs. 18%). Schuckit, Goodwin, and Winokur (1972) found that those half siblings of alcoholics who were and were not raised by an alcoholic parent failed to differ in their incidences of alcoholism. All of these findings are against the social transmission of alcoholism. In support of the hypothesis, however, Cadoret, O'Gorman, Troughton, and Heywood (1985) found that being raised by an alcohol abusing adoptive parent did relate to alcohol abuse in the 20-year-old adoptees.

Others have attempted to decipher aspects of the childhood environment of FHPs raised at home which are associated with transmission of the alcoholic pattern. Although their methodology was poorly articulated, Wolin, Bennett, and Noonan (1979) attempted to relate particular qualitative familial responses to parental alcoholism to the transmission of alcoholism (defined here as becoming alcoholic or marrying an alcoholic). Those families in which the alcoholic was not around much and there was no discussion of the alcoholism, exhibited the least transmission. Those families in which the alcoholic was intoxicated while participating in family rituals and who received a great deal of censorship were midrange in transmission. Those families in which the alcoholic was intoxicated during family rituals and who was not censored, exhibited the most transmission. It may be that the homes exhibiting the most transmission were representatives of a subculture in which intoxication is expected and therefore not worthy of comment. It is known that such subcultures have high incidences of alcoholism. McCord's (1988) finding is in line with the view that attitudes toward drinking will determine adult alcoholism in the ACA (Adult Child of an Alcoholic). McCord found that paternal alcoholism was more likely to be emulated by the son when the mother held the father in high esteem.

Rather than increasing the incidence of alcoholism, being raised in an alcoholic home probably promotes teetotaling. High rates of abstinence are found among adult relatives of alcoholics (Hall, Hesselbrock, & Stabenau, 1983a; Harburg, Davis, & Caplan, 1982; Lucero, Jensen, & Ramsey, 1971). Harburg, Davis, and Caplan's (1982) community survey data suggested that the drinking styles of heavy drinking or abstinent parents tend to be less often replicated by offspring than does the more modal pattern of moderate drinking. Actually, this would be expected if parental behavior had no impact. The children would be found to emulate the society's modal response. In terms of the general impact of parental drinking habits on the habits of the children, Gabrielli and Plomin's (1985) data suggest that children's drinking habits are influenced more by the cultural group of which they are members rather than familial drinking habits. Of course, these two variables are often confounded in the real world. The joint impact of common culture and genetic influences probably accounts for the higher rates of alcoholism observed among FHPs.

Characteristics of Children of Recovering Alcoholics

The previous studies have examined offspring of alcoholics who were either unrecovered or undifferentiated as to recovery. Some researchers have specifically selected children of recovering alcoholics. Children of recovered alcoholics and controls have not been found to differ on self-esteem, locus of control, ratings of family environment, mood and physical symptoms or perception of parents (Billings & Moos, 1983; Callan & Jackson, 1986). In another study, Moos and Billings (1982) reported that children of recovered alcoholics were less depressed than controls. Although it could be argued that children from families having the capacity to recover are just generally better off, the data are also consistent with the interpretation that removing the stress of the drinking, allows symptomatology to remit. Further, there is a correlation between good coping skills in the parents and good coping skills in the children (Billings & Moos, 1983).

Summary

The fact that children of wet alcoholics are at risk for behavioral and emotional problems that are manifested into adulthood cannot be denied. Different problems are identified in different studies, lending support to the idea that there is not some single cause. That is, it is likely that the problems redound, not from alcoholism per se, but from particular stressful events that are more likely to occur in alcoholic families. If alcoholic families are selected for middle or high SES, lack of violence, lack of pathology in the mother, or lack of social disruption, the children do not differ from other children. Further, in recovered samples, children of alcoholics are not found to differ from other children. Certainly, this picture is much more optimistic than suggested by the traditionalists. Particularly, data suggest that not everyone is deleteriously affected by parental alcoholism.

A specific hypothesis of the traditionalists is that support for transmission of alcoholism is promoted through the emotional impact of having an alcoholic parent. Evidence for this is lacking. In contrast, there is support for cultural transmission. That is, alcoholism is higher in cultures that sanction alcohol abuse. Further, there is support for the idea that witnessing an alcoholic parent during one's formative years can promote offspring abstention. The role hypothesizing of the traditionalists has spawned very little empirical investigation. Thus, no empirical evidence exists in support of role taking as standard responses to being the child of an alcoholic.

EMPIRICALLY IDENTIFIED FAMILY
INTERACTION PATTERNS

In addition to research examining characteristics peculiar to wives and children of alcoholics, research has addressed whether particular characteristics describe the family environment of those family units in which there is an alcoholic parent. This section begins with an examination of data regarding the issue of familial denial. Then, data regarding voluntary social isolation by alcoholics is reviewed followed by an examination of the alcoholic husband's participation in family activities. Next, the incidence of violence, social disruption, and divorce are considered. Discussion then turns to perceptions of family members about the quality of life within the family. This includes interpersonal perceptions, the perceptions of alcoholics regarding their spouses, spouses regarding their alcoholic mates, and children concerning their relationships to their parents. A survey of those studies in which the interaction pattern in families has been observed is then presented. Finally, the characteristics of recovering families are explored and the following question is addressed: Which interpersonal familial characteristics are associated with better outcome in the alcoholic?

Is Denial a Familial Conspiracy?

One characteristic imputed to alcoholic families by traditional treatment centers is denial. A problem in evaluating the validity of the imputation is that denial has many meanings. Denial can mean a total failure to attend to information about the drinking and a selective forgetting of all unusual drinking behavior. Another definition of denial allows for recall and awareness of drinking behavior along with a failure to ascribe significance to the events. Such denial might result from having grown up in a culture in which everyone drank excessively such that problematic drinking would be viewed as an expected part of life. Denial of this type would not be a motivated defense mechanism, but rather reflects a lack of information. A third definition of denial allows an awareness that anormative drinking was occurring but a failure to be alarmed by it. Finally, denial could refer to a private awareness and recognition of the significance of the problematic drinking, but a public dissembling in order to save the family embarrassment or to avoid alarming other family members.

Most empirical research regarding denial has compared responses of the alcoholic's report of drinking with that of family members. In the main, investigations have found that alcoholics and family members are in agreement (McCrady, Paolino, & Longabaugh, 1978; O'Malley, Carey, & Maisto, 1986). Some investigators find underreporting by family members compared to the alcoholics (Guze, Tuason, Stewart, & Picken, 1963; Skoloda, Alterman, Cornelison, & Gottheil, 1975) possibly reflecting differential access to information by the family members. Alternatively, however, the finding could stem from a desire to be protective. McAuley, Longabaugh, and Gross (1978) note that an alcoholic and his relatives will agree on a diagnosis of alcoholism when a physician fails to concur. Agreement between the alcoholic and relatives or among relatives regarding the drinking behavior tends to increase when actual status is unambiguous (totally abstinent vs. totally out of control; definitely alcoholic vs. definitely normal) (Orford, 1973; Sher & Descutner, 1986). With regard to diagnostic judgments by relatives, the rate of false positive classifications is lower than the rate of false negatives (Thompson, Orvaschel, Prusoff, & Kidd, 1982). Rimmer and Chambers (1969) find that the disagreement between proband and relatives as to diagnosis of alcoholism is about the same as with other diagnoses (e.g., depression).

If denial can be viewed as a general tendency to deny problems of any type, there is support for denial among the spouses of alcoholics. Orford (1976) found that wives of alcoholics were distinguished by elevations of validity scales on psychological instruments possibly suggesting a tendency not to admit to any disapproved traits.

Social Isolation

Many investigators have found that alcoholic families are more socially isolated (participate in fewer activities outside the family) than do normal families (James & Goldman, 1971; Moos & Moos, 1984; Steinglass, 1981a). Even families in which the alcoholic has been dry for 2 years participate in fewer outside activities and less recreation than control families (Moos & Moos, 1984). Lemert (1960) found that social isolation was more characteristic of Al-Anon families and less characteristic of alcoholic families on welfare.

Further consistent with social isolation, children in alcoholic families compared to controls have been found to rely more on avoidance coping (physical withdrawal, taking solace from food or drink) rather than confiding in friends (Rouse, Waller, & Ewing, 1973).

Summary and Comment.   There is little support for the view that family members fail to correctly label the alcoholism which they witness when alcoholism is extreme. There is support for the view that family members are more isolated than others and that the children confide less than controls. In terms of the impact of social isolation, data suggest that failure to seek social support is dysfunctional. Clair and Genest (1987) found, in a sample of college age ACAs, that failure to seek social support was associated with depression proneness.

Alcoholic Husband's Participation in Family Activities

Sixty-five percent of wives in Orford et al.'s (1975) sample reported that their husbands failed to participate in familial activities. Moos and Moos (1984) found that alcoholics fulfilled fewer familial responsibilities than did their counterparts in normal homes. Orford et al. (1976) found that as drinking increased, the husband's participation in family activities declined. However, whereas personal participation in family activities and general executive control declined, Orford et al. (1976) found that male alcoholics assume greater prerogatives in making decisions about the family's socializing and the couple's sexual activity.

Violence and Social Disruption

Families of alcoholics do experience more family violence, and economic hardship. Booze-Allen and Hamilton (1974) report that 10% of the children in their samples had experienced abuse. Forty-five percent of the wives in Orford et al.'s

(1975) sample reported physical violence. If one selects families in which violence of child abuse has occurred, alcohol is frequently an accompanying feature (el-Guebaly & Offord, 1977). It has been recognized, however, that as the drinking becomes continuous and the alcoholic's physical prowess deteriorates, violence becomes less likely (Coleman & Strauss, 1983).

In alcoholic families, sexual problems (impotence due to drinking, lack of rapprochement, resentment created by infidelity) have been noted (Lemere & Smith, 1973). Sixty-one percent of the alcoholics in Orford et al.'s (1975) sample had allowed their grooming to deteriorate while drinking.

Divorce

Alcoholics marry at the same rate as the general population but separate and divorce at higher rates (Billings, Kessler, Gomberg, & Weiner, 1979). In a study conducted prior to the recent increase in the national divorce rate, problem drinking was cited in 21% of the cases in a divorce court sample (Kephart, 1954). It appears that alcoholism constitutes a risk factor for divorce.

Researchers have assessed the conditions under which alcoholic marriages are likely to end. Not surprisingly, those marriages in which there is greatest amount of hardship (persistent job loss, police involvement, more violence) are more likely to end (Bailey et al., 1962; Jackson & Kogan, 1963; O'Farrell et al., 1981). Greater hardship also precipitates help seeking by the wife (Jackson & Kogan, 1963). Those wives who leave are more likely to be consistent members of the labor force (Bailey et al., 1962). Some have found that infidelity is related to divorce, but there are inconsistent findings (O'Farrell et al., 1981).

Researchers have sought to identify traits in the spouse that increase the probability of divorce. Jackson and Kogan (1963) found that increased manifest anxiety, decreased ego strength, and increased psychoticism were marginal predictors of divorce. O'Farrell et al. (1981) identified (1) influence by others to separate; (2) positive attitudes toward divorce; (3) fear of violence; and (4) a lack of positive components early in the relationship as predictors of divorce. Shyness during childhood predicted toleration of verbal abuse by the spouse. Rae (1972) found that wives of separated alcoholics had scored higher on the MMPI D, Pd, and Manifest Anxiety scales.

Comment.   Most data suggest that poorer mental health in the spouse predicts dissolution of the marriage. The only contrary finding is O'Farrell et al.'s study which suggests that shyness predicts tolerance of verbal abuse. Kogan and Jackson's (1965a) data suggest that wives who remembered a happy childhood are less stressed by their alcoholic marriages. Perhaps there is a heartiness factor among those with happy upbringing that protects against distress despite objective turmoil, which allows for more robust commitment to the marriage.

Inter- and Intrapersonal Perceptions within the Family

A number of researchers have assessed the perceptions of spouses regarding themselves and their mates. In terms of wives expectations, that is, assumptions of how a husband usually behaves, Al-Anons vs. control wives (married to normals) did not differ (Kogan & Jackson, 1963b). That is, alcoholic family members share the same views on relationships as the larger culture. Hence negative perceptions of alcoholics by their wives can be inferred to be violations of commonly shared expectations.

Kogan and Jackson (1963a, 1963b, 1964) and Gynther and Brilliant (1967) found that wives viewed their unrecovered alcoholic husband negatively (socially undesirable, lacking in emotional warmth, gloomy, distrustful, bitter), whether wet or dry, contrary to the Jekyll/Hyde stereotype that might have been predicted. Gliedman, Rosenthal, Frank, and Nash (1956) found that wives viewed husbands more negatively than husbands viewed themselves. Mitchell (1959) examined the discrepancy between husband's self-perception and wife's perception of him. Mitchell failed to detect greater discrepancy between the two perceptions of the husband in alcoholic marriages compared to control spousal pairs.

In research employing similar methodology, Rae and Drewery (1972) and Drewery and Rae (1969) found that husbands view themselves as more feminine than wives view them. This discrepancy is particularly pronounced in couples in which the wife is a high Pd scorer on the MMPI. Wives with the nonelevated Pd scores did not differ from control wives in their views of husband's masculinity, although high Pd wives viewed their husbands as more masculine than did control wives. Gynther and Brilliant (1967) and Orford (1976) found that both the alcoholic and the spouse prefer that the alcoholic be more dominant. Both spouses also prefer that husbands be more affectionate (Orford, 1976). Drinking, in the opinions of both the alcoholic and his spouse, enhances husband's dominance but decreases the display of affection (Orford, 1976).

Interpersonal Perceptions and Perceptions of the Quality of Life within the Family Environment

Moos and colleagues have been pioneers in developing measures that assess the qualities of particular environments. Family members rate their family environment on scales assessing the dimensions of cohesion among family members, expression of feelings and opinions, the presence of conflict, and satisfaction with the family environment. Some of Moos research as well as early work that has assessed similar constructs is reviewed.

Moos and Moos (1984) found that families of relapsed alcoholics scored lower on measures of cohesion, and expression, and higher on conflict. Some have attempted to pin down the particular features associated with drinking that might produce familial unhappiness. Burton and Kaplan (1968) find that drinking severity and family dissension are correlated. Zweben (1986) examined a population of middle-age couples in which the husband had received treatment for alcoholism. The number of drinking relapse days after treatment correlated negatively with marital satisfaction for the spouse but not for the alcoholic. Wives' marital satisfaction appeared to be mediated by the disruption created by the alcoholic's drinking (e.g., degree of participation in family activities, bathing, belligerence). Zweben's results were somewhat consistent with Finney, Moos, Cronkite, and Gamble (1983) who found that the alcoholic's mood was more impactful on predicting marital satisfaction than were drinking impairment factors (amount consumed; trouble with law or job). Family cohesion is higher in those families reporting fewer negative life events and more positive life events (Moos & Moos 1984).

Adult children of alcoholics have been asked to recall their families of origin from the ages of 13 to 18. ACAs recall less family cohesion, less cultural and intellectual stimulation in the family of origin, and more often view their families as unchangeable (Clair & Genest, 1987). Benson and Heller (1987) found that adult daughters of alcoholics compared to controls reported having received less social support from their families, and less consistent affection from their fathers. They reported more parental conflict during their last 5 years at home than did controls. Goodwin et al. (1974) found that FHPs raised at home less often recalled a domineering mother. McCord and McCord (1962) and McCord (1988) investigated alcoholic fathers who had a high incidence of unemployment. They noted that alcoholic fathers could be characterized as either negligent in providing any discipline or as erratically punitive. They were deficient in providing open displays of affection toward their children. They frequently were also lacking in open respect for their wives.

O'Farrell and Birchler (1987) compared the marital satisfaction, perceived marital stability, and perceptual accuracy (one spouse is aware of changes desired by the other spouse) of alcoholics and their wives compared to a marital counseling control group, and a group of control families. The wives in alcoholic families expressed greater marital dissatisfaction, and saw a higher probability of the dissolution of the relationship than wives in the control group but did not surpass dissatisfaction and perceived probability of divorce of wives of couples involved in marital counseling. What was particular to the alcoholic families was that the husbands desired less change and were less dissatisfied than their wives. This difference was greater in the alcoholic families than in the marital counseling control group. Further, the alcoholics were less accurate than their wives and other husbands (both normal controls and marital counseling husbands) in their perceptions about changes desired by the wives.

Observations of Family Interaction

Most of the previous research has assessed static measures of perception, satisfaction, etc. There are studies examining the interaction patterns among family members during in vivo sessions. For example, Jacob and Krahn (1988) and O'Farrell and Birchler (1987) found less positive expression and congeniality in alcoholic families during observed interactions. Billings et al. (1979) and Jacob, Ritchey, Cvitkovic, and Blane (1981) observed there is more expression of hostility in alcoholic marriages than in nonalcoholic marriages rated as happy. Thus, expression of hostility in alcoholic marriages mirrors the hostility found in unhappy marriages in general. Becker and Miller (1976) and O'Farrell and Birchler (1987) observed that increased frequency of interruptions are characteristic of the interactions of alcoholic couples.

The passivity of alcoholics suggested by the surveys of the perceptions of spouses is corroborated in the observations-of-behavior literature. Jacob et al. (1981) found that alcoholics make fewer problem solving statements and fewer directive statements than control males in dyadic interactions with their spouses and their children. Billings et al. (1979) show that alcoholics made fewer statements than either males in distressed marriages or males in happy marriages. Wives of alcoholics make more statements than wives in distressed or happy marriages.

Gorad, McCourt, and Cobb (1971), students of the Bateson and Haley approach to the analysis of communication, have suggested that alcoholics are likely to avoid taking responsibility (being found accountable) for their statements and are likely to manifest a variety of evasive maneuvers. Perhaps consistent with the Gorad et al. hypothesis are observations of the alcoholics behavior during family discussions. Gorad et al. (1971) found avoidance of responsibility in alcoholics as they interacted with their wives. O'Farrell and Birchler (1987) noted more avoidance of responsibility in alcoholics, than husbands from blissful unions, although, the rates did not exceed the phenomenon in husbands in marital counseling. Hernsen, Miller, and Eisler (1973) varied the topic of conversation (alcoholism or other topic) between spouses. When discussing the drinking, wives looked more at their husbands, while the husbands looked away. Becker and Miller (1976) also noted a lack of eye contact from the husband when discussing the drinking. There findings are consistent with a lack of interpersonal responsibility in alcoholics.

There have been attempts to assess the impact of drinking by the alcoholic on marital interaction patterns. Jacob has been a major researcher in this line of investigation. His recruitment of subjects has consisted of advertising in the paper for families in which drinking has been a problem. Jacob pays his families to encourage them to participate. None of the Jacob's families were seeking treatment at the time of his studies and the alcoholic had not embraced an abstinence goal. Jacob then taps a population of alcoholics which probably differs from alcoholics in treatment. Jacob et al. (1981) and Jacob and Krahn (1988) found that alcohol increased the expression of negative affect in alcoholic but not control families. Wives of alcoholics were more likely to disagree when their husbands were drinking. Billings et al. (1979) show that imbibing by either partner increased the amount of conversation in both alcoholic marital couples and distressed couples, but produced no impact on happily married couples.

Contrary to the finding that imbibing will increase negative statements in alcoholic families, are the results of Frankenstein, Hay, and Nathan (1985), who found that spouse's positive verbal behavior increased when alcoholics were drinking. Further, the alcoholics in Frankenstein's sample made more problem-solving statements and were more talkative than their spouses. Frankenstein et al.'s unusual results may be attributable to the fact that the drinking interaction sessions were conducted at the beginning of treatment when hope and positive expectations may have elicited uncharacteristic behavior from alcoholics and their wives.

Steinglass (1981b) observed interactions in families at home during the evening and weekend at randomly scheduled observation periods. All spouses had been married over 20 years and were middle and upper class. Families were categorized according to whether they were stably wet, were stably dry, or had not sustained either wet or dry status for 6 months. Results suggested that in the stably wet families, family members spent less time in each other's physical presence. The transitional families spent the most time together. The stably dry families were characterized by more problem solving, greater emotional disclosure, and open disagreement.

The Discovery of a Powerful Moderator Variable

Subsequent work by Jacob suggests the operation of a moderator variable. Jacob divided alcoholics into steady state drinkers (those who consume approximately the same amount on a daily basis) vs. periodic drinkers (those whose consumption fluctuates dramatically and who sustain long periods of abstention). Neither the steady staters nor the periodics were involved in treatment. Neither group had endorsed an abstinence goal.

The impact of the drinking on family environment differed greatly in the two different groups. In family session in which drinking occurred, steady state drinkers manifested more problem solving and less negative behavior (Jacob & Leonard, 1988). In the episodic drinkers, imbibing resulted in increased negativity and a trend toward less problem solving (Jacob & Leonard, 1988).

Not only were the interaction patterns differentially impacted by drinking in the families of steady staters vs. periodics, but differences were noted on other variables as well. Among steady state drinkers but not the periodics, positive correlations were obtained for the following pairs of variables: between the amount consumed and less elevation of MMPI pathology scales for both the drinker and the spouse; between increased amount consumed and the wife's decreased depression as assessed by the Beck Inventory; between increased amount consumed and wife's increased satisfaction with the marriage; and between increased amount consumed and wife's perceived cohesion of the relationship as assessed by the Locke-Wallace Test and the dyadic adjustment scales (Dunn, Jacob, Hummon, & Seilhamer, 1987; Jacob, Dunn, & Leonard, 1983).

There were differences between the steady staters and periodics beyond the difference in their temporal pattern. The periodics differed from steady staters, in more often drinking away from home, in being more often involved in fights, in experiencing more job loss attributable to drinking, in reporting more neglect of family and occupational responsibilities when drinking, and in more often being arrested for drunken behavior (Jacob, Dunn, & Leonard, 1983).

Comment.   It might be argued that, for the steady state drinkers, there is evidence of the functional nature of the drinking. Drinking tended to be associated with positive events and experiences. Thus, these individuals have little reasons to change their drinking behavior. The periodics do experience distress attributable to drinking. Their periodic patterns may reflect an unsuccessful attempt to be sober. Hence a group, unmotivated to change because of insufficient ill effects of the drinking (the steady staters) is being compared with a group that desires change but has not been successful in achieving the change (the periodics).

Jacob's findings suggest that there is a group of alcoholics (viz., the steady staters) characterized by not having sought assistance for drinking. This group experiences relatively little distress resulting from drinking. In this population, there is evidence that drinking may exert a positive influence on interpersonal family environment. Although it might be argued that this group is inappropriately labeled alcoholic, this group does meet Goodwin's criteria for alcoholism, the MAST criteria, and does self-label as having experienced alcohol problems. In fact, the positive experiences of this group may occur in drinking contexts.

Jacob's findings of a salubrious impact of drinking on family interaction patterns is supportive of the family systems view of Steinglass (see Davis, Berenson, Steinglass, & Davis, 1974). Steinglass and colleagues have advanced the systems thinking perspective, that is, heavy drinking occurs in order to stabilize the family unit. According to this perspective, the drinking serves a function for the family unit. The results for the steady staters support this view.

Familial Characteristics Associated with Better Outcome

Families manifesting greater affection and family cohesion at intake have better outcomes (Orford, Oppenheimer, Egert, & Hensman 1977; Orford, Oppenheimer, Egert, Hensman, & Guthrie, 1976). In addition to family cohesion and less conflict being predictors of good outcome, active recreational orientation contributes to positive outcome (Moos, Bromet, Tsu, & Moos, 1979). Those marriages in which the wife views the husband positively and the husband believes that his wife views him positively produce better outcomes (Orford et al., 1976). Those men whose wives trust and accept them, as assessed at intake, also display better outcomes (Cadogan, 1973).

Alcoholics who are married to the high Pd scoring wives are less likely to achieve sobriety than are those with the low Pd scoring wives. This is particularly likely to be the case for those families in which economic dislocation has redounded from the drinking (Rae, 1972). Marriages in which the wife is more dominant, a correlate of high Pd in the wife, have poorer outcomes (Orford et al., 1977). It should be recognized that these findings are not necessarily reflecting a causal mechanism in the behavior of the wife. Rather, it could be that the high Pd scoring wives may marry primary ASP alcoholics, the group with the worst treatment outcomes.

There is evidence that spouse's involvement in treatment is associated with positive outcome. Wives who opt for active participation in treatment have husbands exhibiting better outcomes and less treatment dropout (Ewing, Long, & Wenzel, 1961; Janzen, 1977; MacDonald, 1958; Smith, 1969; Wright & Scott, 1978). Those with intact marriages vs. the divorced have better prognosis. Single alcoholics have lower recovery rates (Billings & Moos, 1983). There is a correlation between the number of hospital admissions an alcoholic has experienced and the number of marriages he has had (O'Farrell et al., 1981).

Summary and Comment

Data suggest that families sustaining more harmonious relationships, in which family members have better coping skills, are those that produce better treatment outcomes. Willingness of the spouse to participate in treatment also is a positive factor. The correlational nature of the findings must be considered; data cannot be used to infer that harmonious relationships, better coping skills, or spousal support causes better outcome. It is equally likely that these factors reflect the gravity of the alcoholism which is the causative factor in determining outcome.

Characteristics of Recovering Families

Orford et al. (1977) find that in families in which the husband has been sober for a year, there is more open display of affection by the husband toward the wife. Recovering families have not been found to differ from normal families on measures of congruence between spouse's perception of mate and self-perception of mate, family cohesion, expression of positive affect, familial organization, and measures of familial conflict (Moos & Moos, 1984). In recovering families, family interaction patterns revert to male dominance or egalitarian patterns (Orford et al., 1977). Husbands assume as much responsibility in recovering families as in control homes (Moos & Moos, 1984). However, there are specific differences between families of recovered alcoholics and control families. Recovering families do differ from control families in terms of fewer recreational activities and lower participation in outside events. Recovering families have fewer arguments than control families (Moos & Moos, 1984). Moos, Finney, and Chan (1981) differentiated types of social activity. Recovered alcoholic families did not differ from community controls in terms of participation in religious and organized social activities, but were lower on informal social contacts. Recovered alcoholics perceive a more extensive network of social support than do community samples.

In contrast to the above sanguine picture, Clifford (1960) finds that wives are sometimes disappointed that sobriety does not bring the hoped for benefits. Orford et al. (1977) cite that the wives' negative view of the husband persists 12 months into sobriety. Jackson (1954) has cautioned that, as the drinking progresses, the wife may become accustomed to attributing all problems in the marriage to the drinking and will thus fail to identify and resolve the normally occurring conflicts in the marriage.

Summary of the Family Environment Studies

Results of the family environment studies do suggest that families of alcoholics are less healthy and less likely to be perceived positively by family members than are families in which there is no pathology. Data also suggest that particular features of alcoholism may account for the dysfunction. Familial dysfunction is more likely in families in which the drinking has created social problems. When social problems are not created by the drinking, increasing amounts of alcohol consumption does not create greater familial dysfunction. Further, in recovered families, there is no evidence of greater dysfunction compared to control families.

The observations of interaction patterns in families, do support the view of a more responsibility avoiding, less active participating alcoholic father. There is also support for decreased positive interactions, increased display of hostility, and more avoidance of each other's physical presence.

The conclusion drawn as to characteristics of families of alcoholics will vary enormously depending upon the selection process used to recruit the alcoholic family. When families of alcoholics in treatment or wives in Al-Anon are examined, pathology is found. Such might be expected given that such individuals have mobilized themselves to seek help because they were distressed. If, however, populations are recruited through response to adds in the newspaper soliciting those with drinking problems, different results emerge. Jacob and colleagues have used the latter procedure to recruit alcoholic families for study. They find evidence of the adaptiveness of the drinking, in that it is associated with increased family harmony. More specifically, Jacob et al. note that this surprising association is discernible if two distinct groups of alcoholics are distinguished, viz., those who drink daily (steady state drinkers) and those who abstain for long periods and then drink excessively for a short duration of time (periodics). Support for the adaptiveness of drinking is found only in the group of steady state drinkers.

Spousal participation in treatment emerges very clearly as a positive factor increasing the chances of the alcoholics recovery. Further, good will between the spouses is certainly a correlate of better prognosis. The review of wife's reactions to the drinking, which are associated with better outcome, suggest that some enabling behaviors do not predict less recovery. Indeed, some enabling type behaviors may reflect greater investment by the wife in the marriage, which is associated with a high rate of recovery.

CHAPTER SUMMARY

In this chapter the empirical literature regarding the characteristics of spouses and children of alcoholics was reviewed. In both groups, support for the presence of symptomatology associated with stress was strongly supported. There was suggestion that symptomatology was created by the social consequences of the heavy drinking rather than being associated with the presence of alcoholism in the home per se. When samples of spouses and children of recovering alcoholics were selected, symptomatology did not differ from controls in either group.

There was support in the spouse literature for the prototype alcoholic spouse who was raised in a dysfunctional family of origin, married a man whose alcoholism was active, who domineered her husband, whose husband was less likely to recover, and who did not improve when the alcoholism remitted. This type of spouse was more likely to be distinguished by a high Pd score on the MMPI rather than simply exhibiting elevations on the stress scales of the MMPI. Children of alcoholics exhibit diverse emotional and behavioral problems similar to children exposed to other types of stressors.

There have been attempts to identify unique features of children of alcoholics which are not found in children exposed to other types of stressors. Increased conduct disorders emerged as a unique characteristic of children of alcoholics. There was little support for the idea that growing up in an alcoholic home will increase the risk for alcoholic drinking. Rather, the effect of growing up in an alcoholic home promotes abstention. There was little evidence in support of the roles suggested by the traditionalists.

The literature on observations of familial interaction patterns suggested less familial harmony. In family interactions, alcoholics could be characterized as less active in terms of problem solving and participation. They made more responsibility avoidant maneuvers.

Support was found, in particular groups of alcoholics, for the system's theory hypothesis that drinking serves a function in the family environment. In steady state drinkers (those who daily drink roughly the same amount) who are not seeking treatment, drinking not only improves family interaction, but amount consumed during the week correlates with better mental health and more marital satisfaction in the spouse.

Increased familial harmony, and family participation in treatment emerged as correlates of successful recovery. When the spouse is invested in the relationship, the husband is more likely to recover.

8 Treatment of the Family Members

This chapter address family treatment in alcoholism. The topic can be divided according to the objectives of the treatment. One goal is to improve the mental health of family members. Another is to modify the behavior of family members in ways that will promote sobriety in the alcoholic. A third goal is to treat the relationship between the drinker and his/her spouse. Individual clinicians sometimes strive for one, and sometimes for more, of these goals.

This chapter begins with approaches that focus on the mental health of individual family members. We follow with a section that examines the literature suggesting which spousal behaviors might promote abstinence in the drinker. Finally, we present a review of the emerging research investigating treatment aimed at improving the spousal relationship in alcoholic marriages. Summaries are provided at appropriate parts and specific suggestions for treatment are offered.

THE MENTAL HEALTH OF FAMILY MEMBERS

The standard type of treatment for family members in most traditional treatment centers concerns itself primarily with their mental health. An attempt is made to promote helpful attitudes for coping with the stress of the situation of living with an alcoholic. Usually catharsis is encouraged. Through the formation of self-help groups, social support is offered. Both catharsis and social support are also utilized when family members report physical abuse.

There are no outcome studies that directly test the effects that the traditional approaches have on self-esteem, the self-concept, general well being, or absence of specific problems. Thus, there is no directly relevant evaluative literature. However, there is a more general research literature that offers indirect suggestions as to what is and what is not most likely to be helpful. Researchers have conducted studies on the phenomenon of catharsis, and there is a broad literature on how and when social support is effective. Further, family members sometimes speak of themselves, or think of themselves, as having been victimized. This may or may not involve their having experienced physical abuse. A reasonable question to ask, is whether it is helpful for people who are in fact victimized to think of themselves that way. Fortunately there is a research literature addressing that and related questions. Thus, there are literatures that can be tapped to shed some indirect light on questions that are relevant to the treatment of alcoholic families.

The research literature that should be reviewed for indirect light on questions concerning the mental health of alcoholic families, involves experimental tests of general psychological questions. For example, how do observers evaluate victims? If they sometimes evaluate them negatively, what factors will lead to negative evaluations, and what would prevent that? Are there circumstances that lead people who are victimized to seek out further situations in which they are victimized? The general principles that have emerged from such research can be logically related to therapeutic situations. The relevant research and theory is summarized here. However, the theory and logic will be of less interest to some readers than the final conclusions on what would be most helpful to clients. Therefore, concluding segments of several sections of this chapter offer bottom lines on what can be gleaned about treating families of alcoholics and some specific suggestions are made concerning therapy.

The Empirical Literature on Personal Misfortune and Victimization

In this section the literature pertaining to persons who have been victimized is reviewed. The purpose in reviewing this literature is to provide a basis for speculating which cognitive adjustments and therapeutic interventions might be most useful for victims. Research is available to suggest which types of adjustments are associated with salubrious outcomes along a number of dimensions. There are answers to the question of what adjustments are likely to lead a victim to seek out further victimization, what adjustments are associated with better coping and better mood in the victim, and what type of adjustments will be admired by observers and therefore more likely to elicit social support from the environment. The purpose of this section is to identify useful adaptations worthy of promotion by treatment providers.

Before reviewing the empirical literature on trauma and victimization which may be relevant to some spouses and children of alcoholics, a caveat is warranted. Many alcoholics are not abusive, neglectful, irresponsible, or untrustworthy. Hence, the concept of victimization will not be germane for a good number of family members. Although Booze-Allen and Hamilton (1974) report a sample statistic of 28% of abusive behavior on the part of the alcoholic parent, the percentage of relatives of alcoholics who are indeed abused will vary enormously as a function of the particular sample selection. The stereotype that living with an alcoholic is synonymous with abuse, however, exists and is probably veridical in many cases. Even when there is no physical abuse, the self-concept of having been victimized can affect a person's life-adjustment. Interfering with this self-perception, or encouraging it, then offers alternative philosophies in dealing with family members. It is important to see what the research literature suggests about that role.

The Psychological Impact of Being a Victim

Beyond the damage created by tragedy, there are psychological and social costs associated with being a victim. Happy, well functioning people are those with a sense of control over events. Exposure to uncontrollable events can result in dysphoria, a sense of helplessness and a vitiation of goal directed activity (Seligman, 1975). The belief that meaningful contingencies elude one's control creates an aversive state. Tragedy (such as occurs for cancer victims, flood victims, parents of terminally ill children) challenges the victims' beliefs in the controllability of outcomes, extracting a cost beyond that of the loss itself.

In addition to the psychological costs, there are social costs attendant with being a victim. Lerner (Lerner & Miller, 1978) has demonstrated that observers who view an individual suffering through no fault of his/her own will derogate the victim. Lerner has invoked the concept of just world to explain this phenomenon. The just world holds that people want to believe that outcomes are related to their behaviors. When observers view a victim's undeserved suffering, the observers' beliefs of a controllable ordered world are challenged. The observers will reinstate their sense of fairness by inventing reasons why the victim is worthy of the persecution, that is, they will derogate the victim.

Although victim derogation has been demonstrated, the responses of observers to victims can be moderated by the behavior of the victim. A rape victim who presents herself as happy 6 months after the rape will be liked more by those who hear her story than a rape victim who gives the same account of the event but indicates that she is still suffering from the experience (Coates, Wortman, & Abbey, 1979). Persons who are happy despite their prior victimization are admired and liked more than nonvictims (Kleck, Ono, & Hastorf, 1966). Putting on a happy face then does invite more observer approval for a victim. Victims who believe they are suffering in the service of a worthy cause do not elicit derogation (Godfrey & Lowe, 1975).

Given the psychological and social costs that can be associated with being a victim, it is not surprising that those suffering a tragedy will resist viewing themselves as victims. That people do resist this perception is attested to by the finding that for many of those suffering great misfortune (flood victims, parents of dying children), their perceived quality of life returns to control levels within 6 months after the calamity (Taylor, Lichtman, & Wood, 1984), although such is not necessarily the case when spouses are killed in auto accidents (Lehman, Wortman, & Williams, 1987.). There are several avenues of research that have examined the mechanisms through which people experiencing tragedy avoid the conclusion that they are victims.

Taylor et al.'s (1984) research has identified the processes employed by breast cancer victims to challenge their victim status. Taylor et al. found that (a) breast cancer victims employ downward social comparison strategies. Those who have had lumpectomies will compare themselves to those who have had mastectomies. Those who have had mastectomies will compare to those whose cancer has metastasized, etc. Victims tend not to compare themselves with those who were more fortunate. (b) Cancer victims often invent scenarios that suggest how it could have been worse. (c) Many believe that they are coping with their illness better than the average cancer victim, although Taylor et al.'s data suggested that this perception of better than average coping was not supported by the data. (d) Many focus on their blessings rather than their illness. In Taylor et al.'s study, 60% believed that their perceptions and view of life had changed for the better as a result of their illness.

Cancer patients then employ a wide variety of strategies to reinstate their nonvictim statuses. The Taylor et al. (1984) research establishes that cancer victims do indeed actively resist being victims. Unfortunately, Taylor et al. did not evaluate the impact of these cognitive strategies on mental health or quality of life. Hence, no definitive statement regarding the utility of the strategy can be made. All we have from this research is a model of what some people have done, rather than data germane to what has been functional for them.

Others have examined the attributional processes of sufferers. This area of research suggests that victims frequently do blame themselves, rather than accepting the belief that they were passive victims (Chodoff, Friedman, & Hamburg, 1964). Researchers have differentiated self-blame into behavioral self-blame vs. characterological self-blame (Janoff-Bulman, 1979). Behavioral self-blame attributes tragedy to some behavior of the victim that was either performed or neglected. Characterological self-blame attributes the tragedy to some stable trait in self that will continue to render one worthy of victimization. Janoff-Bulman (1979) makes the prediction that those who accept behavioral self-blame will be the best adaptors as such individuals are able to reinstate their sense of control after it has been challenged.

Janoff-Bulman's hypothesis has been supported by consistent data in a number of areas. Among accident victims rendered paraplegic, cancer victims, parents of infants with perinatal complications, and parents of cancer stricken children, an association between behavioral self-blame and better coping (Tennen, Affleck, & Gershman, 1986) and behavioral self-blame and belief in future control (Tennen et al., 1986) has been found. The data are mixed for rape victims (Meyer & Taylor, 1986), victims of miscarriage (Madden, 1988), and is negative for burn victims (Kiecolt-Glaser & Williams, 1987). As Shaver and Drown (1986) have noted, there is reason to expect some inconsistency in this relatively new research area. Confusion in the literature may be attributable to the differential tapping of three related concepts: causality, responsibility, and blameworthiness. Being the cause of an event is not equivalent to being responsible for an event. An external force may cause an event, although one can be responsible for the outcome caused by an event if one has the capability of acting to disrupt the process put into play by the external event. Blameworthiness assumes conditions beyond those required for responsibility and causality. Blameworthiness generally assumes that the outcome could have been foreseen and may further require intentionality. In the literature, in constructing dependent measures, researchers have not been self-conscious as to which concept (causality, responsibility, blameworthiness) they were assessing. Inconsistency in the literature will probably remain until distinctions are made regarding the construct being measured and valid dependent measures for each construct are established.

In the literature there is sufficient evidence to suggest that behavioral self-blame is not deleterious to the victim. It would be going beyond that data to say that behavioral self-blame is itself improves coping. The research in the area is all correlational. Although it could be that self-blame is the cause of better coping, another possibility is that persons who view themselves as responsible for everything are better equipped to cope with all manner of stress. Future research may address the question of whether behavioral self-blame can cause better adaptation. At this point, it does appear to be better than characterological self-blame.

Comment.   Usually clinicians begin with the assumption that it is deleterious to view a bad situation in a positive light. Clinicians also assume that it is unhealthy for a victim to identify ways in which his/her behavior might have interrupted the process of victimization. The research just reviewed suggests that seeing positives in a bad situation and recognizing that what has happened could have been worse are strategies that are adopted by cancer victims. Victims of a large number of events also identify behaviors that might have prevented their plight and which might help to avert future tragedy. There is reason to believe that these strategies are adaptive. These strategies may help to prevent the process of victim derogation by observers and may provide the victim with a sense of control over future outcomes. Hence, the assumptions made by clinicians and the implied interventions are called into question. Challenging behavioral self-blame or challenging the framing a bad situation in a positive light may be counterproductive. The clinician may wish to respect these strategies and recognize the adaptive nature of these adjustments.

Choosing to Suffer

The discussion thus far has examined persons who have been victims of one discrete process or event. There are persons whose victimization occurs repeatedly and predictably. One such group is battered wives. Miller and Porter (1983) have observed how battered wives, many of whom have been repeatedly victimized, differ from those whose victimization is not repeated or predictable. Examining a population of battered women, Miller and Porter found that these women failed to engage in the usual attributional inquiry of "why me?" or "why did this happen?" Perhaps their lack of questioning reflects a self-concept that includes an expectation of mistreatment. When events are expected as part of a person's identity, there is no need to ask why.

It is known that daughters of alcoholics more often marry alcoholics than would be expected on the basis of chance. In the preceding chapter, the case was made that the marriage of daughters of alcoholics to alcoholics may be accounted for by common subcultural membership. It is possible, however, that even when the impact of common subcultural membership is removed, FHP daughters will more often choose to marry alcoholics. Hence, an additional explanation is required. Traditional doctrine would explain the fact that daughters of alcoholics choose to marry alcoholics in terms of the unsatisfied emotional needs deriving from the alcoholic family of origin. An emotionally needy daughter would choose a husband just like Dad so as to obtain what she did not receive in the family of origin. Alternative explanations referencing the self-concept rather than unmet emotional needs can also be proffered. Perhaps enduring the trauma of an alcoholic home induces changes in the self-concept which make a subsequent choice to suffer more likely. It is this latter possibility to which the next section is devoted.

There is a literature that speaks to the issue of those events that lead to choosing to suffer on a repeated basis. The research suggests that particular changes in self-concept can be induced that will mediate volunteering to suffer.

A number of studies have demonstrated that persons who are assigned to suffering through random selection, will subsequently volunteer for suffering. The experimental paradigm has been to tell subjects that they have either been selected to eat worms and drink quinine water or they have been selected to participate in the control condition involving participation in an innocuous task. When the experimenter tells those subjects who expect to suffer that there are enough persons in the worm eating condition so that the subject has his/her choice of eating the worm, participating in a task involving shock, or participating in the control condition, those believing they were going to suffer more often chose to suffer (Comer & Laird, 1975).

In a choosing to suffer study, Comer and Laird (1975) measured subject's change in self-percept after assignment to suffer and prior to the choice to suffer. Additionally, changes in the subject's view of eating worms was also examined. Comer and Laird assessed whether subsequent to assignment to eat worms subjects would (a) see themselves as more worthy of suffering; (b) view themselves as more brave; (c) see themselves as suffering for science; or (d) change their view of the task such that eating worms would not be as disturbing. The results suggested that all of the above occurred. Subjects most often used only one of the strategies. Those subjects for whom cognitive alterations failed to occur, were unlikely to choose to suffer.

Some cognitive alterations led to volunteering to suffer in new domains. Those subjects who perceived themselves as more brave or more self-sacrificing, were willing to volunteer to receive shock as well as to eat the worm. For subjects who failed to change their self-percepts in this global manner (they had decided that eating worms was palatable) there was no increased volunteering for suffering in general.

In subsequent research, a number of explanations have been supported for the choosing to suffer effect. Sometimes suffering now is seen as a way to avoid future more severe suffering. This type of thinking seems to mediate subjects choice to suffer in the present even when they are aware that possible future suffering will be determined by random processes (Curtis, Smith, & Moore, 1984).

The literature on choosing to suffer demonstrates that after persons have been subjected to suffering they can experience alterations in their cognitions about themselves that will increase subsequent volunteering to suffer. Some of these cognitive alterations do not connote a victim status, e.g., the subject instead decides he/she is brave, or a martyr for science. There were a number of percept changes that probably occur in the real world that were not represented in the experiment. For example, deciding one is "born to loose" is well represented in literature and music but was not available to Comer and Laird's subjects.

Desirable Responses or Undesirable Responses to Suffering

Responses to victimization can be evaluated in terms of the considerations suggested by each of the reviewed literatures. Desirable responses should allow a retention of a sense of controllability, should avoid inviting victim derogation by the observer, should preclude mediation of volunteering for further suffering. An additional criterion, not discussed in the literature but which is certainly important, suggests itself. A response can be evaluated as to whether it promotes harmonious relations with others. All of these criteria will be considered in examining the four responses to suffering that have been reviewed in the literature.

The ensuing discussion evaluates several possible reactions to suffering. The four responses are the following: (1) Deciding one is brave or self-sacrificing in the service of a worthy cause; (2) deciding one deserves to suffer by virtue of prior sin or poor character; (3) displaying anger and protesting against the suffering; and (4) refusing to recognize that one is suffering. The present discussion identifies adaptive ways of coping with victimization. It is important to consider whether particular responses to victimization are useful. Many family members of alcoholics might be construed as having been victimized. The clinician might wish to consider what might be a more helpful reaction to the situation.

Bravery and Self-sacrifice

An individual who decides he/she is brave or devoted to self-sacrifice is probably utilizing a strategy similar to Taylor et al's subjects who decided they were coping better than average with their cancer. Such individuals are not victims in the sense that the world will feel sorry for them. Such individuals inspire admiration, not pity. There is little empirical data suggesting how this response is related to coping responses. Seeing one's self as brave or self-sacrificing, being positively valued traits, might enhance self-esteem and result in good mood. Godfrey and Lowe's (1975) study suggests that victims who regard themselves as suffering in the service of a worthy cause receive positive evaluation from others. This type of response would lead to further choosing to suffer, but such an individual would probably not be labeled as a social problem.

Deserving to Suffer

The literature on attributional processes in learned helplessness situations suggests that individuals who explain their suffering in terms of characterological defect will experience depression. Such individuals exhibit bad mood and performance deficit (Petersen & Seligman, 1983). The Comer and Laird study suggests their cognitive schemas will lead to further choice to suffer. A person who believes he/she is born to suffer may gravitate to situations in which he/she will again suffer. The victim derogation literature suggests this response will lead to derogation by others. In victim derogation studies, derogated victims had responded passively and looked as if they were suffering. Although the deserving to suffer response will be derogated, it is also known that the depressed are sometimes reinforced by the immediate sympathetic response they elicit from others (Coyne, 1976). A sad demeanor then might be immediately reinforced by others, but later scorned and avoided. There are those who manifest the "born to lose" phenomenon who display a stoic exterior rather than a sad exterior. These individuals may receive a little better evaluation from others, since their suffering is not readily apparent.

Angry Indignation

In the Comer and Laird experiment, indignant individuals were probably among the subjects who did not volunteer to eat the worm despite the fact that they had been originally assigned to do so. Such individuals would not be expected to continue to choose to suffer. In a study in which persons were victimized by being forced to work for uncontrollable outcomes, those who protested their fate and expressed anger were viewed as admirable by observers of the scene (Littrell, 1981).

There is a type of angry response that might result in further choosing to suffer. Some spouses of alcoholics become locked into downward social comparisons with their alcoholic mates. They dwell, not on their own victimization, but rather on the exasperating nature of the alcoholic's behavior. The negative view of the alcoholic by means of the comparisons, may offer some positive self-esteem to the spouse. To the extent that this type of comparison is necessary for self-esteem maintenance, the spouse will stay in the relationship or select other such relationships that might allow for the negative contrast.

The angry, indignant response can create other negative effects. Some angry, indignant people become hypervigilant so as not to choose, by mistake, a second situation in which they will suffer. The schema of being abused is ever present in their awareness. Their thresholds are low for viewing themselves as abused given ambiguous objective facts. Such a prepotent organizing schema may not be conducive to developing warm interpersonal relationships. If one is vigilant to those situations which carry the potential for abuse, then one is perhaps too ready to see others as persecutors.

Denial or Refusal to Recognize Suffering

The adaptation of refusing to recognize suffering and seeing the positive aspects in a bad situation is a recognized response to uncontrollable trauma. Taylor et al.'s breast cancer victims who viewed themselves as better off than others is an example. Such a response was also represented in the Comer and Laird experiment by the individual who decided that the worms were not so unpalatable. For spouses of alcoholics, framing the home situation as not so bad, or concentrating on the positive aspects of the situation, constitute exemplars of this general strategy. There are considerations that help to evaluate whether this strategy is adaptive.

One criteria for evaluating a response to victimization is to ask whether the response will result in victim derogation by observers. The research of victim derogation suggests that when persons who were victimized present themselves as cheerful, such as might occur when victims view their situation in a positive light, victim derogation does not occur. Thus, on the dimension of evaluations from others, the response of framing a situation in the positive light should be labeled as adaptive.

A second criteria for evaluating a response to victimization is to ask whether the response is associated with better mental health in the victim. Research on coping strategies provides support for the belief that framing a situation in a positive light is a functional strategy on one possible index of mental health viz., reduced physical symptomatology. Scheier, Weintraub, and Carver (1986) categorized their subjects as optimists, persons who generally believed that the future would be bright, or pessimists, persons who held negative views of future outcomes. In an earlier study, optimists had been found to report fewer physical symptoms than pessimists. Scheier et al. sought to determine whether optimists vs. pessimists differed in terms of the cognitive coping mechanisms they would employ given a problem. Clear differences emerged. Given a stressful event, the optimists engaged the strategy of changing the objective external situation or seeking social support. When the objective circumstances were beyond control, the optimists made light of the situation or found some beneficial aspect of the situation. In contrast, the pessimists, in dealing with all problems, relied on catharsis or refusing to think about the problem. The Scheier et al. findings do suggest that the strategy of framing a situation in a positive light is a strategy of optimists who experience less symptomatology. Unfortunately, the findings of the Scheier et al. studies are correlational and preclude a causal interpretation. However, it does offer some support for the idea that viewing a bad situation in a good light is adaptive. In a related study, examining the coping strategies of a sample of ACAs, Clair and Genest (1987) found that employing the coping mechanisms of focusing on the positive aspects of situations was related to decreased depression proneness. The correlational data is, therefore, consistent with the view that framing a situation in a positive light is associated with better mental health in the individual.

Refusing to recognize suffering or framing a bad situation in a positive light might be labeled denial by traditionalists. A spouse of an alcoholic who frequently sees the positive side of things despite repeated embarrassing situations and unmet obligations would be labeled as "in denial." Denial is viewed as particularly bad by those who subscribe to the idea that external events cause emotions rather than one's interpretation of events as the critical factor in emotions. For those adopting the former view, a person exposed to abusive situations will realize negative physical outcomes elicited by these events even if the person finds positive aspects in the events. An individual exposed to objectively bad events will be aroused on measures of blood pressure and cortisone in the blood, mediators of ill health. The increased blood pressure and increased adrenal gland secretions will create health problems even when the individual labels the situation in optimistic terms and does not recognize his/her high blood pressure or increased adrenal gland secretions.

Not everyone accepts the concept that external events cause emotion. Albert

Ellis clearly sees interpretations of events as the cause of arousal (Zastrow, 1985). A person who interprets an objectively abusive situation in a positive way, may avoid having his/her blood pressure increased or his adrenal glands induced to secrete cortisone and adrenaline. Perceiving the positives in the situation may preclude high blood pressure and adrenal gland secretion. Hence, if a person does not interpret objectively negative events as bad, some of the negative consequences of these events will not occur.

Whether high blood pressure and adrenal gland secretions are elicited by events or one's interpretation of events has probably not been definitively answered. There are data on both sides. Conditioning of negative emotions clearly occurs. That is particular stimuli can elicit autonomic reactions (increased blood pressure and adrenal gland secretion), even when the cognitive implications of these stimuli are not processed. Thus, repeated exposure to a bad situation will result in the situation itself, independent of cognitive events, causing emotional reactions. However, when the stimuli eliciting an emotion are complex, cognitions clearly become a large factor in determining the emotional responding that is evoked. Discrimination of changes in the situation and interpretations of events, become part of the standard responses in the situation. In such cases, interpretations can be a filter for pain. Empirical literature offers few clear conclusions. For any particular individual who appears to be "in denial," the question of deleterious emotional responding might be addressed empirically. Any spouse who professes contentment with his/her objectively negative situation, can be evaluated as to frequency of illness and elevation in blood pressure.

Are people who do not know that they are being abused, better off when they are convinced that they are? The answer is probably ambiguous. If a person truly has better options, he/she is better off negatively evaluating the current situation and leaving. If a person is developing physical problems resulting from his/her current situation, then getting disgusted and leaving is also good. On the other hand, a person in a relatively dismal situation, may have achieved the best of all possible worlds for himself/herself. If one views the situation as good and there is no evidence of ill effects on health, nothing is gained by offering a different perspective on the situation.

In reality, any particular set of objective circumstances will probably be difficult to judge. One way of dealing with this issue is for the therapist to avoid evaluating for the client whether he/she is in a bad situation. If the client is involved in group therapy, lots of different perspectives on the issue will be available and the client can choose his/her own perspective on the matter.

Summary

In reviewing the responses toward victimization, the strategy that clearly emerges as dysfunctional is characterological blame (attributing problems to a stable trait in the victim.) It results in negative mood, failure to act effectively in new situations, further choice to suffer, and victim derogation. The strategies of suffering for a worthy cause, being angry and indignant, and denial produce mixed outcome. The value judgments of the client should be the determining factor as to whether these responses become targets of intervention or not.

THERAPY FOR THE SAKE OF THE FAMILY MEMBER

Issues of the Self-concept

The process of therapy allows patients to talk about trauma and express event congruent emotions. The therapist has a great deal of latitude in guiding the emotional response, the attitudinal stance toward the event, and the meaning the patient eventually ascribes to the event. It would seem wise to be self-conscious about supporting particular responses.

The goal of the therapist should be to direct the family member to alterations in self-concept that will allow a sense of controllability over outcomes, will elicit appreciation or admiration of the family member from others, will result in eschewal of further suffering, and will promote positive relationships with others. Although therapists often encounter patients at a stage when self-concept adjustments have already occurred, some are in the process of adjusting. This is particularly likely to be the case for children. The therapist should be very self-conscious about inadvertent reinforcement for those adjustments that will lead the patient into further suffering. Sympathy may be counterproductive as it can reinforce a "born to lose" self-percept in the family member.

Family members can present with already well developed self-percepts which will lead them to seek out suffering. The therapist has the option of exploring with patients the choices that their self-schema imply and the payoffs to which these choices entitle. Transactional analysis offers a structure and set of interventions for this type of exploration.

Self-disclosure and Emotional Expression

A number of studies are consistent with the notion that allowing a person to talk about trauma or think alone about the trauma will decrease ruminations and produce a long-term salubrious impact on health (Pennebaker & Beal, 1986; Pennebaker & O'Heeron, 1984). Unfortunately some of this literature has lacked sufficient experimental control. Further, the mechanisms responsible for the salubrious effect have not been identified. A cognitive restructuring resulting in a sense of control, self-esteem building, and a view of the world as benign could be the active component responsible for the beneficial impact demonstrated in these studies. The extent to which emotional expression per se is responsible for the salutary effect has not been evaluated.

Catharsis

Catharsis or emotional expression is a primary goal of many approaches to therapy. Some believe that if emotions are allowed expression, the force behind these emotions will be dissipated. It is assumed that crying will eventually make people less sad and expressing rage will eventually make people less angry. Fortunately, there are empirical data as to the impact of emotional expression on the subsequent force and frequency of the emotion. The data are generally against the hypothesis that expression will dissipate the force of an emotion (Geen & Quanty, 1977; Tedeschi, Smith, & Brown, 1974; Wills, 1981). In fact, people become more angry when allowed to cathart (express) their anger. Allowing expression of fright, seems to enhance the experience of fear as well (Tesser, Leone, & Clary, 1978). Conclusions regarding sadness are less clear. The impact of expression of sadness on later feelings has not been evaluated empirically.

Researchers have found that dissipation of emotion, following expression does occur under some circumstances. When the process of emotional expression allows for cognitive restructuring the magnitude of the emotion to the event can dissipate (Bohart, 1977; Green & Murray, 1975). That is, one can learn to view a frightening situation in a way that makes it less frightening. One can view a provoker in a way that creates less anger. Cognitive restructuring might further include seeing the situation from a perceived aggressor's perspective, seeing oneself as more powerful than was previously assumed, finding new coping resources, etc. In order to be beneficial, catharsis must be accompanied by cognitive restructuring.

There is a more specific danger associated with angry catharsis. Expressing or venting anger exerts an influence on the venter's attitude toward the source of the anger. That is, the process of angry catharsis polarizes the views of the venter toward the target of the anger. When attitudes are assessed toward the target of the anger, increased negativity toward the target is found following the angry expression (Bohart, 1977; Geen, Stonner, & Shope, 1975; Mallick & Mc-Candless, 1966). Thus there is a danger that venting among spouses or children of alcoholics without cognitive restructuring will result in increased negativity of feelings toward the alcoholic and increased rather than decreased family tension.

There is a further danger that can eventuate when catharsis is emphasized. Sometimes emotional expression becomes the norm in therapy groups. A therapist's attention to cathartic displays may operate as reinforcement. The patient learns to expect reinforcement for emotional displays. Emotional expression then switches from being a respondent (conditioned response) to an operant (a bid for reinforcement). Such operant emotional displays often take on an insincere quality. Wegscheider (1985, pp. 253–255), a traditionalist discussed in Chapter 6 of this Volume, seems to be aware of this phenomenon. She remarks upon patients who seem to gravitate toward emotional catharsis but fail to exhibit meaningful alterations in their lives.

A Role for Emotion in Therapy

If one rejects catharsis as a goal for its own sake, emotions can still retain an important role in therapy. Examining the client's emotional reactions to events can provide information. (E.g., Do I become tense, when drinks are being served at a social function? Am I sad when considering the prospect of being in the same situation 20 years from now?) Information about emotional reactions is usually best explored through here and now fantasies which elicit emotion in the therapy session. The information gained from such processes can furnish guides for future planning. Further, Berkowitz (1990) has found that persons who have an opportunity to recognize their anger, correct for their irritation when evaluating others. That is, they are able to block cognitive distortions that are attributable to their emotional state.

People often present to therapy sessions in a state of arousal. A patient who comes to a particular therapy session in an emotional state may immediately feel better if given an opportunity to cry or self-disclose. In the case of anger the process may polarize attitudes and it is not clear that arousal will attenuate as a result of expression per se. However, on the positive side, the process of being heard and understood by the therapist may provide relief and good feeling. Aside from emotional satisfaction for the patient, emotional expression can have a positive effect on the relationship between the client and the therapist. The therapist may wish to allow expression in order to strengthen the therapeutic relationship. There are things that the therapist can do to minimize possible negative impact of expression of anger. In order to avoid the negative effect of attitude polarization, the therapist should stay alert for opportunities for reframing the situation in some beneficial way. There are expected benefits that can accrue from emotional expression in a group context as well. When therapy is conducted in a group, there is reason to believe that emotional self-disclosure will facilitate the subjective experience of social support and group cohesion (Mayer & Dollar, 1987).

Skill Development in Labeling Emotions

The chapter on genetic markers (Vol. II, Chapter 6) advanced the possibility that FHP people inherit an autonomic nervous system which obscures the recognition of emotional arousal. The FHPs probable deficiencies in recognizing and labeling emotion should be addressed by therapists. FHPs can be expected to be "out of touch" with their feelings. They need training in how to discern and be aware of what is happening in them. Research does offer suggestions about useful strategies for training people to recognize their emotions.

A here and now approach strategy can be useful. Placing FHPs in contexts in which they can observe emotions in other people might help to develop discriminations of emotional events in themselves. Dimberg's (1982) research suggests that the natural response to watching emotion expressed by others is observer mimickery. Further, observers recognize emotions in others by creating a congruent state in themselves (Zajonc & Markus, 1982). The process of watching and labeling emotional expression in others will help bridge the connection between kinesthetic events and the emotional label. This process will be facilitated by a therapist who asks the FHP to comment on what he/she observes. The therapist can further assist by providing feedback when the FHP exhibits a particular emotional expression.

In teaching the recognition and labeling of arousal a there and then approach (talking about prior emotions) might also be useful. Talking about emotions (what emotions are usually evoked under particular conditions) might provide FHPs with schema for how they might feel given particular events. Pennebaker's work (1982) suggests that when people have schema for particular internal events, like symptoms or emotions, they will scan for confirmatory information. Without the schema, people tend to ignore internal events or physical sensations. Hence talking about emotions, such as occurs with Claudia Black's sentence completion techniques, could assist in learning to recognize emotions and label them.

Social Support and Group Identification

The general salubrious impact of social support has received wide recognition (Cobb, 1976). That association with supportive others would be beneficial for codependents and FHPs is an obvious corollary. The finding of increased social isolation among the families of alcoholics suggests that they constitute a group who might be deficient in social support. Hence incorporating social support into their therapy makes sense.

A question remains as to whether groups of codependents are the appropriate support group for family members or whether a mixed therapy group might be more beneficial. Considerations pro and con suggest themselves.

Considerations Favoring Homogeneity of Group Composition

Schachter's (1959) early work suggests that when people are exposed to the prospect of receiving shock they will choose to be in the presence of others who are about to experience the same distress rather than waiting alone or waiting with unthreatened individuals. Latane, Eckman, and Joy (1966) found that people who endured a shock that was conjointly experienced liked each other more than people in groups who had not experienced a mutual ordeal. Extrapolating from this experimental work, it would seem that groups composed of persons who have experienced similar trauma might more quickly develop mutual liking and stronger bonds.

Another benefit of homogeneous composition suggests itself. Shaver's (1969) victim derogation research suggests that the more that observers can take the role of victim, the less likely they will derogate the victim. Hence, being in a group with similarly victimized others might result in more understanding and less victim derogation. This consideration suggests that homogeneous groups of FHP are likely to be more beneficial than heterogeneous groups.

A homogeneous group might provide greater information on the normative responses to growing up in an alcoholic family than would a heterogeneous group. There are beneficial effects that can be expected to derive from the provision of information regarding the impact of being raised in an alcoholic home situation. When individuals are given information about normative responses in a situation, they are less likely to draw inappropriate conclusions about themselves, and less likely to act on their inappropriate conclusions (Wilson & Linville, 1982). For example, the FHP who is informed that having a low self-concept is context normative may begin to doubt the legitimacy of his/her low self-esteem. Rather than assuming that the low self-esteem derives from accurate observation of behavior, the FHP may come to attribute the low self-esteem to the environment. He or she may then select goals and aspirations that are more in keeping with true ability. In such a way, accurate information could help people reevaluate inappropriate beliefs about themselves, and, as a consequence, act in a more realistic manner.

Considerations Favoring Heterogeneity of Group Composition

There are some potential drawbacks that may occur in a homogeneous group. Latane et al. (1966) found that those subjects who endured a shock experience in pairs rated the shock as more painful than subjects who experienced the shock individually. Apparently, when persons share an aversive experience, they tend to sensitize each other to the aversive qualities of the experience or disinhibit each other in censoring a negative label for the experience. Coates and Winston (1983) have reviewed the literature on homogeneous support groups for victims of spousal death, rape, and bereaved parents. They attempted to ascertain whether there is evidence of a contagion effect wherein depression might be increased by the group experience. They concluded that the evidence did not support such an effect. They also concluded, however, that at least for the leaderless groups, there was little evidence that the group experience decreased depression either. Although empirical evidence is scanty and mixed, danger of sensitizing persons to negative emotions is probably greater in homogeneous groups. The clinician should be cognizant of this danger.

Participating in a group of FHPs or codependents may exert a labeling effect. Viewing oneself as ACAs or codependent may become an organizing template for one's personality. Once established this label may afford a self-handicapping strategy. (Self-handicapping is discussed in Chapters 11 and 12 of Volume II.) Basically, self-handicapping is a self-protective excuse which when invoked in the face of failure precludes being labeled as lacking in ability. An example of a self-handicap might be maintaining anxious behavior so that a failed test can be blamed on test anxiety rather than lack of ability. The label ACA could become a self-handicap if one attributes failure to the status.

There is a literature examining the drawbacks and benefits of self-handicapping. In fact, there is evidence that persons will mention some form of trauma in their lives given situations high in evaluative threat (DeGree & Snyder, 1985). Fortunately, the evidence suggests that having a self-handicap does not imply that people will exert less effort in preparing for a demanding situation (Tucker, Vuchinich & Sobell, 1981). Further, the availability of a self-handicapping excuse can attenuate performance anxiety (Harris & Snyder, 1986). In general, then, self-handicaps can be functional. Whether offering a readily available self-handicap in the form of an ACA label is good or bad will probably depend on whether the codependent needs to remain in a compromised objective situation in order to utilize the strategy. Perhaps past trauma is enough to qualify for the beneficial effects. To their credit, most self-help groups do focus on how the affected family member can actively alter circumstances in the present rather than blaming the past. This suggests that self-help groups dissuade their members from maintaining situations that create disadvantage.

A study by Burk and Sher (1990) does suggest an additional negative impact of the label COA (child of an alcoholic). These researchers found that both peers and mental health professionals evaluated a teen more negatively when this teen was described as a COA. Surprisingly, additional information that the teen was high functioning did not offset the negative label for the professionals. Reflecting upon the results of their study, the authors speculated whether targeted groups for COAs might create an iatrogenic negative label for those who participate.

Comment.   There are both pros and cons to establishing a homogenous rather than a heterogeneous group experience for alcoholic family members. On balance the pros seem to outweigh the cons. The negative ramifications of the cons can be avoided.

Outcome Research on Alateen

As mentioned in the beginning of this chapter, there has been little empirical investigation evaluating the impact of Al-Anon or Alateen on the mental health of participants. One uncontrolled study surveyed ACAs attending twelve steps meetings at one point in time. Twenty-five percent of the group said they were doing better as a result of the group (Cutter & Cutter, 1987). Although client satisfaction is important, it does not constitute proof of efficacy. A controlled study by Hughes (1977) compared long standing Alateen attenders with FHP adolescents who were nonattenders or attenders of their first meeting. Better psychological functioning was found among the long-term attenders. Although his study might be interpreted as supportive of a positive impact for Alateen, other explanations exist. It is likely that more parents of long-term Alateen attenders were recovering alcoholics. It is known that children of recovered alcoholics are less distressed than children of wet alcoholics. This confound may explain the study's findings. To date, little solid outcome data on support groups is available.

Therapeutic Suggestions Concerning the Mental Health of Family Members

The research on victimization and responses to suffering does suggest that children of alcoholics and their spouses are likely to exhibit special problems that should be recognized and addressed in treatment. The process of victimization can result in self-concept changes that will lead the victim to choose future situations in which to suffer, which will be derogated by others, and which will afford low self-esteem and negative emotions. For those who present with less than optimal adjustments, the therapist can guide the exploration of alternatives.

Emotionally rehashing traumatic events is a process that has the potential for creating enhanced dysfunction. Individuals who present with mild or no resentment, can be induced to feel very resentful. On the other hand, emotional expression does have a function. It can foster bonds between people in group therapy and bonds from the client to the therapist. The process of rehashing a stressful event when combined with cognitive restructuring, can result in an enhanced sense of strength. Emotional expression does have a place but caveats need to be considered.

The literature suggests that social support deficits are probably more common among alcoholic family members than among the general population. Incorporating provision of social support into therapy is therefore desirable. The issue of whether a homogeneous or heterogeneous support group is more beneficial has not been addressed empirically. Rationale can be generated in both directions, although the stronger case probably rests with homogeneous composition.

Research presented in the chapter on genetics suggests that children of alcoholics are likely to be deficient in recognizing and labeling emotions. Providing schema for the experience of emotion and providing practice in recognizing emotions in others constitute interventions that might aide clients in discerning emotional signals in themselves.

CHANGES IN THE SPOUSE TO BENEFIT THE ALCOHOLIC

Thus far, the discussion has centered on those changes that might be made for the sake of the family member to benefit the family member herself/himself. Although the empirical literature offers few clear conclusions as to which behaviors in the spouse will promote abstinence in the alcoholic, there are some suggestive findings. A wife's participation in treatment, greater trust by the wife at treatment outset, and harmonious familial relationships have all been identified as factors associated with good outcome on the drinking dependent variable. However, causal inferences cannot be derived from such correlational data. Wives self-selected into treatment in studies that identified wife participation as a positive factor in alcoholic husband's treatment outcome. It may be that wives of husbands with less severe alcoholism are more willing to be cooperative. With the exception of one study that is reviewed in the next section, there is no clear basis for inferring that participation by wives causes less relapse. The same argument can be made for trust and family harmony. Rather than harmony and trust enhancing chances for sobriety, those alcoholics with greater capacity for achieving sobriety may well also have enhanced capacity for inspiring trust and participating in harmonious interpersonal relationships. Even though the evidence does not allow the inference that trust and harmony in the family will cause reduced relapse, a therapist might well promote these phenomena. The therapist can be reasonably confident that such goals will not undermine recovery.

An alcoholic's opportunity for recovery might be enhanced by a supportive family. A therapist who wishes to promote family support must consider the next question of "what constitutes support?" The empirical literature does not offer much suggestion as to which specific behaviors seem supportive. The alcoholic can be consulted as to what will be most helpful. The following might be encouraged: discussion about whether to serve liquor in the home, discussion about whether to entertain drinking relatives, discussion about the impact of the spouse's drinking on the recovering alcoholic, discussions about how the spouse might be most useful if the spouse observes signs that she/he believes are relapse precipitants, discussions about how the spouse could best respond in the event of relapse. Since the perception of support will vary according to the particulars of each relationship it is important for discussions to occur.

The traditional approach does offer advice about specific behaviors of spouses. There is empirical data that can be brought to bear in evaluating some of the specific advice which traditionalists offer to wives of alcoholics. The traditional approach does emphasize a specific change the spouse should make to benefit the alcoholic, viz., relinquishing codependent behaviors, including impassioned protests against drinking. There has been little evaluation regarding whether the chances for recovery increase when the spouse quits enabling. There is the empirical work of Orford et al. (1975) and Schaffer and Tyler (1979). Examination of coping styles in wives associated with good and bad outcomes suggest that verbal attacks against drinking predict good outcomes whereas verbal attacks against the man are associated with negative outcomes. Thus, vehement disapproval of drinking does enhance chances of sobriety. Many behaviors discouraged by traditionalists (e.g., throwing out bottles, going out to fetch the alcoholic) are associated good prognoses.

Traditionalists also address the issue of divorce and separation. Data exist that speak to the impact of these events on recovery from alcoholism. There is some evidence that threats of divorce or separation are often the impetus for initiation of treatment for the alcoholic (James & Goldman, 1971). However, if the family dissolves and the alcoholic continues to drink, his chances of achieving sobriety when he eventually attempts it will be decreased. Further, Schaffer and Tyler (1979) found that divorce and separation threats employed as coping mechanisms by the wife were negatively related to husband's sobriety during the follow-up period. These findings support the traditionalist view that empty threats of divorce by wives should be forgone. However, pressure to recover is a useful strategy.

As part of the insistence on the relinquishing of enabling and codependent behaviors, traditional treatment places strong emphasis on inculcating the belief that the alcoholic's drinking is beyond the control of family members. Joan Jackson's writings suggest that many spouses move naturally first through a period of anger and assiduous effort to control and then into a period of despair and inactivity. This progression mirrors the predictions of Wortman and Brehm (1975) for persons laboring under uncontrollable circumstances which were initially perceived as controllable. The prediction is that the first phase will be reactance (anger and renewed persistence) eventually supplanted by learned helplessness (depression and inactivity). Hopefully, in a third phase, the family member will redirect his/her focus to aspects of family life that offer predictable and responsive interactions.

Although many individuals will eventually move from the reactance phase to the learned helplessness phase, the pull of the reactance phase should not be underestimated. Detachment may be difficult to instill in the spouse. Research suggests that whenever individuals engage in behaviors that seem to be directed toward a goal, that goal will seem controllable even when the actor realizes the event is randomly determined (Langer, 1975). Other research suggests that once people begin to work assiduously toward a goal, even information that a successful goal is improbable does not result in cessation of activity (Brockner, Shaw, & Rubin, 1979; Rubin & Brockner, 1975). Further, there is evidence that persons who work eagerly toward a goal that appears to be unreachable, will be perceived as admirable (Littrell, 1981). This research offers a possible explanation of why altering spouses beliefs about the possibility of controlling the alcoholism, and getting them to decrease their efforts in this regard, will be difficult.

Whereas it may be difficult for the spouse to relinquish a sense of control, it might be possible to direct their endeavors in a more effective direction. Reactance theory holds that an eliminated choice will always seem more attractive (Wortman & Brehm, 1975). When spouses throw out bottles and nag, they are actively limiting the alcoholic's choices. Reactance theory would predict that the drinking will be all the more attractive to the alcoholic under such circumstances. Spouses can no doubt understand this and could direct their efforts in a more profitable direction, e.g., displaying concern, noticing responsible behaviors.

Frequently, spouses seek help before the alcoholic and wish advice on what to do regarding their alcoholic mates. A modification of the Al-Anon approach can be suggested. The spouse might discuss with her mate the problem drinking behaviors she has observed and the difficulties that have ramified from the drinking. Diagnosis and blame should be avoided. Emphasis should be placed on solutions and options for seeking information. Should the alcoholic spouse refuse treatment, the nonalcoholic spouse's participation in treatment might well enhance the probability of the alcoholic's future engagement. The spouse's description of the admirable characteristics observed in recovering alcoholics at the treatment center may provide the alcoholic with models to emulate. The evaluation of this approach vs. alternative approaches should be a concern of future research.

Outcome Research

There have been few controlled studies in which wives were randomly assigned to treatment designed to make changes in them in order to decrease the drinking of the alcoholic. Although those alcoholics whose wives participate in treatment do produce better outcomes, in most studies self-selection was allowed. Hence conclusions cannot be drawn as to efficacy of approaches designed to change the spouse in order to change the alcoholic. There are a handful of outcome studies. These studies evaluated the creation of changes in the spouse to induce changes in the alcoholic. First, we review a study in which group therapy for wives vs. couples therapy was contrasted. Then, the impact of behavior therapy for wives is discussed. Finally, a study in which Al-Anon was evaluated is reviewed.

McCrady et al. (1986) compared treatment for wives in a spouses group to conjoint treatment of husband and wife. This study observed random assignment. Results from the study suggested that treatment for the wife (in a spouses only group) was not as effective as treatment for the relationship. There was a slight suggestion that treatment for the wife, in which her behavior was the focus, was actually less effective than not including her in treatment. Treatment in which wives were the focus resulted in an increase in relapse frequency during the follow-up period, produced greater elevation in the liver scores of the alcoholic, and resulted in greater marital dissatisfaction. The authors speculated that in the condition in which wives discussed their marital relationships with other wives, focusing on the family distress heightened the stress and made the wives acutely aware of dissatisfactions. In this treatment condition, there was no opportunity to practice and identify new ways of relating interpersonally, as husbands were not present during the treatment. Thus, only frustration was highlighted and possibly increased. This frustration probably ramified into negative effects on the drinking outcome.

Behavioral therapists have published the results of their attempts to teach spouses new ways to relate to their alcoholic husbands. An early effort to teach behavioral principles to wives to modify the drinking behavior of the alcoholic failed to measure the impact on the drinking, but did find little satisfaction in the wives (Cheek, Franks, Laucius, & Burtle, 1971). Subsequent efforts in which wives were randomly assigned to disease concept Al-Anon participation approach or a behavioral techniques approach yielded more optimistic findings for the behavioral approach (Sisson & Azrin, 1986). More of the husbands in the behavioral group were induced to enter treatment. Further, there was more sobriety in the husbands in the behavioral group 3 months after treatment initiation than in the Al-Anon type group. In the behavioral groups, wives kept records of husbands' drinking. They positively reinforced sobriety and identified sober periods when husband would be more receptive to entreaties to enter treatment. They also scheduled family activities which precluded drinking. As in Al-Anon, wives were taught to desist interdicting the negative consequences to the husband's drinking. They were taught to leave the situation when signs of violence became apparent and press charges if violence ensued. They were taught to ignore the alcoholic when drinking and to remind him, in a neutral tone of voice, that his sober behavior was preferred. Three of the wives in the behavioral groups left their husbands until he agreed to treatment, although no separations occurred in the traditional group. After the drinker came to treatment, marital therapy and antabuse were part of the treatment package.

Al-Anon. There has been little evaluation of Al-Anon. Gorman and Rooney (1979) did provide a relevant study, however, indicating that exposure to traditional philosophy will change the self-reported behavior of spouses. They found a positive correlation between Al-Anon exposure and decrease in frequency of particular behaviors. These correlations remained statistically significant after statistically removing the effects of husband's sobriety. The following behaviors declined in those attending Al-Anon for long duration: (1) covering for one's husbands lying, although not lying to the boss or making good on bad checks; (2) blaming circumstances for drinking; (3) making husband comfortable while drinking; (4) nagging, preaching, and coaxing; (5) hiding and throwing away bottles; (6) emotional outbursts after husband's drinking; (7) checking up on husband's drinking; and (8) having life revolve around drinking.

The decline in some coping mechanisms were less related to participation in Al-Anon. Rather, these behaviors declined when the drinking ceased. They were (1) learning to live without fear of repercussions; (2) refusing invitations; (3) refraining from normal activity; (4) feeling if husband really cared he would quit drinking; and (5) lying to the boss.

Gorman and Rooney's self-report of wives suggests that they do change their coping srategies as a result of Al-Anon participation, but whether such changes exert a positive influence cannot be inferred from their study. However, findings from the Schaffer and Tyler's study, previously discussed, suggested that not making the husband comfortable while he drinks does enhance chances for sobriety.

Whereas the data suggest that those who participate in Al-Anon value it and find solace in the experience, Pattison, Courlas, Patti, Mann, and Mullen (1965) remark upon the inappropriateness of this type of group for some populations. For their sample of lower-class Blacks and White Appalachian mountaineers, the authors felt that Al-Anon's middle-class orientation was too foreign and alienating.

TREATING THE RELATIONSHIP

There is an emerging emphasis on treating the relationship (interaction patterns) in alcoholic families, rather than directing treatment solely to the intrapersonal issues of each family member. As discussed in Chapter 7, data are consistent with the hypothesis that marital harmony will enhance the probability of successful abstinence in the drinker. There are a few studies in which investigators have treated the marriage with the hope of affecting better marital adjustment to, in turn, realize improvement on drinking measures. These studies are now reviewed.

Outcome Literature of Couples Therapy

Steinglass (1979) and Steinglass, Davis, and Berenson (1977) have applied the concepts of family systems theory to treatment of alcoholic families. Their treatment is directed toward the alteration of interaction patterns, although the goal is to ameliorate the drinking and secondarily to improve the relationship. In the family systems treatment, alcoholics are not enjoined to stop drinking and exposure to traditional concepts has not been part of the therapy. Treatment occurs in multiple couples groups. Observation of interaction patterns is integral to the therapeutic process. The therapist models and directs new behavior. Evaluation has consisted of pre–post comparisons rather than comparison to a control group. Evaluation of the efficacy of this treatment has found support for improvement in couples communication and improvement in the mood of spouses. Improvement on drinking measures and marital satisfaction have not been noted.

Cadogan (1973) evaluated a 5-session couples group through comparison with a control group to which random assignment was observed. Both the couples group and the control group alcoholic member had participated in traditional alcoholism inpatient treatment for the alcoholic. The experimental treatment being evaluated was a form of aftercare. The couples group focused on feeling expression, problem solving, and improved communication. The follow-up results at 6 months favored the couples group. Although the two treated groups failed to differ on trust and communication measures, there was less drinking observed in the couples group. Unfortunately, Cadogan did not control for the fact that the couples group had participated in aftercare whereas the controls did not. Hence the efficacy of couples therapy per se cannot be inferred from his study.

Corder, Corder, and Laidlaw (1972) allowed patients to self-select into a couples program rather than remaining in the control coup. All alcoholics, in the experimental and control groups, participated in the standard 3-week hospital program. In the experimental group the latter 4 days of hospitalization were devoted to couples activities. The couples therapy included analysis and discussion of videotaped interaction between the couples, familiarization with transactional analysis game theory concepts, instructions for recreational activities, and aftercare planning. At 6 month follow-up, there was less drinking, less unemployment, and more aftercare attendance noted in the experimental group. Family interaction was not assessed. Unfortunately, conclusions regarding efficacy are limited by lack of random assignment.

McCrady et al. (1986) compared 3 treatment program packages. None of the couples in the study were currently attending AA and Al-Anon. Few traditional concepts were presented in any of the groups. The first treatment package treated the drinker alone. In the no spouse involved condition, abstinence of the drinker was fostered through self-monitoring, stimulus control, training in refusing drinks, plus relaxation and assertive training. The second treatment package added a component designed to change the behavior of the spouse for the benefit of decreasing the alcoholism. Spouses participated in a therapy group for spouses. Goals were to increase the spouse's expression of feelings regarding the drinking, to decrease the spouse's reinforcement for the drinking, to decrease those spousal behaviors that might cue the drinking, and to decrease spouse's enabling behaviors. The third treatment package included all of the interventions of the other two packages while adding components specifically targeted toward improving the marital relationship. Spouses were involved in conjoint sessions with the drinker. Targeted goals included increasing positive interaction, increasing joint recreational activities and promoting communication. Results favored the third approach in terms of duration in therapy, compliance with homework assignments, and measures of enhanced marital satisfaction. (Interestingly marital satisfaction decreased over the course of follow-up for all groups with the decrease in satisfaction being less pronounced in the third approach). Improvement in drinking behavior was evident in all groups, although the third group improved more rapidly and relapse was less pronounced.

McCrady, Paolino, Longabaugh, and Rossi (1979) randomly assigned couples to one of three types of treatment. Although all couples had all agreed to the joint hospitalization of both spouses, only one group was actually called upon to have the spouse in the hospital. The first group was a control in which the spouse was not included in the hospitalization or the therapy. In the second group the spouse was hospitalized with the alcoholic. Couples groups and spouse groups were added to the program. In the third group, spouses participated in all therapy activities as did the spouses in the second group, but differed from the second group in participating as outpatients rather than inpatients. This offered a check on the usefulness of hospitalization for the spouse.

In the couples groups topics included general marital issues (sex, finances, children, work, leisure time) as well as topics specific to the drinking (how drinking had impacted the marriage, each spouse's feelings about the impact, and how each individual might have acted in a manner which exacerbated the drinking). Alternatives for change were highlighted. In the spouses group, the philosophy of powerlessness over the drinking and detachment was promoted. Self-focus rather than focus on the alcoholic was encouraged.

Outcome assessment was conducted at 6–8 months posthospitalization. No differences among the groups were observed on measures which included drinking status (abstention, control drinking, problem drinking), impairment from drinking, utilization of aftercare, mental health measures, or marital adjustment. The authors remarked, however, that only in the 2 couples groups did pre–post differences on drinking quantity measures reach statistical significance. This study offered tentative support for including spouses in treatment.

O'Farrell, Cutter, and Floyd (1985) randomly assigned alcoholics and their spouses to 10 weeks of outpatient therapy consisting of (a) drinker alone group; (b) multiple couples group focused on interaction between spouses; or (c) multiple couples group in which behavioral therapy constituted the treatment. All alcoholics had been hospitalized prior to the outpatient treatment and all treatments emphasized the goal of abstention. The results of 3 month follow-up assessment favored the behavior therapy treatment on marital adjustment measures. All alcoholics displayed pre–post improvement in drinking, although the behavioral therapy group exceeded interactional therapy without differing from the no marital treatment group. The specific components of the behavioral therapy treatment which differed from the interactional treatment included: an antabuse contract for the drinker, assignments for shared recreational activities, and specific attention to daily caring behaviors.

Hedberg and Campbell (1974) compared behavioral family counseling, systematic desensitization, shock aversion therapy, and covert sensitization. There was random assignment to conditions. Abstention and control drinking goals were allowed. The behavioral treatment provided immediate feedback to couples as they interacted, as well as offering instruction in behavioral concepts. Results at 6 months follow-up favored the family counseling on percentage of patients who attained their drinking goals. Family counseling was especially effective for patients embracing an abstinence goal.

Summary and Comment

Studies reviewed in the prior chapter have established that alcoholics stay in treatment longer and manifest greater drinking improvement when the spouses are involved in treatment. Although an association is found, results do not imply a causal association.

Studies comparing treatment programs in which alcoholics are treated alone vs. treatment programs in which alcoholics and spouses receive treatment simultaneously provide modest support for the inclusion of spouses in treatment. No efficacy was demonstrated in the McCrady et al. (1979) study. In the Cadogan (1973) and Corder et al. (1972) studies superior results were achieved for the treatments involving the spouse, although neither study was adequately controlled. The McCrady et al. (1986) and Hedberg and Campbell (1974) studies did demonstrate better results on drinking measures given spouse involvement.

If spouses are to be involved in treatment, the question as to which type of involvement will result in greatest improvement becomes relevant. Options include providing educational information for spouses without targeting specific behavioral changes; promoting changes in the spouse's behavior targeted toward a reduction in the drinking or targeted toward enhancing the spouse's mental health; and targeting changes in the relationship as the therapeutic goal. McCrady et al. (1986) compared therapy for changing the spouse's behavior (via participation in a spouses only group) such that drinking would decrease vs. involving the spouse in couples therapy to promote better marital adjustment. The approach that included focus on the marital relationship as well as changes in the spouse to benefit sobriety proved superior to changing the spouse alone on the outcome of drinking amelioration. Therapy focusing on the relationship does allow better results. Although the importance of including an improved relationship goal has received modest support, studies comparing the form of the intervention (multiple couples groups, couples with the therapist, concurrent but not conjoint spouses and drinkers) focused on improved interaction have yet to be conducted.

A final conclusion can be inferred from the studies of marital therapy. Drinking does not get better if a drinking goal and drinking focus are not part of the therapy. In the Steinglass study, even when the relationship is treated and does improve, the problem drinking does not necessarily improve. It would seem that if benefits are to be realized in terms of drinking amelioration, the therapist does need to focus and address the issue.

Additional Recommendations for Treating the Relationship

The empirical research reviewed suggests that the marriage does not always improve with the alcoholic's sobriety. As Jackson has noted, as the drinking progresses, wives who attribute all problems in the marriage to the drinking, are likely to neglect interpersonal sources of marital dissatisfaction. Clearly, alcoholic marriages will have their share of interpersonal issues to resolve. Further, in those families in which family problems are noted at intake, sobriety is associated with increased dysphoria in the alcoholic (Vannicelli, Gingerich, & Ryback, 1983). Perhaps alcohol numbs against the impact of a bad marriage. A bad marriage in a recovering persons requires specific attention.

Orford (1975) cautions that in considering the issue of alcoholic marriages, the vast literature on marital therapy and family relationships need not be reinvented. Certainly, any clinician endeavoring to treat alcoholic marriages should be thoroughly acquainted with the family treatment literature and marital assessment instruments. Nevertheless, there are issues that are more likely to arise in alcoholic marriages than in other situations. Suggestions for dealing with some of these issues are now proffered.

Assessment of the Relationship. In treating the alcoholic family, consideration should be directed toward how the relationship can best be altered to meet the needs of each spouse. This should include assessment of what each spouse expects to derive from the relationship. Areas of possible expectation include: emotional support, whether reciprocal or unilateral; sense of identity and belonging, either derived by being one's spouse or via extended family; consensual validation via shared perceptions of the world or a shared value system; mutual enjoyment from shared areas of interest or amusement; financial security; and admiration such that one spouse admires the other and this admiration becomes an esteem enhancer for the admired spouse. The behavior of each spouse should be changed such that each partner's expectations are better met. Included in the appendix are family questionnaires which offers the clinician insight into the structure of the relationship and how the drinking has been responded to in the past.

Reassignment of Responsibility. It is probable that newly recovered families will be grappling with reallocation of role responsibilities. A thorough assessment of how time is spent by each family member; who exerts executive control in major areas of responsibility (disciplining the children, financial planning, cleaning, grocery shopping, decision making, leisure time planning); expectations of each spouse for the ideal allocation should be made. Areas of disagreement need to be negotiated.

Sex. Sex is likely to be an area of needed negotiation and adjustment. Because alcohol decreases anxiety, and anxiety often inhibits sexual performance, sexual anxiety may emerge as a problem when drinking stops. On the other hand, physical impairment due to drinking may have created impotence. Thus sexual performance can constitute a considerable adjustment issue for both spouses, which should be addressed by the therapist.

Resentments and Lack of Trust. Issues of resentment and lack of trust are often acutely felt by spouses in early recovery. The clinical literature offers few directives regarding the most useful way to approach these issues. The following approach, which has been used clinically by the author but has not been evaluated empirically, is tentatively proffered.

The alcoholic should be instructed in reflective listening techniques so that he/she can provide empathic concern while listening to the suffering of the spouse. The alcoholic should be strongly cautioned that true empathy cannot be achieved if while listening, one takes a self-focus with concerns about feeling responsible and guilty for prior events.

The spouse should be allowed to vent. However, the spouse should also reflect on what he/she wants to achieve. If retribution and inducing guilt are the objectives, the spouse should realize that such an outcome may represent a Pyrrhic victory. Guilty, depressed people are difficult to live with and have difficulty sustaining harmonious relationships.

For the issue of trust, AA's "one day at a time" philosophy is often useful. Alcoholics are not in a position to guarantee their sobriety to themselves or others. An alcoholic can make an objective assessment of his/her probability of success. Such an objective assessment process could occur conjointly between the spouse and alcoholic and might well produce beneficial fallout. The results of the assessment will either offer reassurance to both parties or not. Such a detached assessment, without pressure or demand, is less likely to effect the outcome in a deleterious manner.

A skit in which the above points are dramatized is provided in the Appendix Section. This skit is designed to allow for exploration of possible responses by participants. It has been used by the author as part of the educational program in an alcohol treatment program.

References

Al-Anon (1984). *Al-Anon family groups.* New York: Al-Anon Family Group Headquarters, Inc.

Alcoholics Anonymous (1976). *Alcoholics Anonymous: The story of how many thousands of men and women have recovered from alcoholism.* New York: Alcoholics Anonymous World Services, Inc.

Alcoholics Anonymous (1985). *Twelve steps and twelve traditions.* New York: Alcoholics Anonymous World Services, Inc.

Bailey, M. B., Haberman, P., & Alksne, H. (1962). Outcomes of alcoholic marriages: Endurance, termination or recovery. *Quarterly Journal of Studies on Alcohol, 23,* 610–623.

Beardslee, W. R., Son, L., & Vaillant, G. E. (1986). Exposure to parental alcoholism during childhood and outcomes in adulthood: A prospective longitudinal study. *British Journal of Psychiatry, 149,* 584–591.

Becker, J. V., & Miller, P. M. (1976). Verbal and nonverbal marital interaction patterns of alcoholics and nonalcoholics. *Journal of Studies on Alcohol, 37,* 1616–1624.

Bennet, L. A., Wolin, S. J., & Reiss, D. (1988). Cognitive, behavioral, and emotional problems among school-age children of alcoholic parents. *American Journal of Psychiatry, 145,* 185–191.

Benson, C. S., & Heller, K. (1987). Factors in current adjustment of young adult daughters of alcoholic and problem drinking fathers. *Journal of Abnormal Psychology, 96,* 305–312.

Berkowitz, A., & Perkins, H. W. (1988). Personality characteristics of children of alcoholics. *Journal of Consulting and Clinical Psychology, 56,* 206–209.

Berkowitz, L. (1990). On the formation and regulation of anger and aggression: A cognitive-neoassociationistic analysis. *American Psychologist, 45,* 494–503.

Billings, A. G., Kessler, M., Gomberg, C. A., & Weiner, S. (1979). Marital conflict resolution of alcoholic and nonalcoholic couples during drinking and nondrinking sessions. *Journal of Studies on Alcohol, 40,* 183–195.

Billings, A. G., & Moos, R. H. (1983). Psychological processes of recovery among alcoholics and their families: Implications for clinicians and program evaluators. *Addictive Behaviors, 8,* 205–218.

Black, C. (1982). *It will never happen to me!* Denver: M. A. C.

Black, C., Bucky, S. F., & Wilder-Padilla, S. (1986). The interpersonal and emotional consequences of being an adult child of an alcoholic. *International Journal of Addictions. 21,* 213–231.

Bohart, A. C. (1977). Role playing and interpersonal-conflict reduction. *Journal of Consulting Psychology, 24,* 15–24.

Booz-Allen & Hamilton, Inc. (1974). *An assessment of the needs of and resources for children of alcoholic parents* (Contract No. ADM 41-74-0017). Rockville, Md: National institute of alcohol abuse and alcoholism.

Brockner, J., Shaw, M. C., & Rubin, J. Z. (1979). Factors affecting withdrawal from an escalating conflict: Quitting before it's too late. *Journal of Experimental Social Psychology, 15,* 492–503.

Budenz, D. (1981). *The family illness off alcohol/drug dependency.* Middleton, WI: Progressive Literature.

Burk, J. P., & Sher, K. (1990). Labeling the child of an alcoholic: Negative stereotyping by mental health professionals and peers. *Journal of Studies on Alcohol, 51,* 156–163.

Burton, G., & Kaplan, H. M. (1968). Marriage counseling with alcoholics and their spouses-II: The correlation of excessive drinking behavior with family pathology and social deterioration. *British Journal of Addiction, 63,* 161–170.

Cadogan, D. A. (1973). Marital group therapy in the treatment of alcoholism. *Quarterly Journal of Studies on Alcohol, 34,* 1187–1194.

Cadoret, R. J., O'Gorman, T. W., Troughton, E., & Heywood, E. (1985). Alcoholism and antisocial personality. Interrelationships, genetic and environmental factors. *Archives of General Psychiatry, 42,* 161–167.

Callan, V. J., & Jackson, D. (1986). Children of alcoholic fathers and recovered alcoholic fathers: Personal and family functioning. *Journal of Studies on Alcohol, 47,* 180–182.

Chafetz, M. E., Blane, H. T., & Hill, M. J. (1971). Children of alcoholics: Observations in a child guidance clinic. *Quarterly Journal of Studies on Alcohol, 32,* 687–698.

Cheek, F. E., Franks, C. M., Laucius, J., & Burtle, V. (1971). Behavior-modification training for wives of alcoholics. *Quarterly Journal of Studies on Alcohol, 32,* 456–461.

Chodoff, P., Friedman, S. B., Hamburg, D. A. (1964). Stress, defenses and coping behavior: Observations of children with malignant disease. *American Journal of Psychiatry, 120,* 743–749.

Clair, D., & Genest, M. (1987). Variables associated with the adjustment of offspring of alcoholic fathers. *Journal of Studies on Alcohol, 48,* 345–355.

Clifford, B. J. (1960). A study of the wives of rehabilitated and unrehabilitated alcoholics. *Social Casework, 41,* 457–460.

Cloninger, C. R., Bohman, M., & Sigvardsson, S. (1981). Inheritance of alcohol abuse: Cross-fostering analysis of adopted men. *Archives of General Psychiatry, 38,* 861–868.

Coates, D., & Winston, T. (1983). Counteracting the deviance of depression: Peer support groups for victims. *Journal of Social Issues, 39,* 169–194.

Coates, D., Wortman, C. B., & Abbey, A. (1979). Reactions to victims. In I. H. Frieze, D. Bar-Tal, & J. S. Carroll (Eds.), *New approaches to social problems.* San Francisco: Jossey-Bass.

Cobb, S. (1976). Social support as a moderator of life stress. *Psychosomatic Medicine, 38,*(5), 300–314.

Coleman, D. H., & Strauss, M. A. (1983). Alcohol abuse and family violence. In E. Gottehil, K. A. Druely, T. E. Skolada, & H. M. Waxman (Eds.), *Alcohol, drug abuse, and aggression* (pp. 104–124). Springfield, IL: Charles C. Thomas.

Combs-Orme, T., & Rimmer, J. (1981). Alcoholism and child abuse. *Journal of Studies on Alcohol, 42*, 273–287.

Comer, R., & Laird, J. D. (1975). Choosing to suffer as a consequence of expecting to suffer: Why do people do it? *Journal of Personality and Social Psychology, 32*, 92–100.

Corder, B. F., Corder, R. F., & Laidlaw, N. C. (1972). An intensive treatment program for alcoholics and their wives. *Quarterly Journal of Studies on Alcohol, 33*, 1144–1146.

Corder, B. F., Hendricks, A., & Corder, R. F. (1964). An MMPI study of a group of wives of alcoholics. *Quarterly Journal of Studies on Alcohol, 25*, 551–557.

Cork, M. (1969). *The forgotten children.* Toronto: Paperjacks.

Coyne, J. C. (1976). Toward an interactional description of depression. *Psychiatry, 39*, 28–39.

Curtis, R. C., Smith, P. F., & Moore, R. (1984). Suffering to improve outcomes determined by both chance and skill. *Journal of Social and Child Psychology, 2*, 165–173.

Cutter, C. G., & Cutter, H. S. G. (1987). Experience and change in Al-Anon family groups: Adult children of Alcoholics. *Journal of Studies on Alcohol, 48*, 29–32.

Davis, D. I., Berenson, D., Steinglass, P., & Davis, S. (1974). The adaptive consequences of drinking. *Psychiatry, 37*, 209–215.

DeBlois, C. S., & Stewart, M. A. (1983). Marital histories of women whose first husbands were alcoholic or antisocial. *British Journal of Addiction, 78*, 205–213.

DeGree, C. E., & Snyder, C. R. (1985). Adler's psychology (of use) today: Personal history of traumatic life events as a self-handicapping strategy. *Journal of Personality and Social Psychology, 48*, 1512–1519.

Deniker, P., De Saugy, D., & Ropert, M. (1964). The alcoholic and his wife. *Comprehensive Psychiatry, 5*, 374–383.

Dimberg, U. (1982). Facial reactions to facial expressions. *Psychophysiology, 19*, 643–647.

Drake, R. E., & Vaillant, G. E. (1988). Predicting alcoholism and personality disorder in a 33-year longitudinal study of children of alcoholics. *British Journal of Addiction, 83*, 799–808.

Drewery, J., & Rae, J. B. (1969). A group comparison of alcoholic and non-alcoholic marriages using the interpersonal perception technique. *British Journal of Psychiatry, 115*, 287–300.

Dunn, N. J., Jacob, T., Hummon, N., & Seilhamer, R. A. (1987). Marital stability in alcoholic-spouse relationships as a function of drinking pattern and location. *Journal of Abnormal Psychology, 96*, 99–107.

Edwards, P., Harvey, C., & Whitehead, P. C. (1973). Wives of alcoholics: A critical review and analysis. *Quarterly Journal of Studies on Alcohol, 34*, 112–132.

el-Guebaly, N., & Offord, D. R. (1977). The offspring of alcoholics: A critical review. *American Journal of Psychiatry, 134*, 357–365.

el-Guebaly, N., & Offord, D. R. (1979). On being the offspring of an alcoholic: An update. *Alcoholism: Clinical and Experimental Research, 3*, 148–161.

Ervin, C. S., Little, R. E., Streissguth, A. P., & Beck, D. E. (1984). Alcoholic fathering and its relation to child's intellectual development: A pilot investigation. *Alcoholism: Clinical and Experimental Research, 8*, 362–365.

Ewing, J. A., Long, V., & Wenzel, G. G. (1961). Concurrent group psychotherapy of alcoholic patients and their wives. *Internation Journal of Group Psychotherapy, 11*, 329–338.

Finney, J. W., Moos, R. H., Cronkite, R., & Gamble, W. (1983). A conceptual model of the functioning of married persons with impaired partners: Spouses of alcoholic patients. *Journal of Marriage and the Family, 45*, 23–34.

Frankenstein, W., Hay, W. M., & Nathan, P. E. (1985). Effects of intoxication on alcoholics' marital communication and problem solving. *Journal of Studies on Alcohol, 46*, 1–6.

Gabrielli, W. F., Jr., & Plomin, R. (1985). Drinking behavior in the Colorado adoptee and twin sample. *Journal of Studies on Alcohol, 46*, 32–38.

Geen, R. G., & Quanty, M. B. (1977). The catharsis of aggression: An evaluation. In L. Berkowitz (Ed.), *Advances in experimental social psychology* (Vol. 10). New York: Academic Press.

Geen, R. G., Stonner, D., & Shope, G. L. (1975). The facilitation of aggression by aggression. *Journal of Personality and Social Psychology, 31,* 721–726.

Gliedman, L. H., Rosenthal, D., Frank, J. D., & Nash, H. T. (1956). Group therapy of male alcoholics with concurrent group meetings of their wives. *Quarterly Journal of Studies on Alcohol, 17,* 655–670.

Godfrey, B. W., & Lowe, C. A. (1975). Devaluation of innocent victims: An attribution analysis within the just world paradigm. *Journal of Personality and Social Psychology, 31,* 944–951.

Goodwin, D. W., Schulsinger, F., Knop, J., Mednick, S., & Guze, S. B. (1977). Psychopathology in adopted and nonadopted daughters of alcoholics. *Archives of General Psychiatry, 34,* 1005–1009.

Goodwin, D. W., Schulsinger, F., Moller, N., Hermansen, L., Winokur, G., & Guze, S. B. (1974). Drinking problems in adopted and nonadopted sons of alcoholics. *Archives of General Psychiatry, 31,* 164–169.

Gorad, S. L., McCourt, W. F., & Cobb, J. C. (1971). A communications approach to alcoholism. *Quarterly Journal of Studies on Alcohol, 32,* 651–668.

Gorman, J. M., & Rooney, J. F. (1979). The influence of al-anon on the coping behavior of wives of alcoholics. *Journal of Studies on Alcohol, 40,* 1030–1038.

Gorski, T. T., & Miller, M. (1982). *Counseling for Relapse Prevention,* Independence, MO: Independence Press.

Green, R. A., & Murray, E. J. (1975). Expression of feeling and cognitive reinterpretation in the reduction of hostile aggression. *Journal of Consulting and Clinical Psychology, 43,* 375–378.

Guze, S. B., Goodwin, D. W., & Crane, J. B. (1970). A psychiatric study of the wives of convicted felons: An example of assortative mating. *American Journal of Psychiatry, 126,* 115–118.

Guze, S. B., Tuason, V. B., Stewart, M. A., & Picken, B. (1963). The drinking history: A comparison of reports by subjects and their relatives. *Quarterly Journal of Studies on Alcohol, 24,* 249–260.

Gynther, M. D., & Brilliant, P. J. (1967). Marital status, readmission to hospital, and intrapersonal and interpersonal perceptions of alcoholics. *Quarterly Journal of Studies on Alcohol, 28,* 52–58.

Gynther, M. D., Presher, C. H., & McDonald, R. L. (1959). Personal and interpersonal factors associated with alcoholism. *Quarterly Journal of Studies on Alcohol, 20,* 321–333.

Haberman, P. W. (1964). Psychological test score changes for wives of alcoholics during periods of drinking and sobriety. *Journal of Clinical Psychology, 20,* 230–232.

Haberman, P. W. (1966). Childhood symptoms in children of alcoholics and comparison group parents. *Journal of Marriage and the Family, 27,* 152–154.

Hall, R. L., Hesselbrock, V. M., & Stabenau, J. R. (1983a). Familial distribution of alcohol use: I. Assortative mating in the parents of alcoholics. *Behavior Genetics, 13,* 361–372.

Hall, R. L., Hesselbrock, V. M., & Stabenau, J. R. (1983b). Familial distribution of alcohol use: II. Assortative mating of alcoholic probands. *Behavior Genetics, 13,* 373–382.

Harburg, E., Davis, D. R., & Caplan, R. (1982). Parent and offspring alcohol use: Imitative and aversive transmission. *Journal of Studies on Alcohol, 43,* 497–516.

Harris, R. N., & Snyder, C. R. (1986). The role of uncertain self-esteem in self-handicapping. *Journal of Personality and Social Psychology, 51,* 451–458.

Hedberg, A. G., & Campbell, L. (1974). A comparison of four behavioral treatments of alcoholism. *Journal of Behavior Therapy and Experimental Psychiatry, 5,* 251–256.

Heller, K., Sher, K. J., & Benson, C. S. (1982). Problems associated with risk overprediction in studies of offspring of alcoholics: Implications for prevention. *Clinical Psychology Review, 2,* 183–200.

Hersen, M., Miller, P. M., & Eisler, R. M. (1973). Interactions between alcoholics and their wives: A descriptive analysis of verbal and nonverbal behavior. *Quarterly Journal of Studies on Alcohol, 34,* 516–520.

Hughes, J. M. (1977). Adolescent children of alcoholic parents and the relationship of Alateen to these children. *Journal of Consulting and Clinical Psychology, 45,* 946–947.

Jackson, J. K. (1954). The adjustment of the family to the crisis of alcoholism. *Quarterly Journal of Studies on Alcohol, 4,* 562–586.

Jackson, J. K., & Kogan, K. L. (1963). The search for solutions: Help-seeking patterns of families of active and inactive alcoholics. *Quarterly Journal of Studies on Alcohol, 24,* 449–472.

Jacob, T., & Bremer, D. A. (1986). Assortive mating among men and women alcoholics. *Journal of Studies on Alcohol, 47,* 219–22.

Jacob, T., Dunn, N., & Leonard, K. (1983). Patterns of alcohol abuse and family stability. *Alcoholism: Clinical and Experimental Research, 7,* 382–385.

Jacob, T., Favorini, A., Meisel, S. S., & Anderson, C. M. (1978). The alcoholic's spouse, children, and family interactions: Substantive findings and methodological issues. *Journal of Studies on Alcohol, 39,* 12331–1251.

Jacob, T., & Krahn, G. L. (1988). Marital interactions of alcoholic couples: Comparison with depressed and nondistressed couples. *Journal of Consulting and Clinical Psychology, 56,* 73–79.

Jacob, T., & Leonard, K. (1986). Psychosocial functioning in children of alcoholic fathers, depressed fathers, and control fathers. *Journal of Studies on Alcohol, 47,* 373–380.

Jacob, T., Leonard, K. E. (1988). Alcoholic-spouse interaction as a function of alcoholism subtype and alcohol consumption interaction. *Journal of Abnormal Psychology, 97,* 231–237.

Jacob, T., Ritchey, D., Cvitkovic, J. F., & Blane, H. T. (1981). Communication styles of alcoholic and nonalcoholic families when drinking and not drinking. *Journal of Studies on Alcohol, 42,* 466–482.

James, J. E., & Goldman, M. (1971). Behavior trends of wives of alcoholics. *Quarterly Journal of Studies on Alcohol, 32,* 373–381.

Janoff-Bulman, R. (1979). Characterological versus behavioral self-blame: Inquiries into depression and rage. *Journal of Personality and Social Psychology, 37,* 1789–1809.

Janzen, C. (1977). Families in the treatment of alcoholism. *Journal of Studies on Alcohol, 38,* 114–130.

Johnson, V. (1980). *I'll quit tomorrow.* New York: Harper & Row.

Kammeier, M. L. (1971). Adolescents with families with and without alcohol problems. *Quarterly Journal of Studies on Alcohol, 32,* 364–372.

Kephart, W. M. (1954). Drinking and marital disruption: A research note. *Quarterly Journal of Studies on Alcohol, 15,* 63–73.

Kiecolt-Glaser, J. K., & Williams, D. A. (1987). Self-blame, compliance, and distress among burn patients. *Journal of Personality and Social Psychology, 53,* 187–193.

Kleck, R., Ono, H., & Hastorf, A. H. (1966). The effects of physical deviance upon face-to-face interaction. *Human Relations, 19,* 425–436.

Kogan, K. L., Fordyce, W. E., & Jackson, J. K. (1963). Personality disturbance in wives of alcoholics. *Quarterly Journal of Studies on Alcohol, 24,* 227–238.

Kogan, K. L., & Jackson, J. K. (1963a). Role perceptions of wives of alcoholics and of nonalcoholics. *Quarterly Journal of Studies on Alcohol, 24,* 627–639.

Kogan, K. L., & Jackson, J. K. (1963b). Conventional sex role stereotypes and actual perceptions. *Psychological Reports, 13,* 27–30.

Kogan, K. L., & Jackson, J. K. (1964). Patterns of atypical perceptions of self and spouse in wives of alcoholics. *Journal of Studies on Alcohol, 25,* 555–557.

Kogan, K. L., & Jackson, J. K. (1965a). Some concomitants of personal difficulties in wives of alcoholics and nonalcoholics. *Quarterly Journal of Studies on Alcohol, 26,* 595–604.

Kogan, K. L., & Jackson, J. K. (1965b). Stress, personality, and emotional disturbance in wives of alcoholics. *Quarterly Journal of Studies on Alcohol, 26,* 486–495.

Langer, E. J. (1975). The illusion of control. *Journal of Personality and Social Psychology, 32,* 311–328.

Latane, B., Eckman, J., & Joy, V. (1966). Shared stress and interpersonal attraction. *Journal of Experimental Social Psychology, Supplement 1*, 80–94.

Lehman, D. R., Wortman, C. B., & Williams, A. F. (1987). Long-term effects of losing a spouse or child in a motor vehicle crash. *Journal of Personality and Social Psychology, 52*, 218–231.

Lemere, R., & Smith, J. W. (1973). Alcohol-induced sexual impotence. *American Journal of Psychiatry, 130*, 212–213.

Lemert, E. M. (1960). The occurrence and sequence of events in the adjustment of families to alcoholism. *Quarterly Journal of Studies on Alcohol, 21*, 679–697.

Lemert, E. M. (1962). Dependency in married alcoholics. *Quarterly Journal of Studies on Alcohol, 23*, 590–609.

Lerner, M. M., & Miller, D. T. (1978). Just world research and the attribution process: Looking back and ahead, *Psychological Bulletin, 85*, 1030–1051.

Littrell, J. (1981). *How the probability of success alters the evaluation of behavior.* Unpublished doctoral dissertation, A.S.U.

Lucero, R. J., Jensen, K. F., & Ramsey, C. (1971). Alcoholism and teetotalism in blood relatives of abstaining alcoholics. *Quarterly Journal of Alcohol, 32*, 183–185.

Macdonald, D. E. (1956). Mental disorders in wives of alcoholics. *Quarterly Journal of Studies on Alcohol, 17*, 282–287.

Macdonald, D. E. (1958). Group psychotherapy with wives of alcoholics. *Quarterly Journal of Studies on Alcohol, 19*, 125–132.

Madden, M. E. (1988). Internal and external attributions following miscarriage. *Journal of Social and Clinical Psychology, 7*, 113–121.

Mallick, S. K., & McCandless, B. R. (1966). A study of catharsis of aggression. *Journal of Personality and Social Psychology, 4*, 591–596.

Manning, D. T., Balson, P. M., & Xenakis, S. (1986). The prevalence of type A personality in the children of alcoholics. *Alcoholism: Clinical and Experimental Research, 10*, 184–189.

Mayer, M. E., & Dollar, N. J. (1987). *Issues in small group communication.* Phoenix, AZ: Prospect Press.

McAuley, T., Longabaugh, R., & Gross, H. (1978). Comparative effectiveness of self and family forms of the Michigan Alcoholism Screening Test. *Journal of Studies on Alcohol, 39*, 1262–1267.

McCord, J. (1988). Identifying developmental paradigms leading to alcoholism. *Journal of Studies on Alcohol, 49*, 357–362.

McCord, W., & McCord, J. (1962). A longitudinal study of the personality of alcoholics. In D. J. Pittman & C. R. Snyder (Eds.), *Society, culture, and drinking patterns* (pp. 413–430). New York: Wiley.

McCrady, B. S., Noel, N. E., Abrams, D. B., Stout, R. L., Nelson, H. F., & Hay, Wm. M. (1986). Comparative effectiveness of three types of spouse involvement in outpatient behavioral alcoholism treatment. *Journal of Studies on Alcohol, 47*, 459–467.

McCrady, B. S., Paolino, T. J., & Longabaugh, R. (1978). Correspondence between reports of problem drinkers and spouses on drinking behavior and impairment. *Journal of Studies on Alcohol, 39*, 1252–1257.

McCrady, B. S., Paolino, T. J., Longabough, R., & Rossi, J. (1979). Effects of joint hospital admission and couples treatment for hospitalized alcoholics: A pilot study. *Addictive Behaviors, 4*, 155–165.

Meyer, C. B., & Taylor, S. E. (1986). Adjustment to rape. *Journal of Personality and Social Psychology, 50*, 1226–1234.

Miller, D., & Jang, M. (1977). Children of alcoholics: A 20-year longitudinal study. *Social Work Research and Abstracts, 13*(4), 23–29.

Miller, D. T., & Porter, C. A. (1983). Self-blame in victims of violence. *Journal of Social Issues, 39*, 139–152.

Mitchell, H. E. (1959). Interpersonal perception theory applied to conflicted marriages in which alcoholism is and is not a problem. *American Journal of Orthopsychiatry, 29,* 547–559.

Moos, R. H., & Billings, A. G. (1982). Children of alcoholics during the recovery process: Alcoholic and matched control families. *Addictive Behaviors, 7,* 155–163.

Moos, R. H., Bromet, E., Tsu, V., & Moos, B. (1979). Family characteristics and the outcome of treatment for alcoholism. *Journal of Studies on Alcohol, 40,* 78–88.

Moos, R. H., Finney, J. W., & Chan, D. A. (1981). The process of recovery from alcoholism: I. Comparing alcoholics patients and matched community controls. *Journal of Studies on Alcohol, 42,* 383–402.

Moos, R. H., & Moos, B. S. (1984). The process of recovery from alcoholism: III. Comparing functioning in families of alcoholics and matched control families. *Journal of Studies on Alcohol, 45,* 111–118.

Nici, J. (1979). Wives of alcoholics as "repeaters". *Journal of Studies on Alcohol, 40,* 677–682.

Nylander, I. (1960). Children of alcoholic fathers. *Acta Paediatrica Stockholm, 49,* 1–134.

O'Farrell, T. J., & Birchler, G. R. (1987). Marital relationships of alcohol, conflicted, and non-conflicted couples. *Journal of Marital and Family Therapy, 13,* 259–274.

O'Farrell, T. J., Cutter, H. S. G., & Floyd, F. J. (1985). Evaluating behavioral marital therapy for male alcoholics: Effects on marital adjustment and communication from before to after treatment. *Behavior Therapy, 16,* 147–167.

O'Farrell, T. J., Harrison, R. H., & Cutter, H. S. G. (1981). Marital stability among wives of alcoholics: An evaluation of three explanations. *British Journal of Addiction, 76,* 175–189.

O'Gorman, P. A. (1976). Self-concept, locus of control, and perception of father in adolescents from homes with and without severe drinking problems. *Dissertation abstracts international, 36, 5156A.* (University Microfilms, N. 76-4189)

O'Malley, S. S., Carey, K. B., & Maisto, S. A. (1986). Validity of young adults' reports of parental drinking practices. *Journal of Studies on Alcohol, 47,* 433–435.

Orford, J. (1973). A comparison of alcoholics whose drinking is totally uncontrolled and those whose drinking is mainly controlled. *Behavior Research and Therapy, 11,* 565–576.

Orford, J. (1975). Alcoholism and marriage: The argument against specialism. *Journal of Studies on Alcohol, 36,* 1537–1563.

Orford, J. (1976). A study of the personalities of excessive drinkers and their wives, using the approaches of Leary and Eysenck. *Journal of Consulting and Clinical Psychology, 44,* 534–545.

Orford, J., & Guthrie, S. (1968). Coping behavior used by wives of alcoholics; a preliminary investigation. *International Congress on Alcohol and Alcoholism, Abstracts 28th,* p. 97.

Orford, J., Guthrie, S., Nicholls, P., Oppenheimer, E., Egert, S., & Hensman, C. (1975). Self-reported coping behavior of wives of alcoholics and its association with drinking outcome. *Journal of Studies on Alcohol, 36,* 1254–1267.

Orford, J., Oppenheimer, E., Egert, S., & Hensman, C. (1977). The role of excessive drinking in alcoholism complicated marriages: A study of stability and change over a one-year period. *International Journal of Addictions, 12,* 471–495.

Orford, J., Oppenheimer, E., Egert, S., Hensman, C., & Guthrie, S. (1976). The cohesiveness of alcoholism-complicated marriages and its influence on treatment outcome. *British Journal of Psychiatry, 128,* 318–339.

Paolino, T. J., McCrady, B. S., & Kogan, K. B. (1978). Alcoholic marriages: A longitudinal empirical assessment of alternative theories. *British Journal of Addictions, 73,* 129–138.

Parker, D. A., & Harford, T. C. (1988). Alcohol-related problems, marital disruption and depressive symptoms among adult children of alcohol abusers in the United States. *Journal of Studies on Alcohol, 49,* 306–313.

Pattison, E. M., Courlas, P. G., Patti, R., Mann, B., & Mullen, D. (1965). Diagnostic-therapeutic intake groups for wives of alcoholics. *Quarterly Journal of Studies on Alcohol, 26,* 605–616.

Pennebaker, J. W. (1982). *The psychology of physical symptoms.* New York: Springer Verlag.

Pennebaker, J. W., & Beal, S. K. (1986). Confronting a traumatic event: Toward an understanding of inhibition and disease. *Journal of Abnormal Psychology, 95,* 274–281.

Pennebaker, J. W., & O'Heeron, R. C. (1984). Confiding in others and illness rate among spouses of suicide and accidental-death victims. *Journal of Abnormal Psychology, 93,* 473–476.

Peterson, C., & Seligman, M. E. P. (1983). Learned helplessness and victimization. *Journal of Social Issues, 2,* 103–116.

Prewett, M. J., Spence, R., & Chaknis, M. (1981). Attribution of causality by children with alcoholic parents. *International Journal of Addictions, 16,* 367–370.

Rae, J. B. (1972). The influence of the wives on the treatment outcome of alcoholics: A follow-up study at two years. *British Journal of Psychiatry, 120,* 601–613.

Rae, J. B., & Drewery, J. (1972). Interpersonal patterns in alcoholic marriages. *British Journal of Psychiatry, 120,* 615–621.

Rae, J. B., & Forbes, A. R. (1966). Clinical and Psychometric characteristics of the wives of alcoholics. *British Journal of Psychiatry, 112,* 197–200.

Rhodes, J. (1984). *Differences in character roles between adolescents from alcoholic and non-alcoholic families.* Unpublished dissertation at ASU.

Rimmer, J., & Chambers, D. S. (1969). Alcoholism: Methodological considerations in the study of family illness. *American Journal of Orthopsychiatry, 39,* 760–768.

Roberts, K. S., & Brent, E. E. (1982). Physician utilization and illness patterns in families of alcoholics. *Journal of Studies on Alcohol, 43,* 119–128.

Rouse, B. A., Waller, P. F., & Ewing, J. A. (1973). Adolescent's stress levels, coping activities, and father's drinking behavior. *Proceedings, 81st Annual Convention, APA.*

Rubin, J. Z., & Brockner, J. (1975). Factors affecting entrapment in waiting situations: The Rosencrantz and Guildenstern effect. *Journal of Personality and Social Psychology, 31,* 1054–1063.

Schachter, S. (1959). *The psychology of affiliation.* California: Stanford University Press.

Schaffer, J. B., & Tyler, J. D. (1979). Degree of sobriety in male alcoholics and coping styles used by their wives. *British Journal of Psychiatry, 135,* 431–437.

Scheier, M. F., Weintraub, J. K., & Carver, C. S. (1986). Coping with stress: Divergent strategies of optimists and pessimists. *Journal of Personality and Social Psychology, 51,* 1257–1264.

Schuckit, M. A., Goodwin, D. A., & Winokur, G. (1972). A study of alcoholism in half siblings. *American Journal of Psychiatry, 128,* 1132–1136.

Schulsinger, F., Knop, J., Goodwin, D. W., Teasdale, T. W., & Mikkelsen, U. (1986). A prospective study of young men at high risk for alcoholism. *Archives of General Psychiatry, 43,* 755–760.

Seligman, M. E. P. (1975). *Helplessness: On depression, development, and death.* San Francisco: Freeman.

Shaver, K. G. (1969). Defensive attribution: Effects of severity and relevance on the responsibility assigned for an accident. *Journal of Personality and Social Psychology, 14,* 101–113.

Shaver, K. G., & Drown, D. (1986). On causality, responsibility, and self-blame: A theoretical note. *Journal of Personality and Social Psychology, 50,* 697–702.

Sher, K. J., & Descutner, C. (1986). Reports of paternal alcoholism: Reliability across siblings. *Addictive Behaviors, 11,* 25–30.

Sisson, E. W., & Azrin, N. H. (1986). Family-member involvement to initiate and promote treatment of problem drinkers. *Journal of Behavior Therapy and Experimental Psychiatry, 17,* 15–21.

Skoloda, T. E., Alterman, A. I., Cornelison, F. S., & Gottheil, E. (1975). Treatment outcome in a drinking-decision program. *Journal of Studies on Alcohol, 36,* 365–380.

Smith, C. G. (1969). Alcoholics: Their treatment and their wives. *British Journal of Psychiatry, 115,* 1039–1042.

Stabenau, J. R., & Hesselbrock, V. M. (1983). Family pedigree of alcoholic and control patients. *International Journal of the Addictions, 18,* 351–363.

Steinglass, P. (1979). An experimental treatment program for alcoholic couples. *Journal of Studies on Alcohol, 40,* 159–182.

Steinglass, P. (1981a). The impact of alcoholism on the family. Relationship between degree of alcoholism and psychiatric symptomatology. *Journal of Studies on Alcohol, 42,* 288–303.

Steinglass, P. (1981b). The alcoholic family at home: Patterns of interaction in dry, wet, and transitional stages of alcoholism. *Archives of General Psychiatry, 38,* 578–584.

Steinglass, P., Davis, D. I., & Berenson, D. (1977). Observations of conjointly hospitalized "alcoholic couples" during sobriety and intoxication: Implications for theory and therapy. *Family Process, 16,* 1–16.

Steinhausen, H., Gobel, D., & Nestler, V. (1984). Psychopathology in the offspring of alcoholic parents. *Journal of the American Academy of Child Psychiatry, 23,* 465–471.

Tarter, R. E. (1976). Personality of wives of alcoholics. *Journal of Clinical Psychology, 32,* 741–746.

Tarter, R. E., Hegedus, A. M., Goldstein, G., Shelly, C., & Alterman, A. I. (1984). Adolescent sons of alcoholics: Neuropsychological and personality characteristics. *Alcoholism: Clinical and Experimental Research, 8,* 216–222.

Taylor, S. E., Lichtman, R. R., & Wood, J. V. (1984). Attributions, beliefs about control, and adjustment to breast cancer. *Journal of Personality and Social Psychology, 46,* 489–502.

Tedeschi, J. T., Smith, R. B., & Brown, R. C. (1974). A reinterpretation of research on aggression. *Psychological Bulletin, 81,* 540–562.

Tennen, H., Affleck, G., & Gershman, K. (1986). Self-blame among parents of infants with perinatal complications: The role of self-protective motives. *Journal of Personality and Social Psychology, 50,* 690–696.

Tesser, A., Leone, C., & Clary, E. G. (1978). Affect control: Process constraints versus catharsis. *Cognitive Therapy and Research, 2,* 265–274.

Thompson, W. D., Orvaschel, H., Prusoff, B. A., & Kidd, K. K. (1982). An evaluation of the family history method for ascertaining psychiatric disorders. *Archives of General Psychiatry, 39,* 53–58.

Tucker, J. A., Vuchinich, R. E., & Sobell, M. B. (1981). Alcohol consumption as a self-handicapping strategy. *Journal of Abnormal Psychology, 90,* 220–230.

Vannicelli, M., Gingerich, S., & Ryback, R. (1983). Family problems related to the treatment and outcome of alcoholic patients. *British Journal of Addiction, 78,* 193–204.

Wegscheider, S. (1981). *Another Chance.* Palo Alto, CA: Science and Behavior Books, Inc.

Wegscheider-Cruse, L. (1985). *Choice making.* Pompano Beach, FL: Health Communications, Inc.

Werner, E. E. (1986). Resilient offspring of alcoholics: A longitudinal study from birth to age 18. *Journal of Studies on Alcohol, 47,* 34–40.

Whalen, T. (1953). Wives of alcoholics; four types observed in a family service agency. *Quarterly Journal of Studies on Alcohol, 14,* 632–641.

Whitfield, C. L. (1980). Children of alcoholics: Treatment issues. *Maryland State Medical Journal,* June, 86–91.

Wills, T. A. (1981). Downward comparison principles in social psychology. *Psychological Bulletin, 90,* 245–271.

Wilson, T. D., & Linville, P. W. (1982). Improving the academic performance of college freshmen: Attribution therapy revisited. *Journal of Personality and Social Psychology, 42,* 367–376.

Wilson, C., & Orford, J. (1978). Children of alcoholics: Report of a preliminary study and comments on the literature. *Journal of Studies on Alcohol, 39,* 121–142.

Woerner, P. I., & Guze, S. B. (1968). A family and marital study of hysteria. *British Journal of Psychiatry, 114,* 161–168.

Woititz, J. G. (1983). *Adult Children of Alcoholics.* Florida: Health Communications, Inc.

Wolin, S. J., Bennett, L. A., & Noonan, D. L. (1979). Family rituals and the recurrence of alcoholism over generations. *American Journal of Psychiatry, 136,* 589–593.

Wortman, C. B., & Brehm, J. W. (1975). Responses to uncontrollable outcomes: An integration of reactance theory and the learned helplessness model. In L. Berkowitz (Ed.), *Advances in experimental social psychology* (Vol. 9). New York: Academic Press.

Wright, K. D., & Scott, T. B. (1978). The relationship of wives's treatment to the drinking status of alcoholics. *Journal of Studies on Alcohol, 39,* 1577–1581.

Zajonc, R. B., & Markus, H. (1984). Affect and cognition relationships and human development. In C. E. Izard, J. Kagan, & R. B. Zajonc (Eds.), *Emotion, cognition, and behavior.* Cambridge, England: Cambridge University Press.

Zastrow, C. (1985). *The practice of social work.* Chicago: Dorsey Press.

Zweben, A. (1986). Problem drinking and marital adjustment. *Journal of Studies on Alcohol, 47,* 167–172.

Appendix A

Federal Regulations Pertaining to Confidentiality in Alcohol and Drug Treatment Programs

HIGHLIGHTS FROM THE REGULATIONS PERTAINING TO CONFIDENTIALITY ISSUED BY THE DEPARTMENT OF HEALTH AND HUMAN SERVICES IN THE FEDERAL REGISTER ON JUNE 9, 1987

These regulations were initially authorized by section 408 of the Drug Abuse Prevention, Treatment, and Rehabilitation Act (21 U.S.C. 1175). They were amended and transferred by Pub. L. 98-24 to section 527 of the Public Health Service Act which is codified at 42 U.S.C. 290ee-3. Questions regarding this information should be directed to Jane Galloway (301) 443-3200 (phone number provided in the Federal Register).

Any treatment center which provides alcohol and drug treatment and receives any kind of federal aid, including tax exemption, is bound by the rules. Such agencies include those which are certified to receive medicare payment and agencies which are certified to dispense a controlled substance in the treatment of a drug or alcohol client. Violation of the regulations is a criminal offense. The law provides that a fine of up to $500 should be imposed upon the first offense, and fines of up to $5000 should be imposed for each subsequent violation. Violations are to be reported to the US attorney general of the regional office in which the offense occurred. Violations occurring in methadone programs are reported to the Food and Drug Administration.

Release of information: Only a patient can read his/her own record without securing a release. A patient may sign a release allowing disclosure of information to another source. This release must specify the nature of the information to

323

be provided, the agency and individual (identified by names and function) to whom the information is disclosed, and the duration of time for which the release extends which should be apposite to the purpose of the disclosure, and a specification of any conditions under which the release is automatically revoked. The name of the treatment program must be listed on the release. Any disclosed information should be accompanied by the patient's signed release as well as a statement which informs regarding the federal prohibition against secondary disclosures. The following words should be included in the accompanying explanation of the regulations:

> This information has been disclosed to you from records protected by Federal confidentiality rules (42 CFR Part 2). The Federal rules prohibit you from making any further disclosure of this information unless further disclosure is expressly permitted by the written consent of the person to whom it pertains or as otherwise permitted by 42 CFR Part 2. A general authorization for the release of medical or other information is NOT sufficient for this purpose. The Federal rules restrict any use of the information to criminally investigate or prosecute any alcohol or drug abuse patient.

It should be noted that a patient may revoke a release at any time. At which time, the release is voided.

Exceptions to a signed release: The law provides that disclosures can be made in the case of medical emergencies. If an emergency disclosure occurs, such disclosure must be made to a medical person. The occurrence of the disclosure must be documented in the patient's record. The documentation should include the name of the individual providing the information, the affiliation of the individual to whom it was provided, the name of the individual making the disclosure, the date and time of the disclosure, and the nature of the emergency. A treatment program which is hospital based does not require a release to discuss information pertinent to treatment with another unit in the same hospital.

Other exceptions to the rule include compliance with a court order. Incidents of child abuse should be reported to authorities, however information not specifically pertinent to the abuse incident should not be provided. This particular exception does not extend to civil or criminal proceedings which might redound from the reported neglect or abuse. Also unprotected is information in the face of existing threat to a third party. The program can provide information to the police if the patient has committed a crime against the agency. However, disclosure should be limited to information pertinent to the crime, which may include the patient's address, last known whereabouts, and status as a patient. If legal action is brought against the agency by the patient, information in the patient's record can be used in legal defense without securing written permission from the patient.

Court ordered disclosures of confidential information can be made without the patient's permission is the case of investigations or prosecutions of an extremely serious crime. Extremely serious crimes include homicide, rape, kidnapping, armed robbery, assault with a deadly weapon, and child abuse or neglect. Although selling illicit drugs is not automatically included in the definition of a serious crime under the federal regulations, they allow that a judge can determine that drug trafficking constitutes an extremely serious crime.

The information in the patient's record may be used for program evaluation and research purposes provided the specific identity of the patient is protected by those engaged in the enterprise. Information may be provided for medicare audits.

It should be noted that the exceptions to the rule, allow but do not compel disclosure.

Conditions which are not exceptions: If the criminal justice system refers an individual to treatment as a condition of disposition of any criminal proceedings against the patient or as part of parole or other release from custody, the patient must sign a release before information can be conveyed. The information released by the patient can only be used to fulfill the purposes indicated in the release.

The Definition of Protected Information: The statutes protect information in the record. Restrictions apply to any information obtained by the program for the purpose of diagnosis, treatment, or referral. Whether the patient is or is not a patient in a particular agency is also protected information, unless one is simply affirming that an individual is a patient in a general hospital. Inquiries regarding an individual who has never been a patient, can be answered in the negative, however, affirmative answers can never be given without a signed release. Persons making inquiry should be sent a copy of the laws which govern confidentiality.

Patients cannot be required to wear identification badges off the agency campus, although such identification can be required within the confines of the agency.

Who Is Effected by these laws: Any agency which receives federal funding is expected to comply with the federal regulations. Federal funding is defined broadly to include those assisted by the IRS through allowance for income tax deductions for contributions or through a tax exempt status. School based prevention programs are included if they provide diagnosis and referral. Psychiatric treatment facilities are included if they offer alcoholism diagnosis, treatment, or referral for treatment. Institutions, for example general hospitals and emergency rooms, which offer a broad range of services, are not governed by these rules. Also excluded is the case in which the federal government pays for the alcohol or drug treatment of a federal prisoner but the program itself is not included. The

Veteran's Administration has its own rules and is not included under these regulations.

If a treatment agency contracts with an external laboratory, this laboratory is bound by the same confidentiality rules as is the treatment facility. Written agreement must be secured with the external facility.

Informing Patients of Their Rights: At the time of admission to the program, the federal government recommends that patients receive a written statement outlining their rights. They should be informed of their rights to confidentiality as well as the limitations on confidentiality. The following is a suggested statement which might be provided to patients.

The confidentiality of alcohol and drug abuse records maintained by this program is protected by Federal law and regulations. Generally, the program may not say to a person outside the program that a patient attends the program, or disclose any information identifying a patient as an alcohol or drug abuser UNLESS: 1. the patient consents in writing; 2. the disclosure is allowed by a court order; 3. the disclosure is made to a medical personnel in a medical emergency or to a qualified personnel for research, audit, or program evaluation.

Violation of Federal law and regulations by a program is a crime. Suspected violations may be reported to appropriate authorities in accordance with Federal regulations.

Federal law and regulations do not protect any information about a crime committed by a patient either at the program or against any person who works for the program or about any threat to commit such a crime.

Federal laws and regulations do not protect any information about suspected child abuse or neglect from being reported under State law to appropriate State or local authorities.

(See 42 U.S.C. 290dd-3 and 42 U.S.C. 290ee-3 for Federal laws and 42 CFR Part 2 for Federal regulations.)

(Approved by the Office of Management and Budget under Control No. 0930-0099.)

Issue Pertinent to Minors: According to some state laws, minors cannot receive treatment without the consent of their parent. In order to secure parental permission, the minor must sign a release allowing the treatment program to communicate with the parent. The minor must also be willing to sign a release prior to the time that a bill is presented to the parents. There is an exception to the rule pertaining to the issue of requiring minor permission in order to contact parents to obtain permission to treat or to inform regarding other conditions which pose a threat to the life or physical well being of the minor or other individuals. Three conditions must obtain: (1) the program director believes the minor lacks the capacity to make a rational decision on the issue; (2) the situation must pose a substantial threat to the physical well being of the minor or to the well being of another person; and (3) such threat would be eliminated through notification of the parent.

If a state law requires parental permission for treatment of the minor, any release of information must be signed by both the parent and the minor.

Issues Pertinent to the Incompetent or the Deceased: The consent to release provided by a guardian is sufficient without the additional consent of the incompetent individual. A program director can determine that a patient, who has not been adjudicated, is incompetent and can disclose patient status in order to obtain third party payment. An agency can disclose the cause of death without the deceased's permission, but may not label this person as a patient receiving treatment for drug or alcohol abuse.

Protection of Records: When not in use, federal regulations mandate that records be locked. There must be a written policy governing access to records. There are specific regulations governing the securing of records in the event that the program is sold or closed.

Undercover Agents: Federal regulations explicitly forbid the knowing enrollment as a patient or the knowing employment of an undercover agent. However, if a program is suspicioned to employ person engaged in criminal misconduct, an undercover agent can legitimately be allowed. The program director is to be informed, if the program director is not among the suspected. The regulations forbid the prosecution of patients with information obtained in the course of an undercover investigation of the program itself.

SAMPLE CONSENT FORM

1. I (name of patient) [ ] request [ ] authorize:
2. Name or general designation of the program to which the disclosure is made

---

3. To disclose: (kind and amount of information to be disclosed)

---

4. To: (name or title of the person or organization to which disclosure is to be made)

---

5. For (purpose of the disclosure)

---

6. Date (on which this consent is signed)

---

7. Signature of the patient

---

8. Signature of parent or guardian (where required)

---

9. Signature of person authorized to sign in lieu of the patient (where required)

---

10. This consent is subject to revocation at any time except to the extent that the program which is to make the disclosure has already taken action in reliance on it. If not previously revoked, this consent will terminate upon: (specific date, event, or condition)

Appendix B

Marital Communications Skit

COMMUNICATION SKIT

The following is the dialogue from a skit that was performed as part of an outpatient treatment program for alcoholism. The audience for the skit consisted of alcoholics and their spouses who were jointly attending the program. The purpose of the skit is to dramatize some advantageous ways in which to discuss past transgressions of the drinker and some useful ways to deal with probable resentments in the spouse.

Leader (to audience): Tonight we're going to concern ourselves with how couples in early sobriety can best communicate about the issues which are often of concern.

Two rehearsed counselors John and Mary are playing the roles of a drinker and a codependent attending the program. Mary and John are driving home. This is a conversation that we believe might happen.

John: Mary, I'm curious about what you talk about in your codependents group. You haven't really said much about the program.

Mary: Well, since I've been in the program, I've realized how angry I am with you. I don't think I'll ever be able to forgive what you've done to me or the children.

STOP ACTION

Leader (to audience): Place yourself in Don's shoes. How would you be feeling at this point?

Need to elicit following points:

1. "I know she's justified, I really feel bad."

(1b). Despair, feeling sorry for self, don't know what to do, (1c) need to defend; (1d) hopeless

2. Angry—"Here I am, spending all my time going to this recovery program trying to treat my disease. She still isn't satisfied. I might as well be drinking."

3. Trying to be perfect—"She's right. I can never ever drink again. I'll make it up to everyone. I'll work so hard to earn their forgiveness. They'll never be unhappy with me again."

Leader (to audience): Ok, let's try another one. Let's have this conversation occur at home. John had a flat tire and is 1 hour late coming home from work. This is a conversation several hours later, in the living room, after dinner.

John: It was really uncomfortable changing that tire in the heat. Sorry the dinner was held up.

Mary: When you didn't come home on time, I thought you probably had stopped for a drink. It reminded me of how it had been. I started remembering all of the embarrassing moments and horrible situations you placed me in. You know, I don't know if I'll ever be able to forgive you.

Leader (to audience): What might John be feeling here. (elicit the same 3 moods as before: guilt/dysphoria; anger; resolve to be perfect)

Leader (to audience): Let's see how John might act given each of these feelings. (to John) John, pretend you're feeling guilty. What might you say to Mary. Mary why don't you begin the action again.

Mary: Well, since I've been in the program, I have realized how angry I am with you. I don't think I'll ever be able to forgive what you've done to me or the children.

John: (turns away and stage whispers to himself) I feel so bad. I just can't respond. (Looks sad and looks away)

Leader (to audience): Let's evaluate the impact of Don's guilty response on both himself and on Mary. John, in the role of feeling guilty, what do you think the impact would be on you?

John: I think I would be sitting there not really listening further to Mary. I'd start thinking about all the events in my drinking days that I'm sorry for. I'd feel sad. I'd want to get away from the situation and be alone. I'd be too occupied with the past and unable to hear what Mary is saying.

Leader: Mary, how would you feel if John sat there looking sad and withdrawn.

Mary: Well, I might feel a little sorry for him. I might also be angry, that I can't even get mad at him. I have to forget about my feelings and think about him. More than anything else, I'd feel alone, like no one really heard what I was saying. If he stayed sad and withdrawn for any length of time, I'd really feel alone.

Leader: Let's move on. Let's look at how John might act if he feels angry. Ok, start the action.

Mary: I really am getting in touch with my anger. I don't think I'll ever be able to forgive what you've done to me or the children.

John: Here I am rearranging my schedule to treat my disease. I'm doing everything I can. What more can you want. The trouble with you, Mary, is you're never satisfied. I'm just not going to put up with the way you used to be. You know, Mary, the program says you're just as sick as I am. You better be getting treatment for yourself.

Leader (to audience):   What do you think? How are both John and Mary going to feel as a result of this interaction. Let's focus on John first and then Mary.

Pull from audience: John might think, if I quit for Mary and don't remember that I quit for myself, I'll feel like drinking again. I might feel like doing something to retaliate— "If she doesn't appreciate this, why should I stop drinking? I might as well be drunk." Mary might think, this is more of the same. I'll never be happy living with him.

Leader: (to audience) Let's look at the trying to be perfect response. We'll play out how this interaction might look.

Mary: I'm really getting in touch with my anger. I don't think I'll ever be able to forgive what you've done to me or the children.

John: I know. I'll just never drink again. I'm going to start Little League with the kids. I'll take you to the movies every week. I'll be much nicer to your mother. I'll make it up to you. I'll make you happy.

Leader: (to audience) Let's evaluate this one. I think it's harder to see how this response might lead to problems. What's the impact on John, on Mary.

Pull from audience—for John—this is all or nothing thinking. (a) If he gets into a "be perfect," when he falls from grace, he might be back to drinking. Further, given the magnitude of the task, he might be less likely to try in the first place. John might be expecting his sobriety to achieve the impossible. He is setting up unrealistic expectations of sobriety. (b) He's also less likely to be legitimately assertive with Mary or to discipline the kids when they need it. The result might eventually be, "This is too hard, why don't I just give up?" for Mary—"be perfect"—response from John might be ok, for a while. Probably she will be aware that there might be a backlash.

Leader (to audience): Let's focus on Mary. When Mary says:

Mary: I don't think I'll ever be able to forgive what you've done to me or the children.

Leader: What is Mary feeling (possibly feeling alone and discounted; she may feel that since no one has listened in the past, she will have to state her feelings very strongly)

We know that communication serves two purposes. First, it conveys information about content and feelings. Second, it produces an impact on the listener. What impact do you think Mary wants to produce in John? What does she want from John? What does she want to happen? (Place the list on the board.)

Should get the following list—

EMPHASIZE THAT THESE ARE ALL NATURAL HUMAN RESPONSES THAT PEOPLE MAKE GIVEN THE CONTEXT. WE'RE NOT SAYING ANYONE IS BAD. BECAUSE THEY ARE SUCH PREDICTABLE RESPONSES, WE'RE WARNING YOU, SO YOU HAVE A CHOICE.

1. Mary wants reassurance from John that it won't happen again. She may fear so much that it will happen again, that she's getting mad in advance.

2. Mary wants to get back at John and make him feel bad.

3. Mary wants John to be in an "I'll be perfect." She wants to be pampered for a change.

4. Mary wants her feeling acknowledged. Mary may not be aware of this want. When she gets it she might feel surprisingly good.

Leader (to audience): Let's look at each of these wants and evaluate them in terms of (1) whether its possible for them to be met by John, and (2) in terms of if they are met, will the resulting situation be good for John, for Mary, for the relationship. (Go through the list)

1. reassurance—this would be ok, but it's impossible to give. John can't read the future any better than Mary. John can share his feelings about his sobriety. Both Mary and John, together can make an educated guess about long-term possibilities.

2. John feels badly—John gets depressed and is withdrawn and boring.

3. John tries to be perfect. This could feel ok for Mary for a while. John, however, might eventually feel put upon. At some point the scales of retribution might seem balanced, at which point there might be a backlash. In John's mind being perfect, especially if his perfection is not appreciated, might entitle him to another drunk.

4. Mary's feelings could be acknowledged by John. This is called reflective listening. John can do it. Mary could feel better.

Leader (to audience)   Let's go back to a typical scene and see if we can make this interaction a good one for everybody. Mary, let's begin with you. As you know, if you know what response you want from someone else, you're going to be more likely to get it. Do you know what you want to happen?

Mary: Yes, I want John to really listen to me, to take my perspective, and to acknowledge some awareness of what I experienced.

Leader: John, do you know what kind of things to say to yourself so you can stay directed to the task of listening to Mary, hearing what she is saying, and then letting her know you have heard?

John: Yea, but I'd like help from the audience. I've prepared these statements that might go on in my head. I want the audience to help me get my thinking in order. I want to have a dialogue between the reflective listening perspective and the other three. Can I have 4 volunteers from the audience.

(Each volunteer is given a script of the dialogue with their part underlined. Each wears a sign labeling his role.)

THE ACTION

Mary: Well, since I've been in the program, I really have realized how angry I am at you. I don't think I'll ever be able to forgive what you've done to me or the children.

Angry self-statement volunteer: That woman is never satisfied. What more can I possibly say. I'm getting fed up. She has no right to be giving me a hard time now.

Reflective listening volunteer: (to angry) I'm not going to worry about whether Mary has a right to say what she is saying right now. I really don't care right now who is wrong or right. I'm just going to hear her out.

Guilty self-statement volunteer: I feel so bad. I can remember everything I've done. God, I feel awful.

Reflective listening volunteer: (to guilty) I'm not going to worry about what I did in the past. I'm going to pay attention to Mary's needs.

Trying to be perfect self-statement volunteer: I'll make it up to her. She'll see. I'll think of everything I can do.

Reflective listening volunteer: (to be perfect) I'm not going to problem solve about what I can do in the future. I'm going to listen right now.

Reflective listening volunteer: (to John) John, relax and hear Mary's pain. Respond to Mary as a person in pain. Don't worry right now about where the pain came from or who caused it. That's not the point.

Mary: Look, John, I can see a lot's going on in your head. Perhaps, I can help you deal with me. Just listen. Don't feel guilty, don't try to fix things or me—that's not your job, and don't argue or defend yourself. Please, listen and let me know you understand.

John: nods

Mary: Well, I still am full of resentment and anger. I think I'd like to feel good about us and our marriage. My angry feelings seem to get in the way.

John: I'm sure you're angry. Can you tell me some of the specific things which hurt you.

Mary: Well, yeah. That night, at the kid's birthday party. My folks were at the house. You were late. You didn't call. Then, you showed up drunk. My feelings just all flooded in. I was angry, embarrassed, hurt—all mixed up together.

John: God, that must have been awful for you. I guess I would have felt the same things you did. There's a whole lot of things I'm sorry both of us had to go through.

Leader (to audience): Well, that's how we envision communication which might work. Of course, sometimes, it won't work out this well-but, this was an example of how it could work out well.

Our advice to the drinker is (1) avoid getting hooked into the nonproductive feelings—guilt, trying to be perfect, anger; and (2) reflective listen—that means, listen, hear, and acknowledge that you've heard. The reflective listening usually feels good for the spouse.

We do realize that for some drinkers, the spouse wants the drinker to feel bad, to try to be perfect, or to give the family reassurance. In that kind of situation, the drinker needs to realize what is happening. The drinker needs to be aware that he or she is being asked to give something impossible or something which could jeopardize his/her sobriety or the long term relationship. If the drinker realizes that he/she is in the predicament of being asked to give something he/she can't give, it's best to relax and remember the serenity prayer. You're in one of those situations you can't control, have the wisdom to know it.

For spouses, sometimes the alcoholic will be angry, defensive, and depressed. The same advice applies to you.

Our advice to the spouse is (1) know what you want, and (2) before asking for what you want, evaluate whether you really want it. Think about whether your want is impossible for your spouse to supply and whether if you get what you want, it will be good for you, your spouse, and your marriage.

It's all right to express or talk about your desire for reassurance or even the urge to want to hurt back. It's possible for your spouse to understand these feelings and emphathize with them. However, sometimes its best to evaluate whether you'll be happy if you get what you request.

(Ask for questions)

Leader: I'd like to make a final statement about trust and love. Often spouses are concerned because they can no longer trust or love the drinker. Here's a perspective for thinking about trust and love.

Trust and love are by products of good interaction between people over a period of time. If they're not there now, there is nothing anybody can do about it for the present. What can be done right now, is spending quality time together, caring, meeting today's needs. Eventually the by products will be there.

Don't fight, argue or worry about whether trust and love are present right now. The appropriate perspective is whether you are enjoying the time together now.

Appendix C

Topics Which Might Be Covered in a Group Comprised of Alcoholics

GROUP TOPICS

Family Issues

Who in the family has objected most to your drinking and why? How did they express their objections (watching you, throwing out bottles, hollering, extracting promises)? How did you feel about the objections? How else could members have expressed themselves so that you would have been influenced? Was there anyone who used a good approach?

Did anyone enable you (buying bottles, rescuing)? What is the relationship to this person now?

Did you drink out of spite? Out of guilt? Did you feel guilty? What did you do with the guilt (do more work than your share, not object to things which should have been objected to? Do things to make up for the drinking? Become defensive and drink all the more?)

What was your reaction to the notion that codependents are also sick? How is this statement meaningful for your particular situation, i.e., how did your spouse respond to the stress of the drinking?

Where will the problems be now that you aren't drinking—role changes, decision making? Is spouse willing to relinquish control? Do you anticipate non-alcohol related problems which will be more noticeable for you now that you're not drinking?

Spouses resentments: how will you deal with the external situation (reflective listening, ignoring, leaving scene); how will you deal with internal feelings-keep from becoming rebellious, depressed and guilty, feeling like its not worth it?

What kind of support do you want from your family for your sobriety?

Have you discussed with your spouse: your feelings about his/her drinking, whether you want him/her to tell you when she sees signs of relapse, when his/her watching you will be perceived by you as supportive and when it will feel accusatory, whether to serve liquor in your home, whether he/she can be of help when you are both in the company of drinkers, how he/she should respond to a relapse? How could you bring up these topics? If you don't want to discuss these topics do you know what your objections are?

Attitudes Toward Alcohol

Where did your attitudes toward drinking develop? What was your family's attitude toward intoxication? What type of drinking did you see in your family? How did you feel about your family members? About their drinking?

In high school, what were the drinking practices of the people you knew? Was getting drunk admired? How did you feel about people who refused to drink? What peer pressure did you experience?

How do you feel about the drinking attitudes you accepted? Would you want your children to grow up with the same attitudes?

Where are the manifestations of the old attitudes? Do you expect nondrinkers to be dull people? Do you resent nondrinkers (why at this point)?

What kind of activities do people who don't drink engage in?

Attitudes Toward Alcoholism

What was your stereotype of an alcoholic? Has that been altered as a result of being here in this program?

What do you view as the origin of alcoholism in general? What did you used to think? To what did you attribute your own drinking?

How would you intervene, if at all, with an alcoholic friend?

Will you share your alcoholism and recovery with your friends, family, kids? What might their reactions be? Since most people don't know how to react to someone else's sobriety, how can you take the lead in helping them to relax around you?

If you aren't going to share your alcoholism, do you know why you are reluctant (shame, fear of discrimination)? Do any of these factors have implications for your sobriety (lack of social support, nagging sense of shame)?

Have you seen recovered alcoholics who are no longer ashamed of the alcoholism? What happened to them so that they are no longer ashamed? How did they develop pride?

Recovery

What's your theory on why people quit drinking? Do they want a better life or do they fear the consequences of continued drinking? How about for you?

How long did you think about recovery without doing anything about it? How close did you come? What stopped you, fear of not being able to succeed? Lack of motivation because the situation was not extreme enough?

Is it possible for persons who aren't sure whether they are alcoholic to quit drinking? What will be the special problems for them? What thoughts might lead to a drift back into drinking?

What have you noticed about yourself or your day now that you aren't drinking? How do you expect you and your life to be different a year from now—both in terms of new problems which will be all the more noticeable, and achieving things you weren't able to consider before? Has quitting drinking made you more confident about tackling other goals?

Some people avoid the urges to drink by having a picture in their minds of how they are different and what they have accomplished, what picture could you use? If you think back to the reasons you quit drinking in the first place, what's on your list?

Some drinkers began looking forward to drinking at 3 PM. If you were one of them, do you now find that you are more involved in your afternoon?

What about quitting for someone else? What will you do when they let you down or lack appreciation for your sobriety?

Frequent AA topics: commitment, detachment, gratitude, resentments, criticizing/controlling, surrender/compliance, powerlessness, denial

Relapse

Group discussion about individual views on the most likely precipitants to relapse/ Provide empirical findings.

Some believe that relapse is more likely to occur when you encounter situations in which you used to drink. In what contexts did you use (gregarious, while working, alone, in particular places—bars, parties); were there particular times during the day? Did you use alcohol to alter your mood (drank when angry, sad, lonely, happy, after argument, when not feeling appreciated)? How will you handle each of the bad mood types? What will you do about the urges which might be there in places where you might experience a conditioned urge? Might you be particularly vulnerable when in a good mood or after having achieved something? Do you have other ways to celebrate so you won't feel deprived? Have you experienced any attitude change toward those factors (hassles, aggravations) you believe (or used to believe) caused your drinking? How do you feel about having been controlled by these events? Did you drink to get drunk?

Excuses can be a sign to discover that you may be vulnerable to relapse. Use the information. Introduce the idea that an excuse used as a justification for drinking is irrelevant in terms of consequences. The consequences of drinking will be there even if you don't deserve them (i.e., if you have an excuse).

How will you structure time differently? Fantasize about using weekend time.

Discuss your behavior when you are sober vs. when you are drinking. Which corresponds with your more valued self? How can you develop positive drinking qualities (more self-disclosing, more emotionally expressive, more gregarious, fewer inhibitions, more assertive) in your sober self?

One precursor to relapse is the coaxing of friends. Which friends will be disappointed when you don't drink? How will they show their disappointment? How will you feel? How will you handle these feelings? Do you have a way to turn down drinks. Role play. What response will your assertion receive? How will you handle the response of others?

Do you intend to see drinking friends? What might be the cues for you that you need to leave (feeling deprived)? What changes do you think occur in people so they don't feel deprived or left out when they're around drinkers (pride in their sobriety, learning how to get into a silly mood without drinking)? What arrangements do you need to make with your spouse so you can gracefully leave the scene? Are you planning on living a completely withdrawn life in order to avoid temptations to drink? Discuss the dangers in such a strategy.

When you consider the people you have seen in the group, do you form impressions of who will be likely to maintain abstinence. What qualities do you look for? What about these qualities in yourself? Are there particular thought patterns that might alert you to a relapse in yourself?

How much do you think it is good to worry about staying sober? Is there a way to avoid being complacent without being nervous and apprehensive?

People who make commitments to their sobriety (perform observable behaviors frequently) maintain abstinence longer. Which behaviors will exemplify commitment for you?

People who reward themselves for their sobriety do better than those who don't feel they deserve anything. Are you planning on building in reinforcements in your life as part of your new life style? Are you a person who believes that by being sober you are just breaking even rather than having a source of pride? Is this a general pattern?

How to handle urges and cravings: wait 5 minutes, distract self, leave scene, engage in an alternative rewarding behavior, predicting situations in which cravings are likely to occur

Responses to Relapse

Explain Abstinence Violation Syndrome which consists of feeling guilty after drinking, making no distinction between failing badly and a small violation, taking a small violation as indicative that sobriety is impossible so why try.

What's a good mental attitude to take after a slip? Deciding you need to work harder, learning from the experience, don't focus on the guilt/embarrassment but rather on what to do now

Have those who have relapsed talk about their embarrassment in returning to AA meetings or their reluctance to talk about the slip at AA meetings. How did they overcome this?

Talk about responses to failure in other areas which have been most productive for you.

Discuss cognitive dissonance notion, that after you violate your value system there will be a tendency to alter your attitude defensively (defend your behavior). Where has this happened? How can you keep it from happening?

Role Plays

You come into work 30 minutes late due to a flat tire. No one believes you. You can tell that they believe you had been drinking. Someone makes a smart remark. How do you feel? What emotions do you feel like expressing?

Someone is legitimately angry with you. How can you handle it? (reflective listening). How can you avoid guilt while planning how to do it differently in future? Practice self-statements.

Making Amends

To whom do you feel you need to make amends. How might you do this?

Who is most likely to be resentful about your drinking, or to have a negative view of you? How will they communicate their attitudes? How will you handle it? (Particularly relevant for persons who are returning to work after leave).

General Therapy Issues

Emotions—which ones do you display, don't display; which are troubling? which emotions have you felt but not displayed? How do you feel about emotional people?

Techniques for discriminating emotions in oneself, i.e., developing labeling of kinesthetic feedback: Have the individual give feedback to others about when they are displaying emotions; develop templates for emotions for example by discussing general issue such as "how do you know when you're uncomfortable?"

Assertion: In what contexts are you assertive? In what contexts aren't you? Were there occasions when you wished you were assertive? What are your attitudes toward assertive and nonassertive people? Do you have favorite models of assertion? How are you similar to or different from nonassertive people?

Values—what are they, where did they come from, which ones are apparent?

View of self, self-description; what type of people can't you stand? Which type of people do you like (interpersonal style), most admire for their values, feel most comfortable around?

Is it easier for you to give positive or negative strokes? How do you do it, when have you held back, why?

Where have you been willing to be focus of attention? When have you held back? How do you feel about people who frequently are the center of attention? How can you develop having something to say (observing other's styles)?

Rejection: When has it happened to you? When have your rejected others?

Practice reflective listening
Interpersonal relationships: When do you feel irritable, resentful, assume the worst, misperceive people? Is there any difference in your nondrinking self?

Build social skills.

Problems with procrastination.

Problems with self-consciousness.

Feeling entitled to have fun.

Boredom—lack of interest in life.

DRINKING INFORMATION WHICH CAN SERVE AS GROUP TOPICS

1. Is the drinker a binger or does drinking occur with regular frequency? If the drinker imbibes with regular frequency, list day of the week and the amount drunk during each time interval.

2. If the drinker is a binger, what is the usual duration of the binge? How frequent are the binges?

3. How long has the drinker maintained the above pattern?

4. Does morning drinking occur? Is a drink needed in the middle of the night?

5. How much does the drinker intend to consume? Does the drinker intend to become intoxicated or drunk? Would he/she begin drinking if he could only have one drink?

6. How intoxicated does the person usually become? (Ask would anyone know you have been drinking, how might they know?)

7. Does the person skip meals? If they eat do they feel like drinking after eating?

8. Does the person manifest any personality changes when drinking? (more aggressive, assertive, generous, open and friendly, more able to approach opposite sex, more relaxed, maudlin, more willing to self indulge, less obsessive and concerned about responsibilities, more labile, more willing to be the center of attention)

9. What are the expectancies for drinking—does the individual expect to feel better, to exhibit a more positive personality (ask about assertion)?

10. What does the person do when he/she drinks?

(a) wants to be around others? wishes to be in a bar or party type atmosphere? wants to be alone?

(b) does the person perform chores or watch TV while drinking?

(c) does the person sit and daydream about unfulfilled aspirations?

(d) If the person begins drinking in a bad mood, does he preserve the mood (sit and brood) or does he alter the mood? Does he seek sympathy from others if he feels he has been wronged? Does he seek to change the bad mood by partying with others or by just generally feeling relaxed and relieved?

11. Which moods are most likely to precipitate drinking? angry, bored, lonely, depressed, taken advantage of, unappreciated/neglected, happy, criticized, pressured or overworked, told what to do, told not to drink, criticized for drinking? What feelings or events might precipitate a slip?

12. How much time does the person spend thinking about his/her drinking? Does he/she arrange affairs to accommodate his/her drinking? Does he/she protect his/her supply. Will he/she plan to have enough for the morning?

13. How does the person regard his/her drinking? Is there a pride in being a heavy drinker? Does the person consider himself to be a hard luck story? Does the person consider his wet alcoholic status to be his ineluctable state? Is he embarrassed? Does he deny or underrepresent the extent of his drinking?

14. Why treatment now? How did he decide that his drinking was a problem?

15. When was the first occasion when the individual wondered about his/her drinking? What was the concern? Was anything done to act on the concern (see doctor, try to cut down)? What happened?

16. What reason does the person endorse for wanting to alter his/her drinking? (alcohol is ruining my health, against my religion, function better at the job, self disgust, want to make something of life, doesn't like getting sick, spouse is upset, trouble with law, might lose job)

17. Has the person's drinking just recently become a problem? Was the change precipitated by a major life alteration (divorce, job loss, new job, death, major painful illness)?

18. When began drinking? former drinking patterns? Have there been periods of controlled drinking?

19. Which of the following pertain? withdrawal symptoms (specify which ones) blackouts, dts, seizures, hallucinations, increased tolerance, decreased tolerance, sneaking, preoccupation, gulping, guilt, taking medications; drug use

20. Specify in which life areas alcohol is creating a problem and how: family, legal, job, health, own sense of adequacy, memory and cognitive functioning, mood when not drinking

21. Any prior treatment for drinking or psych problems? Persons reactions to treatment?

22. Has the person ever purposefully remained abstinent? If the person has purposefully remained sober for a protracted duration, what was the quality of the person's sober life? (contrast quality of sober life with drinking life) How were cravings to drink or interpersonal pressures to drink handled?

23. What has precipitated relapse in the past?

24. For those who consider themselves inveterate alcoholics and who strive to maintain abstinence, what are their thoughts after they slip and have one drink? Do they feel so guilty they continue to escape guilt by further drinking? Do they feel they have blown it and that there is no distinction between one drink and three weeks of drinking? Do they feel they deserve 3 weeks of drinking? Do they fear facing repercussions? Do they wait for external factors to stop them? Do they fear withdrawal symptoms?

25. How do relatives, friends, boss feel regarding the drinking? How are attitudes expressed? How does the person feel about the reactions of others? Does he/she sneak drinks? Does he/she feel he/she owes an apology to anyone? Does he/she feel guilty? Does he/she avoid the family?

26. Eating, exercise, and sleeping pattern?

27. Who will object to the individual's sobriety? Number of friends or relatives who will be supportive of the sobriety.

28. What major obstacles are there in the person's life which have resulted from the drinking and will be making life difficult?

29. How optimistic is the person about being able to stay sober? Has the person thought about a plan? Does she/he have any way of envisioning a sober life?

30. Describe the person's motivation for sobriety. What is the genesis of the motivation (fear or aspiration)?

Appendix D

Intake Interview Forms

This appendix contains forms to be used for garnering information on incoming patients. There are 5 forms. One form contains questions to be completed about the patient (with drinker or spouse) by the therapist. Another form, to be completed by the drinker, gathers information about the drinker. The third form is to be completed by the spouse and provides data about the spouse's responses to the drinking. A fourth form is completed by the spouse and provides information about the spouse's subjective response to his/her marriage. A fifth form is completed by the drinker and provides information about the drinker's subjective responses to his/her marital relationship.

The forms presented here are not proffered as validated instruments which predict future behavior. They are presented to assist beginning clinicians. Regardless of the work setting, everyone gathers information during the intake process and enters it in the record. Given this requirement, it becomes important to have some idea of what information usually appears in an intake interview summary. The new clinician may find these forms useful in guiding data gathering.

GENERAL INTAKE INTERVIEW
TO BE COMPLETED BY THE THERAPIST

Intake Date:
Interviewer name:
Client's name:

General Information

1. Who was present for the interview? (Indicate whether spouse accompanied the patient to the interview even if they were not included in the interview itself.)

2. What is the presenting problem?

3. Who made the referral?

4. How long has the presenting problem been a concern?

5. List the persons residing in the patient's home.

name & relationship	age	descriptors	drug use	pt's attitude re: person

6. Does the drinker have a familial history of alcohol or drug abuse? Describe.

   What was the drinker's response to the family drinking problem?

7. Does the drinker's spouse have a familial history of alcohol or drug abuse? Describe.

   What was the spouse's response to the family drinking problem?

8. List the dates and descriptors of past marriages/love relationships for the drinker.

Dates	Descriptors	Reason for termination

9. List the dates and descriptors of past marriages/love relationships for the spouse.

Dates	Descriptors	Reason for termination

10. Provide a job history for the drinker beginning with the current job.

Type of job	Dates of employment	Quality of interaction with boss	Quality of interaction with peers	Attitude re: job	Reason for leaving

11. Provide a job history for the spouse beginning with current job.

Type of job	Dates of employment	Quality of interaction with boss	Quality of interaction with peers	Attitude re: job	Reason for leaving

12. Specify drinker's education level.

13. Specify spouse's education level.

14. How does the drinker structure his/her free time?

15. How does the spouse structure his/her free time?

16. Describe the drinker's social support system. Who are the significant others? What type of support is provided and with what frequency? How satisfied is the drinker with the support provided?

17. Describe the spouse's social support system. Who are the significant others? What type of support is provided and with what frequency? How satisfied is the spouse with the support system?

18. Describe the sex life of the drinker and the spouse.

19. List the health problems of the drinker.

20. List the health problems of the spouse.

21. How satisfied is the drinker with life? Indicate what he/she would wish to change.

22. How satisfied is the spouse with life? Indicate what he/she would wish to change.

23. Comment upon the drinker's childhood.

24. Comment upon the spouse's childhood.

DESCRIPTIVE INFORMATION

Complete this information for each person seen during the interview.

1. Who is being described?

2. Describe the person's affect.

3. Describe the person's speech.

4. Describe the person's dress, grooming, and posture.

5. Describe the person's social skills and manner of relating to the interviewer.

6. List significant personality descriptors.

7. Describe the person's comfort level during the interview &/or attitude about the interview.

8. Do you suspect that the person has a major mental illness (schizophrenia, organicity, MDI, personality disorder)? Specify the reason for your suspicion.

9. Describe the quality of the interaction among the persons who were present for the interview.

DRINKING INFORMATION

1. Who was the informant for this information?

2. If the drinker imbibes with regular frequency, complete the following. List the drinker's average intake for the hours and days listed. List by number of drinks. If the drinker imbibes 2 or 3 nights per week but not necessarily the same nights, arbitrarily pick several nights for which to provide the information.

	Mon.	Tues.	Wed.	Thur.	Fri.	Sat.	Sun.
7–9am							
9–11am							
11–2pm							
2–4pm							
4–7pm							
7–9pm							
9–12pm							
12–3am							
3–7am							

3. How long has the drinker maintained the above pattern?

4. Is the drinker a binge drinker?

   What is the usual duration of a binge?

   How frequent are the binges?

5. Who in the drinker's life has noticed his/her intake?

6. Who objects to the drinker's imbibing?

   How are the objections manifested?

   How does the drinker respond to the objections?

7. Specify the drinker's concerns regarding his/her drinking; what is the basis for the concern? When did the concern develop?

8. Check those consequences which have occurred as a result of the drinker's imbibing.

   drinking on occasions when the drinker has not wanted to drink
   drinking more than the drinker wishes on an occasion (loss of control)
   blackout (list the date of first blackout _____)
   morning drinking
   memory problems when not drinking
   violence when drinking
   DWI (list dates _____)

absenteeism
tardiness at work
threats from spouse
drinking at work
reprimand at work
lost job (list dates _____)
jail time (list dates and charges)
skipping meals
sneaking drinks
lying regarding drinking

9. Has the drinker ever evidenced withdrawal symptoms? List dates and symptoms.

10. Has the drinker ever been medically detoxed? List dates and type of detox.

11. In what context does the drinker usually imbibe, i.e., what is he/she usually doing while he/she drinks?

12. Does the drinker drink more or less than friends?

13. Which moods generally precipitate drinking?

14. Does the drinker usually purposefully seek intoxication?

15. How intoxicated does the drinker usually become? List behavioral symptoms.

16. Does the drinker manifest pride as he/she speaks about his/her drinking?

17. Has the drinker sought treatment before? List dates and type.

18. Who will object to the drinker's abstinence?

19. List any prior periods of abstinence; reasons for quitting and reasons for resuming consumption.

    Dates   Why quit   Why resume

20. When did the drinker begin drinking?

21. What was the drinker's pattern of drinking prior to the present pattern?

    Dates of prior patterns   Description of prior patterns

22. What does the drinker wish to do regarding his/her drinking? Indicate feelings and endorsed goal.

23. When was the drinker's last drink?

    What withdrawal symptoms is the drinker presently manifesting?

24. Describe the drinker's other drug usage. Specify type of drug used, amount taken and history.

25. Specify spouse's attitude toward the drinking and what he/she does when the drinker drinks. Indicate the informant on this question.

26. Is there a family history of manic depressive illness or schizophrenia? Indicate the family member.

DISPOSITION
(With brief rationale)

1. Will the drinker be detoxed?

2. What treatment is planned?

3. List possible treatment goals.

4. What factors are likely to impair the treatment goals?

5. What are the patient's expectations regarding the efficacy of treatment?

6. Will feedback to the DWI center be necessary?

7. Has the patient taken antabuse in the past? Did the patient abuse the antabuse?

INFORMATION FROM THE MEDICAL RECORD

1. Circle those lab scores which are elevated.

   GGT   SGPT   SGOT

2. Indicate the number and type of physical problems related to alcohol for which the client has been seen in the last two years. If the client is a spouse indicate the number and type of stress related physical complaint for which the client has been seen in the last two years.

3. How many times did the patient cancel and reschedule prior to contact on this referral?

DRINKER'S INTAKE QUESTIONNAIRE

What is your present occupation?

How long have you been employed at your present job?

What job did you hold before your present job?

How long were you employed at this job?

What hours do you presently work?

who lives in your home besides you? (List relationship and age)

If you are presently married or in a love relationship, how long have you been married or in a relationship?

What were the approximate dates of any previous marriages?

check those areas in which you are presently experiencing problems in your life

_____ marital or mate problems

_____ problems with children

_____ problems with parents or relatives other than those in immediate family

_____ chronic pain or health problems

_____ problems with work other than those created by drinking

_____ drinking

_____ financial problems

_____ emotional problems (tension, depression, stress, anxiety, etc.)

_____ poor self esteem

_____ other (specify)

Was coming here your idea and not primarily someone else's?

If coming here was not your idea, do you believe that it is a good thing that you are here?

    yes   no   unsure

If coming here was not your idea, and you don't believe that it is a good thing that you are here, how much do you resent being here?

no resentment	slight resentment	moderate resentment	great resentment

What is your goal with regard to your drinking right now?

_____ continue to drink at my present level, but obtain information regarding alcoholism

_____ reduce my drinking

_____ quit drinking completely

_____ don't know

_____ do nothing

Before coming here, have you ever wondered whether you had a drinking problem?

If yes, how long ago did you begin to wonder if you had a drinking problem?

Have you ever sought out information regarding alcoholism?

If yes, how long ago was it?

Have you ever attended AA?

If yes, how long ago was it? (give approximate years if you can)

Have you ever been treated for a drinking problem before?

If yes, give approximate date or dates.

Who in your life thinks you drink too much?

_____ spouse or lover	_____ children
_____ boss	_____ me
_____ fellow employees	_____ everybody
_____ doctor	_____ no one
_____ relatives outside of immediate family	

Do you believe you have a drinking problem?

      yes   no

If yes, when did your drinking problem being, give the year _____

Have you ever tried to quit drinking?

      yes   no

If yes, please indicate the month, the year, and the duration of your sobriety.

If, in the past, you have been purposefully abstinent for over a two week period, indicate what factors led you to drink again (on the last occasion). How long had you been thinking about returning to drinking? Where were you and with whom were you when you broke your abstention? A day later how did you feel about your drinking?

When did you have your last drink? (list the date and hour)

Have you ever been medically detoxed? (please list the dates)

Have you ever had a seizure in conjunction with withdrawal?

At what age did you begin your drinking?

List any health problems you are presently experiencing.

If you were feeling depressed, would you tell your spouse?

      yes   no

If yes, how would you expect to feel afterward?

better   the same   worse

If you were complimented at work, would you tell your spouse?

yes   no

If you had an argument with a friend, would you tell your spouse?

yes   no

If yes, how would you expect to feel afterwards?

better   the same   worse

If you had a problem at work, would you tell your spouse?

yes   no

If yes, how would you expect to feel afterwards?

better   the same   worse

If you were feeling vaguely anxious, would you tell your spouse?

yes   no

If yes, how would you expect to feel afterwards?

better   the same   worse

Have you initiated discussion with your spouse regarding your drinking?

yes   no

If yes, how did you feel afterward?

better   the same   worse

If you were feeling depressed, is there a friend with whom you would discuss it?

yes   no

If you had a problem at work, is there a friend with whom you would discuss it?

yes   no

If you had a problem with your spouse, is there a friend with whom you would discuss it?

yes   no

If your car was not running, is there a friend whom would give you a ride to work?

yes   no

If you were complimented at work, is there a friend whom you would tell?

yes   no

If you wanted to express your opinion about some issue on the news, is there a friend with whom you could talk?

yes   no

Do you attend church?

yes   no

Do you belong to any groups or clubs? (include bridge clubs, bowling leagues, etc.)

How many group or club meetings do you participate in per month?

How many times per month do you get together with relatives?

How many times per month do you get together with friends?

How often do you drink? (Check the appropriate response)

_____ daily

_____ several days out of the week

_____ once a week

_____ several times a month

_____ several times per year

_____ once a year

Have you ever had what you consider a binge?

yes   no

What was the longest period of continuous (non-stop save for sleep) drinking you have ever experienced?

If you drink with a regular frequency, complete the following. List your average intake for the hours and the days listed. List by number of drinks (a drink = one beer; one 4 oz. glass of wine; or one oz of hard liquor). If you drink 2 or 3 nights per week but not necessarily the same nights, arbitrarily pick nights for which to provide the information.

	Mon.	Tues.	Wed.	Thur.	Fri.	Sat.	Sun.
7–9am							
9–11am							
11–2pm							
2–4pm							
4–7pm							

7–9pm							
9–12pm							
12–3am							
3–7am							

How long have you maintained the pattern indicated on the question above?

_____ less than one year

_____ between one to three years

_____ between three to seven years

_____ between seven to ten years

_____ more than ten years

What periods in your life do you consider to have been your periods of most heavy drinking? List approximate ages.

During the period of your most heavy drinking, how frequently did you drink?

_____ daily

_____ several days out of the week

_____ once a week

_____ several times a month

_____ several times per year

_____ once a year

How much did you typically consume per day when you were drinking at your heaviest?

What was the most you would consume per day?

Which of the following has happened to you as a result of your drinking?

_____ seizures

_____ internal shakes while sobering up

_____ hang over

_____ blackouts (loss of memory for periods while drinking)

_____ hallucinations

_____ tardiness at work

_____ absenteeism from work

_____ reprimand at work

_____ boss has threatened to fire if I don't quit drinking and/or get treatment

_____ lost job (list year or years)

_____ DWI (list year or years)

_____ marital disputes

_____ jail time

_____ needed a drink in the middle of the night

_____ spouse has threatened to divorce if I don't quit drinking and/or get treatment

_____ no problems

Do you have trouble remembering things?

yes   no

About how many days of sick time do you use per year?

Are you afraid that your drinking is getting worse?

yes   don't know   no

Have you ever taken a valium or other type of tranquilizer for over a one month period?

yes   no

Have you ever found yourself drinking when you had not wanted to, or planned not to?

yes   no

Have you ever been surprised by the amount you drank the day before?

yes   no

Do you remember to eat meals when you drink?

yes   no

If you drink with your friends, do you drink more, about the same, or less than they do?

more   about same   less

What percentage of your drinking is done in each context? Indicate by circling the appropriate word next to each.

alone at home	all	most	some	little	none
at home with my spouse	all	most	some	little	none
at home with friends	all	most	some	little	none
in a bar with strangers	all	most	some	little	none

at work with others	all	most	some	little	none
at work alone	all	most	some	little	none
with friends other than at a bar or at home	all	most	some	little	none

If you ran into a friend while you were drinking, how would he/she know that you were drinking? (Check those items which apply)

_____ they could not tell

_____ I would be more relaxed than usual

_____ I might be more argumentative or belligerent

_____ my speech would be slurred

_____ I might have trouble walking

_____ loss of bladder control

Do you panic because you fear you may not have a drink when you need it?

yes   no

Have you ever tried to hide your drinking?

yes   no

Have you ever lied about your drinking?

yes   no

Can you perform better at work after you have had a drink?

yes   no

Please complete these questions if your goal is to quit drinking. Pick the three most important reasons you have for wanting to quit drinking. Place a "1" by the most important reason, a "2" by the second most important reason, and a "3" by the third most important reason. If you have less than three reasons, you may indicate less than three.

my spouse is threatening to divorce me

alcohol is ruining my health

my doctor has instructed me to quit, although I believe my doctor is overreacting

I will function better at my job

drinking is against my religion

I'm disgusted with myself

I want to make something out of my life

I don't like getting sick

there are many things I would rather spend money on

my spouse is upset with my drinking

I'm hurting my friends and family, although they do not harass me

my drinking is getting me in trouble with the law

I'm afraid my drinking might become worse

I might lose my job

I want to help my spouse quit drinking by quitting myself

Other _____

Will your friends be disappointed if you quit drinking?

    yes   no

Do you believe that you will need the help of treatment in order to stop drinking?

    definitely will not   unsure   definitely will

Do you believe you will need to attend AA in order to stop drinking?

    definitely will not   unsure   definitely will

Do you believe you will have to change your friends in order to stop derinking?

    definitely will not   unsure   definitely will

Do you believe that you will have to make major life style changes in order to stop drinking?

    definitely will not   unsure   definitely will

Which of the following could interfere with your ability to maintain sobriety? Check those which apply.

    _____ feeling too carefree

    _____ an argument with my boss

    _____ being unfairly overworked or underpaid

    _____ being treated unfairly

    _____ being unfairly criticized

    _____ an argument with my spouse

    _____ being suspected of drinking when I haven't

    _____ stress or tension

    _____ feeling blue

    _____ feeling bored

_____ trouble with my children

_____ pressure from friends to drink

_____ expectations from others that I drink

_____ embarrassment over refusing a drink

_____ financial problems

_____ urges to drink

_____ failing to remember the harm alcohol has caused

_____ being in the presence of others who are drinking heavily

_____ feeling tired

_____ physical pain

_____ getting an "I don't care attitude"

_____ problems with my parents

_____ nothing could interfere with my sobriety

_____ other (specify your thoughts) _____

SPOUSE'S INTAKE QUESTIONNAIRE

Some of the questions on this form refer to your spouse. If you have a girlfriend or boyfriend rather than a spouse, substitute those words.

What is your present occupation? (you need not list the company for whom you work)

How long have you been employed at your present job?

What job did you hold before your present job?

How long were you employed at this job?

What hours do you presently work?

List the persons with whom you live and their ages. List in the form: daughter–age 6; wife–age 40, etc.

If you are presently married or in a love relationship, how long have you been married or in a relationship?

List the approximate dates of any previous marriages (for example, 1942–1960)

Check those areas in which you are presently experiencing problems in your life

_____ marital or mate problems

_____ problems with children

_____ problems with parents or relatives other than those in immediate family

_____ chronic pain or health problems

_____ my spouse's drinking

_____ problems with my job

_____ concern over my spouse's job

_____ financial problems

_____ emotional problems (tension, depression, stress, anxiety, etc.)

_____ poor self esteem

_____ other (specify) _____

Of the problems in your life listed above, circle those which are a direct result of your spouse's drinking.

Did someone (perhaps your doctor) suggest that you come to this appointment, or did you seek out these services on your own?

suggestion from another   sought out services myself

How sure are you that you need to be here?

/   /   /   /   /   /   /

very sure   very unsure

Do you believe that your spouse has a drinking problem?

yes   no

Have you ever wondered in the past if your spouse had a drinking problem?

yes   no

If yes, when did you begin to wonder if your spouse had a drinking problem?

_____ less than a year ago

_____ about a year ago

_____ more than 2 years ago

_____ more than 10 years ago

_____ more than 15 years ago

_____ more than 20 years ago

Have you ever sought out information regarding alcoholism?

yes   no

If yes, give approximate dates _____

Have you ever attended Alanon?

    yes   no

If yes, give the approximate dates _____

Have you ever been treated for stress associated with your spouse's drinking problem before?

    yes   no

If yes, give the appropriate date _____

Who in your life thinks you should seek help for your stress? (Check appropriate response)

_____ spouse or lover   _____ children
_____ boss   _____ me
_____ fellow employees   _____ everyone
_____ doctor   _____ no one
_____ parents

How worried are you about your spouse's drinking?

   /   /   /   /   /   /   /
not at all   extremely

Is your spouse presently drinking?

    yes   no

If your spouse is presently sober, when did your spouse quit drinking?

Please check the type of help you hope to obtain by coming here today.

_____ ideas about how to stop my spouse's drinking

_____ direction to help me obtain a separation or divorce

_____ help for my moodiness or stressed condition

_____ information regarding alcoholism

_____ some explanation regarding why my spouse drinks

_____ help to decide whether or not to separate or divorce

_____ an explanation regarding why I married an alcoholic

_____ I'm unsure

Have you ever considered divorce or separation in the past?

    yes   no

Are you presently considering divorce or separation?

    yes   no

Have you ever actually separated from your spouse?

If yes, please list the approximate dates.

If you were feeling depressed, would you tell your spouse?

yes   no

If yes, how would you expect to feel afterwards (circle one)

better   the same   worse

If you were complimented at work, would you tell your spouse?

yes   no

If you had an argument with a friend, would you tell your spouse?

yes   no

If yes, how would you expect to feel afterwards?

better   the same   worse

If you had a problem at work, would you tell your spouse?

yes   no

If yes, how would you expect to feel afterwards?

better   the same   worse

If you were feeling vaguely anxious, would you tell your spouse?

yes   no

If yes, how would you expect to feel afterwards?

better   the same   worse

Have you initiated discussion with your spouse regarding his/her drinking?

yes   no

If yes, how did you feel afterward?

better   the same   worse

If you were feeling depressed, is there a friend with whom you would discuss it?

yes   no

If you had a problem at work, is there a friend with whom you would discuss it?

yes   no

If you had a problem with your spouse, is there a friend with whom you would discuss it?

yes   no

If your car was not running, is there a friend who would give you a ride to work?

yes   no

If you were complimented at work, is there a friend that you would tell?

yes   no

If you wanted to express your opinion about some issue on the news, is there a friend with whom you could talk?

yes   no

Do you attend church?

yes   no

Do you belong to any groups or clubs? (include bridge clubs, bowling leagues, etc.)

How many group or club meetings do you participate in per month?

How many times per month do you get together with relatives?

How many times per month do you get together with friends?

How often do you drink? (Check the appropriate response)

_____ daily

_____ several days out of the week

_____ once a week

_____ several times per year

_____ once a year

How many aspirins do you take per week on the average?

Do you have trouble remembering things?

yes   no

If you work, about how many days of sick time do you use per year?

Are you afraid that your spouse's drinking is getting worse?

yes   no

Have you ever taken valium, librium, dalmane or any other tranquilizer for over a month period?

yes   no

Do you presently take valium, librium, dalmane or any other tranquilizer on a daily basis?

yes   no

During the last two months have you taken more than two tablets of valium, librium, or dalmane?

    yes   no

Do you eat regular meals?

    yes   no

Within the course of a day, how many times do you think about your spouse's drinking?

    never   occasionally   frequently   very frequently

During the last two weeks circle those problems which you have experienced.

    headache   diarrhea   backache   chest pain

Were either of your parents heavy drinkers?

    yes   no

Have you ever been exposed to alcoholism before in someone you've been close to? Indicate the relationship.

_____ mother	_____ father
_____ uncle	_____ aunt
_____ grandparent	_____ brother or sister
_____ former spouse or mate	_____ boyfriend or girlfriend

Which behaviors have you performed in the last month

_____ watched your spouse's alcohol consumption while out in public

_____ thrown out liquor

_____ looked for hidden bottles

_____ attempted to influence my spouse to stop drinking by crying or screaming

_____ lost my temper

_____ broke down in tears

_____ purchased liquor for my spouse

_____ been unable to sleep while waiting for spouse to come home drunk

_____ called in sick for spouse who had hangover or was drinking

_____ talked for over 30 minutes to a friend or relative about my spouse's drinking

_____ checked in the refrigerator or elsewhere to determine how much my spouse had had to drink

_____ spoken to my children about my spouse's drinking

_____ been embarrassed due to my spouse's drinking

_____ avoided getting together with friends for fear of embarrassment over my spouse's drinking

Who in your environment knows that you believe your spouse has a drinking problem? (Answer this question only if you believe your spouse has a drinking problem.)

_____ my children   _____ my inlaws

_____ my relatives   _____ a close friend

_____ the people with whom I
work

other (specify) _____

To what about your spouse's drinking do you most object? (Check those items to which you most object.)

_____ my spouse is not living up to potential

_____ he/she becomes visibly intoxicated

_____ he/she becomes irritable or violent when drinking

_____ he/she falls asleep when drinking

_____ he/she never comes home and doesn't phone when drinking

_____ he/she looks terrible (for example, doesn't shave; put on make-up; bathe) when drinking

_____ his/her drinking is jeopardizing his/her job

_____ he/she might receive a DWI or hurt someone while driving

_____ too much money is spent on drinking

_____ he/she lies about drinking or hides his/her drinking

_____ he/she broods when drinking

Does your spouse do the majority of his/her drinking at home?

drinks at home   drinks away from home

What are you usually doing when your spouse is drinking?

_____ watching TV

_____ go to bed to avoid an argument

_____ talk to a friend or relative on phone, usually about the drinking

_____ argue with spouse

_____ leave the house and go to a friend's

_____ leave the house on an errand

_____ other (specify) _____

Have you discussed your spouse's drinking with him or her?

yes   no

Have you ever requested that your spouse promise to quit drinking?

yes   no

Check those words which describe you well.

_____ warm	_____ impulsive
_____ irritable	_____ nervous
_____ caring	_____ understanding
_____ moody	_____ thoughtful
_____ rebellious	_____ independent
_____ generous	_____ concerned about others
_____ responsible	_____ hard working
_____ shy	_____ hard to get to know
_____ kind	_____ intelligent
_____ domineering	_____ passive
_____ confident	_____ submissive
_____ worried	_____ selfish
_____ unreliable	_____ outgoing
_____ charming	_____ confident
_____ often the center of attention	_____ likable

Have you stopped inviting your friends to your home because you didn't know what would happen?

Have you put off achieving personal goals because too many things were happening or you just were too fatigued?

Have you maintained the responsibilities to your job, home, and children in the way you have wished?

How have your feelings changed toward your spouse over the years? Compare your feelings and beliefs about your spouse over the years of your marriage. Are there differences?

How have you changed since the development of your spouse's drinking? Which changes have you liked? Not liked?

EVALUATION OF THE MARITAL RELATIONSHIP BY THE DRINKER

Check those activities in which you participated last weekend.

_____ watched TV

_____ visited friends

_____ played with my children

_____ went grocery shopping

_____ went to movie

_____ ate out other than at a fast food restaurant

_____ played cards

_____ went to a party

_____ went bowling

_____ went fishing

_____ other (specify) _____

Circle those activities which you check above which you did with your spouse.

During the last week which activities have occurred between you and your spouse?

_____ argued for over 10 minutes

_____ exchanged short, angry remarks

_____ hugged each other

_____ attempted to solve a problem regarding the children

_____ talked about a TV program together while we were watching it

_____ talked together for more than 5 minutes about a mutual friend or a relative

_____ talked about an event which had occurred at work (can be either spouse's work)

_____ talked about what had occurred during the day after coming home from work

_____ discussed finances for over 10 minutes

_____ ate dinner without having the TV set on

Who takes major responsibility for each of the following activities in your family? (Leave blank those activities which don't occur in your family

preparing meals	myself	my spouse	equally shared
making sure the grass is cut	myself	my spouse	equally shared
grocery shopping	myself	my spouse	equally shared
paying bills	myself	my spouse	equally shared
preparing the children for school	myself	my spouse	equally shared
praising the children for good report card	myself	my spouse	equally shared

monitoring whether children are home on time	myself	my spouse	equally shared
scolding children when appropriate	myself	my spouse	equally shared
planning social activities	myself	my spouse	equally shared
remembering birthdays (children's, relatives)	myself	my spouse	equally shared
cleaning	myself	my spouse	equally shared
calling service departments when appliance requires repair	myself	my spouse	equally shared
changing car oil	myself	my spouse	equally shared

Check those words which best describe your spouse.

_____ warm	_____ understanding
_____ impuslive	_____ moody
_____ irritable	_____ thoughtul
_____ caring	_____ rebellious
_____ generous	_____ worried
_____ concerned about others	_____ selfish
_____ responsible	_____ irresponsible
_____ hard working	_____ outgong
_____ shy	_____ center of attention
_____ hard to get to know	_____ charming
_____ kind	_____ witty
_____ intelligent	_____ assertive
_____ domineering	_____ confident

Which words do you believe your spouse would check in describing himself or herself?

_____ warm	_____ understanding
_____ impulsive	_____ moody
_____ irritable	_____ thoughtful
_____ caring	_____ rebellious
_____ generous	_____ worried
_____ concerned about others	_____ selfish
_____ responsible	_____ irresponsible
_____ hard working	_____ outgoing

_____ shy   _____ center of attention
_____ hard to get to know   _____ charming
_____ assertive   _____ domineering
_____ kind   _____ witty
_____ critical   _____ confident

Which words do you believe your spouse would check in describing you?

_____ warm   _____ understanding
_____ impulsive   _____ moody
_____ irritable   _____ thoughtful
_____ caring   _____ rebellious
_____ generous   _____ worried
_____ concerned about others _____ selfish
_____ responsible   _____ irresponsible
_____ hard working   _____ outgoing
_____ shy   _____ center of attention
_____ hard to get to know   _____ charming

Check those areas which you believe are strengths in your marriage.

_____ sex life   _____ agreement on raising
                                       children
_____ agreement on how to   _____ support in the area of
        spend money   my career choice
_____ agreement over how to _____ agreement over how to
        interact with my   interact with spouse's
        relatives   relatives
_____ my satisfaction with   _____ concern or consideration
        my spouse's career   from my spouse
_____ agreement over how to _____ agreement over mutual
        spend free time   friends
_____ agreement over major
        life values

Check those areas which you believe are problems in your marriage.

_____ sex life   _____ agreement on raising
                                       children
_____ agreement on how to   _____ support in the area of
        spend money   my career choice
_____ agreement over how to _____ agreement over how to
        interact with my   interact with spouse's
        relatives   relatives

_____ my satisfaction with my spouse's career

_____ lack of concern or consideration from my spouse

_____ agreement over how to spend free time

_____ agreement over mutual friends

_____ my feelings over past hurts from my spouse

_____ my spouse's bad feelings over past hurts

_____ my drinking

_____ my spouse's drinking

_____ disagreement over major life values

_____ I can't rely upon my spouse for emotional support

_____ I can rely upon my spouse to fulfill his/her share of household responsibilities

Check those areas which your spouse believes are problems in your marriage.

_____ sex life

_____ agreement on raising children

_____ agreement on how to spend money

_____ support in the area of my career choice

_____ agreement over how to interact with my relatives

_____ agreement over how to interact with spouse's relatives

_____ my satisfaction with my spouse's career

_____ lack of concern or consideration from my spouse

_____ agreement over how to spend free time

_____ agreement over mutual friends

_____ my feelings over past hurts from my spouse

_____ my spouse's bad feelings over past hurts

_____ my drinking

_____ my spouse's drinking

_____ disagreement over major life values

Check those areas which your spouse believes are strengths in your marriage.

_____ sex life

_____ agreement on raising children

_____ agreement on how to spend money

_____ support in the area of my career choice

_____ agreement over how to

_____ agreement over how to

interact with my
relatives

interact with spouse's
relatives

_____ my satisfaction with
my spouse's career

_____ concern or consideration
from my spouse

_____ agreement over how to
spend free time

_____ agreement over mutual
friends

_____ agreement over major
life values

How likely is it you will be married to your present spouse two years from now?

/   /   /   /   /   /   /

likely   unlikely

Which topics have you spent more than 20 minutes talking about with your spouse in the last week?

_____ money

_____ children

_____ relatives

_____ TV or movie

_____ occurrence at work

_____ purchase for the house

_____ transportation arrangement of family member

_____ annoying habit of my spouse's

_____ annoying habit of mine

_____ other (specify) _____

Circle the conversations which you regard as having been pleasant or productive conversations.

What percentage of the interactions with your spouse are enjoyable?

In your daily life, what percentage of your good times are spent with your spouse?

Is your spouse a contributing factor in making your pleasant times enjoyable?

yes   no

In your daily life, what percentage of your tense, angry, unpleasant times are spent with your spouse?

Is your spouse a contributor in creating your hard times?

yes   no

Have you asked your spouse to change his/her behavior in the last week?

yes   no

If yes, what change did you request?

Did you want your spouse to do something differently during the week that you didn't bring up?

yes   no

If yes, what request didn't you make?

Why not?

If you make a request of your spouse what response are you most likely to receive?

_____ he/she will ignore me

_____ he/she will become defensive and won't hear me

_____he/she will listen, agree to my request, but won't follow through

_____ there will be an argument

_____ he/she will listen and we can come to an agreement which will be honored

_____ he/she will turn the tables and criticize me

Overall how would you evaluate the quality of your marital relationship?

/   /   /   /   /   /   /

bad   good

Check those statements which you feel describe your marital relationship.

_____ I view my spouse and myself as a permanent family unit

_____ If my spouse were complimented or insulted, I would experience similar emotions as he/she

_____ Many of the intense positive feelings which I experience have been connected with my spouse

_____ I spend much of my time thinking about or attending to my spouse's emotional needs

_____ I spend much of my time thinking about or attending to my spouse's physical needs

_____ during the month I have noticed admirable characteristics in my spouse

_____during the month I have been appreciated by my spouse

Have you and your spouse discussed your drinking?

yes   no

Who initiated the discussion?

Describe your mood during the discussion.

Describe your spouse's mood during the discussion.

What point did your spouse wish to convey to you during the discussion?

What point did you wish to convey to your spouse?

Did you feel the conversation accomplished anything?

Does your spouse object to your drinking?

How were your spouse's objections conveyed to you?

How do you wish your spouse would respond to you when you are drinking?

Do you believe that your spouse should ever talk to you regarding your drinking?

yes   no

If yes, how should he/she initiate the conversation?

Have you ever been worried about your own drinking?

yes   no

If yes, did you mention your concern to your spouse?

yes   no

If yes, did you feel better after talking with your spouse?

yes   no

EVALUATION OF THE MARITAL RELATIONSHIP
BY THE SPOUSE

Check those activities in which you participated last weekend.

_____ watched TV

_____ visited friends

_____ played with my children

_____ went grocery shopping

_____ went to movies

_____ ate out other than at a fast food restaurant

_____ played cards

_____ went to a party

_____ other (specify) _____

Circle those activities which you checked above which you did with your spouse.

During the last week which activities have occurred between you and your spouse?

_____ argued for over 10 minutes

_____ exchanged short, angry remarks

_____ hugged each other

_____ attempted to solve a problem regarding the children

_____ talking about a TV program together while we were watching it

_____ talked together for more than 5 minutes about a mutual friend or a relative

_____ talked about an event which had occurred at work (can be either spouse's work)

_____ talked about what had occurred during the day after coming home from work

_____ discussed finances for over 10 minutes

_____ ate dinner without having the TV set on

Who has taken major responsibility for each of the following activities in your family during the last 2 months? (Some activities may not be relevant in your family)

preparing meals	myself	my spouse	equally shared
making sure the grass is cut	myself	my spouse	equally shared
grocery shopping	myself	my spouse	equally shared
paying bills	myself	my spouse	equally shared
getting the children ready for school	myself	my spouse	equally shared
praising the children for good report cards	myself	my spouse	equally shared
monitoring whether children are home on time	myself	my spouse	equally shared
scolding children when appropriate	myself	my spouse	equally shared
planning social activities	myself	my spouse	equally shared

remembering birthdays (children's, relatives)	myself	my spouse	equally shared
cleaning	myself	my spouse	equally shared
calling service departments when appliance requires repair	myself	my spouse	equally shared
changing car oil	myself	my spouse	equally shared

How satisfied are you with the current distribution of responsibilities?

Very unsatisfied   Neutral   Very Satisfied

Are there expectations which you used to have for your spouse that you no longer hold (paying the bills on time, help with the children, picking you up on time when you need a ride, emotional support)? Explain how things have changed.

Check those words which best describe your spouse.

_____ warm	_____ understanding
_____ impulsive	_____ moody
_____ irritable	_____ thoughtul
_____ caring	_____ rebellious
_____ generous	_____ worried
_____ concerned about others	_____ selfish
_____ responsible	_____ irresponsible
_____ hard working	_____ outgoing
_____ shy	_____ center of attention
_____ hard to get to know	_____ charming
_____ assertive	_____ domineering
_____ kind	_____ witty
_____ critical	_____ confident
_____ relates well to persons at work	_____ concerned about children
_____ respected by others	_____ good at his/her job
_____ intelligent	

Which words do you believe your spouse would check in describing himself or herself in the last 2 months?

_____ warm	_____ understanding
_____ impulsive	_____ moody
_____ irritable	_____ thoughtul
_____ caring	_____ rebellious

_____ generous   _____ worried
_____ concerned about others   _____ selfish
_____ responsible   _____ irresponsible
_____ hard working   _____ outgoing
_____ shy   _____ center of attention
_____ hard to get to know   _____ charming
_____ assertive   _____ domineering
_____ kind   _____ witty
_____ critical   _____ confident
_____ relates well to persons at_____ concerned about
work   children
_____ respected by others   _____ good at his/her job
_____ intelligent

Which words do you believe your spouse would check in describing you?

_____ warm   _____ understanding
_____ impulsive   _____ moody
_____ irritable   _____ thoughtul
_____ caring   _____ rebellious
_____ generous   _____ worried
_____ concerned about others   _____ selfish
_____ responsible   _____ irresponsible
_____ hard working   _____ outgoing
_____ shy   _____ center of attention
_____ hard to get to know   _____ charming
_____ assertive   _____ domineering
_____ kind   _____ witty
_____ critical   _____ confident
_____ relates well to persons at_____ concerned about
work   children
_____ respected by others   _____ good at his/her job
_____ intelligent

Check those areas which you believe are strengths in your marriage.

_____ sex life   _____ agreement on raising
children
_____ agreement on finances   _____ support in my work
_____ agreement over how to   _____ agreement over how to
interact with my relatives   interact with spouse's
relatives

_____ my satisfaction with my _____ my spouse's
spouse's career   consideration of me
_____ agreement over how to _____ agreement over mutual
spend free time   friends
_____ agreement over major
values

Check those areas which you believe have been problems in your marriage over the last 2 months.

_____ sex life   _____ agreement on raising
                                           children
_____ agreement on finances _____ spouse's support for my
                                           career
_____ agreement over how to _____ agreement over how to
interact with my relatives   interact with spouse's
                                   relatives
_____ my dissatisfaction with _____ spouse's lack of concern
spouse's career   for me
_____ disagreement over how _____ disagreement over
to spend free time   friends
_____ my feelings over past _____ my spouse's feelings
hurts   over hurts
_____ my drinking   _____ my spouse's drinking
_____ disagreement over life _____ my spouse's failure to
values   provide me with
                                   emotional support
_____ my spouse's unreliability in
performing share of work

How likely is it you will be married to your present spouse two years from now?

/   /   /   /   /   /   /
likely   unlikely

What topics have you spent more than 20 minutes discussing with your spouse in the last 2 months?

_____ money

_____ children

_____ relatives

_____ TV or movie

_____ occurrence at work

_____ purchase for the house

_____ transportation arrangement for family member

_____ annoying habit of my spouse's

_____ annoying habit of mine

_____ other (specify) _____

Circle the conversations which you regard as having been pleasant or productive conversations.

What percentage of the interactions with your spouse have been enjoyable during the last two months? (provide a number between 0–100).

In your daily life during the last 2 months, what percentage of your good times are spent with your spouse?

Has your spouse been a contributing factor in making your pleasant times enjoyable?

    yes   no

In your daily life during the last 2 months, what percentage of your tense, angry, unpleasant times have been spent with your spouse?

Has your spouse been a contributing factor in creating your hard times?

    yes   no

Overall, how would you evaluate the quality of your marital relationship?

    /   /   /   /   /   /   /

bad   good

Check those statements which you feel describe your marital relationship.

_____ I view my spouse and myself as a permanent family unit

_____ If my spouse were complimented or insulted, I would experience similar emotions as he/she

_____ Many of the intense positive feelings which I experience have been connected with my spouse

_____ Many of the intense negative feelings which I experience have been connected with my spouse

_____ I spend much of my time thinking about or attending to my spouse's emotional needs

_____ I spend much of my time thinking about or attending to my spouse's physical needs

_____ During the month I have noticed admirable characteristics in my spouse

_____ During the month, I have been appreciated by my spouse

Have you asked your spouse to change his/her behavior in the last week?

yes   no

If yes, what change did you request?

Did you want your spouse to do something differently during the last week that you didn't bring up?

yes   no

If yes, what request didn't you make?

If you make a request of your spouse what response are you most likely to receive?

_____ he/she will ignore me

_____ he/she will become defensive and won't hear me

_____ he/she will listen, agree to my request, but won't follow through

_____ there will be an argument

_____ he/she will listen and we can come to an agreement which will be honored

_____ he/she will turn the tables and criticize me

Do you feel apprehensive when your spouse is in the company of drinking persons?

yes   no

If yes, how does your apprehension affect your spouse?

/   /   /   /   /   /   /
Annoys him/her   Doesn't affect   he/she feels cared
                                                              about

Do you worry about whether your spouse has been drinking?

yes   no

If yes, how does your concern affect your spouse?

/   /   /   /   /   /   /
Annoys him/her   Doesn't affect him/her   he/she feels cared
                                                              about

If your spouse came home late due to some unforseeable circumstance, would you suspect that your spouse had been drinking?

yes   no

If your spouse was in a bad mood, would you suspect that your spouse was drinking or was going to have a drink?

yes   no

If yes, how does this affect you?

/   /   /   /   /   /   /
Annoys me   Doesn't affect me   I feel cared about

In the last 2 months approximately how many discussions of your spouse's drinking have occurred between you and your spouse?

Which behaviors have you performed in the last month?

_____ watched your spouse's alcohol consumption while out in public

_____ thrown out liquor

_____ looked for hidden bottles

_____ attempted to influence my spouse to stop drinking by screaming or crying

_____ lost my temper

_____ broke down in tears

_____ been unable to sleep while waiting for spouse to come home drunk

_____ called in sick for spouse who had a hangover or was drinking

_____ talked for over 30 minutes to a friend or relative about my spouse's drinking

_____ checked in refrigerator or elsewhere to determine how much my spouse had had to drink

_____ spoken to my children about my spouse's drinking

_____ been embarrassed due to my spouse's drinking

_____ avoided getting together with friend's for fear of embarrassment over spouse's drinking

_____ felt guilty over my spouse's drinking

_____ believed I was responsible for my spouse's drinking

_____ purchased liquor for my spouse

Answer the following questions if your spouse is presently sober.

Have you and your spouse discussed his/her preference about whether you drink around your spouse?

        yes   no

Who initiated the conversation?

Have you and your spouse discussed his/her preference about whether friends drink around your spouse?

Who initiated the conversation?

Have you and your spouse discussed whether to have alcoholic beverages available for guests?

    yes   no

Who initiated the conversation?

If you noticed that your spouse had an urge to drink would you discuss it with your spouse?

    yes   no

Is there some possible change in you which your spouse feels might strengthen the probability of his/her maintaining abstinence?

    yes   no

What is it?

Author Index

Subject Index

403